Reincarnation Refuted

Evidence, Logic and Common Sense

Stephen Blake M.Sc. (Lond)

Grosvenor House
Publishing Limited

All rights reserved
Copyright © Stephen Blake M.Sc. (Lond), 2014

The right of Stephen Blake M.Sc. (Lond) to be identified as the author of this
work has been asserted by him in accordance with Section 78
of the Copyright, Designs and Patents Act 1988

The book cover picture is copyright to Inmagine Corp LLC

This book is published by
Grosvenor House Publishing Ltd
28-30 High Street, Guildford, Surrey, GU1 3EL.
www.grosvenorhousepublishing.co.uk

This book is sold subject to the conditions that it shall not, by way of
trade or otherwise, be lent, resold, hired out or otherwise circulated
without the author's or publisher's prior consent in any form of binding or
cover other than that in which it is published and
without a similar condition including this condition being imposed
on the subsequent purchaser.

A CIP record for this book
is available from the British Library

ISBN 978-1-78148-687-0

Acknowledgements

This book began several years ago following a series of exchanges I had with readers of *Psychic World* on the question of reincarnation. The editor, the late Ray Taylor, saw fit to publish my letters sparking off an interesting debate amongst the readership. Although I disagreed with much of their views, their comments and criticisms proved to be of inestimable value in the preparation and writing of this book. I would like to thank them for taking the trouble to reply to my letters. Over the years I have corresponded with many people on the question of reincarnation but one person deserves special mention, Dr. Susan Martinez. I would like to thank her for her continued stance against the doctrine and for her thoughtful and insightful comments about the Refutation. Most of all, however, I would like to thank James Webster for suggesting that I write the book, and for his unwavering support throughout the long and exhausting process of producing it. The many conversations I have had with James over the years have been a constant source of inspiration. I would also like to thank Grosvenor House Publishing Ltd for their help and support during the production stages of the book. Finally, I would like to thank the reader for engaging with a book that will challenge their view of the world.

Book Dedication

To my friend and colleague James Webster without whose support and encouragement this book would never have been written.

Contents

PART 1: BELIEF AND LOGIC	1
Chapter 1: Waking the Dead	3
Chapter 2: Believing the Impossible	49
Chapter 3: Proving a Negative	87
Chapter 4: The Problem with Karma	115
PART 2: SEEN AND UNSEEN	155
Chapter 5: Strange Encounters	157
Chapter 6: Spirit Influence	192
Chapter 7: Mind and Body	233
Chapter 8: Suggestive of What?	260
PART 3: TIME AND ETERNITY	299
Chapter 9: Newton's Universe	301
Chapter 10: Law and Disorder	342
Chapter 11: The Unreality of Time	376
Chapter 12: From Here to Eternity	413
MATHEMATICAL APPENDIX	441
BIBLIOGRAPHY	449
INDEXES	457

Preface

The word 'reincarnation' is repeated so often it is thought by many to be a fact. It is the purpose of this book to show that reincarnation is *not* a fact, has never been a fact and - more importantly - cannot happen. I am aware that this contradicts a fundamental tenet of the Eastern religions and opposes the grain of New Age thinking but there are very good reasons for supposing that reincarnation is impossible - reasons that will become abundantly clear as the book progresses. After many years of study and research into religion, science and the paranormal, I have come to the conclusion that reincarnation is not only a false and misleading doctrine but a hindrance to spiritual progress. That individuals should wish to believe in such an indemonstrable concept as reincarnation is itself a topic worthy of study but, whatever the reasons, it is evident that the steady trickle of media commentary in support of the doctrine has played a critical part. While the majority of spiritualistic publications have found it profitable to promote the idea of reincarnation, either as a fact or a possibility, this book is dedicated to the task of explaining why it cannot happen. As such the reader will encounter ideas never seen or discussed in the reincarnationist literature.

Although reincarnation is normally associated with the great religions of the East, this is not a religious book in the usual sense of the word, nor is it a book about religion. The reader will not be bombarded with quotations from the scriptures nor be asked to accept any religious precept other than the existence of an eternal creative force. All that is required is an open mind and a willingness to engage in straightforward logical arguments. With the exception of some parts of Chapter 4 and the mathematical appendix, the book is accessible to everyone.

Written largely with reincarnationists in mind, or those who regard reincarnation as a possibility, this book will also be of interest to those who wish to see how logical arguments can be used to dismantle a religious or political ideology. If after having read this book the reader is willing to critically examine any doctrine or idea put to him or her - whatever its source - before accepting it as the gospel truth, the book will have served a useful purpose. The thesis of this book can be summed up in three statements: (a) there is no evidence for reincarnation, (b) the doctrine of reincarnation is logically incoherent, (c) reincarnation violates commonsense.

* * *

Chapter 1: Waking the Dead has been organised as a conversation between myself and two believers in reincarnation. This has a twofold purpose: (a) to provide an introduction to the many issues surrounding the subject, and (b) to submit the arguments *for* the doctrine to direct scrutiny. While the characters are imaginary their opinions are quite real.

Chapter 2: Believing the Impossible looks at reincarnationism in conjunction with a belief system that provides reincarnationism with much of its legitimacy - Darwinism. As we shall see, both "isms" have many features in common, not the least of which both lack a credible *modus operandi*. Following an outline of reincarnationism in the West and its portrayal on the World Wide Web, we conclude by showing that biological evolution - reincarnationism's outward justification - could never have happened the way Darwin envisaged.

Chapter 3: Proving a Negative deals with the oft repeated claim that reincarnation cannot be refuted because "you can't prove a negative." Following a discussion of inductive reasoning and its relationship to statements that cannot be refuted, we show that the claim, when applied to the doctrine of reincarnation, is a category mistake. In the second part of the chapter, we introduce the Temporal Postulates and prove that systems incorporating concepts of individuality, immortality and reincarnation are logically incoherent. The chapter concludes by proving another negative: that no events are connected in necessary causal relationships.

Chapter 4: The Problem with Karma analyses a key component of reincarnationist philosophy: the doctrine of karma. Explaining how karma must work in practice if the personality is to be liberated from the cycle of rebirths, we show how it may be quantified and analysed with the tools of mathematics and probability theory. We then present a number of propositions, chief of which is that karma cannot be eliminated in practice leading, in turn, to what I have called the Impossibility Theorem - a universal statement asserting that reincarnation cannot be a fact of nature. The chapter ends with a further analysis of karma showing it to be fundamentally incoherent. For readers with a mathematical background the proofs are provided in the Mathematical Appendix.

Chapter 5: Strange Encounters begins with a light-hearted conversation with an imaginary gentleman who believes he is more than one person. This prepares the ground for a serious analysis of multilocation (of which bilocation is a special case) and the strange phenomenon of circumscriptive replication i.e. the physical occupation of two or more places at once. The question, whether or not these and other phenomena, such as the physical phenomena of mediumship, the exteriorisation of sensibility and motivity, community of sensation and shared memories undermine the concept of individuality is discussed in detail.

Chapter 6: Spirit Influence looks at the spiritual constitution of the self, the phenomena of spirit possession and how discarnate personalities can impress the minds of psychically sensitive people with their thoughts, feelings and memories. Once dismissed as superstition, spirit possession is now engaging the attention of anthropologists, psychiatrists and public health officials. A proven instance of spirit possession - the case of Lurancy Vennum - first brought to the world's attention in 1928 by Dr. E. Winchester Stevens is reviewed at length.

Chapter 7: Mind and Body discusses mind-body interaction showing that correlated birthmarks - often touted as evidence for reincarnation - belong to a group of paranormal phenomena that include, among other things, stigmata, hypnotically induced burns and maternal impressions.

Chapter 8: Suggestive of What? is a critical analysis of Dr. Ian Stevenson's best-known work: *Twenty Cases Suggestive of Reincarnation.* We show that Dr. Stevenson reached his principal conclusion - that reincarnation is the best possible explanation of past life memories and correlated birthmarks - only by misrepresenting the facts. As we shall see, such phenomena have a much more plausible explanation than that proposed by Dr. Stevenson. We review a number of Stevenson's cases showing that one in particular - the case of Jasbir - cannot possibly be an instance of reincarnation demonstrating that Stevenson will opt for the reincarnation explanation even when it is manifestly untrue. A number of his cases show that obsessive belief in reincarnation can lead to identity confusion, mental illness and suicide.

An idea much loved by reincarnationists, who frequently maintain that everything and everyone is subject to it, is the so-called Law of Cause and Effect: that actions in this life have consequences (i.e. karma) that can only be resolved in future incarnations; hence the need for reincarnation. Chapter 9: Newton's Universe traces the origin of the 'law of cause and effect' to the collapse of the old geocentric astronomy of Ptolemy, its replacement with the heliocentric models of Copernicus and Kepler, the conflict between Galileo and the Catholic Church, and the triumph of Newtonian physics. The chapter concludes with a discussion of how the concept of causal necessity spread to areas beyond the physical sciences - especially to the field of political economy - and how Newtonian methods were incorporated into the technical apparatus of traditionally 'non-scientific' disciplines.

Chapter 10: Law and Disorder continues the discussion of causal necessity, revealing that the law of cause and effect was controversial from the very beginning. Having been contested by a number of distinguished classical thinkers such as Hume and Peirce, it collapsed as a fundamental principle of science with the arrival of the quantum at the beginning of the twentieth century. Modern philosophers such as Jaegwon Kim and John Mackie still maintain that the concept of causation is problematical. The chapter concludes with a discussion of the phenomenon of 'deterministic chaos,' arguably the final 'nail in the coffin' of causal certainty.

Chapter 11: The Unreality of Time establishes the reasons for believing that time is unreal - an idea traceable to Plato, Aristotle, Parmenides of Elea, Sextus Empiricus, and Augustine. More recently, it is associated with the Cambridge philosopher John McTaggart. The Chapter concludes with a discussion of the Reduction Principle and how it relates to the scientific theory of spontaneous creation out of nothing espoused by Stephen Hawking, and to a fundamental precept of the great religions.

In Chapter 12: From Here to eternity, we show how various concepts of the soul have been enlisted in the reincarnationist cause and why they have singularly failed to provide a rationale for reincarnation. We then discuss the issue of human immortality and consider whether or not an eternal being can be a person. The chapter concludes with a presentation of the Refutation as a system of formal propositions, chief of which is that the human self does not reincarnate.

* * *

Refutations of reincarnation are sometimes dismissed as so much 'armchair' theorising, inferior in every way to empirical research and contrary to personal experience - an idea espoused by those who have convinced themselves that past life memories permit of only one interpretation. In reply to this, it must be said that no amount of data can demonstrate anything without an underlying theory to support it or give it meaning. Only when a theory has been formulated can the data be reckoned as 'empirical evidence.' While reincarnation research is notable for the amount of data it has accumulated, it is notable for the absence of any coherent or testable theories. Secondly, the reader should be aware that the doctrine of reincarnation is itself the product of 'armchair' theorising and as such should be subjected to the normal tests of logical consistency.

Another stratagem used to counter refutations of reincarnation is to say that because reincarnation means different things to different people, it is unclear what is being refuted. The implication is that whatever version of reincarnation is refuted, all other versions remain intact. Unfortunately for proponents of this view, reincarnation is refuted not by analysing the multitudinous beliefs about reincarnation - an approach not pursued in this book - but by establishing the true nature of human spirituality. The flat Earth doctrine was refuted not by analysing the meaning of the word 'flat' but by establishing the *true* shape of the Earth.

It is a curious fact that while diversity of meaning is supposed to inhibit refutations of reincarnation, it does not, apparently, inhibit discussions of reincarnation. Individuals who attend conferences on reincarnation and, more importantly, speakers who deliver lectures at conferences on reincarnation, are generally relaxed and unconcerned about this potential source of confusion. Communication proceeds smoothly, papers are delivered happily and fees accepted gratefully – and no one ever complains that reincarnation means different things to different people. Furthermore, empirical research into reincarnation is never bedevilled by such issues; researchers get on with the job and cheerfully announce that their findings support the doctrine of reincarnation. Significantly, the *European Values Survey (2002)* had no difficulty phrasing the question: "Do you believe in reincarnation, that is, that we are born into this world again?"

There are two kinds of refutation in this book: a mathematical refutation based on the unviability of karma (discussed in Chapter 4) and a logical refutation based on the unreality of time. The logical refutation was first published as a brief outline in James Webster's anthology *The Case Against Reincarnation: A Rational Approach (2009)* - a book that may be regarded as a companion volume to this one. Since then, I have made a number of changes, the most notable being the use of the term 'self' in place of 'soul' and the introduction of the so-called Temporal Postulates enabling the propositions of the Refutation to be developed in a more systematic and orderly manner. This 'two-pronged' approach means that if one accepts the scientific concept of the *unreality* of time (as does the author) then reincarnation is refuted by the Temporal Postulates. On the other hand, if one believes that time is *real* (as do a number of philosophers) then reincarnation is refuted by the Impossibility Theorem. Either way, reincarnation is refuted.

* * *

"Every journey begins with the first step," to quote an old saying. Whatever the reader's beliefs, hopes or aspirations, I hope the journey is an interesting and eventful one!

PART 1
BELIEF & LOGIC

Chapter 1
Waking the Dead

It was a warm, sunny morning in late Spring, and the sweet-scented smell of may blossom toyed gently with the aroma of freshly ground coffee as it drifted along the tree-studded avenues of Bloomsbury. I had just purchased Dr. Carl Wickland's *Thirty Years Among the Dead* and *The Gateway of Understanding* - records of his communications with obsessing spirits - and was relaxing in a small snack bar near the British Museum, sipping hot coffee and enjoying a freshly prepared salad sandwich. Dr. Wickland contradicted everything I had read about reincarnation to date. Reincarnation does *not* happen, advanced spirits do *not* teach it, and belief in it retards the progress of the soul beyond death. Even more alarming is how children can be controlled by obsessing spirits attempting to reincarnate in their bodies.

Sitting opposite me was John Faraway - a firm believer in reincarnation. Glancing somewhat furtively at Wickland's books, he said:

"Actually, the evidence for reincarnation is overwhelming. Many people regard it as an indisputable fact."

"What evidence?" I replied.

"Memories of past lives retrieved under hypnotic regression; spontaneous recall of past lives, particularly among children; the work of Dr. Ian Stevenson - he's proven that reincarnation happens; the writings of people like Allan Kardec and Helen Blavatsky, the Edgar Cayce readings; communications from the other side; channelled writings, and so on, not to mention a host of distinguished philosophers who have professed a belief in reincarnation. In fact, three quarters of the world believe in it."

"You do realise," I said, "belief is not synonymous with fact and, in any case, belief in reincarnation throughout most of the world is based on religious conviction not on empirical evidence."

"Maybe," he replied, "but so many facts about reincarnation have been accumulated it has been proven beyond a reasonable doubt."

"I think you are confusing facts with evidence; the two things are completely different. For example, evidence – however persuasive - that X murdered Y is not the same as the *fact* that X murdered Y because the evidence may be circumstantial or, maybe, X was framed. It's perfectly possible that X did *not* murder Y."

"Ok, but the existence of past life memories proves that reincarnation happens."

"Not necessarily," I replied, "If you compare the number of people who don't have any memories of past lives with the number of people who do, then you must admit that the evidence *against* reincarnation is overwhelming."

"All that means is that not everyone reincarnates. It doesn't mean that no one reincarnates."

"With respect, you misunderstand the doctrine of reincarnation. Any Hindu or Buddhist will tell you that everyone reincarnates – without exception."

"I don't believe that," returned Faraway, "I think we choose whether or not to reincarnate."

"It makes no difference what you believe," I said, "everyone – according to the doctrine of reincarnation – is subject to karma; and karma is the motive force for reincarnation. If karma is in operation then everyone reincarnates; if it isn't then no one reincarnates. Choice doesn't come into it."

"I certainly believe in karma," replied Faraway somewhat thoughtfully.

"Then you are forced to believe that everyone reincarnates."

"How can I be forced to believe something against my will?"

"It's a question of logic; one thing implies the other. If you accept, say, the axioms of arithmetic then you must accept that $2 + 2 = 4$. By the same token, if you accept that karma is in operation then you must accept its principal implication, namely, that everybody reincarnates. You could, of course, deny that $2 + 2 = 4$, or deny that karma compels people to reincarnate, but you would only be deluding yourself."

"Ok, if karma is in operation then research into past life memories will prove that everyone reincarnates."

"If karma is *known* to be in operation," I replied, "research into past life memories would be pointless since everyone would automatically believe in reincarnation. But of course in Hinduism and Buddhism karma is regarded as an absolute truth which means that Hindus and Buddhists aren't really bothered about proving reincarnation. Of course, they're more than happy to announce apparent cases of reincarnation if and when they arise but they do it largely for Western consumption, rarely for themselves."

"If one implies the other," replied Faraway, "then memories of past lives are empirical evidence of karma."

"The problem with empirical evidence is that people interpret it in ways that uphold their view of the world."

"What do you mean?"

"Well, centuries ago it was believed that the Earth was at the centre of the universe and astronomical data was interpreted accordingly. That meant the Sun, stars and planets orbited the Earth. When the geocentric view of the universe was abandoned in favour of Sun-centred models, astronomical data was reinterpreted and the Earth and planets were then found to orbit the Sun. In other words, the same set of data was interpreted in two completely different ways. Believers in reincarnation are no exception; they interpret past life memories in ways that support their belief in reincarnation."

"That's very interesting," replied Faraway, "but if, say, Albert Smith has a memory of a past life then, surely, that's a record of Albert Smith's former life and that means there can be only one interpretation – that Albert Smith has lived on Earth before."

"You say that Albert Smith has a memory of a past life but, in practice, most memories of past lives are retrieved during regression therapy and turn out to be little more than fantasies or the result of suggestions by the therapist. But, let us suppose, for the sake of argument, that Albert Smith does have memories which he believes relate to a former life. Firstly, a memory of a past life – however obtained - and a record of a past life are two completely different things. A record of a past life, say, the life of the English King Henry VIII, forms part of the historical record and is contained in documents, letters, biographies and oral communications passed down from one generation to the next. But, a memory of a past life is no more a record of a past life than a dream of a past life or a fantasy of a past life."

"In other words," returned Faraway, "my memories of going to the theatre yesterday afternoon are no more than fantasies?"

"No, I am not saying that. There's a big difference between your memories of going to the theatre yesterday afternoon and Albert Smith's memories of a previous life because, in your case, you remember yourself as John Faraway whereas Albert Smith – according to you - has memories of being a completely different person, let us say Daniel Boone."

"I don't think there's any real difference."

"Let me put it this way. If Jo Bloggs claimed to be you i.e. John Faraway - because he remembered going to the theatre yesterday afternoon - you would dispute it immediately because you know yourself to be John Faraway and nobody else. In other words, your particular memories belong to you and no one else. On the other hand, you are saying that because Albert Smith believes he has memories of being Daniel Boone he can be both Albert Smith *and* Daniel Boone i.e. the person he is *now* and the person he *was* two hundred years ago. In other words, you are claiming that Albert Smith can be two completely different people."

"Surely not," retorted Faraway, "because only Albert Smith now exists."

"That's not the point," I replied, "there's no real difference between your claim that Albert Smith was Daniel Boone two hundred years ago or the claim that Albert Smith was Daniel Boone last week or even the claim that Albert Smith was Daniel Boone five minutes ago. All these claims are saying the same thing: that Albert Smith *is* Daniel Boone - the time factor is irrelevant."

"I don't see that."

"Well, you claim, presumably, to have been John Faraway when you were born thirty two years ago, and also claim to have been John Faraway ten years ago, and claim to have been John Faraway yesterday, and claim to have been John Faraway five minutes ago. All that means is that you claim to be John Faraway *now*. By the same token, if Albert Smith claims to have been Daniel Boone two hundred years ago then he is claiming to be Daniel Boone now. Of course that would make Albert Smith at least two hundred years old! Adding the phrase: 'in a previous life' merely confuses the issue."

"I'm still not convinced."

"Let me put it another way. Claiming that the Moon is Mars doesn't become less ridiculous by saying that the Moon was Mars two thousand years ago or even two million years ago. Like the Moon and Mars, Albert Smith and Daniel Boone are unique entities and none of them can be anyone else either now, in the past or in the future. The point is that people do not mutate into other people. Albert Smith cannot claim to have been Daniel Boone unless Daniel Boone had somehow mutated into Albert Smith - which is, of course, absurd. While you would dispute Jo Bloggs' claim to be *you*, Daniel Boone is no longer around to dispute Albert Smith's claim to be *him*; that's the only reason anyone would make such a claim in the first place. If Jo Bloggs turned up and also claimed to have been Daniel Boone in a previous life, it would be blindingly obvious that both were deluded or telling lies."

"Ok, how do you explain the fact that Albert Smith has memories of being Daniel Boone in a previous life?"

"Actually, that would be an inference not a fact. It may be true that Albert Smith has some memories which can be correlated with the life of Daniel Boone, as shown in the historical record, but that's not the same as having memories of *being* Daniel Boone in a previous incarnation. Memories of previous lives are often incidental and sometimes traumatic. Just because someone possesses a few snapshots doesn't mean they own the whole album."

"Yes, but it's very likely that whoever possesses the snapshots – to use your metaphor - also owns the whole album."

"Not necessarily. But, that brings us back to my original point about interpreting the evidence to uphold one's view of the world. If someone is predisposed to believing that people in possession of snapshots own the whole album then obviously they will make the appropriate inference; but there are no independent grounds for making it. In fact, the snapshots may have been borrowed, stolen, found, faked or copied."

"That may be true," returned Faraway, "but you still haven't explained how Albert Smith could have acquired Daniel Boone's memories in the first place."

"We are assuming, of course, that Albert Smith *has* acquired some of Daniel Boone's memories. In practice this would be extremely difficult to verify, even for a famous personality like Boone, because memories of past lives can rarely be linked to the historical record. However, let us suppose, for the sake of argument, that Albert Smith has a memory of signing a particular document as Daniel Boone and also remembers the contents of this document, and suppose further that the original document signed by Daniel Boone turns up sometime later and matches up with Smith's memory; then one could reasonably assert that Albert Smith has a memory that correlates with a specific incident in the life of Daniel Boone. But, that's a very long way from saying that Albert Smith was Daniel Boone in a previous life or even that Albert Smith possesses Daniel Boone's memories."

"How else can it be explained?" replied Faraway.

"You make the mistake of assuming that *any* explanation is better than no explanation. In fact, no explanation is better than the wrong one."

"Yes, but do *you* have another explanation?"

"Actually, the phenomenon is well known to spiritualists and psychical researchers; it's called spirit possession or obsession. This happens when people still living in a physical body fall under the sway of discarnate spirits."

"What exactly do you mean by discarnate spirits?"

"By discarnate spirits, I mean discarnate personalities i.e. people who have shed their physical body and passed on to the spirit side of life, or non-human entities who have never occupied a physical body but inhabit dimensions close to the Earth. In a sense we are all spirits, incarnate or discarnate. Spirit influence can range from possession by malevolent or mischievous entities – sometimes referred to as 'demonic possession' - obsession by earthbound spirits, or by spirits wishing to establish links with people on Earth. Very often spirit entities convey bodies of teaching for the benefit of humankind. Some teachings can be helpful, some completely false. Depending on the communicating spirit and the character of the medium or channel, spirit influence can be for good or ill. In general like attracts like but there's no hard and fast rule. For example, a weak-willed person may fall prey to mischievous spirits; children are very often obsessed by spirits because the very young are highly impressionable. Many selfish, materially minded people, on quitting the physical body at death, find they cannot pass on to higher spheres of consciousness and, instead, hang around in dimensions close to the Earth attempting to relive their former lives. Such spirits may be attracted to the auric light of someone still living in a physical body - like a moth to the flame of a candle. When this happens their respective auras become entangled and they impress each other with their thoughts, feelings, and memories. Sometimes a discarnate spirit may attach itself to a living person in order to experience - albeit second-hand - the person's feelings and emotions, occasionally encouraging them to commit terrible crimes. Serial killers have often said a voice inside them told them to do it."

"Can you be more specific?"

"Suppose, for example, a woman gets burned as a witch in seventeenth century England, fails to free herself from the Earth's magnet pull and, as a discarnate personality, becomes attached to a person living in twenty first century New York – call him Y. Not all incidents need be violent or traumatic but the incidents usually have significance for the earthbound personality and it is this that prevents the personality from passing on. In any event, the discarnate witch will impress Y - albeit it unwittingly - with memories of being burned. Under hypnotic regression, or even in dreams, Y may then experience the trauma of being burned. In fact the experience may be so real it could be misinterpreted as a previous life event."

"You mean Y re-lives the trauma?"

"No. It would be incorrect to use the word, 're-live' because that implies Y has lived through the experience before i.e. in a previous life. However, the obsessing witch may also impress Y with other memories so that Y discovers he possesses information relating to the historical time period in question; in rare cases it may be possible to check these facts against the historical record. It is the possession of inaccessible information – whose authenticity is confirmed by experts - that distinguishes fantasies created by the subject's own subconscious mind from memories impressed by discarnate personalities."

"Ok," replied Faraway, "but some people have memories of several lives. How do you explain that?"

"A person may be obsessed by several discarnate personalities, each one impressing the host with its memories and character traits. When this happens the obsessed person may exhibit mood swings and personality changes depending on which personality is in control."

"That's very interesting but is there any evidence that this sort of thing happens?"

"Well, when someone is regressed by a hypnotherapist and reports memories of a previous life - *real* memories, not confabulations - they are really reporting memories that have been impressed on their minds by a discarnate personality. Normally, these memories lie below the threshold of consciousness but can easily surface under hypnosis or even in dreams. For example, Dr. Helen Wambach regressed many subjects and found they possessed fairly detailed knowledge of recondite things known only to experts. The hypnotherapist, Arnall Bloxham regressed clients over a period of twenty years and built up a large record of past life memories. Like Helen Wambach's subjects, Bloxham's clients possessed knowledge of things that were verified at a later date. These cases - and many more - merely show how discarnate personalities can impress psychically sensitive people with their knowledge and memories."

"But," replied Faraway, "Dr. Ian Stevenson proved that reincarnation happens."

"I assume you are referring to Dr. Stevenson's, *Twenty Cases Suggestive of Reincarnation* reporting the spontaneous recall of past lives among young children in the Indian subcontinent and other parts of the world?

Faraway nodded.

"Actually, Dr. Stevenson proved nothing of the kind. What he *did* show was that explanations are culturally biased. In areas of the world where belief in reincarnation is the norm, reincarnation, unsurprisingly, is the main explanation for past life memories. More importantly he showed that departed souls who believe in reincarnation hang around trying to reincarnate in the bodies of children. Before the child is born, the departed soul - now a discarnate personality - can impress the child with birthmarks via the mother as 'maternal impressions' resembling wounds it may have received on Earth. After the child is born - normally when the child is about 2 or 3 years old - the obsessing personality may impress the child with memories of its life on Earth. Both influences may be present in any one child."

"Ok," replied Faraway, "but is there any evidence that this sort of thing happens?"

"Yes, from Dr. Ian Stevenson's own research. If you study the case of Jasbir in *Twenty Cases Suggestive of Reincarnation*, you will find that Jasbir was impressed with the memories of a discarnate personality who, on Earth, was known as Sobha Ram. It is definitely not a case of reincarnation because Jasbir and Sobha Ram were contemporaries of one another for the first three years of Jasbir's life. Since Sobha Ram died while Jasbir was still alive he could not have reincarnated in Jasbir's body."

"Mmm", Faraway mused, "I'll study that particular case but I'm still not clear how spirit influence works"

"Spirit influence works through telepathy, hypnotic suggestion, stigmatization and in ways that have no counterpart on the Earth side of life. It is well known that hypnotists, through the power of suggestion alone, can cause marks and wounds to appear on a subject's body. The point is that if a hypnotist can do it then so can a discarnate personality, the only difference being that one is *incarnate* and the other *discarnate*. Sir William Barrett FRS, who was Professor of Physics at the Royal College of Science for Dublin from 1873-1910 showed in a series of experiments how remarkable physiological changes can be produced in a hypnotised subject merely by conscious or subconscious mental suggestion. For example, a red scar or a painful blister can be induced on a subject's body merely by suggesting the idea. If a hypnotist can produce such startling effects on another person's body, a discarnate personality will have no problem impressing an unborn child with birthmarks. We know this can happen because Stevenson's monograph, *Reincarnation and Biology* is full of such cases."

"Is there any evidence - other than reincarnation research - which supports your spirit obsession theory?"

"Actually, spirit obsession is a fact, not a theory, though some people refer to it by other names or misdiagnose it as schizophrenia or some other mental illness. Some of the most original research of this kind was carried out by Dr. Carl Wickland in the first decades of the twentieth century." (I gently tapped the books in front of me.)

"I've never heard of him," replied Faraway.

"Then you should read his books. They record his work with patients obsessed by discarnate personalities."

"Ok, if I find the time, but can you give me any *real* examples of spirit obsession?"

"Well, Dr. Wickland records the case of a small boy called Jack T. living in Chicago. The boy had been perfectly normal till the age of five when he began to worry about things unusual in a child of his age and to behave in ways typical of an adult. He constantly fretted over his looks, talking about his ugly and homely appearance and lay awake at night muttering strange things. At times he had an uncontrollable temper and all efforts to pacify him proved ineffective. The boy's condition became so serious that his family contacted Dr. Wickland's Institute for help. Dr. Wickland's wife, a powerful psychic and medium, concentrated for the boy and was able to attract an entity whose actions and expressions were just like those of the disturbed boy. Speaking through Mrs Wickland, the entity said his name was Charlie Herrman. He was aware that he had died and had tried to reincarnate as a child. In life he had been homely and ugly looking with pock marks on his face and shunned by those around him. His only desire was to become good looking so that folk would accept him. Before he died someone had told him that people reincarnate and become whatever they wished to be. As a result he had become trapped in the boy's aura from which he couldn't escape; this led to outbursts of temper. However, Mrs Wickland's concentration had freed him, and for this he was very grateful. Charlie Herrman was then told about spiritual progress and the need to forget self and to help others. His homely and ugly appearance was a product of his thinking and would vanish when he discarded old ideas. He then showed great willingness to go with the spirits who, he said, had come to help him. A few days later, the boy's mother wrote to Dr. Wickland informing him of a remarkable change in her son's behaviour. She said: 'Jack is now a boy again and has been very good this week, really like he used to be.' Jack remained perfectly normal and made excellent progress at school."

"That's a very interesting story," replied Faraway, "but how do we know that Charlie Herrman wasn't a product of Mrs Wickland's own mind?"

"Because seven years later a member of the Herrman family read Dr. Wickland's book *Thirty Years Among the Dead*, recognised the description of Charlie Herrman outlined in the chapter on theosophy and reincarnation, and wrote to him. A copy of the letter was published in Dr. Wickland's book *The Gateway of Understanding*."

I leafed through the book and showed Faraway a copy of the letter:

I have just read 'Thirty Years Among the Dead'. On page 333, opening your chapter, 'Theosophy,' you describe the case of one Charlie Herrman, who lived all his life near Raymond, Illinois. He died in middle age, about twenty-five or thirty years ago. He was never spoken of by any other name than 'Charlie,' and he and his parents used the double 'r' in spelling 'Herrman,' though my father's folks simplified the spelling thus: 'Herman.' He, Charlie, had smallpox which left his eyesight greatly impaired and his face full of pock marks.'

Most Sincerely Yours, (Signed) ---------------- Herman.

"Couldn't the boy's condition be the result of a personality disorder?" replied Faraway.

"I think you mean a 'dissociative identity disorder.' As I understand it, DID is a psychiatric diagnosis – somewhat controversial in the profession - in which a person displays several distinct identities each with its own way of perceiving and interacting with the environment. If that were true, it would certainly rule out reincarnation as a possible explanation. But, in the case I have just outlined, by far the simplest explanation is the one given by Dr. Wickland i.e. obsession by a discarnate personality. Any other explanation would be so convoluted as to stretch credibility to breaking point. For example, it would need to take into account the involvement of Mrs Wickland, the letter from the Herrman family attesting to Charlie's existence, and the sudden improvement in the boy's condition. In any case, Jack T.'s obsession shouldn't be judged alone but in conjunction with all the other cases of obsession brought to Dr. Wickland's attention."

"Well," replied Faraway, "even if Charlie Herrman did obsess the boy, that doesn't prove that Herrman won't reincarnate at some later date. The point I am making is that spirit obsession doesn't disprove reincarnation; they could both be true."

"I think you have missed the point," I replied. "The point is that memories of past lives, knowledge of obscure facts, or even correlated birthmarks are not suggestive of reincarnation. If Charlie Herrman had obsessed Jack T. in the prenatal stage of his development, it is quite possible that his skin blemishes would have been impressed upon Jack T. as birthmarks. As it happened, Charlie Herrman wanted to start life as a five year old."

"If that's true, why didn't Jack T. have memories of Charlie Herrman's life?" replied Faraway.

"We don't know that he didn't; he may not have spoken about them. In any case, in a non-reincarnationist culture impressed memories will not be rationalised as memories of a previous life; they may just remain in the mind as incoherent images. Rationalisations are *acquired* from parents and friends or from external sources, such as the mass media."

"I don't see how birthmarks can be impressed on a child at the prenatal stage," puzzled Faraway.

"The physiological mechanism, like so many things relating to mind-body interaction, is unclear. In fact, Dr. Stevenson believed the phenomenon to be paranormal. However, it's not difficult to imagine what is happening. When a strong believer in reincarnation dies and becomes a discarnate personality it will attach itself to a pregnant woman in the mistaken belief it can reincarnate."

"Isn't that the same as reincarnation?" interrupted Faraway.

"No, because the unborn child is the expression of an existing individuality. The discarnate personality would, so to speak, be surplus to requirements. The point is that the foetus, being at the most impressionable stage of its development, can be impressed with birthmarks and defects by the discarnate personality, probably via the mother as maternal impressions."

"I've never heard of maternal impressions," replied Faraway.

"It's when a pregnant woman receives a shock - like witnessing a man being beheaded - and then gives birth to a baby with a red mark round its neck. This is a well-documented phenomenon. In a similar way, a discarnate personality can impress a pregnant woman with powerful images of wounds it may have received at its passing - like bullet wounds in the stomach. Although the mother may not receive conscious images of the wounds - the process probably operates below the threshold of consciousness - they are, nevertheless, transmitted to the foetus, and the child is born with birthmarks corresponding to the bullet wounds. It works just like maternal impressions. After birth, the discarnate personality will transfer its attachment to the child and impress it with memories of its last days on Earth, especially if the passing was a violent one. These memories, according to Stevenson's research, surface when the child is about 2 or 3 years old. Stevenson's monographs are full of such cases. Although Stevenson regarded these cases as evidence of reincarnation, he can be proven to be wrong."

"You say that the unborn child is the expression of an existing individuality," Faraway continued, "but how do you know?"

"Because," I replied, "the self is associated with its physical expression from conception to death. Anything else is totally arbitrary. Where would you draw the line? Does life begin 30 days after conception? 60 days? 90 days? When the umbilical cord is cut? When the child is born? Legal definitions prove nothing and, in any case, vary from one generation to another and from one culture to another."

"In other words," replied Faraway, "if a woman terminates her pregnancy, she is murdering the child?"

"No, I am not saying that. The woman may have every legal and moral right to terminate the pregnancy, say if she has been raped, but it is still the destruction of a life. Killing in self defence is still the destruction of a life."

"Ok, if spirit obsession is a fact," continued Faraway, "why do reincarnation researchers always interpret past life memories and correlated birthmarks as evidence of reincarnation?"

"Well, research can be a costly enterprise. If someone spends a lot of time and money - usually money obtained from a research foundation - investigating reports of past lives, he or she would be disinclined to return 'empty-handed.' But, more to the point, reincarnation researchers must already believe in reincarnation as a theoretical possibility otherwise they wouldn't spend so much time investigating it. One doesn't investigate things without a prior belief in their existence – what would be the point?"

"Yes, but Helen Wambach, who wrote *Life Before Life*, started off as a sceptic but changed her mind in the face of overwhelming evidence."

"If Helen Wambach had really been a sceptic, as claimed, she could have easily interpreted the data differently."

"But doesn't that argument apply to people who believe in spirit obsession? Are they not interpreting the evidence to uphold their beliefs?"

"No. Although memories of past lives and correlated birth marks confirm that discarnate personalities exist, none of these things are necessary to prove that they exist; their existence has been proven by other means. By contrast, reincarnation research has nothing but past life memories and correlated birthmarks."

"If reincarnation doesn't happen," returned Faraway, "why do most spirits teach it?"

"Most spirits who communicate anything at all are usually close to the Earth, either because they desire to influence earthly affairs or because they have not shed their materiality; either way their spiritual vision is limited. Since – as you say – three quarters of the world believe in reincarnation, the majority of those 'passing on' will be believers and since they will remain close to the Earth waiting to reincarnate it follows that the majority of communicating spirits will believe in reincarnation. The obsession the majority of communicating spirits have with the doctrine of reincarnation is merely a reflection of the state of affairs on Earth; it has nothing to do with spiritual truth."

"Many spirits who have communicated through famous mediums in the past – like Edgar Cayce – seem pretty advanced to me," replied Faraway.

"Well," I replied, "Edgar Cayce's spirits may seem advanced from *our* point of view but from higher spiritual spheres they might look fairly mediocre."

"But, Edgar Cayce's spirits were of such great service to sick people I don't believe they could have been mistaken about reincarnation."

"There is this presumption that, because Cayce's spirits provided useful remedies for people's ailments, everything else they uttered must have been the absolute truth. They may have been right about some things but were wrong about others – reincarnation being one of them. You also assume that Cayce's spirits were totally impartial. When individuals pass over they carry their beliefs and prejudices with them - remember the case of Charlie Herrman. The spirits who communicated through Edgar Cayce already believed in reincarnation – they may have been Buddhists or Hindus - and would automatically interpret any impressed memories as belonging to a previous life of the subject. Religious attachment to ideas can be extremely difficult to shake off. Buddhists, Hindus, Christians and Muslims do not cease to be Buddhists, Hindus, Christians and Muslims when they pass over; they can remain loyal to their faiths for a very long time, and Edgar Cayce's spirits would have been no exception. Although Cayce himself didn't believe in reincarnation, people who contacted him often did. In spiritualist circles it is a well-known fact that communicating spirits often reflect 'sitters' beliefs about all kinds of things. But in any case, a subject doesn't need to believe in reincarnation - merely be the recipient of impressed memories."

"Cayce's spirits gave information about past lives that were later confirmed," replied Faraway. "For example, Cayce gave a life reading to a blind musician who later regained his vision in one eye following suggestions by Cayce's spirits. As it happened, this man had a passion for railroads and a great interest in the Civil War. Cayce told him that he had been a soldier in the South, in the army of Lee, and that he had been a railroad man by profession; his name had been Barnett Seay and the records of Seay could still be found in the state of Virginia. Sometime later the man searched the records in the state capitol at Richmond and found the record of one Barnett Seay, standard-bearer in Lee's army who had entered and been discharged from the service in such and such a year. That seems pretty conclusive to me."

"Conclusive of what?" I replied. "The blind musician – let us call him Y – had a passion for railroads and a tremendous interest in the Civil War. If Y had been obsessed by the spirit of Barnett Seay, it would easily account for his special enthusiasm – even obsession - for those subjects. Furthermore, the obsessing spirit would have impressed Y with its memories. Impressed memories - like any other memories - can be 'read' by communicating spirits. Since Cayce's spirits already believed in reincarnation, it is unsurprising that they should have interpreted Y's impressed memories as belonging to a previous incarnation. The subsequent discovery of one 'Barnett Seay' in the Richmond records means only that a person called Barnett Seay existed – nothing more. The case of Charlie Herrman proves that subsequent confirmation of existence does not imply reincarnation. It follows that Y was no more a reincarnation of Barnett Seay than Jack T. was a reincarnation of Charlie Herrman."

"But," replied Faraway, "if Y had been obsessed by the spirit of Barnett Seay, wouldn't Cayce's spirits have known about it"

"Why should they have known? I think you credit Cayce's spirits with more powers than they actually possessed. Impressed memories may be indistinguishable from naturally acquired memories. Although Cayce's spirits were typical of those who teach reincarnation, other spirits warn against it."

"What spirits?" queried Faraway.

"The spirit of Helen Blavatsky, co-founder with Colonel Olcott of the Theosophical Society, warned against belief in reincarnation. Communicating through the mediumship of Mrs Wickland she bitterly regretted that she had ever taught it. In Carl Wickland's book *Thirty Years Among the Dead*, she states that: 'A spirit impresses you with the experiences of its life and these are implanted in your mind as your own. You then think you remember your past.' She also states that she tried very hard to reincarnate but spirits told her she could not: 'We progress, we do not come back.' The spirit of Blavatsky is now devoting much effort in persuading earthbound spirits to give up all attempts to reincarnate and to turn their thoughts towards the light."

"There's no way of knowing that that was the spirit of Helen Blavatsky," replied Faraway somewhat testily, "It could have been some impersonating spirit."

"Blavatsky anticipated people's disbelief. She said that people wouldn't believe it was her because the earthly HPB would never have said those things. But this underlines the difficulty of communicating between two worlds; people only accept things that uphold their beliefs."

"Is that the only communication against reincarnation?"

"In *Illuminated Brahminism*, a communication from the spirit of the ancient Indian teacher Ranga Hilyod it is stated that the doctrine of reincarnation is a 'perversion of a great truth' and a 'source of the most pestilent spiritual mischief'; and in *Illuminated Buddhism*, a communication from the spirit of Siddhartha Sakyamuni, it is said that the doctrine of reincarnation 'poisoned' the mentality of India for centuries."

"Yes," replied Faraway, "but, there's no proof that those communications actually came from Ranga Hilyod and Siddhartha Sakyamuni."

"I think you have missed the point", I replied. "What really matters is the spiritual content of the messages, not the source. Spirits who warn against belief in reincarnation are exclusively concerned with the spiritual upliftment of humankind; but spirits who give out information on past lives are merely pandering to the interests of their listeners. For example, Cayce's spirits told Y that he had been a soldier in General Lee's army - in itself a piece of useless information but Y must have found it quite titillating.

* * *

We had been chatting for nearly an hour when a friend of John Faraway's - Alice Toogood - wandered in. Another devotee of the doctrine of reincarnation, she professed a firm belief in karma.

"The doctrine of karma explains all the injustices and inequalities in the world," explained Alice.

"How so?" I enquired.

"Otherwise everything happens by chance. If someone gets shot that's negative karma; winning a fortune is positive karma."

"Why do you add the word 'karma'? Surely it's enough to say: getting shot is bad, and winning a fortune is good?"

"Because," replied Alice, "getting shot is probably a punishment for shooting someone in a previous life, and winning a fortune is probably a reward for generosity.

Bad actions are punished with negative karma, and good actions are rewarded with positive karma. That way the soul gets purified."

"Like punishing and rewarding a child?"

"Exactly."

"That's a strange philosophy," I replied. "What is the point of deferring punishments and rewards to future incarnations? Surely they would be more effective and more just if they were imposed immediately. One doesn't punish a small child by cancelling its 18th birthday party. Hopefully, by then, all childish misdemeanours and transgressions will have been forgiven and forgotten. Besides, how many 18 year olds remember being naughty when they were only three years old? It violates a fundamental principle that people should know exactly why they are being punished. In the doctrine of karma, people are punished for misdemeanours committed in previous incarnations about which they have absolutely no memories; and if they have no memories, they feel they are being punished arbitrarily."

"But," replied Alice, "the soul needs more than one life to learn all the necessary lessons. Since many criminals re-offend, their punishments on earth must have been ineffective. Also, a serial killer cannot be properly punished unless he experiences the act of being murdered over and over again."

"Because particular kinds of punishment are ineffective," I replied, "doesn't mean that a criminal cannot be reformed by other means. Secondly, the notion that a murderer should experience the act of being murdered is a value judgment and, in any case, it is far from obvious that being murdered over and over again will achieve the desired result; it may punish the murderer but it will not necessarily reform him. But, more importantly, doing the same to the perpetrator, as the perpetrator has done to his victim, would make you no better than the perpetrator."

"But," said Alice, "karma, as a law of cause and effect, is totally impersonal. If X murders Y, forces are set in motion that guarantee that X gets murdered – or something equally unpleasant - in his next incarnation, preferably by Y; that way the debt gets settled."

"You mean that karma works as mechanism for settling disputes?"

"Yes," replied Alice.

"That assumes it *is* capable of settling disputes; but there are serious problems with it."

"Such as?" queried Alice.

"To begin with, the soul gets punished twice for only one misdemeanour which means that karma never settles disputes in practice."

"I don't see that!" retorted Alice.

"Well, using your example, suppose X murders Y. Then, according to you, Y must have murdered X in a previous incarnation so that X is merely settling accounts. But, if X is settling accounts then the debt has been settled and that should be the end of the matter. Nevertheless, X is still held morally and legally responsible for the murder of Y in the *present* incarnation and, if caught, will definitely be punished and possibly executed. Hence X gets punished *twice*: once in the incarnation when X is murdered by Y and once in the present incarnation when X is punished for murdering Y. But this additional and unnecessary punishment creates a sense of injustice in the soul of X which is resolved in the next incarnation only by X murdering Y; and so the process continues, each murdering the other in one incarnation after another without end. Rather than settle disputes, karma prolongs disputes. If, on the other hand, X is *not* punished for murdering Y on the grounds that X is merely settling accounts from a previous life, then the same argument would have to be applied to all murderers; indeed, the same argument would have to be applied to *all* perpetrators of any crimes. In the end, nobody on Earth would get punished for anything."

"Ok, that's only one problem. Are there any more?"

"Yes," I replied, "Can you explain why earthly riches are heaped upon the wicked? If this is positive karma, the wicked must have been fairly good in a previous incarnation. If karma purifies the soul, how is it that good people have become so degenerate? Also, many saintly people live in extremely humble circumstances - presumably negative karma. Are you saying that these people were *wicked* in a previous incarnation?"

"Saintly people may have been wicked in *distant* incarnations," replied Alice, "but, through the operation of karma they have gradually been transformed into saintly people. Also, saintly people choose to live in humble circumstances. I see no evidence of negative karma there. Perhaps, their saintliness is their positive karma."

"Ok," I replied, "but can you explain how good people can become wicked?"

"Perhaps, earthly riches are not always indicative of positive karma," replied Alice. "Maybe their wickedness is their negative karma. Wicked people may have been more wicked in previous incarnations, and through the operation of karma have become *less* wicked."

"In other words, karma cannot be taken at face value."

"Precisely," replied Alice.

"Ok, I grant you that, but the problems don't end there," I continued. "On the one hand karma operates as a corrective force by punishing bad actions and rewarding good ones, and on the other hand it imprisons the soul for all time. Ultimately, karma achieves nothing."

"How does karma imprison the soul?"

"Because actions generate karma, and karma compels the soul to reincarnate. When the soul reincarnates, the actions of the next incarnation generate more karma; the process is endless. According to the law of cause and effect, every action sets in motion a chain of effects that continues without end. In the doctrine of reincarnation, the actions of one incarnation, say incarnation N, have karmic consequences which must be worked out in incarnation, N+1. The actions of incarnation N+1, have karmic consequences which must be worked out in incarnation N+2, and so on *ad infinitum.*

"You say that karma imprisons the soul for all time," replied Alice, "but Hindus and Buddhists teach that karma can be controlled and overcome by following a virtuous life and achieving a perfect balance of mind leading, eventually, to the cessation of all karma. The Lord Buddha called it the Noble Eightfold Path. That means that everyone can, in principle, escape the cycle of rebirths."

"In principle," I replied, "but not in practice."

"Why not in practice?" enquired Alice.

"Well," I replied, "a person's ability to control karma is itself determined by karma. Without perseverance, dedication, devotion to duty, obedience, ability to concentrate and meditate, and a willingness to renounce the world, nothing will be achieved. But, these character traits do not fall from the sky, nor are they determined by the personality; as far as the personality is concerned they are *givens*. Character traits can only be determined by karma; hence, the ability to control karma is itself determined by karma. This means that karma cannot be eliminated by design, only by chance."

"Why by chance?" enquired Alice.

"Well, if I ask why your house was burgled last year, you will probably say: 'that is my karma – I must have been a thief in a previous incarnation.' If I ask why you were a thief in that incarnation, you will say: 'that was my karma - I must have been an acquisitive person in an incarnation before that one.' Each time we go back to an earlier incarnation your answer will be the same: 'that was my karma,' with some sort of rationalisation attached. Since present karma is determined by previous actions, and since previous actions are determined by previous character traits which, in turn, are determined by karma, the process goes backwards in time *ad infinitum*. This means that there could never have been a first incarnation which is, of course, nonsense."

"Yes, there must have been a first incarnation," added Faraway, "because all physical things must have a beginning."

"Ok," I replied, "but, what determines the karma of the first incarnation?"

"Well," replied Alice, "since there is no incarnation before the first one, the karma of the first incarnation must be determined by the actions of the first incarnation."

"But, what determines the actions of the first incarnation?"

"I see the problem," replied Alice, "If actions determine karma, the same karma cannot determine the character traits which are responsible for the actions because something cannot determine itself."

"Exactly, and if nothing determines the actions of the first incarnation, they must be the product of chance – like the throw of dice. And if the actions of the first incarnation are the product of chance then, ultimately, all subsequent karma must be the product of chance which means that liberation from the cycle of rebirths is also the product of chance."

"Hmm, I'll think about that," replied Alice.

"But, it also has implications for the ethics of karma," I continued. "If the actions of the first incarnation are the product of chance, the present personality cannot be held morally responsible for them; and since the karma of the present incarnation is, ultimately, traceable back to the actions of the first incarnation, the present personality cannot be held morally responsible for his or her present karma. All inequalities stem from the inequalities of the first incarnation, and since the inequalities of the first incarnation are the product of chance, the law of karma fails as a system of explanation. While it purports to be an even-handed system of correction - handing out punishments and rewards as deserved - it is, in fact, totally arbitrary."

"Couldn't the law of karma make allowances for the inequalities of the first incarnation?" replied Alice.

"No," I replied, "not if the law of karma is impersonal."

"Why is that?" replied Faraway.

"Consider the following example. Two people, let's call them A and B, are competing with each other in a shooting contest; competitor B is blindfolded. When B fires his gun the projectile moves in exactly the same way as if a sighted person had pulled the trigger. The laws of physics do not make allowances for the fact that B is blindfolded and unable to see the target; they are completely impartial and apply even-handedly to everyone irrespective of initial handicaps or advantages. Gravity doesn't make allowances for the difference in heights; a projectile released from the top of a building will take longer to reach the ground than an identical projectile released only a few feet from the ground. Karma, as an impersonal law of cause and effect, must operate in exactly the same way; it cannot make allowances for the inequalities of the first incarnation any more than the laws of physics can make allowances for the initial inequalities between A and B."

Alice sipped her coffee searching for flaws in my argument. Faraway, who had been listening intently, said:

"In spite of what you say, a billion Hindus and Buddhists cannot all be wrong!"

"Actually," I replied, "Hindus and Buddhists disagree on the most fundamental question: the nature of the human self. Hindus believe that the self is immortal whereas Buddhists believe it is an illusion. Actually, the Buddhist concept of rebirth is unclear because no fixed entity is reborn."

"In Buddhism" Alice interjected, "the consciousness in the new person is neither identical to nor entirely different from that in the deceased person but together form a stream of consciousness."

"Maybe," I replied, "but that's self-contradictory."

"Why is that?" Alice queried with some surprise.

"Because in Buddhism there is no permanent self that links one incarnation with another."

"Yes, but why is that self-contradictory?"

"In Buddhism it is taught that all visible things are in a constant state of flux and that nothing has any permanent reality - except nirvana. When this principle is applied to the doctrine of rebirth it is inferred that no permanent self exists. But this is a *non sequitur.* Anything subject to change is neither identical to nor completely different from what it was before it changed; but that does not mean the different states of the thing have nothing in common. For example, a tree continually changes its state from seed to sapling to full maturity until it dies from which it follows that any state of the tree is neither identical to nor completely different from any other state of the tree. Nevertheless, all the states of the tree are related through their common identity, and it is this identity that remains a constant and permanent feature of the process of change. If this were not the case, then the tree in my garden today would be completely different to the tree in my garden tomorrow; and John Faraway today would be completely different to John Faraway tomorrow - which means he could rob a bank today and be free of prosecution tomorrow because, by then, the John Faraway sitting in front of us will no longer exist. Therefore, the claim that nothing is permanent because all visible things are in a constant state of flux is manifestly false. If there were no underlying permanent 'self' that was common to all the different states of consciousness linking one life with another, none of these states of consciousness would have anything in common and it would then not make sense to say that rebirth had taken place. Rebirth necessarily entails a permanent self - contrary to Buddhist teaching that no such thing exists. Hindus abandoned the concept of the impermanent self many centuries ago and teach that the human self is immortal. Obviously, Buddhists and Hindus cannot both be right – which means that one of them is wrong."

"But," countered Alice, "Buddhist's say that all things - not just all *visible* things - are in a state of flux from which it follows that no permanent self exists."

"In that case," I replied," the statement is merely saying: 'nothing impermanent is permanent' - which is a tautology."

"In spite of what you say," replied Faraway, "no one can disprove reincarnation for the simple reason you can't prove a negative."

"Surely that depends on the negative," I replied.

"What do you mean?"

"Well, for example, 'two plus two is *not* equal to five is a negative statement but that can easily be proven by going back to the axioms of arithmetic."

"Yes but reincarnation is different; it's something that happens."

"Reincarnation is something that *allegedly* happens. The principal difficulty with the doctrine of reincarnation is the concept of reincarnation. In all systems of belief that incorporate the notion of re-embodiment, reincarnation is treated as a meaningful activity - like switching overcoats or crossing the road. Given this fundamental idea, believers – and even agnostics – often claim that since you can't prove that something meaningful never happens, and since reincarnation is meaningful, you can't prove that reincarnation never happens. In other words: you can't prove a negative. But the argument is a red herring because the issue is one of logical consistency not possibility; the doctrine of reincarnation is incoherent."

"What exactly do you mean by incoherent?" queried Alice.

"A doctrine or system of thought is incoherent if its parts are logically incompatible with each other. If they are, then the system is self-cancelling or self-refuting. For example, a loving and forgiving God is incompatible with a punishing and revengeful God; God in time is incompatible with God in Eternity; human salvation is incompatible with eternal damnation; human immortality is incompatible with human mortality, and so on. If someone believes in a revengeful and forgiving God they effectively believe in nothing because, taken together, revenge and forgiveness are self-cancelling."

"Yes, but what has that to do with reincarnation?"

"Over the centuries the doctrine of reincarnation has accumulated so much baggage it has become a veritable dog's breakfast."

"What baggage?" returned Alice, "Reincarnation seems pretty straightforward to me."

"Well, philosophers and theologians have always modified doctrines to meet current fads, and the doctrine of reincarnation is no exception. For example, Hindus originally subscribed to the current Buddhist notion of the impermanent self and taught that the individual was destined to be absorbed by Brahman which meant that everyone would eventually be annihilated. However, when the idea of human immortality became fashionable, Hindus integrated it into their own system of thought paying scant regard to logical consistency. In recent times, when Helen Blavatsky's *The Secret Doctrine* was published, reincarnationism upgraded its metaphysical apparatus by several notches and most books on reincarnation appealed to it for support. However, thanks to HPB's outlandish claims about the source of her information plus the work of twentieth century philosophers and logicians, both metaphysics and theosophy were discredited as avenues of truth. But that didn't deter believers. Since the rise of physics in the nineteenth and twentieth centuries, reincarnationists quietly dropped the prefix 'meta' from the word 'metaphysics' and pretended that the doctrine of reincarnation had the support of 'physics.' It began with the reinterpretation of karma as a 'law of cause and effect,' and this soon morphed into its upper case version, The Law of Cause and Effect, suggesting a *universal* law. However, when the 'quantum' was discovered at the turn of the twentieth century, reincarnationism had to change gear once again because the 'law of cause and effect' lost its status as a fundamental principle of science. Gaining inspiration from books like the *Tao of Physics (1975)* by Fritjof Capra, reincarnationists tried hard to incorporate the wonders of quantum physics – or at least the jargon of quantum physics – into their explanatory models. Since then, reincarnationism has become a full-blown industry, spawning so many pseudo-scientific papers and research efforts that HPB would have been truly astonished and – judging by her attitude since passing - truly disconcerted. The point is that the ongoing desire to sell reincarnationism to the masses by dazzling them with the latest intellectual gadgetry, has compromised its logical integrity."

"Why is the doctrine of reincarnation incoherent?" interjected Faraway.

"Well, for example, it claims that the human self is immortal, but immortality and reincarnation are logically incompatible."

" I don't understand that!" retorted Faraway.

"Let me explain. If the human self is immortal it must exist in eternity and if it exists in eternity it must be timeless. If the human self is timeless then all its incarnations are simultaneous; but in that case the human self would have no individuality – contrary to everything we know about human beings. If the human self doesn't incarnate as more than one person at a time then it doesn't reincarnate."

"I don't follow that," replied Faraway.

"Well, do you agree that different people living and working at the same time are unique individuals?"

"Yes, I have no doubt of that."

"Then you agree that each individual has a spiritual identity that distinguishes them from all other individuals."

"Yes."

"In other words, the human self doesn't incarnate as more than one person at a time; if it did, groups of human beings would be like gaggles of geese."

"Yes," agreed Faraway, "but how does that explain your point?"

"Well, you have just agreed that the human self does not incarnate as more than one person at a time because then its incarnations would be simultaneous. Since time – at least to the human self – has no reality, it follows that, if it *did* reincarnate, all its incarnations would be simultaneous. Since human individuality rules out simultaneous incarnations it follows that the human self cannot reincarnate. Because the human self is immortal and uniquely expressive reincarnation cannot happen."

"But surely," replied Faraway, "eternity is the same as infinite time in which case the self's incarnations in time are *not* simultaneous. If the self *does* exist in time then it can occupy different bodies at different points of time in which case reincarnation is possible – at least in principle."

"Actually, the concept of infinite time has been rejected by physicists and philosophers because the universe is of finite duration. Time begins and ends with the physical universe which means that time – however long - cannot be equated with eternity. All philosophers agree that eternity is *timeless*. If – as you say - the human self exists in time it must be perishable or mortal, and mortality is incompatible with immortality. If the human self is immortal it cannot exist in time and that means it exists in eternity. If it exists in eternity then time has no reality and all events and incarnations are simultaneous."

"I'm not clear why the human self cannot exist in time," interjected Alice.

"Because the human self is immortal. What is immortal exists in eternity, and time to eternity is relatively zero. In terms of the finite and the infinite, the finite to the infinite is relatively zero. For example, if you divide a number by infinity you always get zero. This means that relative to the human self time has no reality, and if time has no reality the human self cannot exist in time."

"But you just said that eternity was not infinite time."

"That's correct. Eternity is not infinite *time*; but it *is* an infinite something else – probably beyond definition. Anything finite – time or otherwise – to eternity has no reality. To the human self time has no reality therefore the human self cannot exist in time."

"Let us suppose, for the sake of argument," Alice continued, "that the human self *does* exist in time. Could it then reincarnate?"

"No, because karma cannot work in practice and, without karma, reincarnation cannot happen; both are dependent on one another."

"I don't see why reincarnation depends on karma", said Faraway, "reincarnation could still happen in practice."

"Not so," I replied. "According to the doctrine of reincarnation human spiritual development is subject to karmic law. If reincarnation wasn't a law-governed process it would be totally random; and if it were totally random there would be no relationship whatsoever between actions and consequences. For example, a mass murderer might be rewarded with a huge fortune in his next incarnation. No proponent of the doctrine of reincarnation has ever taught that! If karma cannot work, the doctrine of reincarnation collapses."

"Quite recently," Alice continued, "I saw a book about physics, reincarnation and the soul. Apparently, reincarnation is supported by quantum physics; it's explained in terms of quantum non-locality."

"Firstly, quantum physics supports nothing of the kind. Some physicists, who happen to be Hindus, have tried very hard in recent years to swing the weight and prestige of quantum physics behind the reincarnationist cause and have, in the process, generated a lot of interest amongst the book-buying public. But, all they have done is use the jargon of quantum physics to dazzle their readers. Quantum mechanics – as it is more properly called - can *only* be expressed in the language of higher mathematics. For example, the axioms of quantum mechanics are that (1) all states are vectors in complex Hilbert space, and (2) every physical observable is a Hermitian operator acting on the Hilbert space. If you read any books with the words 'quantum' and 'reincarnation' in the title, you will find that the mathematical content is precisely *zero*, not because the authors wish to make their books more readable, but because there's no physics behind their theories. Secondly, quantum non-locality, or 'action-at-a-distance' as it sometimes called, refers to the faster-than-light communication between the parts of a quantum system such as two photons – an apparent violation of a fundamental principle of modern physics which asserts that nothing can exceed the speed of light. This produces some very strange effects like 'quantum tunnelling' in which a particle at a wall vanishes only to reappear almost instantaneously on the other side. Furthermore, some quantum physicists have argued that particles, before they are actually observed, exist 'everywhere at once' and only materialise when their properties are measured. The superficial resemblance of all this with the apparent behaviour of 'ghosts' and 'spirits' has led some reincarnationists to suppose that all paranormal and spiritualistic phenomena, including UFOs, mystery animals, time-slips - in fact the 'whole gamut' - are explainable in terms of quantum physics. Since quantum particles are apparently unbounded by time and space the next step is to define the human self as a quantum entity and, hey presto, the human self can be everywhere at once occupying different bodies at once even if the bodies themselves are scattered over time. Apparently they have provided a scientific explanation of reincarnation. The problem with this is that, since the human self is timeless, it must incarnate in all its bodies simultaneously; and if it incarnates in all its bodies simultaneously in eternity, it has no individuality in eternity. If the human self has no individuality in eternity, then it has no individuality in time. But, if we insist that the human self does have individuality then it must have individuality in time *and* eternity. Furthermore, we have already seen that the doctrine of karma is futile, and without karma there can be no reincarnation."

"Doesn't obsession by spirits contradict what you have said about the human self being uniquely expressive?" queried Faraway.

"Did you have any particular cases in mind?"

"Take the case of Charlie Herrman. When he was on Earth he expressed himself as Charlie Herrman and when he became a spirit he expressed himself – albeit briefly - through Jack T. If time has no reality for the human self then Charlie Herrman's self must have been expressing itself through Charlie Herrman and Jack T. simultaneously which means that the human self cannot be uniquely expressive."

"I think you have misunderstood the meaning of the term 'uniquely expressive.' To say that the human self is uniquely expressive is just another way of saying that it doesn't incarnate in more than one physical body simultaneously – nothing more."

"But the expressions of Charlie Herrman's self are still simultaneous," protested Faraway, "and that contradicts the idea of unique expression."

"You are confusing 'expressiveness' with 'influence;' the two things are completely different. Jack T's obsession by Charlie Herrman was no more an expression of Charlie Herrman's self than a hypnotized subject is the expression of a hypnotist's self. Charlie Herrman may have influenced Jack T's behaviour but he had certainly not reincarnated as Jack T. An obsessing spirit does *not* incarnate in the body of the person it obsesses."

"That seems to contradict what happens when someone channels information, like Jane Roberts," replied Alice. "Just before Seth began speaking through her, she would sit back in an armchair, take off her glasses and adopt completely different mannerisms; just as though some other entity had occupied her body."

"Appearances can be deceiving," I replied, "Jane Roberts' trance mannerisms were merely an automatic response to Seth's personality - in some ways like a marionette's response to a puppeteer's movements, though the analogy is far from perfect. The problem is that there are no Earthly counterparts to describe what happens on the spirit side of life. The spirit of Ranga Hilyod said that: 'I did teach that all spirits could return to earth to manifest, and influence mortals' but that: 'There were those who could not understand how a spirit could come to earth without being re-embodied in physical life.'"

"It's just occurred to me," said Faraway, "your claim that the human self cannot incarnate in more than one physical body cannot be true."

"How so?"

"Firstly, the human body exists at each point of time from the moment it is born to the moment it dies. Secondly, the human self incarnates in each of these bodies. Thirdly, since the human self doesn't recognise time, all these embodiments must be simultaneous which means that the human self cannot be uniquely expressive."

"Unfortunately, my friend, you are incorrect. The human self expresses itself through one and only one archetypal form. The physical body at each point of time - like the simultaneous shadows of a single object - is merely a reflection of the archetype and has no reality in itself.

To confuse the physical body with the archetype is to confuse the shadow with the substance."

"Well," replied Alice," I have a copy of the Silver Birch Anthology here and it seems to support the idea of reincarnation."

Alice leafed through the book and read out the following extract: *"What incarnates is another aspect of the same individuality, and I do not mean personality. If you visualise man as an individual, who in his earthly life is like an iceberg in which you have one small portion manifesting and the larger portion not manifesting, then that is the end of one incarnation. In a successive incarnation, a portion of the submerged self will come into the world of matter, two different personalities, but one individual. And in spirit life, as progression takes place, it is part of the submerged self that comes to the surface all the time."*

"Well," I replied, "the passage has many undefined terms, but let us take it step by step. Firstly, are we agreed that when Silver Birch uses the term 'personality' he mean 'person'?

"Yes," replied Alice.

"Then by 'two different personalities' Silver Birch means two different people."

"Yes."

"Firstly, what is meant by individuality?"

"That which distinguishes one person from another," replied Alice.

"Ok, but, what is it that distinguishes one person from another?"

"The most obvious thing is our physical bodies. When you see two different bodies, you see two different people," replied Faraway.

"Yes, but suppose they are hidden from sight, say, behind a screen. There might be two people pretending to be one person. How could you tell the difference?"

"That's easy!" returned Faraway. "If I ask the same question twice and hear two different voices, there must be two different people."

"Not necessarily," replied Alice, "because voices can be disguised; one person might be pretending to be two."

"I was wondering," continued Faraway, "if two people are so alike in their physical appearance, behaviour, thoughts, feelings, attitudes and desires that they could not be distinguished from one another, would they still be classed as different individuals?"

"Actually, two people like that could not really exist. At a minimum, each would see the other from a different physical vantage point - they occupy different regions of space - and that alone would create in each of them a different mental state. But, in any case, they must still be regarded as different individuals because individuality is not contingent upon our ability to make distinctions. Individuality is primarily a subjective experience - that which makes us feel uniquely different from other individuals."

"Apart from the physical body," continued Alice, "how can one individual be distinguished from another?"

"Well," I replied, "if we can't see them, we could ask questions and analyse their responses. Assuming that all questions are answered honestly and consistently, one question might be: 'What is your favourite colour?'"

"Right," said Faraway. "If the first response is 'blue' and the second 'green' then two different people must be present."

"Yes," replied Alice, "but, if both responses are 'blue' there might be two people whose favourite colour happens to be blue."

"In other words," I continued, "we need to ask more questions. When the responses differ, we know there are two people present. If the responses are always the same, then only one person is present."

"That seems to clear it up," said Faraway.

"Unfortunately, it doesn't," I replied, "because responses are only expressions of individuality. They allow us to distinguish one individual from another but they don't say what individuality is. But there's another problem. Silver Birch says: *'What incarnates is another aspect of the same individuality, and I do not mean personality.'* In other words, Silver Birch is saying that we cannot distinguish one individual from another by pointing to two different personalities because two different personalities might be one individual. But, that's clearly wrong if the personalities are contemporaries of one another."

"What do you mean?" queried Faraway.

"Well, do you agree that contemporaneous personalities i.e. those living and working at the same time, are different personalities with different individualities?"

"Obviously!" interjected Alice

"Then Silver Birch must be referring to personalities who are *non*-contemporaneous e.g. personalities living and working in different historical time periods."

"Yes," concurred Alice.

"OK, let's continue. The next sentence says: *'If you visualise man as an individual, who in his earthly life is like an iceberg in which you have one small portion manifesting and the larger portion not manifesting, then that is the end of one incarnation.*' That statement is perfectly consistent with only *one* incarnation. In esoteric teaching, the physical body is the smaller, manifesting part, and the remainder is the larger non-manifesting part. Nothing in the statement implies reincarnation."

"Yes, but what about the next statement," replied Alice. She picked up the book and read it out aloud: '*In a successive incarnation, a portion of the submerged self will come into the world of matter, two different personalities, but one individual.*'"

"Well, we have already agreed that two contemporaneous personalities are two individuals. But, can two *non*-contemporaneous personalities be only one individual?"

"Silver Birch says they can be," replied Faraway.

"But, is Silver Birch correct?"

Alice looked amazed.

"Anything can be disputed," I continued. "Nothing should be accepted on authority."

"Ok," replied Faraway, "You're going to tell us he is wrong."

"Well," I continued, "do we all agree that the human self is immortal?"

Both listeners nodded intently.

"At the risk of repeating myself," I continued, "if the self is immortal it exists in eternity.

"Yes," said Faraway, "we've been over this ground before."

"Let me continue. To eternity time has no reality therefore all events are simultaneous. What would appear as a succession of incarnations to Silver Birch would be simultaneous to a being existent in eternity; they would be exactly the same as contemporaneous incarnations are to us.

We have already agreed that two contemporaneous personalities are *two* individuals, and since all incarnations are contemporaneous to an eternal being, it follows that, to an eternal being, two noncontemporaneous personalities are two individuals. But, if two noncontemporaneous personalities are two individuals in eternity then they are *always* two individuals, and that means they are individuals in time. Thus, when Silver Birch says: *'two different personalities, but one individual'* he is clearly mistaken."

"Why should Silver Birch make this mistake?" enquired Alice.

"When Silver Birch was communicating this material he was probably still time-bound; and time-bound personalities think in temporal terms. This seems to be true of all communicating spirits who teach the doctrine of reincarnation. Advanced spirits who have progressed beyond the limitations of time, warn against belief in reincarnation."

"Ok," replied Alice, "but Darwinism is in sync with the doctrine of reincarnation. Both describe evolution from lower to higher forms of life. That's more than just coincidence."

"In Darwin's *Origin of Species*?"

"Yes," continued Alice, "reincarnationists say much the same thing. Consciousness transmigrates from one form to another working its way up the evolutionary ladder eventually transmigrating from one human form to another. Some believe that if the personality has been particularly evil the next life will be lived as an animal. Buddhists believe that the forms are linked together by a stream of consciousness; Hindus would call it the self. Whatever you believe, the evolutionary ladder still exists."

"Yes, that's what they believe," I replied, "but Darwinism is in crisis."

"What do you mean?" interjected Faraway.

"Well, that's another story."

* * *

Time seemed to have flown - if it indeed it ever existed - and our conversation reached a natural conclusion. John Faraway and Alice Toogood left the snack bar while I munched into my salad sandwich.

Chapter 2
Believing the Impossible

Reincarnationism and Darwinism have surprisingly many features in common. Both tell 'stories' of progressive evolution from 'lower' to 'higher' forms of life, and both require continuity between the objects of interest (incarnations in one case, species in the other). However, the similarities do not end there for both posit hierarchies of life (spiritual in one case, taxonomic in the other) and both employ systems of punitive control (misfortune in one case, extinction in the other). While the personality adapts to circumstances, the species adapts to the environment; and both need inconceivable stretches of time for their respective 'actors' to play out their respective roles. Moreover, both are constantly searching for 'missing links' (memories of previous lives in one case, intermediate forms in the other), and both derive comfort from the 'principle of irrefutability.' Merely because no cases of reincarnation have ever been confirmed does not mean that reincarnation does not happen, and merely because no intermediate forms have ever been discovered does not mean that none exist. In other words: "you can't prove a negative." To be sure, reincarnationists claim that cases of reincarnation exist, and Darwinists maintain that intermediate forms have been discovered but, in both cases, the claims fall apart under scrutiny. Crucially, both suffer from 'confirmation bias' i.e. "The tendency to seek or interpret evidence favourable to already existing beliefs and to ignore or reinterpret evidence unfavourable to already existing beliefs." (Michael Shermer, *Why People Believe Weird Things* p.299). As we shall see, this describes reincarnationist Dr. Ian Stevenson and Darwinist Richard Dawkins rather well. But make no mistake, believing that one may have been a duckbilled platypus in a previous life or that one's distant ancestor was a leaf-cutting insect must, by any reckoning, be considered weird.

Despite the absurd nature of the content involved, and the absence of a credible *modus operandi*, both "isms" attract uncritical coverage in the media (films in one case, TV documentaries in the other), and both attract considerable sums of money under the pretext of doing 'field work.' But if the reader is still unclear why it is necessary to attack Darwinism in a book refuting reincarnation, a moment's reflection will reveal that being a monkey in a previous life or being descended from one is saying pretty much the same thing. The point is that both dehumanize humanity in slightly different but equally significant ways. No wonder Charles Darwin is so popular amongst reincarnationists! Needless to say, once the prop of Darwinism has been removed, reincarnationism loses much of its legitimacy.

* * *

As part of a general research effort into beliefs and values across Europe and the Nordic countries, the *European Values Survey (1999-2002)* published data on belief in reincarnation and life after death. The principal question put to respondents was: "Do you believe in reincarnation, that is, that we are born into this world again?" Set within the context of Western beliefs about immortality, individuality and the survival of human personality after death, the question was phrased as simply as possible and was intended to capture the core meaning of the term 'reincarnation.' It was assumed that respondents would understand the meaning of the statement: "We are born into this world again." The survey revealed that belief in reincarnation is greatest in Eastern Europe (27%) followed by the Nordic countries (22.6%) with Western Europe a close third (22.2%). A weighted average of these figures shows that, across the whole of Europe and the Nordic countries, the figure is approximately 25% - a figure that tallies with recent survey results across the United States of America. In Western Europe, Switzerland (36%), Portugal (29%) and the United Kingdom (29%) are significantly above average. In Eastern Europe Lithuania (44%) is well above average, as is Iceland (41%) among the Nordic countries.

One would have expected a small proportion of respondents to express a belief in reincarnation because the question is loaded with the suggestion that reincarnation can happen: "We believe that reincarnation is possible – do you?" Nevertheless, the overall results are surprising because the doctrine of reincarnation is not a precept of Christianity, Judaism or Islam. Although it is not within the scope of this book to examine why people hold such beliefs, it is worth noting that belief in reincarnation may be linked to belief in the survival of human personality after death coupled with an ignorance or misunderstanding of

Spiritualism. The latter teaches that when the physical body is cast aside, the soul progresses to ever more rarefied spheres of existence towards a future state of infinite realisation. For those who believe in reincarnation, immortality in the flesh may be the only kind of immortality that is understood or even desired.

Whatever reasons are adduced, the results are remarkable because the belief that each one of us can be born again into this world as a different person is to believe in something self-contradictory. This follows because the human self is endowed with individuality and it is the expression of this individuality that differentiates one person from another. To believe that a person can be born again into this world as a different person is to believe that the defining qualities of one person can reappear as the defining qualities of a new person; but if the defining qualities of the new person are the same as the defining qualities of the old person, then the new person cannot be different to the old person. This means that Julius Caesar cannot be reborn as Isaac Newton; John Smith cannot be reborn as Janet Brown; and William Shakespeare cannot be reborn as Winston Churchill. Julius Caesar, Isaac Newton, John Smith, Janet Brown, William Shakespeare, and Winston Churchill – like everyone who has ever lived or will live – are different human beings with unique spiritual identities.

Consider the declaration: "I am John Brown." If the "I am" part of the declaration represents the utterance of an immortal being and the "John Brown" part corresponds to the incarnation of that being, the declaration means that an immortal being is expressing itself as "John Brown." Since an immortal being exists in eternity, and since time to eternity is relatively zero (and therefore unreal) it follows that to an immortal being all events are simultaneous. Consequently, there can be no distinction between past, present and future; all exists within an eternal Now, and expressions involving tense are meaningless. An immortal being does not say "I was Julius Caesar" or "I will be Isaac Newton" but "I am Julius Caesar" or "I am Isaac Newton." Furthermore, an immortal being does not say: "I am Julius Caesar and I am Isaac Newton" because an immortal being does not incarnate as more than one person simultaneously; to do so would be contrary to the nature of human individuality.

Vagueness, circularity and inconsistency characterize all definitions of reincarnation and its equivalent expressions: transmigration, re-birth and metempsychosis. For example, consider the following definition of metempsychosis in the Encarta English Dictionary: "The passage of somebody's soul after death into the body of another person or an animal." The principal difficulty here is that the meaning of the term 'soul' is unclear. From the definition alone, we do not know precisely what passes into the body of another person or animal, how this transition is made or what happens to the soul between incarnations. Popular accounts of reincarnation tend to treat the term 'soul' as synonymous with awareness or consciousness or as some psychic entity, and it is here that confusion creeps in because the 'soul' is then treated synonymously with the 'self' or 'spirit' in contradistinction to how it is being used in the definition, namely, as something *possessed*.

Moreover, the passage of the soul after death into the body of another person or an animal is a temporal process. Bodies exist in time and the soul passes into a body and stays there for an interval of time (i.e. the life of the person or animal). Following death, more time passes (it may be seconds or centuries) and the soul passes into another body, and stays there for another interval of time. Throughout the whole process, from birth to death and to rebirth, time passes. But, if one insists that the soul is immortal, then time has no reality for the soul, and if time has no reality there can be no passage of time. If there is no passage of time, there can be no passage of the soul; hence, there can be no metempsychosis of the soul. To add further confusion, some spiritual traditions regard the soul as the temporal abode of the inner self whose primary function is to record the experiences of the personality in the world of matter. But if the soul exists in the temporal world it cannot be immortal (see Chapter 3: Proving a Negative).

As an alternative route to reincarnation, the concept of a greater Self is sometimes invoked as a means of uniting disparate personalities into a greater whole (an allusion to the principle of the one and the many). In this view, the Self re-embodies successively as different personalities in different historical time periods to generate a temporal sequence of incarnations. These incarnations are then called the 'reincarnational selves' of the greater Self. Needless to say, there are problems with the view. Firstly, if the Self is immortal - in which case time has no reality - all the associated incarnations would be simultaneous, and if they are simultaneous they are not successive. Furthermore, if all the personalities are simultaneous then they are coexistent, and if they are coexistent they are unique and separate. Thus, it would be incorrect to say, for example, that personality A reincarnates as personality B or that personality B reincarnates as personality C. All one can say is that the greater Self expresses itself simultaneously as personalities A, B, C; but if such is the case, then the Self cannot be uniquely expressive - contrary to human individuality. Secondly, the designation 'reincarnational selves' is a misnomer because no necessary relationship exists between the concept of the greater Self and the concept of reincarnation. To see this, consider a group of personalities A, B, C coexistent in space, and suppose these personalities are components of a greater Self. Since no temporal order exists between personalities who are coexistent in space, it would be an obvious falsehood to assert that A, B and C are the reincarnational selves of this greater Self. If these personalities are scattered across time instead of space the relationship remains unchanged because they are still coexistent from the greater Self's point of view. It is evident that whatever language is used, all attempts to attribute reincarnation to the temporal activity of a greater Self or group Soul will inevitably fall foul of human individuality and the unreality of time.

In *Reincarnation: Field Studies and Theoretical Issues (1977)* Dr. Ian Stevenson - who spent much of his life investigating cases of past life memories - attempts a quick philosophical route to reincarnation by assuming the existence of an immortal soul and then asking whether an entity that has no ending can have had a beginning. He states: "It is possible to reach the idea of reincarnation through philosophical argument. The quickest route by this method is to assume the existence of the soul and its immortality and then ask whether a soul that has no terminus to its existence can have had a beginning." This is buttressed by a quotation from Schopenhauer: "Whoever believes that man's birth is the beginning must also believe that his death is the end" from which Stevenson concludes: "from the concept of prenatal existence of the soul it is a short step to the idea that the soul had incarnated in other physical bodies before the present one." But, of course, this is a *non sequitur* because Stevenson's use of the past tense in relation to an immortal being is unwarranted (see, for example, D. H. Mellor, 'The Unreality of Tense' in *The Philosophy of Time (1993)*, Robin Le Poidevin and Murray MacBeath, eds.) In the words of philosopher Ayn Rand: existence *is*. An immortal being says: "I am." If the physical body is the incarnation of a being existent in eternity then its body is the physical expression of its individuality; and since human individuality can only be expressed through one physical body at a time, it follows that the human soul cannot simultaneously incarnate in more than one physical body. Hence, it cannot reincarnate.

Much of the confusion in the reincarnationist literature stems from equating eternity with infinite or absolute time – a concept employed by Sir Isaac Newton in *Mathematical Principles of Natural Philosophy (1687)*. As we shall see, the notion of absolute time has been abandoned by modern physicists as non-existent and by philosophers as meaningless. Time – however measured – is necessarily relative to something and this something begins and ends with the physical universe. Since the physical universe is of finite duration time must be finite from which it follows that any eternal being must be timeless. Past, future, beginning and end have no meaning in eternity, therefore Stevenson's quick philosophical route to the doctrine of reincarnation is erroneous.

* * *

On the continent of Europe and in North America, the doctrine of reincarnation grew in popularity following the publication of two major works: (1) a series of channelled writings entitled: *Philosophie Spiritualiste: Le Livre des Esprits (1860)* (translated into English as 'The Spirits Book') edited by Hippolyte Léon Denizard Rivail, who wrote under the pen name Allan Kardec, and (2) *The Secret Doctrine (1888)* published in two volumes by Helena Petrovna Blavatsky. The latter volumes laid the foundations of the theosophical movement and spawned a host of theosophical-related works, first published by the international Theosophical Society at Adyar, India and then by the Theosophical Society of America. However, belief in the transmigration of the soul appeared much earlier. For example, Pythagoras claimed to be a reincarnation of Euphorbus - the Trojan hero killed by the king of Mycenaean. It was also believed by a number of philosophers and mystics such as Plato, St Simon, Prosper Enfantin, St Martin, Fourier, Pierre Leroux, and Jean Reynaud. While Kardec adopted the idea of reincarnation from spirit communications obtained through the mediumship of Celina Japhet, Blavatsky claimed authority from hidden 'masters' secreted in the Himalayas.

Blavatsky, though normally associated with the belief that reincarnation on Earth is virtually limitless, originally taught that it is an exception - like a "two-headed elephant" (see *Isis Unveiled (1877)*, Vol. 1, p. 351.) Colonel Olcott, the principal organiser of the Theosophical Society, maintained that reincarnation only occurs if the physical life is a failure e.g. if a child is stillborn. This view was later modified, and the Eastern doctrine of karma was added to form a grand system - a system that gained adherents outside the theosophical movement. For example, in *A Critical History of the Doctrine of a Future Life (1880)*, the Unitarian clergyman, the Rev. W. R. Alger states that the "theory of the transmigration of souls is marvellously adapted to explain the seeming chaos of moral inequality, injustice, and manifold evil presented in the world of human life." (p. 475).

Needless to say, the doctrines of reincarnation and karma have been powerful tools of political and social repression. By shifting the responsibility for the ills of society onto the victims, the victims are taught that the perpetrators of their misfortune are themselves. This has a twofold purpose: firstly, it deters the victims from pursuing the real perpetrators of their misfortunes and secondly it maintains the powerful and the privileged in their special positions; such people are there by karmic right and no one has any business dislodging them.

Outside France, the teachings of Blavatsky and the Spiritist School were bitterly opposed by leading spiritualists in England and America. William Howitt called the doctrine: "pitiable and repellent" and argued that if it were true "there must have been millions of spirits who, on entering the other world, have sought in vain their kindred, children and friends." In America, Andrew Jackson Davis declared it to be: "a magnificent mansion built on sand." Daniel Dunglas Home, the most accomplished medium in the history of spiritualism, said in a published letter: "I have had the pleasure of meeting at least twelve Marie Antoinettes, six or seven Marys of Scotland, a whole host of Louis and other kings, about twenty Great Alexanders, but never a plain John Smith. I, indeed, would like to cage the latter curiosity." However, Allan Kardec had some followers in England, notably Anna Kingsford who translated his books into English and believed herself to be a reincarnation of the Virgin Mary, and Edward Maitland who believed himself to be St John the Divine.

Since the days of Blavatsky and Kardec, the issue has continued to generate controversy among believers and sceptics alike, and the principal question in the debate, namely, is reincarnation fact or fantasy has never been settled, though some attempts have been made - notably by Dr. Ian Stevenson - to provide the doctrine with an empirical foundation. Unfortunately, his work has tended to fuel rather than resolve the controversy. Stevenson's best-known book, *Twenty Cases Suggestive of Reincarnation (1966)*, documenting his work with children in India, Ceylon, Brazil, Alaska, and the Lebanon was widely criticised for its failure to provide objective evidence for the hypotheses proposed. Critics - rightly or wrongly - argued that memories of past lives originate from selective thinking, confabulation, and the psychological phenomenon of false memories. Furthermore, Stevenson was unable to identify a physical mechanism by which an individual's consciousness could transmigrate from one body to another. This has led to widespread rejection of his conclusion that reincarnation is the best possible explanation of the evidence. (See Chapter 8: Suggestive of What? for a new critique of Stevenson's work.)

In spite of the general scepticism of the scientific community, investigations into past lives - largely through hypnotic regression - have become a popular activity among New Age enthusiasts as a route to personal discovery and conflict resolution. Unfortunately (for them) the use of hypnotic regression to induce or recover memories has been a controversial issue and the supposed clinical benefits strongly disputed. The scientific consensus is that memories recalled during hypnotic therapy are stories created by the subconscious mind using imagination, forgotten information and suggestions by the therapist. Subjects often report that memories created under hypnosis are indistinguishable from, and in many cases more vivid than, actual memories. Moreover, individuals who believe in reincarnation are more likely to report past life memories than disbelievers. Analyses of cases suggestive of reincarnation often reveal archaic speech patterns that are superficially convincing but turn out to be flawed when examined in detail. For example, the speech pattern of a regressed subject believed to have a memory of a past life in 16th century England was found to be a duplicate of that used by film makers and writers of the period who were attempting to convey the atmosphere of 16th century England. In another case, one subject reported historically accurate information relating to the Roman era that, on further investigation, turned out to be identical to that found in a contemporary novel set in the same time period as the individual's memories. When subjects were asked (under regression) to provide information that would allow for verification, their responses were vague and unhelpful. More striking evidence against the reincarnation hypothesis was the absence of commonplace knowledge of the period relating to the past life. For example, a subject who described the life of a Japanese fighter pilot during World War II was unable to provide the name of the Emperor of Japan during the 1940s. (See Wikipedia)

However, the work of some researchers, such as Dr. Helen Wambach, would seem to contradict the above findings. Supposedly motivated by a desire to debunk reincarnation, Dr. Wambach conducted a 10 year survey of over a 1000 subjects. When regressed to 'previous' lives many subjects gave detailed answers to specific questions on a whole range of subjects from clothing, footwear and utensils to money and housing. She found that subjects' recollections were "amazingly accurate" and wrote that "fantasy and genetic memory could not account for the patterns that emerged in the results. With the exception of 11 subjects, all descriptions of commonplace objects were consistent with historical records."

Victor Zammit, whose writings may be explored on the Internet, summarizes Wambach's work as follows: "By doing a scientific analysis on the past lives reported by her 10,000 (sic) plus volunteers she came up with some startling evidence in favour of reincarnation: (1) 50.6 % of the past lives reported were male and 49.4 % were female — this is exactly in accordance with biological fact. (2) The number of people reporting upper class or comfortable lives was in exactly the same proportion to the estimates of historians of the class distribution of the period. (3) The recall by subjects of clothing, footwear, type of food and utensils used was better than that in popular history books. She found over and over again that her subjects knew better than most historians — when she went to obscure experts her subjects were invariably correct."

Since absence of evidence is not evidence of absence, had Dr. Wambach found nothing remotely suggestive of reincarnation, she would not have disproven reincarnation. But what is this "startling evidence" in favour of reincarnation? Apparently 50.6% male and 49.4% female reported past lives – a biological fact! Now, given that a thousand people chosen at random from the electoral roll – or even the local telephone directory - will show similar proportions it can hardly be maintained that such proportions support the reincarnation hypothesis or, indeed, any other hypothesis other than the obvious one that males and females make up roughly similar proportions in the general population. Furthermore we are told that there is an exact correlation between the proportion of people reporting "upper class or comfortable lives" and the proportions computed by historians. Although superficially persuasive, such claims should be treated with caution. Interpersonal comparisons of comfort, discomfort, happiness, misery, ambition, jealousy or any other mental or emotional state and perceived membership of a social class are notoriously difficult to make because they are notoriously difficult to measure. Such correlations – if they exist at all – are highly subjective. To illustrate, if ten people are asked to assign a number from 1 to 100 to rate the 'competence' of a certain politician, the result would likely be a spread of numbers such as: 5, 8, 9, 20, 35, 40, 45, 59, 60, 75, each reflecting the political beliefs and prejudices of the respondent and the meaning attached to the word 'competent.' In the case of the historical study, the meanings attached to the words 'upper class' and 'comfortable' will vary, not merely, from one individual to another but from one epoch to another and from one historian to another. Yet we are asked to believe that the meanings attached to these terms by Dr. Wambach's regressed subjects are identical to the meanings attached to them by modern historians. Finally, we are told that subjects' knowledge of clothing, footwear, food and utensils etc. was "better than most historians" but was confirmed by "obscure experts." This may well be true, but is it indicative of reincarnation or is it indicative of something else? This is an issue we shall explore in Part 2.

* * *

The means by which individuals acquire knowledge and understanding of religious, philosophical and metaphysical matters is itself an area worthy of study and it must be recognised that the World Wide Web has become an increasingly important source of information. Across the Web, ideas, opinions and beliefs about reincarnation, life after death and a host of related topics can be found in abundance. It would be impractical to reproduce even a small proportion here but a few representative samples from sources of varying authority have been selected. According to the Wikipedia: "The word reincarnation derives from Latin, literally meaning, entering the flesh again. The Greek equivalent metempsychosis roughly corresponds to the common English phrase: transmigration of the soul, and also usually connotes reincarnation after death, as either human, animal, though emphasising the continuity of the soul, not the flesh." On another webpage the Wikipedia states that: "Reincarnation is a doctrine or metaphysical belief that some essential part of a living being (in some variations only human beings) survives death to be reborn in a new body. This essential part is often referred to as the spirit or soul, the higher or true self, divine spark, or I. According to some beliefs, a new personality is developed during each life in the physical world, but some part of the self remains constant throughout the successive lives."

The confused origin of reincarnationism is illustrated in the following passages from the Wikipedia: "Philosophical and religious beliefs regarding the existence or non-existence of an unchanging 'self' have a direct bearing on how reincarnation is viewed within a given tradition. The Buddha lived at a time of great philosophical creativity in India when many conceptions of the nature of life and death were proposed. Some were materialist, holding that the self is annihilated upon death. Others believed in a form of cyclic existence, where a being is born, lives, dies and then is re-born, but in the context of a type of determinism or fatalism in which karma played no role. Others were 'eternalists', postulating an eternally existent self or soul comparable to that in Judaic monotheism: the atman survives death and reincarnates as another living being, based on its karmic inheritance. This is the idea that has become dominant (with certain modifications) in modern Hinduism."

The online Llewellyn Worldwide Encyclopaedia provides a definition of reincarnation that has been stripped of Eastern metaphysics: "Reincarnation is the theory that man's soul, or awareness, survives death, and returns at varying intervals to be born into another physical body for the purpose of growing in knowledge, wisdom and self-awareness. Part of the belief is that we each experience life as male and female, as members of the various races and social and economic classes. It doesn't matter one little bit if you remember lifetimes as royalty or as a slave, or a lifetime as a corporation president or a janitor. We have all been there or will be. Status, wealth and social position all disappear at death. Lessons learned and growth gained from the various experiences are what remain, and we are the sum of all of our past experiences."

In the Llewellyn account the soul is undefined but treated synonymously with the self, awareness or consciousness. We are not told if reincarnation is freely chosen or whether it is a law-governed process involving karma. On the nature of reincarnation itself, the author is somewhat confused. At the beginning of the account we are told it is a theory; in the next paragraph, it is called a belief and, within the space of a few lines, it has become a universal truth: "We have all been there or will be."

The Sceptic Encyclopaedia of Pseudoscience gives a minimalist account: "Reincarnation is the belief that when one dies, one's body decomposes, but something of oneself is reborn in another body. It is the belief that one has lived before and will live again in another body after death. The bodies one passes in and out of need not be human. One may have been a Doberman in a past life, and one may be a mite or a carrot in a future life. Some tribes avoid eating certain animals because they believe that the souls of their ancestors dwell in those animals. A man could even become his own daughter by dying before she is born and then entering her body at birth."

One of the most popular accounts of reincarnation is provided at www.himalayanacademy.com/resource. At the time of writing, it was voted the best on an internet survey. The following is an extract from the article: "Hindus know that all souls reincarnate, take one body and then another, evolving through experience over long periods of time. Like the caterpillar's metamorphosis into the butterfly, death doesn't end our existence but frees us to pursue an even greater development." Here, reincarnation is presented as a natural process like the metamorphosis of a caterpillar. As a natural process, reincarnation must obey natural laws; but, what are these laws? Quoting further: "Because certain seed karmas can only be resolved in earth consciousness and because the soul's initial realizations of Absolute Reality are only achieved in a physical body, our soul joyously enters another biological body. At the right time, it is reborn into a flesh body that will best fulfil its karmic pattern." In other words, individuals are compelled to reincarnate by powers beyond their control. In order to rationalise the process of reincarnation, the author presents us with the notion of seed karmas but, once this idea is introduced, it becomes an explanation for reincarnation. The statement: "Hindus know that all souls reincarnate" illustrates the tendency among religious devotees to transform belief into a universal truth. Like the Llewellyn account critical concepts such as the soul, consciousness, Absolute Reality, seed karmas and karmic pattern are left undefined. Furthermore, we are told that the soul reincarnates "at the right time." But what is the right time? Evidently, the right time is when the soul is ready to reincarnate!

* * *

In Hinduism, the term 'soul' is generally considered to be a misleading term since it implies an object possessed, whereas the self signifies the subject who perceives all objects. The existence of the individual self does not require proof as it is self-evident, its quality being primarily consciousness. The individual self is related to Brahman or the supreme Self of the universe (Paramatman) but there is disagreement as to the nature of this relationship. In Advaita Vedanta (non-dualism) the individual self and the supreme Self are one and the same. Dvaita (dualism) regards the individual self as part of the supreme Self but always maintaining its individual identity. Vishishtadvaita (qualified non-dualism) takes a middle path and recognises the individual self as a mode or attribute of the supreme Self. The individual self transmigrates from one body to another based on karmic reactions; and the spiritual goal is self-realization. The process of self-realisation is one of negating all objective concepts and to continually ask:

"Who am I? Am I the body, the senses, the thoughts?" Once all objectivity has ceased, what remains is pure subjective self and through this knowledge one returns to the Source which is the supreme Self. The qualities which are common to both the supreme Self and the individual self are: being, consciousness, and bliss. Liberation or moksha (final release) is liberation from all limitations and unification with the supreme Self.

In Hindu metaphysics, transmigration is not a natural corollary of the Self but a separate component of a composite system; this disjunction may well be a consequence of its mixed origins. As far as it is known it was Shankara who formulated the system of Advaita (non-dualism) (see, for example, J. R, Hinnells (ed.) *Handbook of Living Religions (1984)* p.207.) Advaita Vedanta repudiates the notion of individuality and immortality, declaring that the human spirit has no separate existence from Brahman and that there is no permanent self. Since the non-dualistic position of Advaita Vedanta is not consistent with the view that the individual self has a relationship with God, the twelfth century Hindu sage Ramanuja introduced the system of Vishishtadvaita (qualified non-dualism). While accepting that the self and God were of the same essence, Ramanuja taught that the individual self retained its self-consciousness and was, therefore, able to exist in an external relationship with God. This paved the way for the later theistic developments of Dvaita Vedanta (dualism) in which the individual self maintains its identity.

In Buddhism the concept of reincarnation differs fundamentally from the modern Hindu concept in that there is no permanent self but merely a 'stream of consciousness' that links one life to another. Accordingly, the terms 'I' or 'me' do not refer to any fixed thing but are simply convenient terms that allow reference to an ever-changing entity. The actual process of change is called 'becoming again,' or more briefly 'becoming.' Some English-speaking Buddhists prefer the term 'rebirth' or 're-becoming' since the term reincarnation implies a fixed entity that is reborn. Crucially, the consciousness arising in the new personality is neither identical to, nor entirely different from, the consciousness of the previous personality.

The principal difficulty with the Buddhist concept of a 'stream of consciousness' is that anything neither identical to nor entirely different from something else describes anything subject to change. An object X that has changed its state is neither identical to nor entirely different from the object X before it changed. For example, a ripe tomato is neither identical to, nor entirely different from, the tomato before it was ripe. Although the state of the tomato is continually changing, all the phases of change have 'tomatoness' in common. In other words, 'tomatoness' is a constant or permanent feature of the process of change. In the Buddhist concept of rebirth, the idea that the consciousness arising in the new person is neither identical to nor entirely different from the old consciousness posits a process of change that can be compared directly with the changing states of the tomato. In particular, the 'stream of consciousness' that links one life to another corresponds to the 'stream of tomatoness' that links one state of the tomato to another. Like 'tomatoness,' 'selfness' must remain a constant or permanent feature of the process of change otherwise the various phases of consciousness would have nothing in common. It would then be meaningless to assert that anything had been reborn. Hence, the notion of a 'sequence of related lives' with 'no self tying these lives together' is self-contradictory.

A Darwinian fairytale

Geologists, Sir Charles Lyell (1797-1875) and John Playfair (1748-1819) were the principal advocates of a geological theory called 'uniformitarianism.' Originally conceived by James Hutton (1726-1797), uniformitarianism asserted that the geological character of the earth was determined over long periods of time entirely by slow-moving forces such as erosion and volcanism. The subtitle of Lyell's multi-volume work, *Principles of Geology (1830)* was: "An attempt to explain the former changes of the Earth's surface by reference to causes now in operation."

It was Lyell's brand of uniformitarianism that provided the foundation for Charles Darwin's theory of evolution. Darwin was so impressed with Lyell's theories, that he took Volume 1 of his recently published *Geology* aboard the HMS Beagle on his exploration of the Galapagos Islands. When the Beagle made its first stop at St Jago, Darwin discovered rock formations which, seen through Lyell's eyes gave him a revolutionary insight into the geological history of the island, an insight he applied throughout his travels. Following his later observations on the distribution of animals on either side of the Andes, Darwin wrote in his Journal: "This is merely an illustration of the admirable laws, first laid down by Mr Lyell, on the geographical distribution of animals, as influenced by geological changes."

Lyell's interpretation of geological change as "the steady accumulation of minute changes over enormously long spans of time" was mirrored in Darwin's theory of evolution. In conformity with the Lyellian concept of change through slow and continuous accretions of geological activity, Darwin constructed his theory around the notion of slow and continuous adaptations of species to the environment. In his seminal work, *On the Origin of Species (1859),* Darwin systematically presented evidence in support of his belief that "nature does not make leaps" (natura non facit saltum). To quote from Darwin's Red Notebook: "one species *does* change into another."

The mutual dependence of Lyellian uniformitarianism and Darwinian evolution was highlighted by Lyell himself. Lyell's presidential address to the London Geological Society in January 1837, stressed that geographical continuity of species supported his concept of uniformitarianism. Almost simultaneously, Darwin was claiming that geological continuity supported his concept of evolution. Darwin had always maintained that natural selection caused primitive organisms to evolve slowly and continuously into more complex forms that were fully adapted to their environment. For this to happen, however, species would need long periods of undisturbed tranquillity. Without the "admirable laws, first laid down by Mr Lyell," primitive organisms could never have climbed the evolutionary ladder - it would have been repeatedly kicked away - in the manner proposed by Darwin. But, it is equally true that without the evolutionary "laws" laid down by Mr Darwin, the "admirable laws" of Mr Lyell would lack credibility.

Pole shifts, major climate changes, 'flips' in the Earth's magnetic field, earthquakes, tsunamis, asteroid impacts belie the claim that primitive organisms have slowly evolved undisturbed through countless millennia into the complex species we observe today. According to the latest evidence, the Earth "has gone through periods of abrupt and catastrophic change, some due to the impact of large asteroids and comets on the planet. A few of these impacts may have caused massive climate change and the extinction of large numbers of plant and animal species." (quoted from Wikipedia).

George Cuvier (1769-1832), French naturalist, zoologist and pioneer in the fields of comparative anatomy and palaeontology maintained that many of the geological features of the Earth and the past history of life could be explained by catastrophic events that had caused the extinction of many species of animals. In a 1796 paper entitled *On Living Elephants and Fossils*, Cuvier states that: "All of these facts, consistent among themselves, and not opposed by any report, seem to me to prove the existence of a world previous to ours, destroyed by some kind of catastrophe." According to the University of California Museum of Palaeontology: "Cuvier did not believe in organic evolution, for any change in an organism's anatomy would have rendered it unable to survive. He studied the mummified cats and ibises that Geoffroy had brought back from Napoleon's invasion of Egypt, and showed that they were no different from their living counterparts; Cuvier used this to support his claim that life forms did not evolve over time." If Cuvier was correct then, of course, intermediate forms should not exist. However, Darwin always believed that his theory of continuous evolution was contingent on the existence of such forms and that, without them, his theory was untenable.

The failure since Darwin's time to discover a single intermediate form - a so-called "missing link" - among the countless millions that are supposed to exist, has thrown

Darwinism into crisis. In *Evolution: A Theory in Crisis (1985)* Michael Denton states that: "There can be no question that Darwin had nothing like sufficient evidence to establish his theory of evolution. Neither speciation nor even the most trivial type of evolution had ever actually been observed directly in nature. He provided no direct evidence that natural selection had ever caused any biological change in nature and the concept was in itself flawed because it was impossible to reconcile with the theory of heredity in vogue at the time." (p.70) Furthermore, in *Darwin's Century (1958)*, Loren Eiseley states that: "A close examination of the last edition of the *Origin* reveals that in attempting on scattered pages to meet the objections being launched against his theory the much-laboured upon volume had become contradictory.... The last repairs to the *Origin* reveal how very shaky Darwin's theoretical structure had become." (p.242).

The frustration – and indeed embarrassment – felt by evolutionary biologists over the general failure to discover "missing links" is highlighted by Michael Denton: "The overall picture of life on Earth today is so discontinuous, the gaps between the different types [of species] so obvious, that as Steven Stanley reminds us in his recent book *Macroevolution*, if our knowledge of biology was restricted to those species presently existing on Earth, 'we might wonder whether the doctrine of evolution would qualify as anything more than an outrageous hypothesis.'" (p.157)

In response to the paucity of evidence for continuous evolution, palaeontologists Niles Eldredge and Stephen Jay Gould introduced the concept of 'punctuated equilibrium.' According to standard definitions punctuated equilibrium proposes that most sexually reproducing species will experience little net evolutionary change for most of their geological history, remaining in an extended state called 'stasis.' To quote Gould and Eldredge: "the degree of gradualism commonly attributed to Charles Darwin is virtually nonexistent in the fossil record, and that stasis dominates the history of most fossil species." (See Punctuated equilibria: the tempo and mode of evolution reconsidered. Paleobiology 3 (2): 115-151. p.145). The authors clearly believe that continuity between species is a fiction. However, while they freely admit that the gaps in the fossil record are real enough, they offer no explanation for the un-Darwinian leaps that species supposedly make from one form to another.

More than a century before the crisis in Darwin's theory of evolution, Gregor Mendel, Austrian monk and scientist, had laid the foundations of genetics after cultivating and testing some 29,000 pea plants in his monastery garden. Analysing his results he discovered simple patterns which accounted for the transmission of hereditary characteristics from parent organisms to their offspring, now known as Mendel's Laws of Inheritance. Three decades later, these Laws were rediscovered by the Dutch botanist Hugo de Vries in a long series of plant-breeding experiments and by the German botanist, Carl Erich Correns, who had carried out similar garden pea experiments.

These discoveries – made independently by reputable scientists – revitalised Darwin's theory of evolution which, by the 1890's, had become little more than an intellectual curiosity. The principal problem with Darwin's theory was not that there was no evidence to support it – proponents merely argued that researchers had not looked hard enough for intermediate forms – but that it lacked a credible mechanism for change. Darwin had proposed that change occurred from one generation to the next through minute variations in form making a species more adapted to its environment - like gazelles becoming more agile in order to escape their predators, or monkeys developing longer arms to swing more efficiently from trees. Unfortunately (for Darwin) this alleged tendency has never been observed in nature nor has it been confirmed in the fossil record. But, with the discoveries of Mendel, de Vries and Correns a believable mechanism of change had been provided. De Vries proposed that sudden changes in an organism's hereditary structure - which he called 'mutations' - were the cause of substantial changes in form. This was in stark contrast to Darwin's slow, imperceptible variations. Of course, the great majority of mutations would be disastrous but some would, by pure chance, have survival value. The forms, thus produced, would then survive, prosper and reproduce. Mendelian genetics, combined with the concept of chance mutations, transformed an unsuccessful theory of natural selection into a twentieth century paradigm of biological evolution.

Since the discoveries of Mendel, de Vries and Correns, students of biology, and indeed the public at large, have been told that Darwinian evolution is an indisputable fact and that chance mutations, combined with natural selection, have driven the evolutionary machine. But there have always been problems with this machine, not the least of which is time. If mutations occur randomly, how long would it take for a living organism to be created? In a famous debate between Samuel Wilberforce and T. H. Huxley in Oxford in 1860, Huxley is alleged to have argued that monkeys - provided they had enough energy, paper and longevity - typing randomly on machines would eventually type out an entire Shakespeare sonnet or even a play, like Hamlet. Later versions claim that monkeys could type out the entire works of Shakespeare! This argument is supposed to demonstrate that, given sufficient time, blind, chance mutations, combined with natural selection, could produce the complex species (including human beings) now inhabiting the Earth.

The crucial question is this: could evolution have happened that way? Not according to Oxford mathematician John C. Lennox. In his book: *God's Undertaker: Has Science Buried God? (2007),* Lennox performs a few simple calculations to show that chance mutations could never have produced life as we know it. A similar view is taken by M.I.T. mathematician and probability theorist Gian-Carlo Rota. According to Rota: "If a monkey could type one keystroke every nanosecond, the expected waiting time until the monkey types out Hamlet is so long that the estimated age of the universe is insignificant by comparison . . . this is not a practical method for writing plays." (Quoted in *God's Undertaker*, p.155). Continuing this line of argument, how long would it take monkeys to type out the 23rd Psalm? If a monkey hits one key per second, the average time to produce the word "The" is about 35 hours. To type out the entire Psalm, the universe would need to last for about 10^{1007} years (1 followed by one thousand and seven zeros). The present age of the universe is about 10^{10} years (1 followed by ten zeros.)

In the light of such calculations, it is generally recognised that random processes of the kind proposed by Huxley could never have led to the emergence of complex organisms – let alone human beings. Arch-Darwinist

Richard Dawkins also agrees: "It is grindingly, creakingly, crashingly obvious that, if Darwinism were really a theory of chance, it couldn't work. You don't need to be a mathematician or a physicist to calculate that an eye or a haemoglobin molecule would take from here to infinity to self-assemble by sheer higgledy-piggledy luck."

In *Evolution From Space (1984)*, Astrophysicists Sir Fred Hoyle and Chandra Wickramasinghe state: "No matter how large the environment one considers, life cannot have had a random beginning. Troops of monkeys thundering away at random on typewriters could not produce the works of Shakespeare, for the practical reason that the whole observable universe is not large enough to contain the necessary monkey hordes, the necessary typewriters and certainly not the waste paper baskets required for the deposition of wrong attempts. The same is true for living material. The likelihood of the spontaneous formation of life from inanimate matter is one to a number with 40,000 noughts after it... It is big enough to bury Darwin and the whole theory of evolution. There was no primeval soup, neither on this planet nor on any other, and if the beginnings of life were not random, they must therefore have been the product of purposeful intelligence." (p.176)

Nevertheless, Darwinism plus random mutations remain the current orthodoxy in the biological sciences. The extreme improbability of life appearing spontaneously on Earth – or on any other planet - and its fatal implications for Darwin's theory of evolution resulted in the publication of two books by Richard Dawkins called: *The Blind Watchmaker (1986)* and *Climbing Mount Improbable (1996)*. In these books, he attempts to provide a credible mechanism for evolutionary change. Dawkins agrees that living organisms are so complex that, left to chance alone, they are highly improbable events. In *Climbing Mount Improbable* Dawkins states that this complexity can be handled by "breaking the improbability up into small manageable parts, smearing out the luck needed, going round the back of Mount Improbable and crawling up the gentle slopes, inch by million year inch." (p.67) As we shall see below, Dawkins breaks up this improbability into manageable parts by introducing hidden assumptions that contradict the fundamental postulate of evolutionary theory, namely, that the evolutionary machine is driven by chance, not by design. We shall outline the problem and then discuss Dawkins' 'solution.'

At the top of Mount Improbable is, say, a haemoglobin molecule. This is just a metaphorical way of saying that the spontaneous creation of a haemoglobin molecule is an extremely improbable event. Let us suppose it takes 5,000 steps for the appropriate molecules to bond together to form a haemoglobin molecule. If this happens, then it has climbed to the top of Mount Improbable. In Darwinian theory, incomplete formations have no survival value, therefore all the steps up Mount Improbable must be taken so quickly (i.e. molecules must bond so quickly) that formations do not get eliminated by virtue of incompleteness. This, of course, raises the following question: in what sense can a haemoglobin molecule be regarded as a complete entity without the prior existence of organisms that utilize haemoglobin molecules? Obviously, the haemoglobin molecules have no function without the organisms, and the organisms cannot function without the haemoglobin molecules. Thus, a mutual dependence exists which can only be realised if both haemoglobin molecules and organisms are created simultaneously. However, for the purpose of the present discussion we shall ignore this problem.

At each step, there are two possibilities: one advantageous and one disastrous. As soon as a disastrous step is taken e.g. a wrong molecule is bonded, or a molecule is bonded incorrectly, the formation is demolished. This simple rule incorporates the general Darwinian principle that 'unfit' species or formations do not survive. Therefore, to reach the top of Mount Improbable, 5,000 advantageous steps must be taken very quickly. Conceptually, 5,000 random steps, each with only two outcomes - advantageous or disastrous – is like the throw of 5,000 coins – where each coin has the letter A (advantageous) on one side and the letter D (disastrous) on the other. When throwing coins, it makes no difference whether 5,000 coins are thrown sequentially or whether they are thrown simultaneously; all possible outcomes will be identical. By a well-known result in combinatorial analysis, there are 2^{5000} equally likely outcomes. However, only one outcome will be successful – namely, the outcome with 5,000 advantageous steps. The probability of this outcome is 1 chance in 2^{5000} - a number so small that, in practice, a haemoglobin molecule will never be created. Alternatively, it would need 2^{5000} attempts to create the molecule. If each attempt takes 1 second then 2^{5000} attempts would take approximately 10^{1498} years, a number so large that, by comparison, the current age of the universe is insignificant. This is the problem that Dawkins attempts to address.

We shall show, in numerical terms, how Dawkins reduces the improbability (i.e. increases the probability) of climbing Mount Improbable. To make the calculations manageable we shall use a slippery rock instead of a mountain. Rock Improbable can be climbed in only five advantageous steps. All possible outcomes can be generated by throwing five coins and, altogether, there are 32 ($=2^5$) equally likely outcomes. Only one outcome produces a successful route to the top:

(1) ... A, A, A, A, A

i.e. five advantageous steps. In the Darwinian scenario, disastrous steps are not permitted because an unfit organism will be eliminated by natural selection. The probability of making these five advantageous steps is $1/32 \approx 0.031$ – about 3 chances in 100.

The chances of surmounting Rock Improbable can only be increased if we abandon the Darwinian postulate that unfit organisms are eliminated and permit an organism to make one disastrous step. This means that the organism is allowed six steps in which to reach the top of Rock Improbable. To generate all possible outcomes, six coins are thrown; altogether, there are 64 ($=2^6$) equally likely outcomes. But now, there are seven outcomes which provide seven successful routes. They are as follows:

(1) ... A, A, A, A, A, A
(2) ... D, A, A, A, A, A
(3) ... A, D, A, A, A, A
(4) ... A, A, D, A, A, A
(5) ... A, A, A, D, A, A
(6) ... A, A, A, A, D, A
(7) ... A, A, A, A, A, D

Each outcome represents one route to the top of Rock Improbable. In routes 1 and 7, the final step is redundant because the organism has reached the top and does not need further steps. In evolutionary terms, these redundant steps correspond to harmless additions, like a man with five fingers, or a horse with two tails. There are 57 (= 64 - 7) ways of *not* getting the top such as (A, A, A, A, D, D) or (A, A, A, D, A, D). Since all 64 outcomes are equally likely, the probability of each outcome is $1/64 \approx 0.0156$. But, with seven equally likely routes to the top, the probability of success is now $7/64 = 0.109$ – about 11 chances in 100. The chances of reaching the top have increased by nearly four times.

If we permit the organism to make two disastrous steps, it now has seven steps in which to reach the top of Rock Improbable. There are 128 ($=2^7$) equally likely outcomes – each with a probability of $1/128 \approx 0.0078$. By listing all possible outcomes, or by using a well-known result from combinatorial analysis, it can be shown that there are 29 equally likely routes to the top. Two possible outcomes are as follows:

(1) ... A, A, A, A, A, A, A
(2) ... D, D, A, A, A, A, A

The probability of reaching the top is now $29/128 \approx 0.2266$ i.e. about 23 chances in 100. Continuing, it can be shown that if 3 disastrous steps are allowed (8 steps in total) the probability of reaching the top of Rock Improbable is 0.363; with 4 disastrous steps (9 steps in total) the probability is 0.5; with 5 disastrous steps (10 steps in total) the probability is 0.623. The probability of reaching the top of Rock Improbable steadily increases with the number of permissible disastrous steps. With 20 disastrous steps (25 in total), the probability of getting to the top is a approximately equal to 1 - a virtual certainty. In other words, the improbability of the organism's creation by chance mutations is reduced to zero. We now have Dawkins' method of handling complexity – the abandonment of Darwinism!

In *God's Undertaker*, Lennox uses the monkey-typing metaphor to expose the flaws in Dawkins' argument. This time round, monkeys must type out the Shakespearean phrase: "Methinks it is like a weasel". The phrase has 28 letters (spaces are included) and there are 28 monkeys – one for each letter position. When a letter is typed, it is compared with the target letter and, if correct, it is retained. The successful monkey drops out and the rest carry on typing. As it turns out, monkeys drop out fairly quickly and the target phrase is typed within a reasonable amount of time. Apparently, monkeys can type out Shakespeare's plays! But Dawkins' two hidden assumptions are apparent:

1) The correctness of a letter is determined independently of the correctness of any other letter.
2) A letter can be retained while other correct letters are being generated.

In a Darwinian model this cannot be true. A phrase will only make sense if all individual letters are typed correctly in one trial. Viability derives from the correctness of the whole phrase not from the correctness of individual letters. Correct letters combined with incorrect ones will merely produce phrases of gobbledygook. Since, a phrase of gobbledygook is an unviable formation, it must – according to Darwinian rules - be eliminated. In other words, if a single trial is a failure the whole phrase must be discarded and a new trial begun with nothing pre-typed.

The retention of a correct letter within a phrase of gobbledygook is equivalent to the retention of an advantageous step in an unviable formation of molecules. In the Darwinian scenario, phrases of gobbledygook and unviable formations are both eliminated, but in the Dawkins model they survive. The fallacy of the Dawkins approach is that it assigns correctness to individual letters or steps, whereas correctness can only be assigned to the phrase or the formation as a whole. Lennox easily identifies the circularity in Dawkins' argument. The target phrase - against which randomly selected letters are compared - must already exist! If not, then comparisons cannot be made and the phrase: "Methinks it is like a weasel" cannot be created except by pure chance - the very problem Dawkins is trying to solve. Crucially, the prior existence of the target phrase implies design - exactly what Dawkins denies. In other words, Dawkins assumes what he is trying to prove. The irony, as Lennox points out, is that Dawkins' argument actually strengthens the case for creation by design.

The fallacy of the Dawkins argument can be seen when applied to mutations. For example, a mutation which provides a gazelle's offspring with wings (mutation A) can only be advantageous if it is combined with a mutation which provides it with bird-like feet (mutation B). A gazelle with wings may escape its predators but, without the ability to land safely, it will probably kill itself. Moreover, it cannot be assumed that the gazelle will survive long enough for its offspring to be born with bird-like feet anymore than it can be assumed that an incomplete formation of molecules will survive long enough to become a haemoglobin molecule. Both will be eliminated as unfit organisms. Hence, mutation A cannot improve the survival chances of an ordinary gazelle without mutation B. In other words, mutations A and B must occur simultaneously. Once again, we see that single mutations cannot be deemed advantageous (or disastrous) independently of other mutations and that fitness applies only to the organism as a whole.

Against this, it might be claimed that a single mutation could conceivably produce a gazelle with wings and suitable feet. But, then, one could just as easily claim that a single mutation could turn a frog into a prince. Without theoretical grounds for their existence, multi-purpose mutations must be dismissed as a fantasy. Furthermore, the probability of such a mutation must be weighed against the probability of all other possible mutations. Since, there is no reason to suppose that a mutation, transforming an ordinary gazelle into a flying gazelle with suitable feet, is any more likely than a mutation turning a gazelle into any one of a trillion other things – like an elephant with wings - the likelihood of such an occurrence is practically zero.

The orthodox Darwinian argument is somewhat different. Mutations cause gradual or continuous changes in form. A gazelle is not born with a pair of fully-functioning wings but small appendages which become more and more wing-like with each successive generation. Eventually, gazelles are born that can fly. At the same time, gazelle feet become more and more bird-like. Finally, gazelles are born that can fly and land safely. This may take countless mutations and millions of years but the result is guaranteed. Once again, the argument falls foul of the 'trillion outcome' problem. Why should an ordinary gazelle evolve into a flying gazelle with suitable feet rather than any one of a trillion other things unless it is known in advance that such mutations would improve its chances of survival? This could not be known before it had been tried. Furthermore, gazelles with puny wing-like structures and strange-looking feet - apparently on the way to fully-grown gazelles with wings and bird-like feet - would, in themselves, have no survival value and be quickly eliminated.

Continuous evolution - as proposed by Darwin - must be tested against the fossil record. In the case of flying gazelles there would need to be millions of forms that are midway between ordinary gazelles and flying gazelles. Fossils with larger and larger wing-like appendages and feet becoming more and more bird-like would need to be found in abundant quantities. When all these fossils had been excavated they would need to be carefully sorted, numbered, and indexed and then placed inside glass cases in museums for general inspection. The fossils would need to be carefully laid out, starting with the fossil remains of an ordinary gazelle, showing all the intermediate fossils up to and including the fossil remains of a flying gazelle. In other words, they would need to show a continuous series. Once the fossils had been so organised, it would be possible to create a 'flick movie' showing how the ordinary gazelle had evolved into the flying gazelle. Only then could it honestly be claimed that one had evolved into the other. Suggestive pictures showing how one species has evolved into another without supporting evidence would, of course, be fraudulent. As we have seen, the total absence of intermediate forms belies the claim that one species has evolved into another.

Although, chance mutations cannot account for the organisms or species we observe on Earth, it is widely accepted that chance mutations may produce minor modifications within an existing species such as chaffinches with longer beaks, horses with white manes, and butterflies with black wings etc. This is a well-attested fact and has been called 'microevolution' – a phenomenon observed by Darwin on his exploration of the Galapagos Islands. However, Darwin went far beyond the evidence when he generalised from micro- to macroevolution - the transformation of one species into another. Such a generalisation was never justified in Darwin's time nor has it been justified since in spite of claims to the contrary; nor has it been possible to identify - or even construct - a credible mechanism for evolutionary change.

As a final note, Darwinists often argue that the mere existence of chance mutations – even in microevolution - coupled with the profligacy of Nature is a denial of design and, by implication, a confirmation of Darwinism. For example, it is sometimes said that an acorn tree is extremely wasteful with acorns because thousands are produced whereas only a very few become trees. In reply to this, it must be said that the notion of an 'acorn tree' is an artificial division imposed upon a small aspect of the natural world by naturalists for the purposes of study and research. In reality the natural world is an organic whole without boundaries. What may be 'seen' as a separate organism is, in fact, a part of a greater whole. A leaf is part of a branch, a branch is part of a tree, a tree is part of a forest, and so on until the whole biosphere is embraced. To assert that an 'acorn tree' is wasteful with acorns is like asserting that a branch is wasteful with leaves, or that a forest is wasteful with trees. In reality what appears to be 'wasted' by one organism can be used by another organism with great effect. If the system around the 'acorn tree' is extended to encompass a wider area, the apparent 'wastage' is contained within the system and the 'acorn tree' becomes an element in a wider network of organic and inorganic relationships. In a closed system the Law of Conservation of Energy ensures that one form of energy is, merely, converted to another form, the total amount of energy remaining constant; nothing is lost. The concept of 'wastage' in Nature is nothing more than human prejudice.

Chapter 3
Proving a Negative

It is often claimed that reincarnation cannot be refuted because it is impossible to prove a negative. The 'negative' referred to is the statement:

(S1) ... The human self does not reincarnate.

This is the same as claiming that the following 'positive' statement cannot be refuted:

(S2) ... The human self reincarnates.

The claim that S1 cannot be proven or, equivalently, that S2 cannot be refuted is an allusion to a principle which asserts that a meaningful phenomenon or process cannot be rejected as impossible or non-existent solely on the grounds that no instances of that phenomenon or process have ever been recorded. In other words: the absence of evidence is not evidence of absence. For example, the absence of 'hard' evidence for extra-terrestrial beings does not prove that extra-terrestrial beings do not exist. We shall refer to this as the 'principle of irrefutability.' When this principle is applied to the doctrine of reincarnation, it is maintained that the absence of conclusive evidence for reincarnation neither proves that reincarnation does not happen nor does it prove that reincarnation cannot happen; hence, reincarnation is possible. This is the basis of what may be called the 'agnostic argument' against refutations of reincarnation.

Agnosticism towards reincarnation is a frame of mind between credulity and scepticism and is founded on two premises:

Premise 1: The mode of argument commonly known as 'inductive reasoning' does not produce statements that are logically valid or necessarily true.

Premise 2: All refutations of reincarnation are exercises in inductive reasoning.

As we shall see, the first premise is *true* and the second premise is *false*.

The term agnostic normally refers to someone who believes that nothing is known or can be known about the nature and existence of God. For example, to an agnostic, the statements: "God exists" or "God is vengeful" cannot be refuted or verified by any means whatsoever, therefore it is pointless believing in the truth or falsity of either statement. When applied to the doctrine of reincarnation, however, agnosticism can be of two kinds: strong and weak. In strong agnosticism, it is believed that the statement: "The human self reincarnates" cannot be refuted or verified by any means whatsoever. In weak agnosticism, it is believed that the statement cannot be refuted but can, in principle, be verified.

A statement that cannot be refuted may be false, and a statement that cannot be verified may be true. The point is that no methods exist for proving that an irrefutable statement is false or that an unverifiable statement is true. In the spectrum of beliefs, strong agnosticism is close to scepticism. The strong agnostic asserts that reincarnation cannot in principle be verified or refuted and that all evidence, either for or against reincarnation is irrelevant. Weak agnosticism is close to credulity. The weak agnostic asserts that reincarnation cannot be refuted but modifies this position with the belief that reincarnation is a meaningful concept and can in principle be verified e.g. through empirical research.

When Negatives Cannot be Proven

The claim that negatives cannot be proven or that their corresponding positive formulations cannot be refuted is closely related to the argument that inductive reasoning does not produce statements that are logically valid or necessarily true. Inductive reasoning is a mode of argument that manufactures generalisations on the strength of particular instances of a re-occurring phenomenon or on the basis of incomplete evidence. Suppose, for example, that all crows observed in the past have been black, and that this leads to the inference that all crows observed in the future will be black. The claim that this is not a logically valid inference and may, in fact, be wrong is equivalent to the claim that the statement: "White crows exist" cannot be refuted and may, in fact, be true. In other words, the absence of evidence for white crows does not prove that white crows do not exist. In the same way, the absence of evidence for extra-terrestrial beings does not prove that extra-terrestrial beings do not exist; and the absence of evidence for reincarnation does not prove that reincarnation does not happen.

Inductive reasoning bears a superficial resemblance to a common technique in the field of pure mathematics known as 'proof by induction.' In fact, the two methods are quite different. While mathematical induction is a method of proof, inductive reasoning asserts what is likely to be the case on the strength of incomplete evidence. There are two different kinds of inductive reasoning: generalising and interpretive.

(a) Generalising inferences : proof by induction

This is a technique used in mathematics for proving a formula e.g. $S(n) = n(n + 1)/2$ which gives the sum of the first n digits. Firstly, the formula is checked to see if it is true for $n = 1$. This is usually a trivial exercise. The formula is then assumed to be true for $n = k$ and then proven to true for $n = k + 1$. Since the formula is true for $n = 1$, it follows that it must be true for $n = 2$. Since it is true for $n = 2$, it must be true for $n = 3$, and so on *ad infinitum*. Therefore, the formula must be true for all positive integers greater than or equal to 1. The formula can easily be checked. For example, when $n = 5$ the formula gives the sum of the first five integers i.e. $1 + 2 + 3 + 4 + 5$. By ordinary addition the sum equals 15. Using the formula gives $S(5) = 5(5 + 1)/2 = 15$.

Mathematical induction is similar to showing that every member of an infinite sequence of dominos will topple. It is given that the first domino topples (i.e. $n = 1$ is true). It is then shown that if any given domino in the sequence topples it will cause the next domino in the sequence to topple (i.e. if $n = k$ is true, then $n = k + 1$ is true). Thus, if domino 1 topples, it knocks over domino 2. If domino 2 topples, it knocks over domino 3, and so on *ad infinitum*. Therefore all dominos topple. Of course, the domino metaphor should not be carried too far since any sequence of physical dominos is necessarily finite i.e. there will always be a last domino. On the other hand, the formula S(n) is true for all positive integers n because there is no last integer.

(b) Generalising inferences: inductive reasoning

Suppose a research effort is organised to determine whether or not white crows exist. Since white crows are supposed to be rare, all crows spotted in the early stages of the research are likely to be black. The following hypothetical list shows the results of the first (very brief) survey, followed by a (tentative) conclusion or inference:

Crow #1 is black
Crow #2 is black
Crow #3 is black
Therefore, all crows are black.

The list of observations - in this case the three sightings of black crows - is sometimes referred to as the 'premise.' The final statement: "all crows are black", is the conclusion. The conclusion is an inductive inference (i.e. a generalisation from instances).

Instead of recording observations individually, the results may be presented as follows:

Crow #n is black (n = 1 to 3)
Therefore, all crows are black.

It is evident that the conclusion: "All crows are black" is certainly not warranted from only three observations. Suppose 50,000 observations are made with the following results:

Crow #n is black (n = 1 to 50,000)
Therefore, all crows are black.

Although an inference from 50,000 observations is more likely to be correct than an inference from only three, the inference that all crows are black cannot be made with absolute certainty unless the search is known to be exhaustive – like counting the number of objects in a box. In other words, the inference that all crows are black, though likely to be correct, is not necessarily true and may be wrong.

The domino example discussed above illustrates both mathematical induction and inductive reasoning. Assuming that the dominos are correctly spaced, if the first domino topples, every member of an infinite sequence of theoretical dominos will topple. Physical dominos, on the other hand, illustrate inductive reasoning. If the first domino topples it is likely, but not necessarily true, that every other domino in the sequence will topple. In practice any number of factors may stop the progressive fall e.g. a particular domino may not topple, or some dominos may not have been spaced correctly. In other words, there is no necessary causal relationship between the fall of one domino and the next. Likewise, there is no necessary causal relationship between the sighting of one black crow and the next.

Interpretive inferences
An *interpretive* inference is a statement that gives meaning to a given body of evidence. For example, suppose a by-pass is constructed to divert traffic away from a particular town. Suppose further, that following construction, the number of traffic accidents in the town falls significantly and that the number of accidents on the by-pass is very small. The inference that the net fall in accidents is a direct consequence of the by-pass is an interpretive inference. The inference that net accidents will fall in any locality following the

construction of a by-pass is a generalising inference. Since inductive inferences – either interpretive or generalising - are not logically valid, they may be challenged with assertions that oppose or contradict the principal thesis. Consider the following counter assertions to the claim that by-passes reduce traffic accidents:

> *Counter assertion 1*: Traffic diverted from towns, following the construction of by-passes, will be replaced by new traffic so that the volume of traffic through town centres will remain unchanged.
> *Counter assertion 2*: Accidents occurring on by-passes will be greater in number than the fall in accidents in town centres; hence there will be a net increase in the number of traffic accidents.

If counter assertions 1 and 2 are assumptions or "givens" in regional policy making, then the inference that a particular by-pass has successfully reduced the number of traffic accidents will not be generalised to all by-passes. Instead, special reasons may be adduced to account for the fall in accidents in this particular instance e.g. the implementation of road safety measures. If, however, the counter assertions are gratuitous i.e. without theoretical or empirical foundation, then the generalisation will survive intact. Whether or not interpretive inferences lead to generalising inferences depends entirely on the strength or validity of counter assertions or on the existence of countervailing evidence.

Interpretive and generalising inferences may be represented as simple sequences. When supporting the doctrine of reincarnation, for example, a collection of interpretive inferences may be represented by the positive sequence: 1, 2, 3, . . This sequence represents a number of individual case studies in which each case has provided "satisfactory" evidence (i.e. to the researcher) that each individual under investigation has lived a previous life. When this leads to a generalising inference the sequence becomes: 1, 2, 3 . . . all i.e. cases investigated suggest that the individuals concerned have lived previous lives, therefore everyone reincarnates.

When opposing the doctrine of reincarnation, interpretive inferences may be represented by the null sequence: Ø, Ø, Ø . . . i.e. cases investigated suggest that none of the individuals concerned have lived previous lives. If these results are generalised, the sequence becomes: Ø, Ø, Ø...all Ø i.e. cases investigated suggest that none of the individuals concerned have lived previous lives, therefore nobody reincarnates.

Although, inductive inferences are not logically valid and may result in wrong conclusions, they may also lead to correct conclusions. For example, the statements: "White crows do not exist" and "Extra-terrestrial beings do not exist" cannot be logically inferred from the absence of white crow sightings or the lack of hard evidence for extra-terrestrial beings; nevertheless, each statement may still be true. In other words, an inductive inference may produce a true statement but the truth of the statement is incidental and not a logical consequence of the premises.

In the context of the above discussion, let us compare the two negative statements:

(S1) . . . The human self does not reincarnate.
(S3) . . . White crows do not exist.

S1 asserts that something does not happen whereas S3 asserts that something does not exist. In the case of S3, and similar cases of existence, proof is not possible because one single instance to the contrary could conceivably turn up – given enough time. In this particular case, therefore, a negative cannot be proven.

But can the same be said about something which is alleged not happen? Clearly, it depends on the nature of what is supposed to be happening. For example, if is alleged that it is possible to walk and stand still simultaneously, then research is pointless because it will never be possible to observe anyone doing both simultaneously because the two activities are mutually exclusive. The following negatives are trivially true:

(S4) . . . No person can walk and stand still simultaneously
(S5) . . . No squares have round edges
(S6) . . . $2 + 2 \neq 5$

* * *

Let us consider the collection of all statements that cannot be refuted. We shall refer to these as class X. If a statement cannot be refuted, no means exist by which it can be proven to be false. Since no true statement can be proven to be false, class X contains the set of all true statements. False statements that cannot be refuted also belong to class X. For example, the statement: "Extraterrestrial beings inhabit the star Sirius" may be false but since it cannot be proven to be false, it belongs to class X. A curious property of class X is that false statements that cannot be refuted cannot be identified since any statement known to be false is known to be refuted; hence, it can never be known if such statements exist. Although statements in class X cannot be refuted, some true statements are capable of verification. For example, the true statement: "Cows eat grass" has been verified countless times. Since class X contains all true statements it is non-empty. Consider the following statement:

(S7) ... Bigfoot exists.

Since Bigfoot is, supposedly, a creature indigenous to the Earth, an exhaustive search of the planet – though difficult in practice – would, presumably, settle the issue. In other words, if Bigfoot is not found, then Bigfoot does not exist. Whilst intuitively appealing, such an argument is based on the premise that the Earth is a physical entity capable of being explored, like the interior of a huge box; if a particular item cannot be found, then the item does not exist. Although such ideas accord with some views of the universe, they do not accord with some interpretations of quantum physics nor do they accord with paranormal investigations. If parallel universes (i.e. multiverses) or worlds of higher dimensions interpenetrate the Earth, then systematic exploration of all dimensions of the planet is not merely impracticable it is meaningless since it is not known what is being explored. Furthermore, if these 'other worlds' interact with the Earth, then the appearance of strange creatures or unusual phenomena may well be a product of that interaction. Given the paradigm of a multi-dimensional Earth, no statement asserting the existence of strange creatures or unusual phenomena is capable of being refuted. Nevertheless, this does not inhibit verification. One unambiguous sighting of Bigfoot would be sufficient to prove existence. By contrast, zero observations would not prove non-existence. In other words, the statement: "Bigfoot exists" is capable of verification (if true) but incapable of refutation (even if false). Hence the statement: "Bigfoot exists" belongs to class X.

Self-contradictory statements do not belong to class X because all such statements are self-refuting. Self-contradictory statements embody self-contradictory ideas or incorporate logically inconsistent sub-statements such as: "All circles are square-shaped" or "2 + 2 = 5." Although these statements are obviously self-contradictory, other statements are implicitly self-contradictory and it may be necessary to demonstrate inconsistency by logical or mathematical arguments.

Self-contradictory statements cannot be grouped into a single class because a self-contradictory statement in one system of thought may not be self-contradictory in another. Suppose, for example, it is reported that a certain physical object is capable of occupying two places at once, where "place" is defined as the region of space coincident with the body's volume. In classical physics this cannot happen; if a body is located "here" it cannot be located "there." The obvious inference is that bodies occupying different places at the same time must be different bodies. At the quantum level the situation is very different. According to the 'uncertainty principle' if the momentum of a sub-atomic particle, say an electron, is known *exactly* then its position cannot be determined anywhere in space; instead its position is "smeared" over the entire universe. At the sub-atomic level, everyday notions of "here" and "there" have no meaning. Thus, in the context of quantum physics, the statement: "A body can occupy two places at once" is not necessarily self-contradictory.

There is a well-known theorem in elementary geometry which states that the interior sum of angles of an n-sided polygon is equal to $180(n - 2)$ degrees. For example, when n = 3 (triangle) the interior sum is equal to 180 degrees;

when n = 6 (hexagon) the interior sum is 720 degrees. This result is derivable from basic postulates due to the Greek mathematician, Euclid. Consider the statement:

(S8) ... The interior sum of angles of a 100-sided polygon = 17460 degrees.

By a simple calculation i.e. (17460/180) + 2 = 99, it follows that 17460 is, in fact, the interior sum of angles of a 99-sided polygon. Thus,

(S9) ... The interior sum of angles of a 99-sided polygon = 17460 degrees.

Combining (S8) and (S9) we have:

(S10) ...The interior sum of angles of 100-sided polygon = the interior sum of angles of a 99-sided polygon.

Statement S10 is tautologically true if and only if 100 = 99. But since the equality 100 = 99 is self-evidently false, it follows that S8 is implicitly self-contradictory.

A statement that is self-contradictory in one kind of geometry may not be self-contradictory in another. In spherical geometry, for example, the interior sum of angles of a triangle (formed by the intersection of three great circles on the surface of a sphere) is a number between 180 and 540 degrees. Thus, the statement: "The interior sum of angles of a triangle is equal to 360 degrees," though implicitly self-contradictory in Euclidian geometry, is not self-contradictory in spherical geometry.

Reductio Ad Absurdum

Consider the following statements:

(A1) . . . God exists.
(A2) . . . God does not exist.

Either A1 or A2 is true, but not both. In other words: if A1 is true, then A2 is false. Conversely: if A2 is true, then A1 is false; one statement contradicts the other. Contradictory statements are both logically exclusive and exhaustive. Furthermore, when combined with the logical 'and', they produce a single self-contradictory statement e.g. 'God exists and God does not exist.' A self-contradictory statement is self-cancelling in the sense that it produces nothing – much like the sum of number with its negative e.g. $5 + (-5) = 0$. In order to prove that a system of belief is incoherent - in the sense that its premises are mutually incompatible – one need only show that its premises produce self-contradictory conclusions. Consider the following system of statements:

System B:
(B1) . . . All students are demonstrators.
(B2) . . . All demonstrators are rioters.
(B3) . . . All rioters are looters.
(B4) . . . All looters are arsonists.
(B5) . . . All arsonists are killers.
(B6) . . . All killers should be shot.
(B7) . . . No demonstrators should be shot

Premises B1 to B6 imply that all students should be shot, but premises B1 and B7 imply that no student should be shot. Taken as a whole, the system produces the self-contradictory statement: "All students should be shot and no student should be shot"; hence, the system is self-contradictory. If certain premises are removed a self-contradictory system may become coherent but that will not, of course, ensure that its conclusions are sensible. Removing premise B7 from the system, for example, leads to the absurd conclusion: "All students should be shot."

In the following analysis we shall employ the Temporal Postulates which are:

Postulate I: The Reduction Principle
The temporal to the eternal is unreal.

Postulate II: The Principle of Inclusion
All things belong to the temporal or the eternal.

In the two postulates, the terms "temporal" and "eternal" are treated as nouns rather than adjectives and refer to the temporal and eternal domains respectively. To avoid unnecessary repetition, the word "domain" has been dropped. It will be clear from the context how the terms are being used. Postulate I is a concise way of saying that anything belonging to the temporal is unreal or has no reality in relation to anything belonging to the eternal. (We shall discuss this idea in more detail in Chapter 11.) Postulate II states that nothing exists outside the temporal or the eternal or, alternatively, that everything is included within the temporal or the eternal. Four propositions may be deduced from these two postulates. In some cases, we shall prove the propositions by *reductio ad absurdum* i.e. make an assumption and derive a contradiction thereby proving the original assumption to be false.

Proposition A

The temporal and the eternal are mutually exclusive.

Proof

Anything unreal in relation to the eternal cannot belong to the eternal. Therefore, anything belonging to the temporal cannot belong to the eternal. Furthermore, anything belonging to the eternal cannot be unreal in relation to the eternal. Therefore, anything belonging to the eternal cannot belong to the temporal. Hence, the temporal and the eternal are mutually exclusive. [QED]

Proposition B

Anything belonging to the temporal is of finite duration, and anything of finite duration belongs to the temporal.

Proof

Firstly, consider something belonging to the temporal and assume it is of infinite duration. If it is of infinite duration, it always exists, and if it always exists it belongs to the eternal. But, by Proposition A, nothing belonging to the temporal can belong to the eternal. Since this is a contradiction, the original assumption that something belonging to the temporal is of infinite duration is *false*. Therefore, anything belonging to the temporal is of finite duration. Secondly, anything of finite duration does not always exist therefore it does belong to the eternal. By Postulate II it belongs to the temporal. [QED]

Proposition C

A *mortal* human self belongs to the temporal, and an *immortal* human self belongs to the eternal.

Proof

Firstly, if the human self is mortal it does not always exist, and if it does not always exist it does not belong to the eternal. If it does not belong to the eternal, then it must belong to the temporal (Post. II). Secondly, let us assume that an immortal human self belongs to the temporal. If it belongs to the temporal it is of finite duration (Prop. B), and if it is of finite duration, it cannot be immortal. Hence, an immortal human self is not immortal. Since this result is self-contradictory, the original assumption that an immortal human self belongs to the temporal is *false*. Therefore, an immortal human self belongs to the eternal. [QED]

Proposition D

To an eternal being all events are simultaneous.

Proof

Let us assume, on the contrary, that to an eternal being two events E and F are *not* simultaneous. If they are not simultaneous, then one precedes the other in time. Let us suppose that E precedes F. If E precedes F, then time T elapses between E and F. Thus, an eternal being waits time T from E to F. But, by Postulate I, time is unreal to any being existent in the eternal. Hence, an eternal being waits *no* time from E to F. Since this result is a contradiction, the original assumption that E and F are not simultaneous is *false*. Therefore, to an eternal being, any two events E and F are simultaneous. If any two events are simultaneous, then *all* events are simultaneous. [QED]

We shall now show that the following system is incoherent System T:

(T1) ... God creates.
(T2) ... God preserves.
(T3) ... God destroys

The statement: "God exists in the eternal," is not a temporal postulate but we shall take it to be true. God's creation belongs to the temporal or the eternal (Post. II). Let us assume it belongs to the temporal. If it belongs to the temporal then, to the eternal, it is unreal (Post. I). If God's creation is unreal to the eternal, it is unreal to any being existent in the eternal. Since God exists in the eternal, God's creation is unreal to God. If God's creation is unreal to God, it is not created by God; therefore God's creation is not God's creation. Since this result is self-contradictory the original assumption that God's creation belongs to the temporal is *false*. Therefore God's creation belongs to the eternal.

We now prove that system T is self-contradictory. By premise T1 God creates and, since God's creations belong to the eternal, they always exist. If God's creations always exist they are not destroyed; therefore God does not destroy. But, by premise T3, God destroys. Since this result is self-contradictory we conclude that system T is incoherent.

We shall employ the Temporal Postulates and the propositions above to prove that system U below is incoherent.

System U
(U1) ... The human self is immortal.
(U2) ... The human self is uniquely expressive.
(U3) ... The human self reincarnates

Premise U2 expresses the idea of individuality - that the human self does not incarnate in more than one physical body simultaneously. By premise U1 the human self is immortal and therefore belongs to the eternal (Prop. C). Since the human self belongs to the eternal all events are simultaneous (Prop. D). By premise U3 the human self reincarnates but since all events – and hence incarnations - are simultaneous, the human self expresses itself through all its incarnations simultaneously. Hence, the human self is not uniquely expressive. But by premise U2, the human self is uniquely expressive. Since this result is self-contradictory, we conclude that system U is incoherent.

The arguments above prove that the concepts of immortality, individuality and reincarnation *cannot* form part of a coherent system of thought. However, negation of each premise, in turn, produces three different systems. We shall test the coherence of each one.

System V:

(V1) . . . The human self is immortal.

(V2) . . . The human self is *not* uniquely expressive.

(V3) . . . The human self reincarnates.

System W:

(W1) . . . The human self is mortal.

(W2) . . . The human self is uniquely expressive.

(W3) . . . The human self reincarnates.

System X:

(X1) . . . The human self is immortal.

(X2) . . . The human self is uniquely expressive.

(X3) . . . The human self does *not* reincarnate.

Firstly, consider system V. By premise V3 the human self reincarnates; hence, its expressions are sequential in time. If the expressions are sequential then they are not simultaneous; hence, the human self is uniquely expressive. But, by premise V2 the human self is *not* uniquely expressive. Since this result is self-contradictory, we conclude that system V is incoherent.

Secondly, consider system W. By premise W1 the human self is mortal and, therefore, belongs to the temporal (Prop. C). If the human self belongs to the temporal it exists in time. By premise W3 the human self reincarnates and since it exists in time, its expressions are sequential in time; hence, it is uniquely expressive. Therefore, premise W3 implies premise W2. Furthermore, since a *mortal* human self belongs to the temporal, it has no reality in relation to the eternal (Post. I), therefore nothing in relation to the eternal reincarnates. But, if nothing in relation to the eternal reincarnates then nothing in relation to time reincarnates. But, by premise W3 the human self reincarnates. Since this result is self-contradictory we conclude that system W is incoherent with premise W2 redundant.

Thirdly, consider system X. By premise X1 the human self is immortal and therefore belongs to the eternal (Prop. C). Furthermore, to any being belonging to the eternal, all events are simultaneous (Prop. D). By premise X2, the human self is uniquely expressive and therefore does not incarnate in more than one physical body simultaneously. Since all the expressions are simultaneous, the human self cannot reincarnate. We conclude that system X is *coherent* but with premise X3 redundant.

From the analysis above, it is evident that the issue of reincarnation is one of logical consistency, not of empirical evidence. But this is hardly surprising since changing overcoats – the original metaphor of Chapter 1 - is a process occurring in time. Since time, to an eternal being, has no reality it follows that the human self (if immortal) cannot change its physical bodies in time. Hence, the overcoat metaphor is erroneous. We conclude that strong agnosticism - that reincarnation cannot be refuted or verified - and weak agnosticism - that reincarnation cannot be refuted but may be verified through empirical research - are both category mistakes.

In conclusion, both agnostic arguments assume that the statement: "The human self reincarnates" belongs to class X, whereas it is implicitly self-contradictory. The weak agnostic is much like someone searching for 'square circles' or 'flat solids' or planar triangles with interior sums greater than 180 degrees. Believing in the existence of white crows, extra-terrestrial beings, Bigfoot, the Loch Ness Monster and other cryptids is to believe in the possible but to believe in square circles, flat solids, people who can walk and stand still at the same time, and immortal or uniquely expressive beings who reincarnate is to believe in the impossible. Therefore, the agnostic argument fails.

* * *

We shall now prove another negative: that no events are connected in necessary causal relationships. Causality is often discussed in terms of events; one event is the causal event and another event is the consequent event. Events unfold in time and space. Some events – like the splitting of an atom – happen almost instantaneously and occupy a very small volume of space; other events – like the cooling of a star – may take millions of years and cover large regions of space. In physics events are defined as happenings which occur in infinitesimally small regions of space in infinitesimally small intervals of time. If smaller and smaller regions and intervals are considered – approaching points in the limit - events become 'point events.' Although individual point events are not directly perceivable by the human senses, large collections of contiguous point events are. In fact, the events of ordinary experience may be regarded as large collections of such events.

The game of snooker may be approximated as a series of point events. Suppose a snooker ball is struck by the cue at time zero (event A); the ball rebounds on the opposite cushion three seconds later (event B) and stops two seconds after the rebound (event C). Events A, B and C form a *causal* sequence which may be represented as: A→B→C. Suppose a photograph is taken just as the player hits the ball (event P). Since events A and P occur simultaneously and since the player would need time to react, the photograph could not have caused the shot nor even have been a contributory cause of it. If, on the other hand, the player had anticipated the photograph, then the prior anticipation – rather than the photograph - would have been the cause or a contributory cause. Now, while the cue action (event A) is sufficient to cause the rebound (event B) it is not necessary since the motion of another ball could have caused an identical rebound. Furthermore, the rebound itself was not a necessary occurrence since it could have been prevented by the motion of another ball. In the latter case, event C would not necessarily have occurred. Hence, events A , B and C are not connected in a necessary causal relationship.

John L. Mackie (Reader in Philosophy at Oxford University) argues that a cause of an event is neither a necessary nor a sufficient condition of that event. In a paper entitled: 'Causes and Conditions' published in the *American Philosophical Quarterly (1965)*. He states: "Asked what a cause is, we may be tempted to say that it is an event which precedes the event of which it is the cause, and is both necessary and sufficient for the latter's occurrence; briefly that a cause is a necessary and sufficient preceding condition. There are, however, many difficulties in this account. I shall try to show that what we often speak of as a cause is a condition not of this sort, but of a sort related to this." To illustrate his thesis, Mackie uses the example of a house catching fire. A fire has broken out in a certain house but is extinguished before it is completely destroyed. Fire investigators conclude that the fire was caused by an electrical short-circuit at a certain place. Mackie asks the question: "What is the exact force of their statement that this short-circuit caused this fire?" Clearly, the particular short-circuit was not a necessary condition for the house to catch fire since a short-circuit somewhere else, or the overturning of a lighted oil stove, or any number of things, could also have set the house on fire. Furthermore, the short-circuit was not a sufficient condition since if there had been no inflammable material nearby, or if automatic sprinklers had been installed, the house would not have caught fire. Mackie concludes: "Far from being a condition both necessary and sufficient for the fire the short-circuit was, and is known to the experts to have been, neither necessary nor sufficient for it."

In the light of Mackie's arguments, can it be maintained that a boxer's punch is a necessary and sufficient condition for another boxer to fall onto the canvas? The answer must be *no* since certain conditions must be fulfilled before the event in question can happen and, furthermore, other conditions may be present which could result in the same outcome. For example, when boxer P punches boxer Q, the latter must, at the crucial moment, be exposed or vulnerable to P's punches: this vulnerability may, or may not, be present; hence the punch is not sufficient to cause the fall. Furthermore, the boxer could slip and fall without being punched; hence the punch is not a necessary cause of the fall.

However, this is not to deny that events are connected in causal relationships. Clearly, a murderer causes the death of his victim. The point is that events are not connected in *necessary* causal relationships: the victim may not have died. Later on in this section we shall employ similar arguments to show that events occurring in the lives of individuals living in different historical time periods are not connected in necessary causal relationships. This is merely to say that the lives of individuals are not governed by a law of cause and effect.

We shall begin by showing that no event relationships based on empirical evidence are connected in necessary causal relationships. But first, we must eliminate all event relationships that are the product of artificial constructions. Consider, for example, the following events in which E precedes F:

Event E ... P injures his legs in an accident.
Event F ... P is unable to climb a ladder.

Let us introduce the following assumption:

A1 ... Uninjured legs are necessary to climb a ladder.

Given A1, if P injures his legs in an accident, it follows *logically* that any activity requiring the use of uninjured legs will be impossible. In this scenario E is the causal event and F is the consequent event. But it would be incorrect to say that the events are connected in a necessary causal relationship because in each case the causal connection arises as a logical consequence of an artificial assumption which may or may not be true. Since the assumption is not necessarily true it follows that the corresponding event relationship E→F is not necessarily true. Hence, E and F are not connected in a necessary causal relationship.

However, there is a further difficulty. If P injures his legs in an accident it does not follow that P will attempt to climb a ladder. If he does not, then event F will not happen. In other words, the occurrence of event E does not necessarily entail the occurrence of event F. Once again, the events are not connected in a necessary causal relationship. In order to ensure that event F follows event E it would be necessary to introduce an additional assumption such as:

A2: . . . P will attempt to climb a ladder.

But, then, all we have done is to introduce another assumption which may or may not be true in practice.

To show that no event relationships based on empirical evidence are connected in necessary causal relationships, consider the two events:

E1 . . . X fires a gun at Y.
E2 . . . Y suffers an injury.

Firstly, there is no necessary relationship between the two events because X might miss his target and Y still be injured by a speeding truck. However, let us assume that Y is hit by the bullets from X's gun. Although E1 is the cause of E2, it cannot be asserted that E1 and E2 are connected in a necessary causal relationship because Y might have been wearing body armour, the gun might have jammed, X might have missed, the bullets might have been blank, the gun might have back-fired, and so on. Prior to X firing the gun, the assertion that Y will suffer an injury is, in fact, an inductive inference based on previous experience. In practice, people do not normally wear body armour; guns do not normally jam; gunmen do not normally miss at close range; bullets are not normally blank; and guns do not normally backfire. On the basis of previous experience, then, Y is *likely* to suffer an injury but it does not follow that Y will necessarily suffer an injury because the conditions needed to ensure that Y is injured will not necessarily be present. This merely demonstrates that inductive inferences are not logically valid and cannot, therefore, be used as the basis for a law of cause and effect. If event E3 is defined as follows:

E3 . . . Y does not suffer an injury.

The only logically valid inference that can be made is that if X fires a gun at Y, then either Y will suffer and injury or Y will not suffer an injury. In other words, the inference says nothing.

Let examine the above argument by distinguishing between the scenario *a priori* i.e. before X fires the gun, and the scenario *a posteriori* i.e. after X fires the gun. Before X fires the gun the events E1, E2, E3 exist as potential events i.e. each one is capable of happening. After X fires the gun either the event pair (E1, E2) occurs or the event pair (E1, E3) occurs, but not both. In other words (E1, E2) and (E1, E3) are mutually exclusive. Setting out the scenarios *a priori* and *a posteriori* as a system of statements we obtain the following:

A priori:

E1 ... X fires a gun at Y.
E2 ... Y suffers an injury.
E3 ... Y does not suffer an injury.

A posteriori - outcome 1:

E1 ... X fires a gun at Y.
E2 ... Y suffers an injury.
Events E1 and E2 happen

A posteriori - outcome 2:

E1 ... X fires a gun at Y.
E3 ... Y does not suffer an injury.
Events E1 and E3 happen.

Before the gun is fired either (E1, E2) or (E1, E3) is capable of happening. After the gun is fired only one event pair happens. Now, a necessary relationship between two events is, by definition, always necessary. If the event pair (E1, E2) is necessary *a priori* then it is necessary *a posteriori*. Conversely, if (E1, E2) is necessary *a posteriori* then it is necessary *a priori*. But, if (E1, E2) is necessary *a priori*, then the alternative (E1, E3) is impossible since the events E2 and E3 are mutually exclusive. But, we have already claimed that the pair (E1, E3) is, *a priori*, capable of happening. If (E1, E3) is capable of happening it follows that (E1, E2) is capable of not happening. If (E1, E2) is capable of not happening then, *a priori*, it is not necessary. If (E1, E2) is not necessary *a priori*, then it is not necessary *a posteriori*. It follows that E1 and E2 cannot be in a necessary causal relationship.

The above argument, which follows from the principle that inductive inferences are not logically valid applies to all event relationships that have been formulated on the basis of empirical evidence. Suppose, for example, the causal and consequent events F1 and F2 are as follows and it is assumed that all observations are reported.

F1 ... A crow is observed.
F2 ... A crow is reported to be black.

The proposition: "White crows exist" cannot be refuted because a white crow could conceivably be observed. It follows that F2 is not a necessary consequence of F1; therefore the two events are not connected in a necessary causal relationship. Once again, the only logically valid inference that can be made is that if a crow is observed, then either it will be black or it will not be black which, of course, says nothing. This shows that event relationships based on empirical evidence cannot be connected in necessary causal relationships and, consequently, cannot be the product of a law of cause and effect.

It is easy to show that no event relationships based on natural laws are connected in necessary causal relationships. For illustrative purposes, the Law of Gravity will suffice. The motion of a projectile in a gravitational field can be deduced from the Law of Gravity provided certain conditions are fulfilled. In the case of a freely falling body, the path of the body must be unobstructed, there must be no countervailing forces such as heavy winds and air resistance, and there must be no collisions with other objects. When all these potentially disturbing factors have been eliminated - in a so-called ideal experiment - will the Law of Gravity correctly predict the motion of the projectile. However, this does not demonstrate causal necessity because ideal conditions may or may not be present. In practice potentially disturbing factors can and will divert the projectile from its predicted path. Hence, the projectile will not necessarily follow the path predicted by the Law of gravity. Since this argument is applicable to any other physical law, it follows that physical laws cannot establish necessary causal relationships between events. The fact that physical laws add stability to our experience of the world does not change this result.

We shall now show that events occurring in the lives of individuals living in different historical time periods are not connected in necessary causal relationships. Consider two events, E and F. Event E occurs in the lifetime of individual A, and event F in the lifetime of individual B; the two individuals live in different historical time periods. Let us suppose that events E and F are linked together through a long chain of events as follows:

$E \rightarrow H_1 \rightarrow H_2 \rightarrow H_3 \rightarrow H_4 .... H_{50000} \rightarrow F$

Adjacent pairs of causal and consequent events, such as the pair (H_{38}, H_{39}), are directly connected components of the chain. Since no directly connected pairs of events are connected in necessary causal relationships, it follows that no *indirectly* connected pairs of events are connected in necessary causal relationships. In particular E and F are not connected in a necessary causal relationship. If E and F are not so connected then they cannot be the product of any karmic relationship or the product of a law of cause and effect.

Chapter 4
The Problem with Karma

In the Hindu doctrine of reincarnation - as in most Western versions - many personalities may be associated with one individuality. This means that the reincarnating entity is the eternal self. In the Buddhist doctrine of rebirth, however, no such entity exists, though many personalities are threaded together in a so-called 'stream of consciousness.' This difference of view - though perplexing in some respects - presents no difficulties for the analysis of karma because *all* systems embody the notion of a series of noncontemporaneous personalities linked to one another by some underlying principle; the principle may vary from one system to another, but the concept of a series of connected personalities does not. We shall, therefore, discard the notion of an entity reborn and think in terms of a series of personalities. This series will then represent a complete cycle of rebirths from beginning to end, and each personality in the series will correspond to exactly *one* incarnation.

If reincarnation is a natural phenomenon applicable to everyone it must be governed by natural law; in the doctrine of reincarnation this is the *law of karma*, a law that supposedly determines the quality of a person's life based on actions carried out by personalities in previous incarnations. Actions generate karma (i.e. consequences) and karma must be settled in future incarnations; thus, karma is the motive force for reincarnation. If liberation from the cycle of rebirths is to be achieved, it can be achieved *only* through the elimination of karma.

Now, karma as consequences is a very general idea and refers not only to the external circumstances in which a personality finds itself but also to the internal circumstances, that is to say, the physical, emotional and mental conditions that define the totality of the personality's constitution. Thus, a deformed limb, an aggressive temperament, a high intelligence quotient, or a conscientious attitude towards one's duties will all be karmic in origin.

In much of the literature, karma is analysed as an ethical system in which the present personality is punished or rewarded according to actions carried out by personalities in previous incarnations, but little thought is given to the question of karma's ability to achieve its principal objective, namely, to guide the personality towards liberation through the elimination of karma. In the major Eastern religions it is taught that the detached personality can, through meditation, right-living and general renunciation of the world, take control of karma and eventually eliminate it; but there is a problem with this view because the character traits that underlie the personality's willingness to engage in such activities are themselves an integral part of the karmic load; by detaching itself from karma the personality detaches itself from the willingness to control it - an inherently self-contradictory activity, much like desiring to be desireless or walking and standing still at the same time. This means that karma cannot be eliminated by the conscious personality. As we shall see, karma is the product of chance and, as such, can only be eliminated by chance. Hence, the proper focus of attention should not be on the personality's efforts to eliminate karma but on the motion of karma itself. The question we need to ask, then, is karma capable of achieving its primary objective?

Various analogies can be used to characterise karma e.g. 'baggage' and 'harvest yield' but probably the most useful is to envisage karma as a kind of cosmic bank balance in which 'credits' and 'debits' are carried forward from previous incarnations to be settled by the present personality. The karmic balance is then the sum of the 'debits' and 'credits' and the goal is to achieve a balance of *zero*. Although the balance of karma carried forward from the previous incarnation may be settled in the present incarnation, the actions of the personality in the present incarnation always generate fresh karma that must be settled by the new personality in the next incarnation. Thus to escape the cycle of rebirths, the personality must *not* generate fresh karma in the *present* incarnation. In other words, the balance of karma at the end of the current incarnation must be zero, and for this to be achieved all the negative elements of the personality must be perfectly balanced by the positive elements; this is sometimes referred to as a 'perfect balance of mind.' In the following discussion we shall distinguish between:

(a) karma settled
(b) karma generated.

Karma settled in the present incarnation is karma generated in the *previous* incarnation; and karma generated in the present incarnation is karma settled in the *next* incarnation.

Fundamental to karma is the notion that negative or bad karma weakens the propensity to do bad things, and that positive or good karma strengthens the propensity to do good things - like a system of punishments and rewards. Consequently, karma does not produce a series of random personalities with little relationship to one another but a series of personalities whose members exhibit a slow and steady improvement in the moral and spiritual qualities of their actions. If karma did not lead to a progressive improvement in actions, it would not be capable of functioning as a tool of liberation.

To ensure that karma functions effectively, the response to karma must satisfy three conditions. Firstly, the response must be *positive* i.e. the moral and spiritual qualities of the new personality must be superior to those of the old personality. If the actions of the old personality were reprehensible, the actions of the new personality will be *less* reprehensible. If the actions of the old personality were admirable, the actions of the new personality will be more admirable. Secondly, the response to karma must be *small*. This reflects the slow, evolutionary nature of karma and the need for countless incarnations of suffering and enjoyment before the final goal of liberation is attained. For example, a criminal personality cannot immediately precede an honest law-abiding one. Hence, the moral and spiritual qualities of the new personality will differ only very slightly from those of the old one. Thirdly, the response to karma must be *consistent* between incarnations. Whatever the incarnation, the response to karma must be proportionately the same; this ensures that all personalities in a given series are treated in an equitable manner. Summarizing: the response to karma must be (A) *positive*, (B) *small*, and (C) *consistent*.

Conditions A, B and C may be described as the *rational* response to karma. If any of these conditions are not satisfied, the response is said to be suboptimal or irrational. When the response is suboptimal, karma becomes more difficult to eliminate for a number of reasons. Firstly, negative responses retard the evolution of the personality e.g. regression from honesty to criminality. Secondly, large responses produce greater variability e.g. transmigration from human to insect. Thirdly, inconsistent responses produce spasmodic or random outcomes e.g. different reactions to similar circumstances. The rational response to karma, then, *maximises* the possibility of eliminating it. Of course, it is not being suggested that all responses must be rational - far from it; indeed, in some branches of reincarnationism it is believed that some humans transmigrate to lower animals. The point is that departures from rationality make the goal of liberation *more* difficult to attain.

In the doctrine of karma, actions refer not so much to the particulars of a person's behaviour but to the moral and spiritual qualities of the person's actions. For example, walking across a road to help someone is vastly different to walking across a road to avoid someone. The activities are identical but the actions are different; clearly, motive is all. We then have the following scheme:

(a) the moral and spiritual qualities of the *present* personality's behaviour determine the quality of life of the new personality in the *next* incarnation. Expressed simply, this means that actions determine karma.

(b) The quality of life of the *present* personality determines the moral and spiritual qualities of the personality's behaviour in the *next* incarnation. Expressed simply, this means that karma determines actions.

Up to this point we have assumed a system of single incarnation resolution i.e. a system in which all debits and credits are carried forward from the previous incarnation and settled in the *present* incarnation and, furthermore, that the actions of the present incarnation generate fresh karma which must be settled in the *next* incarnation. Now, it might be thought that karma can be spread over a number of incarnations, like a large debt paid off in instalments (if the karma is very negative) or like an annuity (if the karma is very positive). However, the practicalities and fairness of such an arrangement are highly questionable. Although karma spreading would minimise the impact of negative karma it would dilute the enjoyment of positive karma. Thus, the disadvantages of one would cancel out the advantages of the other. Furthermore, if all the negative karma were diluted, all the hard lessons would be diluted, defeating the purpose of karma. As an alternative arrangement, positive karma could be retained but negative karma deferred to the next incarnation. It is easy to show that this too would be self-defeating. If the present personality X enjoyed all the positive karma and deferred all the negative, the new personality Y would then have to carry *double* the negative karma: the negative karma generated by the actions of X plus the negative karma *deferred* by X. If Y adopted the same arrangement, enjoying all the positive karma and deferring all the negative, the new personality Z would then have to carry *triple* the negative karma: the negative karma generated by the actions of Y plus the (doubled) negative karma deferred by Y. If all subsequent personalities adopted the same strategy, the volume of negative karma deferred would multiply without limit. No personality would ever carry negative karma, the karmic debt would never be settled, and karma as a mechanism for liberation would collapse. It is evident that karma spreading will always be self-defeating because one personality's gain is another personality's loss. It may be argued, of course, that the deferment of consequences to the next incarnation is itself unfair. But, then, this is the very nature of karma; a person is punished or rewarded for no apparent reason. Yet, the deferment of consequences is fundamental to the doctrine of reincarnation for without it there would be no motive for reincarnation.

* * *

Anyone familiar with the elements of engineering will recognize the scheme outlined above as an input-output system with a feedback loop (see fig. 1a.)

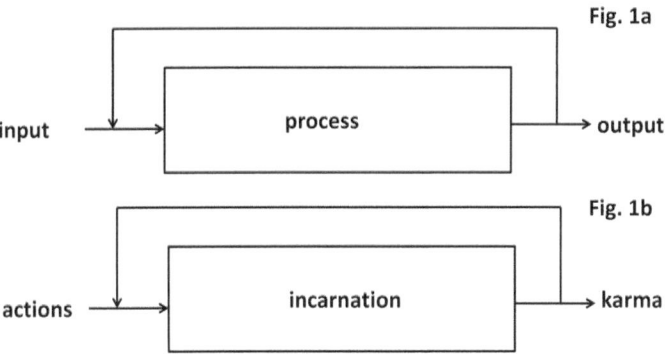

Fig. 1a

Fig. 1b

Consider the manufacture of sliced bread in which uncut loaves are fed into a slicing machine. The uncut loaves are the inputs, and the sliced loaves are the outputs. Let us suppose further that the loaves enter the machine at a higher temperature than normal, causing the bread to crumble. This is detected by a sensor which sends a signal back to a cooling device which lowers the bread's temperature thereby correcting the problem. In fig. 1b actions are the input and karma is the output; actions determine karma, and karma feeds back to actions. For example, the actions of the 120th incarnation determine the karma of the 121st incarnation; and the karma of the 121st incarnation feeds back to the actions of the 122nd incarnation.

In engineering jargon, feedback may be negative or positive. When feedback is negative, the output of the system opposes changes to the inputs with the result that future changes are *weakened*. When feedback is positive, the output of the system reinforces changes to the inputs with the result that future changes are *strengthened*. In the case of the bread-slicing machine, the feedback is negative because the output of ruined loaves, caused by the excessive temperature, triggers off a cooling device that lowers the temperature and reduces the future output of ruined loaves. Negative karma produces *negative* feedback because, by punishing the present personality, it weakens the new personality's propensity to do negative things. Positive karma produces *positive* feedback because, by rewarding the present personality, it strengthens the new personality's propensity to do positive things. (Negative and positive feedback should not be confused with the response to karma which is always *positive* i.e. leading to improvement.)

By definition, a wholly good personality is incapable of doing, feeling or thinking in negative terms, and a wholly bad personality is incapable of doing, feeling or thinking in positive terms. A series of wholly good personalities and a series of wholly bad personalities have different feedback loops as shown in figs. 2a and 2b.

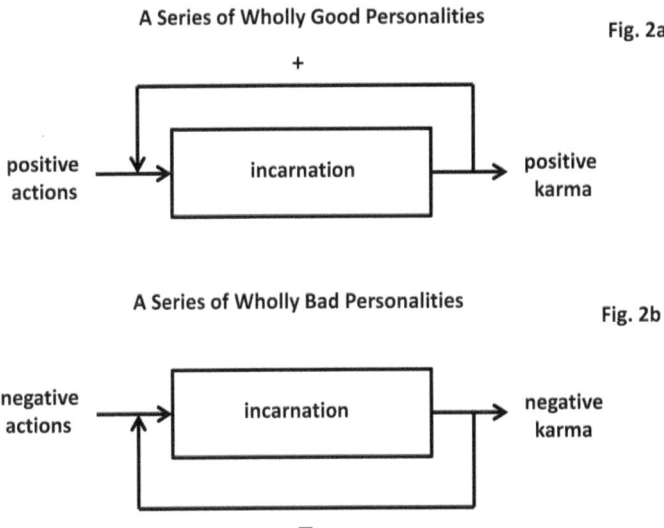

Fig. 2a — A Series of Wholly Good Personalities

Fig. 2b — A Series of Wholly Bad Personalities

The sign attached to the feedback loop shows whether feedback is positive or negative. In general, a personality will be neither wholly good nor wholly bad. Physical, emotional and mental acts will rarely work in harmony and the personality's goals will lack unity of purpose. This means that the feedback mechanism will, in the vast majority of cases, consist of positive and negative loops (see fig. 3a.)

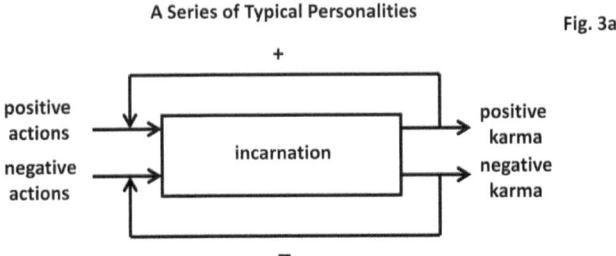

Fig. 3a — A Series of Typical Personalities

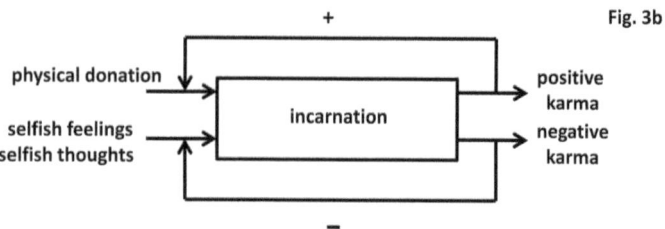

Fig. 3b

The personality will then generate positive karma through positive actions and negative karma through negative actions. In practice most actions will be *impure* i.e. consisting of positive and negative components. For example, a donation to a charitable foundation may be resolved into *three* components: (i) the physical donation, (ii) the feelings behind the donation, and (iii) the thoughts behind the donation. The physical donation will generate *positive* karma, but if it is donated for selfish reasons the feelings and thoughts behind the donation will generate *negative* karma. The net karma will then be the sum of the positive and negative components. Assuming that the donation is made for selfish reasons, the physical donation will pass through the positive loop and the selfish thoughts and feelings behind the donation will pass through the negative loop. Fig. 3b shows how the donation is divided. The feedback mechanism will then encourage donations to charitable institutions but discourage them for selfish reasons.

In general the response to positive karma will be different to the response to negative karma, and the upper and lower loops will function independently. Nevertheless, the output of karma will always be the sum of the positive and negative components. For a series of typical personalities, the negative loop can never become positive since this would usurp the role of the positive side. Whilst the lower can never replace the higher, it may progressively diminish to zero. Thus, the response to negative karma will never be so large as to cause its negative side to become a second positive side; the most that can happen is for the negative side to disappear. This accords with condition B above which asserts that the response to karma must be *small*.

From the discussion above, it is evident that karma is quantifiable: positive numbers corresponding to positive karma and negative numbers to negative karma. Once expressed as a number, karma can be calculated using the operations of arithmetic. For example, a donation to a charitable foundation may earn positive karma of 120 units for the physical donation, 30 units of negative karma for any selfish feelings behind the donation, and 50 units of negative karma for selfish thoughts. The resultant karma is the arithmetic sum of the three numbers:

120 + (-30) + (-50) = 40 units.

Hence, the donation earns 40 units of positive karma. (Note that brackets have been placed around negative karma to draw attention to the negative sign.)

Since karma can be quantified, it can be *ordered*. For example, 1000 units of karma is worth more than 500 units of karma, and (-300) units of karma is worth less than (-10) units of karma. Karma then corresponds to points on the number line (see fig. 4a) and since any point in the number line can correspond to a possible karma, karma can be treated as a continuous variable, like mass or weight.

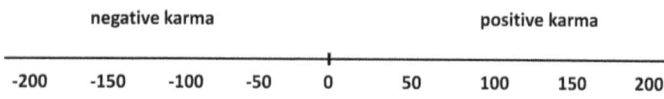

Fig. 4a

Fig. 4b

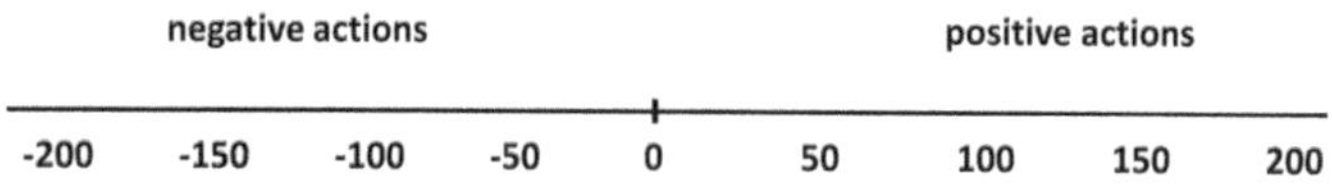

Thus, karma can assume any positive or negative value e.g. 234.23 or (-30.041). Moving along the line from left to right, karma becomes *more* valuable; moving from right to left, karma becomes *less* valuable. For example, a change in karma from (-150) to (-100) (a move from left to right) is a change for the better; a change in karma from 20 to (-130) (a move from right to left) is a change for the worse.

To complete the quantification, it is necessary to quantify actions. Some actions, such as personal services, can be valued in the market place but many actions, such as helping a blind person across the road, cannot be so easily valued. However, a cosmic agency dedicated to the task would experience no difficulty; indeed, it could determine the value of any action by decree; it need only be consistent. As we shall see below, the quantification of actions and karma are inseparable: to measure one is to measure the other. We shall assign positive values to positive actions and negative values to negative actions. As in the case of karma, actions may be represented by points on the number line (see fig. 4b.) Consider the above donation to the charitable foundation. The physical donation might be valued at 100 units, the selfish feelings at (-20) units and the selfish thoughts at (-60) units. The resultant value of the donation is the arithmetic sum of the three numbers:

$100 + (-20) + (-60) = 20$ units.
Hence, the donation is valued at 20 units.

The Axioms of Karma

Since karma is a quantitative system of ethics it must obey certain axioms. These may be stated as follows:

Axiom 1:
When actions are zero, karma is zero.

Axiom 2:
For a given value of actions, there corresponds one and only one value of karma.

Axiom 3:
The greater the value of actions, the greater the value of karma.

In Axiom 1 an action may be zero if the positive and negative components have the same magnitude (the sum will then be zero). Axiom 2 is a statement of causal law. The value of any activity will correspond to one and only one value of karma. Axiom 3 expresses the qualitative (or directional) nature of karma: the greater the magnitude of positive actions, the greater the magnitude of *positive* karma; the greater the magnitude of negative actions, the greater the magnitude of *negative* karma.

Mathematically speaking, Axioms 2 and 3 require that the functional relationship between actions and karma be 'monotonic increasing' in actions. This property is possessed by all of the graphs in fig. 5 with the exception of graph (iv) which is 'monotonic decreasing' in actions.

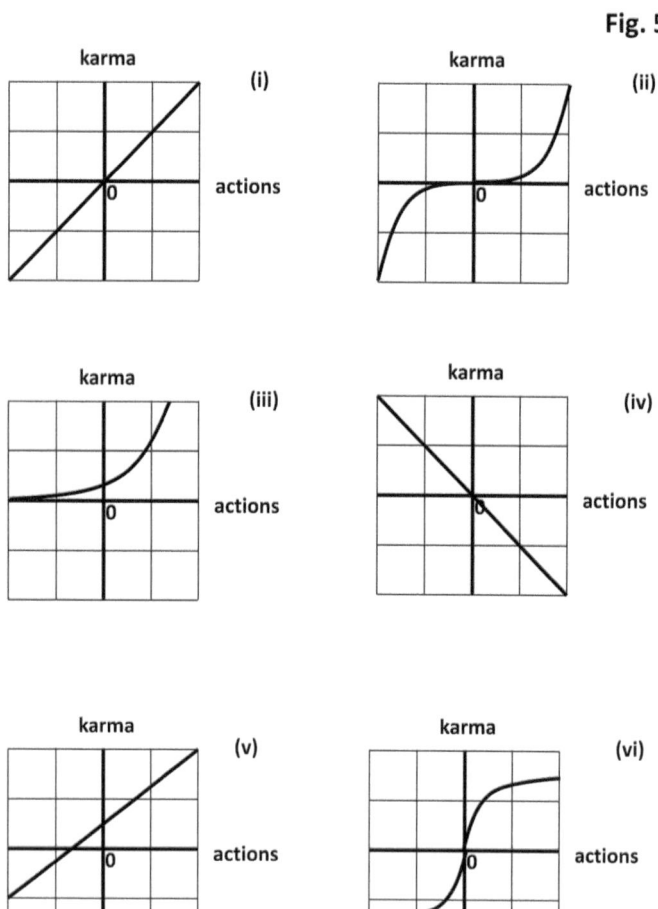

Fig. 5

Only graphs (i), (ii) and (vi) satisfy all three axioms. Graphs (iii) and (v) do not satisfy Axiom 1 since, in either case, when actions are zero karma is not zero. For Axiom 1 to be satisfied, the graph should pass through the origin of coordinates (0, 0). Graph (iv) does not satisfy Axiom 3, since greater values of actions correspond to lower values of karma.

Axiom 3, which expresses the qualitative relationship between actions and karma, is consistent with three broad scenarios: (1) constant returns to actions, (2) increasing returns to actions, (3) decreasing returns to actions. If returns to actions are constant, a unit change in the value of actions will always cause the same quantitative change in the value of karma. Suppose, for example, that actions are currently valued at 30 units and the next day they increase in value by one unit to 31 units causing karma to increase by, say, 15 units. If actions are at a higher level, say 60 units, and increase in value by one unit to 61 units, the increase in karma will still be 15 units. In other words, a one unit increase in the value of actions always causes karma to increase by 15 units. If returns to actions are increasing, the increase in karma would be *greater than* 15 units at higher levels of actions. If returns to actions are decreasing, the increase in karma would be *less than* 15 units at higher levels of actions. In fig. 5 graph (i) shows constant returns, graph (ii) shows increasing returns, and graph (vi) shows decreasing returns.

What is the most reasonable scenario? To answer this question, we need to apply the 'principle of equity.' This means that negative actions should not be punished more excessively than positive actions are rewarded. In mathematical terms, we require that the graph of the karmic function be symmetrical about the origin. Thus, if the graph is traced using a sheet of acetate and then rotated 180 degrees (either clockwise or anticlockwise) about the origin, the two graphs will coincide exactly. Of the graphs satisfying the three axioms, graphs (i), (ii) and (vi) possess this property. If returns to actions are increasing, good personalities enjoy ever increasing amounts of positive karma, and bad personalities suffer ever increasing amounts of negative karma. While such a scheme would discourage bad personalities from accumulating more *negative* karma it would merely encourage good personalities to accumulate more *positive* karma. Instead of terminating the cycle of rebirths, it would serve to extend it. Increasing returns must, therefore, be rejected for this reason alone. If returns are decreasing, good personalities enjoy ever decreasing amounts of positive karma, and bad personalities suffer ever decreasing amounts of negative karma. Clearly, such a scheme would not discourage bad personalities from acts of wrongdoing; indeed, it might encourage them. Either way, it would serve to extend rather than terminate the cycle of rebirths. Therefore, decreasing returns must also be rejected. This leaves constant returns to actions as the only reasonable scenario – graph (i). Constant returns satisfy the principle of equity. For example, if a unit increase in the magnitude of positive actions causes the magnitude of positive karma to increase by 30 units, then a unit increase in the magnitude of negative actions will cause an increase in the magnitude of negative karma also by 30 units. Since, the change in the magnitude of karma will be the same whatever the level of actions, actions are not rewarded or punished in progressively increasing or decreasing amounts. Hence, the treatment of actions is both equitable and symmetrical.

The relationship between karma K and actions A, which we shall call the Law of Karma, can now be represented symbolically as follows:

Law of Karma
(1) .... $K = \alpha A$

The law asserts that the value of karma is proportional to the value of actions. If the value of actions is doubled, trebled, etc. then the value of karma is doubled, trebled, etc. The constant of proportionality α may be determined if we choose suitable units of karma. If we define karma in terms of the actions which produce it this gives a constant of proportionality equal to 1. Formally,

Definition
(2) .... $\alpha = 1$.

Hence, one unit of karma is the product of one unit of actions or, alternatively, one unit of actions produces one unit of karma.

Measuring karma in this manner is like valuing output in terms of the labour input. If it takes 20 man hours to produce 300 bushels of wheat, then 300 bushels of wheat are worth 20 man hours. This method of valuation can be applied to any collection of commodities. Suppose it takes one man hour to produce 15 bushels of wheat, one man hour to dig 3 tons of coal, and one man hour to make 50 ceramic tiles. With constant returns to labour, 600 bushels of wheat, 36 tons of coal, and 800 ceramic tiles will be worth: $(600/15) + (36/3) + (800/50) = 40 + 12 + 16 = 68$ man hours.

Of course, a pure labour theory of value disregards capital input. Furthermore, the input-output coefficients may vary from one worker to another. In the example just discussed, the input-output coefficient for coal is 15, for wheat 3, and for ceramic tiles 50. For a different worker, the coefficients will be different because rates of efficiency vary from one worker to another. However, none of these problems are relevant to the valuation of karma because a person's karma is entirely the product of the previous personality's actions. Consequently, the valuation of karma is identical to a pure labour theory of value in which the input-output coefficient is always unity. With $\alpha = 1$ equation (2) becomes,

(3) .... $K = A$

Fig. 6 shows the relationship between actions and karma.

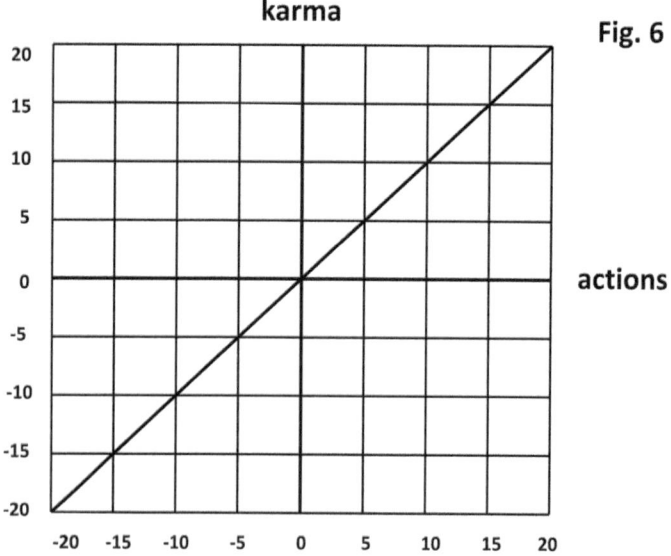

The graph is the set of all points whose first and second coordinates are equal e.g. (-50,-50), (-2,-2), (0,0), (5,5), (103,103). The first coordinate is the value of actions, and the second coordinate is the value of karma. Positive karma worth 500 units is the product of positive actions worth 500 units. Negative actions worth 100 units produce negative karma worth 100 units. Choosing units of karma so that the constant of proportionality is equal to 1 is similar to how the unit of force is defined in Newtonian mechanics.

* * *

We shall now show how karma and actions interact with another. By definition, any action will be the sum of positive and negative components. Let A be the sum of all the personality's actions in a given lifetime and A^G and A^B be the positive and negative components respectively. Then,

(4) .... $A \equiv A^G + A^B$

where the symbol '≡' means 'is defined as.' Let K be the karma generated by the personality and K^G and K^B be the positive and negative components respectively. Then,

(5) .... $K \equiv K^G + K^B$

The feedback mechanism for a typical series of personalities is shown in fig.7.

Fig. 7

A Series of Typical Personalities

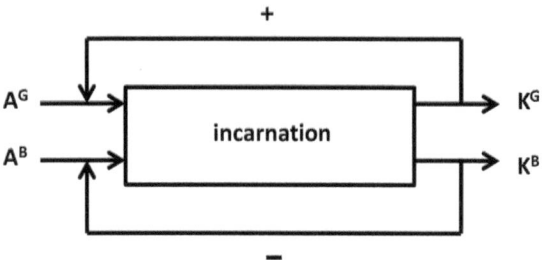

The actions of the previous incarnation generate karma that is settled in the present incarnation, where the value of karma is equal to the value of actions. Symbolically:

(6a) .... $K^G(x) = A^G(x - 1)$
(6b) .... $K^B(x) = A^B(x - 1)$

where $x \geq 2$ refers to the number of the incarnation. Note that x cannot equal 1 since $A^G(0)$ and $A^B(0)$ are undefined. Consequently, $K^G(1)$ and $K^B(1)$ are also undefined because there is no karma in the first incarnation.

Example 1:
If $x = 65$, $K^G(65) = A^G(64)$ and $K^B(65) = A^B(64)$ i.e. karma in the 65th incarnation is equal to the actions of the 64th incarnation.

Example 2:
Incarnation N
Action: a donation to a charity of $1000.

Physical donation valued at 500 units.
Feelings behind donation valued at (-100) units.
Thoughts behind the donation valued at (-200) units.
Incarnation N+1
Action: a donation to a charity of $1500 (allowing for inflation).
Physical donation valued at 500.01 units.
Feelings behind donation valued at (-99.99) units.
Thoughts behind the donation valued at (-199.99) units.

Symbolically, the increase in the value of actions can be represented as follows:

(7a) .... $A^G(x) > A^G(x - 1)$
(7b) .... $A^B(x) > A^B(x - 1)$

where ' $>$ ' means 'is greater than.' The change in actions can be expressed more concisely using the mathematical symbol Δ.

Define,

(8a) .... $\Delta A^G(x) \equiv A^G(x) - A^G(x - 1)$
(8b) .... $\Delta A^B(x) \equiv A^B(x) - A^B(x - 1)$

It then follows from (7) that $\Delta A^G(x) > 0$ and $\Delta A^B(x) > 0$. If actions change from 30 to 30.01 then $\Delta A^G = 30.01 - 30 = 0.01$ (>0). If actions change from (-50) to (-49.99) (a change for the better) $A^B = (-49.999) - (-50) = 0.001$ (>0).

The response to karma may be expressed as a relationship between the karma settled in the present incarnation x and the change in actions from the present incarnation x to the next incarnation (x+1) i.e. a relationship between K(x) and $\Delta A(x+1)$. Since the response to positive karma will in general differ from the response to negative karma we have two equations:

(9a) .... $\Delta A^G(x+1) = f[K^G(x)]$
(9b) .... $\Delta A^B(x+1) = h[K^B(x)]$

where $K^G(x) > 0$ and $K^B(x) < 0$. The symbols f and h mean 'is a function of' or 'is determined by'.

We now consider the functional forms of f and h. Any improvement in actions may be represented as a proportional response to karma. For example, if the proportional response is 0.0002 then the improvement in actions is 0.02 per cent of karma. We shall refer to this as the 'coefficient of response.' By condition C above the response to karma must be consistent between incarnations. This means that the coefficient of response must not change from one incarnation to another. However, it may vary from one series of personalities to another. In mathematical parlance the coefficient of response is *constant* for a given series of personalities. We then have the following response equations:

(10a) .... $\Delta A^G(x+1) = \lambda K^G(x)$
(10b) .... $\Delta A^B(x+1) = \mu K^B(x)$

where λ and μ are the fixed coefficients of response. Actions always improve from one incarnation to another i.e. $\Delta A^G(x+1) > 0$, and since $K^G(x) > 0$ it follows that the coefficient $\lambda > 0$. Moreover, since $\Delta A^B(x+1) > 0$ and $K^B(x) < 0$ it follows that the coefficient $\mu < 0$. The system of karma may then be summed up in six statements, (11a) through to (13b):

(11a) .... $A \equiv A^G + A^B$
(11b) .... $K \equiv K^G + K^B$

i.e. actions are the sum of positive and negative components, and karma is the sum of positive and negative components.

(12a) .... $K^G(x) = A^G(x-1)$, where $x \geq 2$
(12b) .... $K^B(x) = A^B(x-1)$

i.e. positive components of karma are determined by positive components of actions, and negative components of karma are determined by negative components of actions.

(13a) .... $\Delta A^G(x+1) = \lambda K^G(x)$
(13b) .... $\Delta A^B(x+1) = \mu K^B(x)$

i.e. the response to positive and negative karma in each case is a fixed proportion of karma. Disregarding, for the moment, the distinction between positive and negative, the equations of the system may be written more concisely as follows:

(14) .... $K(x) = A(x-1)$
(15) .... $\Delta A(x+1) = \rho K(x)$

where the symbol ρ (rho) is the coefficient of response. Substituting for $K(x)$ in equation (15), we have:

(16) .... $\Delta A(x+1) = \rho A(x-1)$
$\rightarrow$
(17) .... $\Delta A(x+2) = \rho A(x)$

Equation (17) is a second order linear difference equation in x with parameter ρ. The general solution is well known and can be found in any textbook on difference equations. Once the initial conditions have been set – in this case, the actions of the first and second incarnations – the solution expresses the actions of any incarnation in terms of x. Thus, for any incarnation, say the 15,000[th], the actions of that incarnation may be calculated by substituting x = 15,000 into the formula.

Given the coefficient of response ρ, equation (16) shows that the actions of the third incarnation onwards depend on the actions of the first and second incarnations. To see this, substitute x = 2 (the first value of x) into equation (16); then,

(18) .... $A(3) = A(2) + \rho A(1)$

Actions in the fourth incarnation are then:

(19) .... $A(4) = A(3) + \rho A(2)$

Substituting for A(3):

(20) .... $A(4) = A(2) + \rho A(1) + \rho A(2)$
$\rightarrow$
(21) .... $A(4) = [1 + \rho]A(2) + \rho A(1)$.

Actions in the fifth incarnation are:

(22) .... $A(5) = A(4) + \rho A(3)$

Substituting for A(4) and A(3):

(23) .... $A(5) = [1 + \rho]A(2) + \rho A(1) + \rho[A(2) + \rho A(1)]$
$\rightarrow$
(24) .... $A(5) = [1 + 2\rho]A(2) + \rho[1+\rho]A(1)$

The process of substitution may be continued indefinitely. Using the relationship between actions and karma in (14) we can generate the following series of karmas:

(25) .... $K(2) = A(1)$
(26) .... $K(3) = A(2)$
(27) .... $K(4) = A(3) = A(2) + \rho A(1)$

(28) .... $K(5) = A(4) = [1 + \rho]A(2) + \rho A(1)$
(29) .... $K(6) = A(5) = [1 + 2\rho]A(2) + \rho[1 + \rho]A(1)$

and so on. Although karma is determined by the actions of the first and second incarnations, this does not contradict equation (14). Equation (14) expresses immediate cause whilst the solution to equations (14) and (15) expresses ultimate cause. Ultimately, karma is the result of a long series of actions and reactions going back to the first and second incarnations – like a series of snooker ball impacts: actions determine karma and karma determines actions.

Throughout the above discussion, it has been assumed that the actions of the first and second incarnations are different, implying that change has occurred between the two incarnations. In fact, this cannot happen because actions can change only under the influence of karma and this does not operate between the first and the second incarnations (karma in the first incarnation $K(1)$ does not exist because there are no actions before the first incarnation). Actions change in the third incarnation in response to the karma of the second incarnation. Thus, from now on we shall assume that:

(30) .... $A(2) = A(1)$

for both positive and negative actions. Substituting for $A(2)$ in the equation for $K(6)$ we have,

(31) .... $K(6) = [1 + 2\rho]A(1) + \rho[1 + \rho]A(1)$
$\rightarrow$
(32) .... $K(6) = [1 + 3\rho + \rho^2]A(1)$

Hence, karma in the sixth incarnation is determined by the actions of the first incarnation. This result can be generalised to any number of incarnations so that the karma of *any* incarnation is ultimately determined by the actions of the first incarnation. The formula above applies to the components of actions and karma; hence:

(33a) .... $K^G(6) = [1 + 3\lambda + \lambda^2]A^G(1)$
(33b) .... $K^B(6) = [1 + 3\mu + \mu^2]A^B(1)$

It is instructive to see how actions and karma change over many incarnations; this is easily calculated on a spreadsheet using equation (17) as an iteration formulae in both good and bad components and equations (11) and (12). Once the initial actions and response coefficients have been set, the subsequent motion of actions and karma are determined for all time. In fig. 8, Graph 1 has been plotted for $A^G(1) = 100$, $A^B(1) = (-80)$, $\lambda = 0.02$ and $\mu = (-0.02)$. Graph 2 has been plotted for $A^G(1) = 10$, $A^B(1) = (-180)$, $\lambda = 0.02$ and $\mu = (-0.02)$.

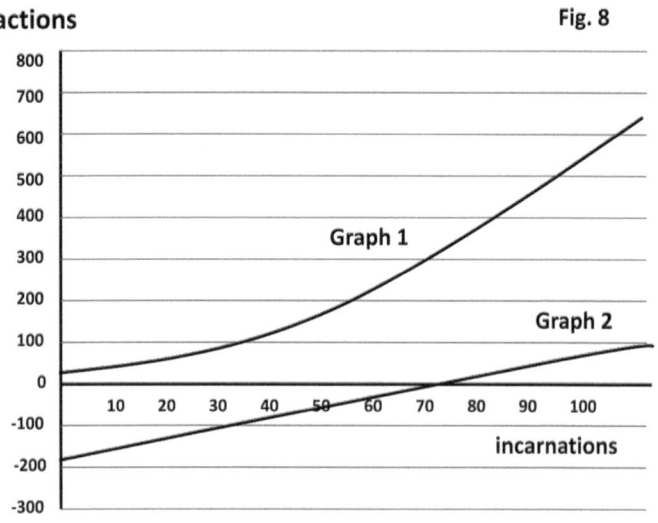
Fig. 8

THE PROBLEM WITH KARMA

Some important features are now apparent. Because actions and karma always increase in value, actions that are initially positive remain positive. Hence, karma can never be eliminated; this happens in the first case. If initial actions are negative, actions and karma steadily increase until they reach zero; this happens in the second case. Thus, liberation can be attained *only* if initial actions are *negative*. But herein lies a problem. Let us look at Graph 2 in more detail. In fig. 9a we have zoomed in towards the point where the graph crosses the incarnation axis.

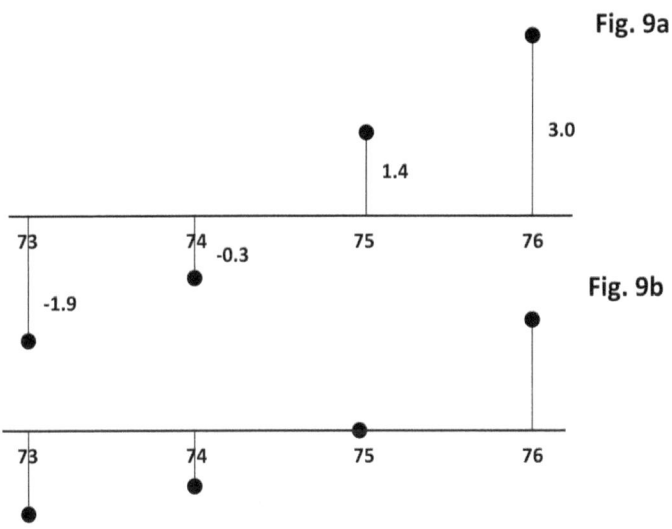

Fig. 9a

Fig. 9b

(The ordinates have been drawn in to show relative sizes.) Actions of (-1.9) in the 73rd incarnation generate karma of (-1.9) that must be settled in the 74th incarnation. Actions of (-0.3) in the 74th incarnation generate karma of (-0.3) that must settled in the 75th incarnation. Actions of 1.4 in the 75th incarnation generate karma that must be settled in the 76th incarnation, and so on *ad infinitum.*

Because the critical value of zero is missed, karma cannot be eliminated. Fig. 9b shows what *should* happen if liberation is to be attained. Actions in the 74th incarnation generate karma that is settled in the 75th incarnation, but actions in the 75th incarnation are *zero,* hence there is no karma to be settled in the 76th incarnation. Liberation is, therefore, attainable at the end of the 75th incarnation. Note that the equations continue to generate karma beyond the 75th incarnation because positive and negative components of actions continue to increase. However, none of this materializes in practice because liberation has already been attained. We shall now investigate the likelihood of the scenario in fig. 9b.

The Mathematics of Karma

Since karma and actions are related to one another by the simple formula $K(x) = A(x - 1)$ it is possible to express the conditions for liberation in terms of either karma or actions. If actions in, say, incarnation 1088 are zero then the karma to be settled in incarnation 1089 will be zero; liberation will then be attained at the end of incarnation 1088. We shall say that a series of personalities attains liberation beyond the first incarnation if there exists an incarnation $x^* > 1$ such that actions $A(x^*) = 0$; liberation will then be attained at the end of incarnation x^*. (If $x^* = 1$, liberation is attained without the necessity to reincarnate.)

Since actions beyond the first incarnation always change for the better (i.e. increase in value) the function $A(x)$ is *monotonic increasing* in x when $x > 1$ (see fig. 8); the same remarks apply to the function $K(x)$. If liberation is to be attained beyond the first incarnation, the graph of $A(x)$ must cross the incarnation axis from below. This can happen only if initial actions (i.e. the sum of positive and negative components) are negative. Furthermore, the graph must cross the axis at an integral point (i.e. an integer.) This integer defines the incarnation in which liberation is attained. If the graph crosses the incarnation axis at a non-integral point (i.e. between incarnations) the point of liberation is missed. Thus, a necessary and sufficient condition for liberation is that the function $A(x)$ has an integral root greater than 1. This root will be the number of the incarnation in which liberation is attained. To find the integral root of the function $A(x)$ is to find the integral solution of the equation:

(34) .... $A(x) = 0$

Ignoring, for the moment, the distinction between positive and negative components, the relationships between actions and karma are as follows:

(35) .... $K(x) = A(x-1)$
(36) .... $A(x+1) - A(x) = \rho K(x)$

Eliminating $K(x)$ from the system, we obtain a second order difference equation:

(37) .... $A(x+1) - A(x) = \rho A(x-1)$

Although the general solution of (37) can be easily determined, it does not permit the variable x to be expressed very easily in terms of the initial actions $A(1)$ and the response coefficient ρ. This difficulty arises because the function $A(x)$ is discontinuous, being defined only on the set of positive integers (i.e. the number of the incarnations). Fortunately, however, since the number of incarnations is large, and the coefficient of response is small, we can replace equation (37) with a 'smooth' approximation that preserves all the principal properties of the original equation. (See Mathematical Appendix). We then obtain the first order differential equation:

(38) .... $A'(x) = \rho A(x)$

where $A'(x)$ is the first derivative of the function $A(x)$. The solution of equation (38) can be found in any book of advanced mathematics and is:

(39) .... $A(x) = A(1) \exp[\rho(x - 1)]$

This gives *two* equations: one for positive components and one for negative components:

(40a) .... $A^G(x) = A^G(1) \exp[\lambda(x - 1)]$
(40b) .... $A^B(x) = A^B(1) \exp[\mu(x - 1)]$

Since actions are the sum of positive and negative components we have:

(41) .. $A(x) = A^G(1)\exp[\lambda(x - 1)] + A^B(1)\exp[\mu(x - 1)]$

where $x \geq 1$, $A^G(1) \geq 0$, $A^B(1) \leq 0$, $\lambda > 0$ and $\mu < 0$. Equating $A(x)$ to zero, we have:

(42) .. $A^G(1)\exp[\lambda(x - 1)] + A^B(1)\exp[\mu(x - 1)] = 0$

After some algebraic manipulation it can be shown that,

(43) .... $x = (1/\alpha)\log_e[-A^B(1)/A^G(1)]+1$

where $\alpha \equiv (\lambda - \mu)$ and $-\infty < x < \infty$. It can easily be seen that, in general, x will not be an integer. Substituting the data we used for constructing Graph 2 into formula (43), i.e. $A^G(1) = 10$, $A^B(1) = (-180)$, $\lambda = 0.02$ and $\mu = (- 0.02)$ we find that x = 73.26. Hence, actions are zero between the 73rd and 74th incarnations. Note that in fig. 9a actions are zero between the 74th and 75th incarnations. The minor discrepancy arises because we used a first order differential equation to approximate a second order difference equation. However, the principal result is the same, namely, that in general, actions will be zero *between* incarnations. What, then, is the probability that actions will be zero *during* an incarnation?

The Probability of Liberation

We begin with the following:

Proposition 1
Liberation is a chance event.

Proof
Within the framework of karma, initial actions are undetermined because karma does not exist before the first incarnation. If initial actions are undetermined they must be the product of chance. In the parlance of probability theory, the components $A^G(1)$ and $A^B(1)$ are random variables. By equation (43) $x=(1/\alpha)\log_e[-A^B(1)/A^G(1)]+1$, where x is the number of the incarnation in which liberation is attained. Since $A^G(1)$ and $A^B(1)$ are random variables and since x is a function of $A^G(1)$ and $A^B(1)$ it follows that x is a random variable. Whether or not liberation is attainable beyond the first incarnation depends on whether or not x is an integer greater than 1. Since the latter is a chance event, it follows that liberation is a chance event. [QED]

A theorem, attributed to the mathematician George Cantor (1845-1918), will help us determine the probability that x is an integer greater than 1. Firstly, the cardinality of a set expresses how many elements the set contains. For example, the cardinality of the empty set Ø is *zero*; the cardinality of a set containing 20 elements is equal to 20, and so on. The set of positive integers $\mathbf{P} = \{1, 2, 3, \ldots \infty\}$ is *infinite*, and its cardinality is denoted **Aleph$_0$**. The set of real numbers $\mathbf{R} = \{x: -\infty < x < +\infty\}$ is also infinite and its cardinality is written as card $\mathbf{R}$. We wish to compare **Aleph$_0$** with card $\mathbf{R}$. Cantor's cardinality theorem says that **Aleph$_0$** < card $\mathbf{R}$. Since $\mathbf{P}$ and $\mathbf{R}$ are both infinite sets, the theorem says that the set of real numbers is of a higher order of infinity than the set of positive integers. Thus, if a number is picked at random from the set of real numbers $\mathbf{R}$, the probability of getting a positive integer is *zero*. Since x in formula (43) is any real number, the probability that x is an integer greater than 1 is zero. Therefore, the probability that a series of personalities attains liberation beyond the first incarnation is *zero*.

Unfortunately, the matter does not rest there because the condition that karma must be completely eliminated for liberation to be possible may be too stringent. In fact liberation may be possible if karma is *almost* eliminated. In other words, there may be little difference in practice between a karma of zero and a karma of, say, 0.0001. In terms of the analysis above, x may come close enough to a positive integer to permit liberation, say for example, if x = 73.0001. If such is the case then karma operates within a small margin of error. But what do we mean by "close" to an integer?

Definition

Let ε be any small number greater than zero; then x is said to be "close" to the integer n if and only if,

$$n - \varepsilon < x < n + \varepsilon.$$

For example if $\varepsilon = 0.0001$, then x is "close" to 156 if and only if $155.9999 < x < 156.0001$. Clearly, $\varepsilon \leq 0.5$. We need, then, to calculate the probability that x is close to *any* integer greater than 1. For this we need the probability density function (pdf) of the random variable x; we shall call it P(x). This can be determined using standard methods of mathematical statistics. If we know the pdf of several random variables, it is possible to calculate the pdf of any function of those random variables. Since x is a function of the random variables $A^G(1)$ and $A^B(1)$ we need only specify the pdf's of $A^G(1)$ and $A^B(1)$; the calculation, then, becomes a routine matter. We note that $A^B(1)$ is a negative quantity; therefore it will be convenient to work with the *positive* quantity $(-1) \times A^B(1) = -A^B(1)$. Furthermore, since initial components are finite in magnitude they each have an upper bound. If $A^G(1)$ and $-A^B(1)$ are measured as fractions of their upper bounds, then $0 \leq A^G(1) \leq 1$ and $0 \leq -A^B(1) \leq 1$. Since initial components are undetermined all values are equally likely; $A^G(1)$ and $-A^B(1)$ are then said to have a *uniform* probability distribution. Under this definition the pdf of actions A is given by the simple formula $P(A) = 1$, where A refers to either $A^G(1)$ or $-A^B(1)$ (see fig. 10).

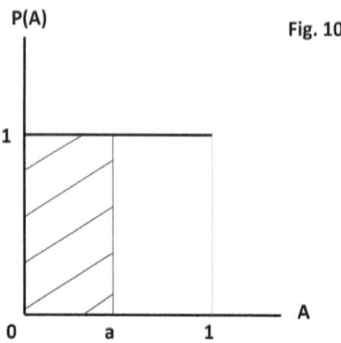
Fig. 10

For example, Pr $(A \leq 0.67) = 0.67$ and Pr $(0.2 \leq A \leq 0.8) = 0.8 - 0.2 = 0.6$. In other words, probabilities correspond to areas under a probability density function. The proof of the following proposition is given in the Mathematical Appendix.

Proposition 2

If the random variables $0 \leq A^G(1) \leq 1$ and $0 \leq -A^B(1) \leq 1$ each have uniform probability distributions, and $\alpha \equiv \lambda - \mu$, then the random variable $x = (1/\alpha)\log_e[-A^B(1)/A^G(1)]+1$ has the following pdf:

(44a) .. $P(x) = (\alpha/2)\exp[\alpha(x-1)]$ for $-\infty < x \leq 1$
(44b) .. $P(x) = (\alpha/2)\exp[\alpha(1-x)]$ for $1 \leq x < \infty$
(See fig. 11)

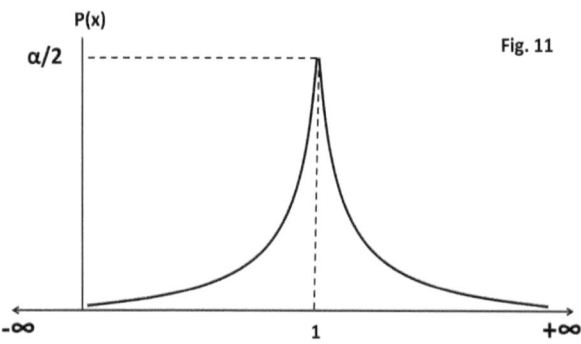
Fig. 11

Given the pdf of x, it is a routine matter to calculate the probability that x is close to an integer greater than 1. In the first instance, we calculate Pr (n - ε < x < n + ε) where n stands for any integer and then compute,

$$\sum \text{Pr} (n - ε < x < n + ε)$$

i.e. sum all the probabilities from n = 2 to ∞. It turns out that $\sum$ Pr (n - ε < x < n + ε) = ε. We summarize this result in the following proposition which is proven in the Mathematical Appendix:

Proposition 3
Let ε be the error in the operation of karma and p be the probability that x is close to an integer greater than 1 then

$$p = ε.$$

In other words, the probability of liberation is equal to the error in the operation of karma. Since this result applies to every series of personalities, one can speak in terms of *the* probability of liberation. With an error of 0.01, for example, the probability of liberation is 0.01. We need, then, to calculate the probability that *every* series of personalities will attain liberation in practice. This is easy to calculate because initial actions are statistically independent. Since the incarnation in which liberation is attained is a function of statistically independent random variables it follows, from the theory of statistics, that the incarnations in which liberation is attained are also statistically independent random variables. From the theory of probability, if E and F are independent events with probabilities p and q respectively, the probability of E and F both happening is p x q. Thus, if ε is the probability of *one* series of personalities attaining liberation, then ε x ε = $ε^2$ is the probability of *two* series of personalities attaining liberation. If N is the total number of series of personalities, then ε^N is the probability of N series of personalities attaining liberation.

One can calculate the size of ε^N by estimating the value of N. Let us suppose, on current projections, that the maximum number of people who will inhabit the Earth at any one time is 10 billion. Since each contemporaneous personality will represent a *different* series of personalities, there must exist at least 10 billion series of personalities. If the error in the operation of karma is, say, 0.1 (quite a large error) then the probability that everyone will attain liberation is $(0.1)^{10,000,000,000}$, a number so small it can be treated as *zero*. Expressed in scientific notation it may be compared directly with Planck's constant:

(45) .. $(0.1)^{10,000,000,000} = 1 \times 10^{-10,000,000,000}$
(46) .. Planck's constant = $6.62606957 \times 10^{-34}$

Compared to ε^N, Planck's constant - which is fundamental to quantum theory - is astronomical. Now, unless every series of personalities can eliminate karma and escape the cycle of rebirths, at least one series will be infinite. Since this is impossible, reincarnation cannot be a fact of nature. This gives us:

The Impossibility Theorem
Let R be the probability that reincarnation is a fact, ε be a small error in the operation of karma, and N be the total number of series of personalities, then $R = \varepsilon^N$.

Since ε is a small number and, in any case is less than a half, and N is a large number, the quantity ε^N is for all practical purposes equal to zero.

A Final Note on Karma

In the previous section, actions were set to zero and the incarnation of liberation was treated as a random variable. An alternative approach is to set the incarnation to a particular number and calculate the probability that karma is almost eliminated. By equation (41) we have:

$$(47) \ldots A(x) = A^G(1)\exp[\lambda(x - 1)] + A^B(1)\exp[\mu(x - 1)]$$

and since $K(x) = A(x - 1)$ we have:

$$(48) \ldots K(x) = A^G(1)\exp[\lambda(x - 2)] + A^B(1)\exp[\mu(x - 2)]$$

where $x \geq 2$. Hence, karma in any incarnation x depends on initial actions and is, consequently, a random variable. It is interesting to see how the probability of almost eliminating karma changes from one incarnation to another; for this we need the pdf of karma. We can simplify the notation if we introduce the following definitions:

$$(49) \ldots p \equiv \exp[\lambda(x - 2)]$$
$$(50) \ldots q \equiv \exp[\mu(x - 2)]$$

Substituting into (48) we obtain:

$$(51) \ldots K(x) = pA^G(1) + qA^B(1)$$

where p and q are constants for any incarnation x. It can be shown (see Mathematical Appendix) that the pdf of K is given by the graph in fig. 12.

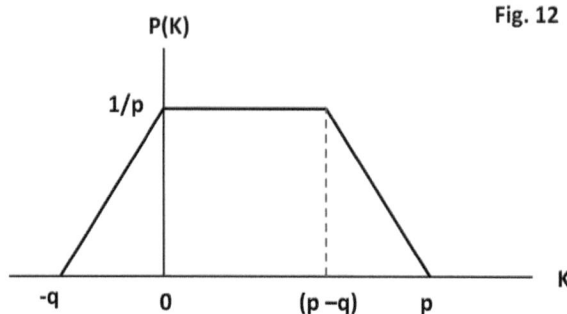

Fig. 12

We wish to find an expression for $\Pr(-\delta < K < \delta)$ where δ is an arbitrarily small number greater than zero. Once the pdf is determined, it is a routine matter to calculate probabilities. It can be shown that,

(52a) .... $\Pr(-\delta < K < \delta) = (2\delta/p) - (\delta^2)/(2pq)$

for $q \geq \delta$.

(52b) .... $\Pr(-\delta < K < \delta) = (q/2p) + \delta/p$

for $q \leq \delta$.

We shall investigate what happens when the number of the incarnation increases. When $q \geq \delta$ the probability is given by (52a).

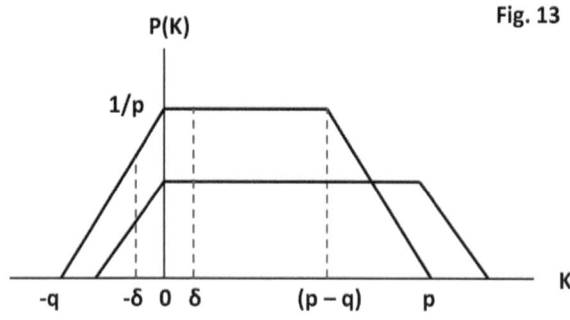

Fig. 13

As x increases (1/p) and q both decrease in value. In fig. 13, the area under the graph between the ordinates $K = -\delta$ and $K = \delta$ *decreases*. When $q \leq \delta$ the probability is given by (52b). As $x \to \infty$, $p \to \infty$ and $q \to 0$ therefore:

$Pr(-\delta < K < \delta) \to 0$.

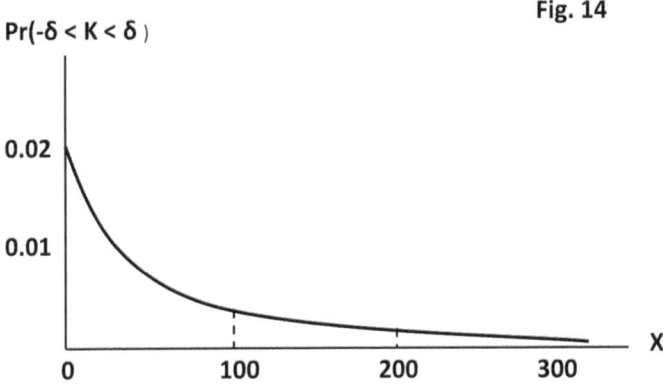

Fig. 14

The graph in fig. 14 has been drawn for:

$\lambda = 0.02$, $\mu = (-0.02)$ and $\delta = 0.01$.

As the number of the incarnation increases the probability that karma is almost eliminated tends to zero. This is contrary to what should happen. As the personality develops the chances of attaining liberation should increase. This proves that the doctrine of karma is fundamentally incoherent.

PART 2
SEEN & UNSEEN

Chapter 5
Strange Encounters

Several weeks following my conversation with John Faraway and Alice Toogood, I found myself in the Charing Cross Road scouring the second hand bookshops for first editions of the Russo-German conflict, 1942-45. I was relaxing in a coffee bar leafing through one of my latest acquisitions when I became conscious of a disturbance. I looked up and saw a tall, wiry man in his sixties, approaching the table, coffee in one hand and sandwich in the other. Hanging from his shoulder was a leather bag.

"May I?" he said
"Be my guest." I replied.

He sat down, put his bag under the table and stirred his coffee.
After a few moments he said:

"You know, I really shouldn't be here."
"Excuse me?" I replied, looking up from my book.
"I have an important engagement."

I looked at him quizzically.

"I should be opening Parliament." he continued.
"Do you mean *at* the opening of Parliament?"
"No, opening Parliament."

I put my book aside and said:

"What do you mean?"
"It's my constitutional duty as Head of State."
"Head of State?"
"Yes, that's right."
"That's very interesting," I replied, not knowing whether he was a comic or merely delusional. "Head of what state?"
"Why, the United Kingdom of course."
"That would make you the Queen of England."
"Naturally – what else?"
"Well, you don't look like the Queen of England to me."

He ignored my comment and took a bite from his sandwich.

"May I ask why you are here and not opening Parliament?"
"I'm taking a short break."
"Won't you be missed?"
"Probably not, there's a pause in the proceedings."
"How do you plan to get back?" I asked him. "The traffic between here and the Palace of Westminster is pretty heavy at the moment."
"That's easy; I'll just refocus."
"Refocus?"
"Yes. It's an act of concentration. When I refocus, I'll be back there straightaway."
"Like superman?"

Of course, I knew that faster-than-light travel was impossible. As he approached the speed of light his mass would approach infinity, attract the mass of the Earth and create an enormous black-hole into which everything would vanish. Needless to say he would miss his appointment with Parliament.

"Oh, no," he replied, "I shall keep my body here and refocus in the Palace of Westminster."

I decided to play along with this gentleman. In any case, he needed no encouragement from me.

"If your body is here, how will you open Parliament? Where will your consciousness go to?"

"To my other body of course."

Before I could reply, he reached out his hand and introduced himself.

"By the way, I'm Arthur J. Doodle."

Well, he just said he was the Queen of England; now he's Arthur J. Doodle.

"Pleased to meet you, but I'm confused. How can you be the Queen of England *and* Arthur J. Doodle?"

"As I said, I have two bodies; one I use when I'm the Queen of England and one I use when I'm Arthur J. Doodle."

When someone makes extraordinary, if not downright absurd, claims there are two courses of action: either one parts company immediately or one elicits further information. I have always been fascinated by the strange and the bizarre and have, over the last thirty odd years, accumulated a substantial collection of works on the paranormal, strange phenomena, UFO's, mystery animals etc. I always keep an open mind but submit everything to the test of reason. I decided, therefore, to question this gentleman further and see if his claims held up under close examination.

"Ok, you have two different bodies. But, if your consciousness is currently focused in the body sitting in front of me, what is your other body doing?"

"It's quiescent."

"You mean it's currently in Westminster Palace doing nothing at all?"

Of course, if the snack bar had had a television set, and if the television had happened to be showing the opening of Parliament, it would have been possible to test his claim. A visibly active i.e. non-quiescent Head of State would have refuted him immediately. On the other hand, a quiescent Head of State would merely have demonstrated consistency; it would not have amounted to verification since she may have been inactive of her own volition. Clearly, Doodle's position was vulnerable to attack: he could be proven wrong, but never right.

"Ok," I continued, "when you've focused into your other body, what will happen to the body sitting in front of me?"

"Nothing at all," he replied, "it will carry on having lunch."

"But will it not become inactive?"

"No, you misunderstand me. Quiescent doesn't mean inactive, it means simply that my consciousness is focused elsewhere."

Here, I begged to differ; that was not my understanding of the word quiescent. According to the Oxford English Dictionary quiescent means: in a state or period of inactivity or dormancy. Doodle paused for a few moments and said:

"That's the dictionary definition. I'm using the word quiescent in a special way. In *my* sense of the word, quiescent means that the body's consciousness is focused elsewhere – nothing more."

"Yes, but if different people use the same word in different ways, communication becomes rather difficult. Would you not agree?"

"I've never had any problems," replied Doodle.

"Ok," I continued, "for the sake of argument, I'll accept your definition of the word quiescent. After you have transferred your consciousness to Parliament your current body will lose all consciousness - which means it will become unconscious - and if it is unconscious it will not be able to carry on eating its - or should I say - your lunch."

"I didn't say that the body sitting here in front of you would lose all consciousness. I simply said that my consciousness would be focused in another body."

"Isn't that the same thing?"

"Certainly not!" he retorted. "It's all a question of emphasis. I can be conscious in two bodies simultaneously and be focused in only one of them."

"You can be conscious in two bodies at once?" I gasped in disbelief.

"Yes, that's right. I can be eating, drinking and talking with you and, at the same time, be focused in another body in another place. At the moment I'm focused here. In a while I shall be focused in Parliament."

"But, if your consciousness can be in two different bodies simultaneously and if you can be doing two completely different things at the same time, why do you need to be focused in only one of them?"

"It's a matter of priorities. Sometimes I need to be more focused in one body, and less focused in another."

"I thought that focussing was all or nothing. If you are focused in one body, then you cannot be focused in another."

"I never said that," replied Doodle.

"Well, it seems to me that if you are conscious in both bodies simultaneously you must be focused in both of them simultaneously."

"Yes, but I am more focused in one body than the other."

"What's the difference?"

"It's a question of control. I have greater control over the body I am more focused in and less control over the body I am less focused in. I really don't see your difficulty."

"Does that mean you have greater control over your body in this snack bar, than you have over your body in the Palace of Westminster?"

"Yes, that's right."

"In that case, why do you say that your body in Westminster is quiescent? Surely, it can carry on opening Parliament while you are sitting here eating your lunch."

"As I've already explained, it's a question of priorities. What is happening in Parliament at the present moment doesn't require my full attention. That is why I am having a break."

"Do you know what is happening in Parliament at this moment?"

"Certainly, all I have to do is refocus."

"Can you tell me?"

Doodle shut his eyes for a few seconds and appeared to concentrate. After a few seconds he said:

"The cellars are being searched by the Yeomen of the Guard."

That, of course, is common knowledge. Since the Gunpowder Plot of 1605, when English Catholics tried to blow up the Houses of Parliament and kill the Protestant King James I, the cellars have been searched ever since. Nowadays, this is done for the sake of form only. But, I wondered, were the cellars being searched at the precise moment Doodle claimed? I only had his word for that. I looked at my watch and noted the time.

"Do you need to be fully focused in your body at Westminster to observe what is happening there?"

"Not really. I can observe things passively."

"I'm confused. If you were not fully focused in Parliament when the cellars were being searched and you were not fully focused here – you had to stop eating and drinking and shut your eyes – then you were less focused in both bodies at the same time instead of being more focused in one and less in the other – which contradicts what you said a few minutes ago."

"On the contrary, I *was* fully focused here."

"In that case why did you stop eating your lunch and shut your eyes?"

"I prefer to do things that way."

"Does that mean you could have carried on having your lunch as normal and, at the same time, observe what was happening in Parliament?"

"Of course, I do that sort of thing all the time."

"Ok, when you are fully focused in Parliament, will I notice any difference here in this snack bar?"

"I don't know," he replied, "that's a matter for you. I may seem somewhat vague and indecisive."

Of course, he might be pretending. How would I know? It would prove nothing at all.

"If I have understood you correctly," I continued, "you are capable of being conscious in both your bodies simultaneously but are more focused in one than the other. Does this mean you have more control over one body than the other?"

"Yes, you could put it that way."

"Doesn't that make life confusing and potentially dangerous? Many things must require your full attention all the time - like delivering a speech, driving a car, crossing the road etc. If you find yourself doing more than one of these important things simultaneously, you need to be fully focused in both bodies at the same time."

"That's no problem, I arrange my affairs accordingly. I make sure my bodies are not doing important things at the same time, so I need only be fully focused in one of them."

"In other words, one body is always playing second fiddle to the other."

"I wouldn't put it that way. When one body is doing something that requires my full attention, I make sure my other body is quiescent."

Suddenly, the proprietor of the snack bar brought in a portable television set. He placed it on a shelf and switched it on. As luck would have it, he wanted to watch the opening of Parliament.

"Never miss 'em," he said.

We both looked towards the television. The Queen was arriving at the Palace of Westminster in a horse-drawn coach, entering through Sovereign's Entrance under the Victoria Tower. I looked at Doodle and said:

"Isn't it about time you refocused?"

He ignored my comment and carried on sipping his coffee. Of course, the opening of the British Parliament is a great state occasion. The Royal Standard is hoisted to replace the Union Flag upon the Sovereign's entrance and remains whilst she is in attendance. Then, after she takes on the Parliament Robe of State and Imperial State Crown in the Robing Chamber, the Queen proceeds through the Royal Gallery to the House of Lords immediately preceded by the Lord Great Chamberlain, the Earl Marshal, the Leader of the House of Lords carrying the Cap of Maintenance on a white rod, and a peer carrying the Great Sword of State. Once on the throne, the Queen, wearing the Imperial State Crown, instructs the House by saying, "My Lords, pray be seated."

The Queen was now seated on her throne. This was a perfect opportunity to test Doodle's claim.

"I assume you are now fully focused in your other body?"

Doodle looked at me rather furtively and said: "Yes."

"Ok, could you raise your left hand i.e. the one in Parliament?"

"I could, but that would be inappropriate at the present time."

At that very moment the Queen glanced across the assembled chamber.

"There, did you see that," said Doodle.

"Yes, but how do I know *you* were responsible? Her Majesty may well have done that of her own volition."

"Well," said Doodle, "if you're going to question everything I say, I see no point in carrying on this conversation."

"Your claim to be the Head of State is so extraordinary, I need some hard evidence."

"You've chosen a poor example. I wouldn't dream of disrupting the opening of Parliament just to prove a point."

"Can you suggest a better example?"

Doodle now seemed fully focused in both bodies – contradicting his claim that he prioritised his activities.

"As it happens, yes, I have more than two bodies."

"You have more than two bodies?" I replied.

By now, nothing Doodle said surprised me.

"How many?"

"Twenty-three."

I thought: "there's no limit to this man's megalomania."

"While we are talking," Doodle continued, "I am currently focused in the body of a lorry driver delivering garden machinery to an address in Clapham Junction, and also focused in the body of a man currently robbing a bank at the end of Charing Cross Road. I won't bore you with the rest."

"Robbing a bank?"

"Yes, can't you hear the police sirens?"

Suddenly there was a commotion outside and two burly police officers stormed in.

"There's been a robbery at the end of the road. Someone was seen running in here."

They cast their eyes around the bar. Everything was calm and peaceful. The proprietor looked away from the television and said:

"No one's come in here for the past ten minutes."

Doodle quietly sipped his coffee, unconcerned at the sudden turn of events.

"Must have the wrong place. Let's try next door."
"You see, I told you," said Doodle with more than a hint of triumph in his voice.
"You just robbed a bank?"
"Yes. I had to shoot the bank clerk. He would have pushed the emergency button."
"Well, you don't seem very concerned. You've just injured another human being. Don't you feel guilty?"
"Not really. It was done by my other body."
"Yes, but you were focused in that body when you shot him, so you must be morally responsible for his injuries."
"Not really. At the precise moment the bank clerk was shot, I was fully focused in another body. I was merely a passive observer."
"But, you were in control of the body that shot the clerk, so that makes you morally and legally responsible."
"Certainly not! I'm responsible for my body's actions *only* when I am fully focused in it."
"If you are not responsible – who is?"
"That's not my concern."
"But you said: 'I had to shoot the bank clerk' and that means you had the intention of shooting him, and if

you had the intention of shooting him that makes you responsible."

"You misunderstand me. When I said: 'I had to shoot him' I meant that I *felt* I had to shoot him. The decision wasn't mine. I was fully focused elsewhere when the gun was fired; therefore, I am not morally responsible."

"If it wasn't your decision, whose was it?"

"Nobody's decision, the gun just went off."

"Let's get this straight," I said, "You claim that you have twenty-three different bodies - including the body of the bank robber - and that you are consciously aware of their behaviour wherever you happen to be focused - or should I say fully focused? If – as you claim – you are expressing yourself in twenty-three different bodies then surely you are responsible for what they do since all these bodies are expressions of your will and intentions. If they are behaving in ways beyond your control then it doesn't make sense to call them your bodies. It's all a question of control."

At this point, Doodle began shuffling his feet. His bag fell over, and wads of bank notes scattered over the floor. He hurriedly gathered them together, picked up his bag and rushed out of the snack bar. I sipped my coffee – it was now cold - and returned to my book.

* * *

Up till now, immortality and individuality have not been discussed at length because the mathematical refutation of reincarnation - based on the unviability of karma - does not depend on any particular concept of the soul or the self or, indeed, on any particular concept of reincarnation. On the other hand, given the Temporal Postulates, it has been shown that any system of premises incorporating the ideas of immortality, individuality and reincarnation is logically incoherent. Mortality and immortality have been defined in terms of class membership. Something is mortal if it belongs to the class of temporal things T, and is immortal if it belongs to the class of eternal things E, where T and E are mutually exclusive and exhaustive. (see Chapter 3). Since it is only the *relationship* between the classes T and E that is of material significance in the logical refutation of reincarnation, T and E have not be defined. To assert that the human self S is immortal, then, is to assert that S belongs to E. Individuality is expressed in terms of what the human self does or does not do. Specifically, individuality requires that the human self does not incarnate in more than one physical body simultaneously, that is to say, individuality and multi-incarnation are incompatible. This accords with commonsense since each person is endowed at birth with only one physical body. Roughly speaking this is to say that the human self is uniquely expressive. The meaning of the expression 'human self' is treated as self-evident.

Although the concept of immortality can be handled most easily in terms of class membership, individuality is potentially compromised by a number of paranormal phenomena that fall under the general headings of bilocation, the physical phenomena of mediumship, the exteriorisation of sensibility, the exteriorisation of motivity, stigmata, obsession, possession, multiple personalities, community of sensation and shared memories. Since individuality is intimately associated with the physical body and to the private world of inner experiences, one's sense of identity may be lost or, at best, confused when the link between personal experiences and the physical body is broken. The aforementioned phenomena might be thought to undermine the integrity of the self in the sense that if all physical, emotional and mental states are experienced *beyond* the body (bilocation, physical materialisation, the exteriorisation of sensibility, the exteriorisation of motivity) or shared *within* the body (community of sensation, shared memories, multiple personalities, stigmata, obsession, possession) one's physical body would serve little purpose and there would be little to distinguish one individual from another. With the exception of bilocation, physical materialisation and the exteriorisation of sensibility and motivity, all of the above phenomena have, in one form or another, been cited as evidence for reincarnation. In this chapter we shall consider the extent to which bilocation, physical materialisation and the exteriorisation of sensibility and motivity lend support to the notion that multi-incarnation is possible.

While multi-incarnation necessarily implies multilocation (because different bodies cannot occupy the same space at the same time) does multilocation – of which bilocation is a special case - necessarily imply multi-incarnation? Before we consider this question we should note that multilocation can mean one of two things:

(a) the simultaneous occupation of different locations by a *physical* body ('circumscriptive replication') or
(b) the simultaneous presence of a person in different places ('phantasmal replication').

The notion of circumscriptive replication has been pondered by Catholic theologians for centuries because, according to the doctrine of the Eucharist, Christ is substantially present – albeit in spirit - in every consecrated Host wherever it is located. According to the Catholic Encyclopaedia, the local extension of a physical body in space is not a *necessary* property of its materiality and may, for instance, be suspended by divine intervention. Although the existence of a physical body in one place is certainly contradicted by its non existence in the *same* place this says nothing *per se* about its existence or non-existence in any other place. In other words, it must be taken as an axiom that circumscriptive replication cannot happen. In fact, it is easy to show that it produces contradictions. Consider the following thought experiment. A snooker ball is simultaneously resting on opposite sides of a table. Let the ball observed at the north end of the table be called A, and the ball observed at the south end be called B. Since A and B are different locations of the same ball, it is meaningless to ask which is the original and which is the replica. Crucially, anything done to one is automatically done to the other. For example, a hole drilled in A will appear in B, and vice versa. Surprisingly, some results are consistent with the mechanics of a particle. Suppose forces Fa and Fb are applied respectively to A and B. Since, in reality, only one ball exists, this would be equivalent to applying one force (Fa + Fb) to *both* A and B. For example, if A is struck with a force F, and B with a force –F (i.e. with equal and opposite forces) then this is equivalent to A being struck with a single force F+ (-F) = 0, and B with a single force F+ (-F) = 0. Hence A and B will both remain undisturbed. This follows because a system of self-cancelling forces applied to a particle will - if at rest - remain at rest (For simplicity, we are ignoring rotational complications). Now, suppose the table is sawn into two parts such that A is on one part and B is on the other, and suppose, further, that the part beneath B is suddenly removed (i.e. the part no longer exists). What happens? There are two possibilities: (1) since the part beneath A is still present, A remains undisturbed but, because A and B are the same ball, B also remains undisturbed, albeit in midair; (2) since the part beneath B is no longer present, B falls to the floor but, because A and B are the same ball, A also falls to the floor, albeit through the table. Since nothing within the problem favours one outcome over the other both can happen but, because both outcomes defy the laws of mechanics, neither can happen. The paradox arises because, from the ball's point of view, the table exists and it does not exist.

Although circumscriptive replication has elements in common with phantasmal replication they describe completely different situations - one paradoxical and the other well-documented. When the two concepts are conflated, they suggest that multi-incarnation is possible. A case in point can be found in Paramahansa Yogananda's *Autobiography of a Yogi (1946)* in which he calls his father's good friend and colleague – the venerable Swami Pranabananda - "the saint with two bodies." In Yogananda's story, his father wishes to deliver a letter to a business associate, Kedar Nath Babu but, unfortunately, has lost his address. However, he informs Yogananda that the letter can be delivered via his friend Swami Pranabananda who "has attained an exalted spiritual stature." When Yogananda reaches the swami's residence in Benares he discovers that his note of introduction is superfluous because the swami is waiting for him. Pranabananda says: "Are you Bhagabati's son?" Mildly surprised, Yogananda hands over the note and explains the purpose of his visit. "Of course I will locate Kedar Nath Babu for you." replies the swami. Suddenly the conversation ceases. In the words of Yogananda: "The saint became gravely motionless. A sphinxlike air enveloped him. At first his eyes sparkled, as if observing something of interest, then grew dull. I felt abashed at his pauciloquy; he had not yet told me how I could meet Father's friend. A trifle restlessly, I looked about me in the bare room, empty except for us two. My idle gaze took in his wooden sandals, lying under the platform seat."

However, the swami soon rouses himself and reassures his visitor that the man he wishes to see will be with him shortly. Again he falls into an "inscrutable silence" and after thirty minutes has elapsed he rouses himself once more, this time, to the sound of Kedar Nath Babu who is approaching the door. Yogananda continues the story: "I heard somebody coming up the stairs. An amazed incomprehension arose suddenly; my thoughts raced in confusion: How is it possible that Father's friend has been summoned to this place without the help of a messenger? The swami has spoken to no one but myself since my arrival!" Yogananda exits the room and halfway down the stairs he meets a thin, fair-skinned man of medium height in somewhat of a hurry:

"Are you Kedar Nath Babu?" asks Yogananda.

"Yes. Are you not Bhagabati's son who has been waiting here to meet me?" he replies.

"Sir, how do you happen to come here?" continues Yogananda.

"Everything is mysterious today! Less than an hour ago I had just finished my bath in the Ganges when Swami Pranabananda approached me. I have no idea how he knew I was there at that time. 'Bhagabati's son is waiting for you in my apartment,' he said. 'Will you come with me?' I gladly agreed. As we proceeded hand in hand, the swami in his wooden sandals was strangely able to outpace me, though I wore these stout walking shoes."

Along the way the swami suddenly stops to ask Kedar Nath Babu how long it will take him to reach his place. Kedar Nath Babu says that the journey usually takes about half an hour. The swami then makes a hasty retreat and disappears into a crowd. After Kedar Nath Babu has told his story, Yogananda is truly astonished:

"I cannot believe my ears! Am I losing my mind? Did you meet him in a vision, or did you actually see him, touch his hand, and hear the sound of his feet?"

"I don't know what you're driving at!" he replies angrily. "I am not lying to you. Can't you understand that only through the swami could I have known you were waiting at this place for me?"

"Why, that man, Swami Pranabananda, has not left my sight a moment since I first came about an hour ago," replies Yogananda.

"Are we living in this material age, or are we dreaming? I never expected to witness such a miracle in my life! I thought this swami was just an ordinary man, and now I find he can materialize an extra body and work through it!"

* * *

Similar cases of bilocation (the simultaneous presence of a personality in *two* different places, near together or far apart) have been recorded throughout history. St. Anthony of Padua (1195-1231) when preaching in the Church of St. Pierre du Queyroix at Limoges in 1226 suddenly remembered that he was due to give a reading at a monastery in another part of the town. According to those present, Anthony suddenly stopped talking, drew his hood over his head and knelt down for several minutes, apparently in deep meditation. At that precise moment, the assembled monks in the monastery chapel saw Anthony leave his stall, read the appointed passage and then suddenly disappear. In the late 16th- to early 17th-century, the Peruvian friar St. Martin de Porres would appear at the sickbeds of fellow monks while apparently engaged in other duties; and in 18th century Italy, St. Gerard Majella is said to have tended to plague victims in different houses simultaneously. The case of St. Alphonse de Liguori is recorded in Charles Richet's *Thirty Years of Psychical Research (1923)*. On 17th September, 1774 Alphonse remained "quiet and dumb" in his cell at Arezzo, taking no nourishment and speaking to no one. Five days later, on 22nd September, he awoke from his apparent trance and said that he had been at the bedside of the dying Pope. According to eyewitness accounts, on the night of 21st September Pope Clement XIV died in Rome attended by Alphonse de Liguori.

More recently, St. Pio of Pietrelcina, the 20th-century Italian stigmatic is believed to have bilocated at will. On one occasion he is said to have materialized in midair over the city of San Giovanni Rotondo during World War II in order to deter U.S. bombers from attacking the city. The following case is recorded by the Catholic Web Services. According to one Father Alberto who met Padre Pio in 1917: "I saw Padre Pio standing in front of the window, looking at the mountain. He was speaking to himself. I approached him in order to kiss his hand, but he did not notice my presence and I noticed that his hand was rigid. At that time, I heard that he was clearly giving absolution and pardon to someone. After a while, Padre Pio shook like awakening from a nap. He looked at me and said; 'you are here. I did not realize it!' After some days, a telegram from Turin was delivered. Someone was thanking the superior of the convent for having sent Padre Pio to Turin to assist a dying person. I realized that the man was dying in the same moment Padre Pio was blessing him in San Giovanni Rotondo. Obviously, the superior of the convent had not sent Padre Pio to Turin, but he had bilocated there."

The materialisation phenomena of mediumship have a number of features in common with bilocation because the material used in the exteriorisation of 'ectoplasmic' forms originates with the medium. In a certain sense the medium 'occupies' two places at once. Whilst physically ensconced inside the 'cabinet' (an enclosed part of the séance room away from the sitters), some part of the medium exists outside it. In her autobiography, *Shadow Land (1897)*, the medium Elisabeth d'Esperance records how, during a materialisation séance, she would feel a strange link between herself and the materialised form, 'Yolande': "There seemed to be a strange link between us. I could do nothing to ensure her appearance amongst us. She came and went, so far as I am aware, entirely independent of my will, but when she had come, she was, I found, dependent on me for her brief material existence. I seemed to lose, not my individuality, but my strength and power of exertion, and though I did not then know, a great portion of my material substance. I felt that in some way I was changed, but the effort to think logically in some mysterious way affected Yolande, and made her weak. The stronger and livelier she became the less inclination I had to think or reason, but the power of feeling became intensified to a painful extent; I do not mean in the physical sense, but the mental, my brain apparently becoming a sort of whispering gallery where thoughts of other persons resolved themselves into an embodied form and resounded as though actual substantial objects."

Elisabeth had to remain immobile because any physical movement, or attempt to regain her normal consciousness, would have weakened the manifestation or brought the séance to an end. Significantly, the materialised forms were extremely sensitive to uninvited physical contact. As Elisabeth records in her book, a sitter, violating the terms of the séance, grabbed one of the forms – believing it to be her in disguise - and forced it to suddenly recoil back into the 'cabinet' leaving Elisabeth seriously injured. During a séance, Elisabeth would frequently become disorientated though still in possession of her reasoning faculties: "No one is taking any notice of me. All eyes and thoughts seem concentrated on the white slender figure standing there with the arms of the two black-robed women around it. It must be my own heart beating so distinctly. Yet those arms round me? Surely never did I feel a touch so plainly. I begin to wonder which is I. Am I the white figure or am I the one on the chair? Are they my hands round the old lady's neck, or are these mine that are lying on the knees of me, or on the knees of the figure if it be not I, on the chair? Certainly they are my lips that are being kissed. It is my face that is wet with tears which these good women are shedding so plentifully. Yet how can it be? It is a horrible feeling, thus losing hold of one's identity. I long to put out one of these hands that are lying so helplessly, and touch someone just to know if I am myself or only a dream – if 'Anna' be I, and I am lost as it were, in her identity."

If, during a séance, a materialised spirit touched anything, it was as if Elisabeth herself touched it. If the spirit touched Elisabeth, it was as if Elisabeth touched herself. If the spirit grasped anything, Elisabeth felt her muscles contract. When, during a particular séance, the spirit was pricked with a rose thorn Elisabeth felt the pain, not the spirit; and when the spirit dipped its hand in hot wax, Elisabeth felt a burning sensation and cried out. If someone embraced and kissed a materialised spirit, Elisabeth would feel the embraces and kisses. In short, Elisabeth's sensibilities were exteriorised and located in the body of the spirit.

It is evident that Elisabeth found these feelings and sensations utterly bewildering, leading her to question her own identity and exact location inside the room. Was she sitting on the chair inside the 'cabinet' or was she the form interacting with the other sitters? Was she truly herself or was she 'Anna'? These feelings usually persisted until the end of the séance but, once over, Elisabeth quickly regained her sense of identity recognising that the physical manifestations were the forms of spirit beings attempting to communicate with their loved ones on Earth. As she recounts in her book, each form expressed a degree of independence characteristic of any human being, coming and going as they pleased and generally acting under their own volition. Although Elisabeth supplied the energy or material for these manifestations – she was often exhausted and dehydrated at the end of a séance - the spirit beings were always in control of the proceedings, she being the passive observer.

Elisabeth's sensitivity to physical contact 'at a distance' is an instance of a well-documented psycho-physiological condition known as the 'exteriorisation of sensibility.' Paul Joire, professor at the Psycho-physiological Institute of France, first drew attention to this phenomenon in a treatise on hypnology in 1892. He found that a hypnotised subject was sensitive to the approach of a sharp instrument, such as a pin, at a short distance from the skin but insensible to contact at the surface of the skin. The distance at which the sensation was experienced depended on the nervous sensibility of the subject and varied, on average, from one to ten centimetres.

In *Psychical and Supernormal Phenomena (1916)*, Joire describes a series of remarkable experiments in which a subject's sensibilities are transferred to physical objects. In one experiment, Joire brings a man to a trance state and blindfolds him to prevent him from picking up clues from those present. Joire then gives him a glass of water to hold between his hands and checks to make sure he is completely insensible to pain by pricking his skin at various points with a pin. He then pricks the surface of the water in the glass and asks the subject what he feels. The subject replies: "You pricked by left hand." He then applies the point of the pin to the outside of the glass but the subject feels nothing. Joire then pricks the surface of the water again and the subject replies: "You pricked by left hand." The experiment is repeated several times with the same results, though eventually the subject loses patience and says: "You are hurting me; you are pricking me."

In another experiment, Joire holds the glass of water at some distance from the subject and finds, once again, that he experiences pricking sensations, though less intensely. The glass of water is then placed on a table in front of the subject with the same results. In a further experiment, instead of pricking the water, Joire pinches it and the subject says: "You are pinching me". The prickings and pinchings are alternated and, each time, the subject makes the appropriate response. Joire then tries different materials such as a glass plate covered in velvet, first placing it between the subject's hands in order to "charge" it with the subject's sensibility, and then moving it some distance from the subject. When the velvet is pricked, the subject experiences the same pricking sensations as before. Some materials are found to be better than others; wood is very good while cardboard is poor. In one of his strangest experiments, Joire uses a piece of putty, shaped to match the general contour of the subject's body, and rests it on a glass plate. The putty figure is sensitised by bringing it close to the subject's body and allowing the subject to hold the glass plate between his hands for a few moments. Joire then stands some distance from the subject holding the glass plate with the figure resting on it. When Joire pricks various parts of the figure the subject feels pricking sensations in the corresponding parts of his body. Joire then cuts off some of the subject's hair and places it on the head of the figure and then pulls it. The subject complains that his hair is being pulled out.

In a final experiment, Joire places the subject before a wall so arranging the lights that his shadow is directly projected on to it. Joire then suggests to him that all his feelings will be transferred to his shadow. Joire then pricks the wall at different points around – but not on - the shadow and the subject is unmoved, experiencing no sensations. However, when the shadow is touched at various points, the subject complains of pains in the corresponding parts of his body. These pains appear to be more acute than in the aforementioned experiments. When Joire scrapes his hand across the head of the shadow the subject says: "You are scratching me." Joire also found that excitation at a distance also left a persistent painful trace similar to the contusion of a mosquito sting.

* * *

Apparently unrelated to the exteriorisation of sensibility is the 'exteriorisation of motivity' in which a spiritualist medium is able to move physical objects or make physical impressions on 'sitters' without normal physical contact. This ability, nowadays referred to as *psychokinesis*, was established beyond a reasonable doubt in a series of séances with the Italian spiritualist medium Eusapia Palladino at the house of the well-known psychical investigator, Albert de Rochas, in 1895. In *Eusapia Palladino and her Phenomena (1909),* Hereward Carringon records the precautions that were taken by the investigators - many of whom were leading researchers in their own fields - to eliminate fraud or trickery: "At a quarter to nine, Dr. Dariex, upon the request of the medium, returned to her right side. He seated himself on the little tabouret, in the angle formed by the medium and M. Sabatier. Eusapia then places her two legs between those of Dr. Dariex, and rests her two feet upon the tabouret. The right arm and the right hand of Dr. Dariex supports her knees and her thighs. In that position, the feet, the legs, the knees, and the thighs of the medium are continually controlled; the contact is constant, so that the least movement of the lower members of the medium can be accounted for. This position of the legs was retained to the end of the séance; at the same time Eusapia rests her head against that of Dr. Dariex, and the latter also shares in the control of the right arm and the right hand, twining his left arm around the arm of Eusapia, in such a manner that the bend of the elbow encircles the lower part of the arm, so that the forearm of Dr. Dariex comes in contact with the forearm of the medium, and his hand rests on the back of her wrist; moreover, by the tips of his fingers, Dr. Dariex touches the hand of M. Sabatier, which holds the right hand of Eusapia. To sum up, he holds the medium in such a manner that he is sure of her lower limbs, her right hand and her right wrist, which do not leave the table, and of her head, which does not leave his head. Dr. Maxwell always holds the left hand; M. Sabatier the right hand very securely." (Quoted in *Eusapia Palladino and her Phenomena,* pp. 57-58).

Having eliminated all possibility of fraud, the following phenomena are observed: ". . . loud raps occurred, the toy piano was brought from the cabinet onto the séance table, and the large arm chair partly rose into the air, its feet keeping time with the music. Invisible hands touched the sitters, pulling their hair and pinching them. Chairs and other articles of furniture were piled onto the table without apparent cause—both hands of Eusapia being well held, it is asserted, at the time. Indeed, Eusapia invariably announced in advance the character of the phenomenon which was about to take place, and asked that the control should be thoroughly verified." (op cit)

Similar phenomena were witnessed when Eusapia visited the Psychological Institute in Paris in 1905. One of the investigators, Nobel-laureate Pierre Curie, reported: "It was very interesting, and really the phenomena that we saw appeared inexplicable as trickery—tables raised from all four legs, movement of objects from a distance, hands that pinch or caress you, luminous apparitions. All in a [setting] prepared by us with a small number of spectators all known to us and without a possible accomplice. The only trick possible is that which could result from an extraordinary facility of the medium as a magician. But how do you explain the phenomena when one is holding her hands and feet and when the light is sufficient so that one can see everything that happens? (Quoted in *Marie Curie: A Life (1995)* p. 208 - Susan Quinn).

Charles Richet, Nobel-laureate in physiology and a leading figure in the field of psychical research, participated in the Curies' investigations of Eusapia and gave the following account of a séance: "It took place at the Psychological Institute at Paris. There were present only Mme. Curie, Mme. X., a Polish friend of hers, and M. Courtier, the secretary of the Institute. Mme. Curie was on Eusapia's left, myself on her right, Mme. X, a little farther off, taking notes, and M. Courtier still farther, at the end of the table. Courtier had arranged a double curtain behind Eusapia; the light was weak but sufficient. On the table Mme. Curie's hand holding Eusapia's could be distinctly seen, likewise mine also holding the right hand. . . We saw the curtain swell out as if pushed by some large object. . . I asked to touch it . . . I felt the resistance and seized a real hand which I took in mine. Even through the curtain I could feel the fingers ... I held it firmly and counted twenty-nine seconds, during all which time I had leisure to observe both of Eusapia's hands on the table, to ask Mme. Curie if she was sure of her control . . . After the twenty-nine seconds I said, 'I want something more, I want uno anello (a ring).' At once the hand made me feel a ring . . . It seems hard to imagine a more convincing experiment . . . In this case there was not only the materialization of a hand, but also of a ring. Everything takes place as though these movements were due to invisible materializations, paradoxical as that term seems. In the course of a séance one is touched ten or twenty times without being able to see anything, even though darkness is not total." (*Thirty Years of Psychical Research (1923)* – pp. 496-497)

* * *

Superficially, bilocation, physical materialisation, and the exteriorisation of sensibility and motivity appear to be unrelated phenomena, but experiments conducted by a number of paranormal researchers suggest they might be different aspects of a single phenomenon. In the 1890's, psychologist Julien Ochorowitz carried out a number of experiments at Warsaw establishing the existence of what he termed a "fluidic double" which, under certain conditions, can detach itself and work independently of the physical body. Conducting a number of experiments in psychic photography with the medium Mlle. Tomczyk he was able him to obtain a photograph of an *etheric* hand on film enclosed inside a bottle, and photographs of objects suspended in thin air (See *Encyclopaedia of Psychic Science (1933)* by Nandor Fodor). In *Modern Psychical Phenomena (1919)*, Hereward Carrington states that: "A number of striking experiments seem to indicate, in the clearest manner possible, that, in addition to our physical body, we possess another body of the same shape, composed of a sort of etheric or semi-fluidic substance, which has given rise to the supposition that it is composed of matter of a different degree of density or solidity than the matter we know. The nature of this etheric body - the 'spiritual body' of St. Paul, is now known; and many experiments have been conducted in an attempt to detach it from the physical body, and with some success." (Carrington, p. 85)

The early literature of psychical research abounds with descriptions of both spontaneous and deliberate detachments of the etheric body and many well-documented cases can be found in *Phantasms of the Living (1886)* by Edmund Gurney, Frederic Myers, and Frank Podmore. The following extract is from *Phantasms*, in which a Mr. S. H. B describes how he managed to transport his consciousness to another location, and is typical of the detachment experience: "On Friday, December 1st, 1882, at 9.30 p.m., I went into a room alone and sat by the fireside, and endeavoured so strongly to fix my mind upon the interior of a house at Kew (viz., Clarence Road), in which reside Miss V. and her two sisters, that I seemed to be actually in the house. During this experiment I must have fallen into a mesmeric sleep, for although I was conscious I could not move my limbs. I did not seem to have lost the power of moving them, but I could not make the effort to do so, and my hands, which lay loosely on my knees, about 6 inches apart, felt involuntarily drawn together and seemed to meet, although I was conscious that they did not move."

Later that night, when Mr. S. H. B retires to bed, he determines to be in the front bedroom of the above-mentioned house at 12 p.m. and remain there until his "spiritual presence" is known to those in the room. The next evening he pays a visit to Clarence Road where he meets Mrs L. who is a married sister of Miss V. During the course of the conversation she remarks that, the previous evening, she had seen him distinctly on two different occasions. (She had spent the night at Clarence Road and had slept in the front bedroom.) At about 9.30 p.m. she had seen him in the passage, walking from one room to another, and at 12 p.m. when she was wide awake, he had entered her bedroom, walked over to her bed and took hold of her hair (which was very long). He then held her hand and gazed intently into it. Mrs L. spoke to the apparition saying: "You need not look at the lines, for I have never had any trouble." She then roused her sister Miss V., who was sleeping with her, and told her about it. When asked by Mr. S. H. B. if she had not dreamed the whole incident - they had met once before at a fancy dress party - she strongly denied it adding that she had forgotten what he looked like but, seeing him again so clearly, recognized him at once.

Although Mr. S. H. B. was as bemused as Mrs L. by his sudden appearance at Clarence Road, the venerable Swami Pranabananda, in Yogananda's story above, was quite nonchalant. Describing his 'visit' to Kedar Nath Babu, he asked: "Why are you stupefied at all this? The subtle unity of the phenomenal world is not hidden from true yogis. I instantly see and converse with my disciples in distant Calcutta. They can similarly transcend at will every obstacle of gross matter." In other words: time, space and matter are illusions of the physical senses. By transcending the physical senses one transcends time, space and matter. The inner self, for whom time, space and matter have no reality, is everywhere and everywhen; hence 'travelling' is the same as 're-focussing'. The 'body' seen and touched by Kedar Nath Babu was, evidently, the swami's etheric double – a body capable of becoming both visible and tangible and manipulating matter when directed to. It should be noted that both Swami Pranabananda's and Mr. S. H. B's hands felt solid to the touch. In the case of St. Anthony of Padua, if he had wanted to turn the pages of his reading material his hands would have had to physically manipulate the pages; and St. Gerard Majella would have needed to be tangibly present in order to tend to the victims of plague.

If all cases of bilocation can be understood as excursions of the etheric body it is easy to see that detachments of the etheric body account for the exteriorisation of motivity. For example, Eusapia Palladino's ability to detach her etheric body during a trance state enabled her to move objects beyond her reach and cause sitters to feel the touch of 'solid hands.' If she was invited to tap sitter A on the shoulder, move a vase of flowers across the room or thump on the table, her etheric body would do exactly that. On those occasions when Eusapia's powers were not forthcoming - a problem experienced by all spiritualist mediums at one time or another - she would be seen attempting to move objects with her feet, an action evidently performed by her etheric body when freely detached. Such behaviour led to the usual charges of fraud and trickery; however it was generally agreed, by those who attended her séances, that the phenomena she produced were genuine.

Interestingly, the etheric body is the possessor of powers and abilities beyond the reach of the physical body such as superfast travel, the penetration of physical matter, and the movement of heavy physical objects. For example, Mr S.H.B's double suddenly appeared in the front bedroom in Clarence Road; Swami Pranabananda's double quitted the room without opening the door and swiftly outpaced Kedar Nath Babu in spite of the apparent handicap of stout walking shoes; the saints travelled to distant locations in their etheric bodies in the twinkling of an eye; and Eusapia Palladino's double managed to raise heavy objects from the floor such as large armchairs and, like many other mediums in the history of spiritualism, the séance room table.

Detachments of the etheric body may also account for séance room materialisations. During a materialisation séance with Elisabeth d'Esperance, the spirit forms bore such a close resemblance to her it is likely that the spirits were controlling Elisabeth's etheric body in order to communicate with members of the circle. Ignorance of how they were produced often led to suspicions that the forms were really the medium in disguise, resulting in accusations of fraud and, in some cases, disruption of the proceedings by inconsiderate members of the circle. However, the fact that these forms operated independently of the medium, coming and going as they pleased, generally exhibiting a will of their own, suggests that they were under the control of an external spirit agency and neither impersonations nor simple bilocations of the medium.

Since the etheric body is an integral part of the human constitution all contacts with that body will be automatically transmitted to the medium as physical sensations. During a d'Esperance séance, when a spirit form was kissed and caressed by one of the sitters, Elisabeth felt that she was being kissed and caressed; when the spirit was pricked with a rose thorn, Elisabeth felt pain. This exteriorisation of sensibility, often present in the trance state, seems to arise when the etheric body is slightly detached from the physical. For example, in the experiments conducted by Joire he found that someone under hypnosis became insensible to pain at the surface of the skin but sensible to pain at a distance of about one to ten centimetres. Evidently, the deeper the trance state the greater the detachment of the etheric body. In cases of bilocation and materialisation the detachment is complete.

Characteristic of the detachment experience is the *inability* to work through the physical and etheric bodies simultaneously. In the case of Swami Pranabananda, when he attempted to transmit Yogananda's message to Kedar Nath Babu, he had to redirect his attention (i.e. refocus) from his physical to his etheric body. (According to Yogananda the swami "became gravely motionless" and "sphinx-like.") But in order to 'return' to Yogananda, he had to redirect his attention from his etheric body back to his physical body. (At that moment the swami disappeared into a crowd). In other words, in order to be with Kedar Nath Babu, he had to 'leave' Yogananda, and in order to be with Yogananda, he had to 'leave' Kedar Nath Babu; the swami was not able to converse with Yogananda and Kedar Nath Babu in two different places at once. In like fashion, our amateur bilocator Mr S. H. B. had to fall into a 'mesmeric sleep,' with arms and legs immobilized, before he could make his presence known at Clarence Road. St. Anthony of Padua remained perfectly still, as if in deep meditation, while he delivered the appointed passage in the monastery chapel at Limoges; St. Alphonse de Liguori remained "dumb and still" in a relative state of incommunicado while he attended the dying Pope Clement in Rome; and St. Pio of Pietrelcina remained transfixed while he blessed a dying person at San Giovanni Rotondo. Elisabeth d'Esperance had to remain physically helpless during a materialisation séance and Eusapia Palladino had to fall into a trance state before she could exhibit her remarkable powers (See Professor Cesare Lombroso's *After Death - What? (1908)* which contains an account of Eusapia's extraordinary abilities). Finally, Professor Joire had to hypnotise his subjects before they could exteriorise their sensibility. But, crucially, throughout the detachment experience everyone retained their personal identities and nobody was mistaken for anyone else. In this sense, they must be contrasted with Arthur J. Doodle who, in effect, claimed to be multi-incarnated - a feat no yogi, saint or medium has ever claimed.

It is evident that if saints, yogis and mediums cannot work through their physical and etheric bodies simultaneously they would be equally unable to work through two or more *physical* bodies simultaneously; and what cannot be achieved by saints, yogis and mediums cannot, *a fortiori*, be achieved by anyone else – as evidenced by Mr S. H. B. Since it can be safely assumed that everyone possesses just one etheric body and, furthermore, since consciousness must be fully focussed in a body in order to control it, and permanently associated with it in order to develop it, we conclude that:

(1) Multi-incarnation is fundamentally impractical.
(2) Multilocation greater than two is impossible.

* * *

The analysis above shows that individuality is not compromised or undermined by any of the paranormal phenomena discussed. But it also shows why arguments that conflate multilocation and multi-incarnation, in order to provide a *modus operandi* for reincarnation, are erroneous. For example, it is sometimes claimed that a spirit can focus in any number of places at once (an allusion to multilocation) from which it follows that it can focus in any number of bodies at once (an allusion to multi-incarnation). If, so the argument goes, a spirit can simultaneously focus in any number of bodies across *space*, it can simultaneously focus in any number of bodies across *time*; therefore reincarnation is possible. The problem with this argument is threefold.

Firstly, if a spirit can focus in *any* number of places at once, it can, in principle, focus *everywhere* at once. Such a spirit would be the possessor of *universal* consciousness, and a spirit with universal consciousness would have little use for physical embodiment of any kind. Secondly, an immortal spirit who focussed in more than one body at a time would not be an individual because all such associations would be simultaneous. The postulate of individuality requires that the human spirit (or self) does not incarnate in more than one physical body simultaneously. Thirdly, to assert that a spirit is capable of focussing in more than one place at a time is self-contradictory since focussing relates to a single point (i.e. the focal point) and not to a group of points.

Chapter 6
Spirit Influence

One of the principal divides in the field of paranormal research is between those who accept the reality of human survival beyond death and those who do not. Whilst a spiritualist, for example, will attribute the phenomenon of table rapping to the activity of discarnate spirits, a materialist will organise tests to determine the presence, or otherwise, of forces yet to be incorporated into the menagerie of physical interactions. Although such divergence of opinion stems from fundamentally different views of the world it also stems from a refusal to entertain unpalatable facts. It is axiomatic in the history of science that facts in conflict with the ruling paradigm are automatically excluded from the domain of discussion until such time as they can be comfortably accommodated within it. According to philosopher of science, Thomas S. Kuhn, scientists do not reject paradigms merely because they are confronted with anomalies or with counter-instances of their own theories (*The Structure of Scientific Revolutions* – p.77). In the case of spiritualistic phenomena, scientists will not change their methods because they are confronted with spiritualistic facts. After more than a century and a half of research into the paranormal, the question of human survival remains a burning issue, not because the evidence is lacking – the evidence is voluminous – but because the evidence cannot be accommodated within the current materialist paradigm which asserts, among other things, that everything – including human consciousness - is governed by *physical* laws. If such an assertion were true then, of course, human beings would be dependent for their existence entirely on the physical body and perish accordingly with its dissolution.

Now, while the paradigm of materialism is contradicted by the facts of spiritualism, it has become a working hypothesis for those in the humanities who would rather be associated with their friends in the social sciences than with their neighbours in the paranormal. In short, investigators who would have followed in the illustrious footsteps of the great pioneers of psychical research such as William Crookes (in England) and James Hyslop (in America), have abandoned the traditional approach to the unseen - which employs minds rather than mechanisms - in favour of materialist methodologies. For investigators with reincarnationist tendencies this is unsurprising because in the reincarnationist view of the world human consciousness needs a physical body for its full expression and a *series* of physical bodies for its continued expression. However, by adopting the materialist approach, reincarnationists have created a problem for themselves, namely, to explain how human consciousness can jump from one physical body to another without falling into the abyss between.

Although some attempts have been made to remedy this difficulty by considering so-called 'consciousness transfer mechanisms' – an essentially tautological device since it is assumed *a priori* that consciousness somehow transfers from one body to another - these approaches merely demonstrate how, in reincarnationism, human consciousness is as dependent on the physical body as it is in materialism, the principal difference being that materialists do not bother themselves with the issue of post-mortem survival. The net outcome is that reincarnation has become a surrogate for survival. By saturating the public consciousness with reincarnationist interpretations of psychical phenomena, researchers and writers have effectively neutralized the principal finding of psychical research, namely, that we all survive bodily death and continue to exist as discarnate spirit beings.

James H. Hyslop who was Professor of ethics and logic at Columbia University and a prominent member of the American Society for Psychical Research in the early part of the twentieth century had no doubt that we all survive bodily death and live on as discarnate spirits. In *Life After Death (1918)* he states: "I regard the existence of discarnate spirits as scientifically proved and I no longer refer to the skeptic as having any right to speak on the subject. Any man who does not accept the existence of discarnate spirits and the proof of it is either ignorant or a moral coward. I give him short shrift, and do not propose any longer to argue with him on the supposition that he knows anything about the subject." (Hyslop, p.306)

From the existence of discarnate spirits and the phenomenon of mind to mind interaction – a fact long established in the field of psychical research - it is a short step to realising that discarnate spirits can influence the incarnate just as much as they can influence the *dis*carnate - the physical body being no obstacle. This influence is often experienced as possession or obsession, conditions that are paranormal in origin but identical in appearance to what psychiatrists have traditionally termed 'split consciousness,' 'secondary personalities,' 'multiple personalities' and 'dissociative identity disorders,' though such epithets merely serve to cloak the underlying phenomena. According to Hyslop: "secondary personality is the doctor's Irish stew. He does not know what it is. In antiquity it was 'demoniac obsession.' At a later period it was 'witchcraft.' Today we call it such things as 'split consciousness' and think we have solved the problem, when, in fact, we have only thrown dust in people's eyes. We have become so accustomed to paradoxes in human knowledge that almost any impossible combination of terms will receive respectful attention, the more impossible the better. What is split consciousness? We can split wood, iron, pumpkins, political parties; but split consciousness, however convenient a term for describing an apparent situation, is a term for our ignorance - a most happy term, to confound a group of people who refer every anomalous thing in the universe to spirits, and to make it unnecessary to inquire minutely into the anomalies of personality." (Hyslop, pp.289-290)

Since the time of Hyslop the methodological approaches of psychiatry have slowly changed. On 19th March, 2012, a conference was held in London entitled: *Spirit Possession and Mental Health*. This Conference was chaired by a consultant psychiatrist, who – at the time of writing - held an Honorary Professorship at the University of Warwick Medical School and was co-director of the Centre for Research in Ethnicity and Mental Health. Other speakers included a Senior Lecturer in Anthropology at University College (University of London) who was also Honorary

Consultant Psychiatrist at Princess Alexandra Hospital, Harlow; a Professor Emeritus in Psychology at Royal Holloway (University of London) and Professor of Abnormal Psychology at New York University in London; and, finally, a holder of an honorary chair at Imperial College (University of London) in the School of Public Health with a doctoral thesis on spirit possession in Ladakh, North India. The aims of the conference were to:

(1) Discuss possible definitions of and different kinds of spirit possession,
(2) Debate the key elements which typify spirit possession.
(3) Discuss who can make a diagnosis of spirit possession and how such a diagnosis might be made.
(4) Compare and contrast how spirit possession might be viewed by clinicians, religious leaders, healers, the "patient", family and community members.
(5) Discuss the value of using the patient's explanatory model of the illness.
(6) Reflect upon the key issues associated with defining what is "normal" and "abnormal".
(7) Discuss folk healing practices in different cultures and "treatment" options including exorcism.
(8) Consider whether there is a need to enhance joint working between mental health professionals and traditional healers.

The conference was addressed to a wide range of professionals, including those from Local Authorities and National Health Service trusts across the UK, Psychiatrists, General Practitioners, Psychologists, Psychotherapists, Counsellors, Early Intervention Teams, Social Workers, Chaplains, Community Faith Leaders & Healers, Community

Development Workers, Educational Establishments, Academics and Policy makers. Judging by the academic background of the speakers it is evident that modern psychiatry has begun to adjust its methods - if not necessarily its view of the world - to cope with the widespread effects of discarnate spirit influence in human society. Without acknowledging that discarnate spirits really exist, psychiatrists can now treat their patients *as if* they did whilst leaving the intellectual apparatus of their discipline intact.

Although the terms 'possession' and 'obsession' are used by psychiatrists, anthropologists and theologians to describe various mental, cultural and spiritual conditions, their meanings, and the distinctions between them, are not always clear. This lack of clarity is due partly to the terms being used interchangeably, and partly because they have been used to describe different things. While psychiatrists speak of 'personality disorders' and 'obsessive-compulsive' complexes, anthropologists speak of 'possession cults' and 'vitamin deficiencies.' On the other hand, priests speak of 'demonic possession' or 'possession by the Devil'. In all cases, a discarnate spirit entity may or may not be present.

Eminent theological scholar, Augustin Poulain (1836-1919) offers the following definitions: "We shall call a person possessed by the demon in the strict sense of the word when at certain moments the latter makes him lose consciousness and then seems to play in his body the part of the soul: he uses, at least to all appearances, his eyes to see with, his ears to listen with, his mouth to speak with, whether it be to those present or his companions. It is he who suffers as if from a burn if his skin is touched with an object which has been blessed. In a word he seems incarnated. We shall call a person obsessed when the demon never makes him lose consciousness but nevertheless torments him in such a manner that his action is manifest: for example, by beating him." (Quoted in *Possession: Demoniacal and Other (1930)* Professor T. K. Oesterreich, p.77)

Poulain, a Jesuit priest, may have regarded all invasions of the mind as demonic in origin, that is to say, as invasions by entities from Hell, though modern priests generally distinguish between 'Satan,' 'demons,' 'unquiet spirits,' 'evil' spirits, and spirits masquerading as the 'dead.' If one believes in the notion of Hell and the existence of such entities - whatever they may be - so be it; but it may well be that the demons of personal experience - as opposed to the demons of mythology - are no more than *very nasty* earthbound spirits who were once incarnated on Earth. Indeed, very nasty individuals have existed throughout human history and it is highly likely that they have become earthbound spirits bent on controlling the lives of people on Earth and generally polluting the psychic atmosphere of the planet.

Although much evidence exists to support this view, there is also evidence to suggest that some invading spirits may be non-human in origin. It is widely believed in paranormal circles, for instance, that certain entities that have never incarnated on Earth - called 'elementals' - exist in non-physical dimensions and occasionally control the bodies of those who open up channels to them in the course of psychic experiments. The language one uses to describe them is, of course, a matter of personal preference but will, ultimately, be determined by one's religious and philosophical beliefs. Whatever the nature of such entities it is evident that they cannot be characterised in any simple way.

Poulain's definitions are operational in the sense that they enable one to distinguish between possession and obsession in terms of what may be *observed*. In cases of possession the subject loses consciousness, but in cases of obsession the subject remains conscious. This accords with the view of highly experienced exorcist, Canon William H. Lendrum, who states that, in cases of possession, loss of consciousness is a common occurrence. (See *The Dark Sacrament* by David M. Kiely and Christina McKenna). It will become clear in the course of the discussion that obsession and possession bear much the same relationship to one another as a partial to a total eclipse, the difference being one of degree, rather than kind. In practice, the two phenomena will have much in common.

It should be noted that Poulain does not fall prey to the common misconception that possession operates from within and obsession from without. In his definitions, Poulain states that a possessing demon seems to play in the subject's body the part of the soul. In other words, occupation of the body is apparent, not real. The within-without dichotomy, and the implicit concept of bodily occupation, is frequently used in the literature but, unfortunately, does not enable the observer to distinguish between the two phenomena in specific cases. For example, in *The Possessed (1995)*, Brian McConnell - a firm believer in the Devil - expresses this relationship as follows: "In obsession, the Devil is said to besiege or sit outside the body of the afflicted. In possession, he sits within the body." (p.32) Thus, to diagnose the correct condition one must know where the Devil is situated in relation to the body.

The principal difficulty with the concept of occupation when applied to a possessing spirit is that a non-physical entity cannot be said to occupy the space of the physical dimension. In *Apparitions (1953)* philosopher G. N. M. Tyrrell states: "Space is, after all, a conception which cannot be separated from the perceived properties of physical objects, and I cannot see how a distinction can be drawn between physical and non-physical ('metetherial') occupation of space; nor, indeed, that non-physical occupation of space means anything." (Tyrrell, p.47). In other words, space has no meaning without reference to physical objects. This means that the location of a physical object can *only* be determined in relation to other physical objects. Since non-physical things cannot have spatial relationships with physical things (they exist in different dimensions), it follows that non-physical things cannot be located in space. An apparition may appear to be in front of a wall, below a ceiling or above a floor but the relationship is only illusory. If non-physical things - such as possessing spirits - cannot be located in space, then they cannot be said to *occupy* space, and if they cannot occupy space, then they cannot occupy the physical bodies of their hosts.

In reply to objections that apparitions seem to be aware of their physical surroundings and behave as if they were located there, Tyrrell states: "There is undoubtedly evidence to show that apparitions behave *as if* they were aware of their surroundings and therefore of being at a particular place among them; but behaving *as if* aware is not the same thing as *being* aware or we could say that the figures on the cinematograph screen were consciously aware of being there." (Tyrrell, p. 48)

The phenomenon of bilocation, which would seem to contradict the claim that non-physical entities cannot occupy space, is dealt with by Tyrrell in the following way:

"There is a small amount of evidence that the apparition of a living person can be seen at a place in space and that the person afterwards remembers viewing the scene from that identical position.(See case 36, p.116). There are also cases of 'travelling clairvoyance,' quoted in Chapter IV, in which the sensitive describes a distant scene as from a particular point of view. But, perverse as it may seem, I am not prepared to accept this as evidence that the conscious self of the sensitive actually *occupied* that spatial point of view. I carry my perverseness even further than that and refuse to admit that the conscious self of a person who is talking to me in the same room is present in that room, or, indeed, is anywhere in space." (Tyrrell p. 48)

Tyrrell's arguments are not negated by the existence of other paranormal phenomena such as the physical materialisations of mediumship, the tangible manifestations of the etheric body, or the haunting of houses. If the manifestations of spirit entities can be lowered in vibration to the extent that they *behave* like physical objects, this merely reinforces the point that only physical or physical-like things can occupy the space of the physical dimension.

A corollary of the above is that the inner self cannot be said to occupy the physical body. Interestingly, this result may be obtained in another way. In esoteric teaching, the inner self is the source of mutually interacting fields of energy that enable the self to communicate with the universe at large i.e. with the non-self. These living fields of energy, which might more aptly be called 'bodies' or 'vehicles of expression,' vibrate at different frequencies and function within the corresponding dimension of consciousness. The field of energy with the lowest frequency manifests in the physical dimension as the physical body. Since the self and its fields of energy are component parts of a composite whole, they cannot exist as separate and independent entities. Where there is the self, there will be living fields of energy, and where there are living fields of energy, there will be the self. Taking an example from physics, a charged particle cannot exist in isolation from the field it generates. Where there is a charged particle (assumed at rest) there will be an electrostatic field, and where there is an electrostatic field, there will be a charged particle. Hence, the particle cannot be said to occupy the field it generates. Since the physical body is no more than a field of energy, the self cannot be said to occupy the physical body. Furthermore, if the self does not occupy the physical body when the body is a vehicle of expression, then it cannot cease to occupy the body when it ceases to be a vehicle of expression i.e. when the physical body dies. In other words, control of the physical body, whether by the self or by a possessing spirit, is not a form of 'sock-puppetry.'

If possession does not mean occupation, what does it mean? Generally speaking, to possess something means to own it, like a house or a car. But, ownership without control is futile. According to standard definitions, to possess someone means to take control of the person's body or mind, especially in a supernatural manner - a definition that accords with Poulain. In the *Oxford Companion to the Body (OCB)*, spirit possession is a transcendental experience which has material, bodily manifestations such as trance (i.e. loss of consciousness) and muscle rigidity. In effect, the self becomes dissociated from the physical body. According to the *OCB:* "the 'embodiment' of the spirit(s) lies in the discrepancy between the usual behaviour of the person who is possessed (that is, the behaviour displayed by that person when in their usual state of consciousness and as a recognized member of the community) and the transformation that occurs in their behaviour when they are possessed by the spirit(s). Thus the 'embodiment' of spirits impinges on the possessed person's selfhood, and raises interesting psychoanalytical questions about dissociation, and how the dissociated parts of the self might be linked in a larger whole."

In *Possession, Demoniacal and Other (1930)* philosopher and psychologist Professor T. K. Oesterreich states that possession is manifested in *three* ways. Firstly, the possessed takes on a new *physiognomy*. This is illustrated in the case of a girl who is possessed by the spirit of a 'dead' man: "As often as the demon took possession of her she assumed the same features which this man had had in his lifetime and which were very well marked, so that it was necessary at every attack to lead N. away from any person who had known the deceased, because they recognized him at once in the feature of the demoniac." (Oesterreich, p.17)

Changes in physiognomy also occur in trance mediumship. Théodore Flournoy (1854-1920), professor of psychology at the University of Geneva, conducted a series of investigations with the gifted medium, Hélène Smith. He noticed how her physical features would change to reflect the earthly characteristics of the possessing spirit. In his book, *From India to the Planet Mars (1899)*, Flournoy states: "Leopold (Cagliostro) succeeds in incarnating himself only by slow degrees and progressive stages. Hélène then feels as though her arms had been seized, or as if they were absent altogether; then she complains of disagreeable sensations, which were formerly painful, in her throat, the nape of her neck, and in her head; her eyelids droop; her expression changes; her throat swells into a sort of double chin, which gives her a likeness of some sort to the well-known figure of Cagliostro." (Flournoy, p.105).

Hélène's bearing and gait also change: "All at once she rises, then, turning slowly towards the sitter whom Leopold is about to address, draws herself up proudly, turns her back quickly, sometimes with her arms crossed on her breast with a magisterial air, sometimes with one of them hanging down while the other is pointed solemnly towards heaven, and with her fingers makes a sort of masonic sign, which never varies." (Flournoy, p.105)

The second characteristic of possession, noted by Oesterreich, is the change of *voice*. The following example is from *Névroses et idée fixes (1889)*, by Pierre Janet: "It was a very extraordinary spectacle for us who were there present to see this wicked spirit speak by the mouth of the poor woman and to hear now the sound of a masculine, now that of a feminine voice, but so distinct the one from the other that it was impossible to believe that only the woman was speaking." (Janet, p.384). Hélène's voice also changed to reflect the personality of Cagliostro: "Soon after a series of hiccoughs, sighs, and various noises indicate the difficulty Leopold is experiencing in taking hold of the vocal apparatus; the words come forth slowly but strong; the deep bass voice of a man, slightly confused, with pronunciation and accent markedly foreign, certainly more like Italian than anything else." (Flournoy, p.105)

The third and most important characteristic of possession, noted by Oesterreich, is the presence of a strange individuality. This is evident in the following German case of 'demonic' possession: "Since Shrove Tuesday (February 10th, 1892) a man called Müller and his wife noted astonishing phenomena in their eldest son M. who was ten years old. He could no longer say a prayer without getting into extraordinary rages, nor suffer near him any object which had been blessed, was guilty of the coarsest offences towards his parents, and showed in his features such a transformation that they were forced to believe that something extraordinary had taken place." (Quoted in Oesterreich, p. 25).

The boy's parents, having tried conventional methods of treatment without success, turned to the local vicar for help who immediately referred him to the convent of the Capuchins at Wemding. Following the customary benedictions, M. responded so aggressively the nuns could only think of his condition as 'demonic.' Moreover, he showed a degree of physical strength impossible for a boy of ten; three grown men were unable to contain him. Needless to say, his stay at the convent was a failure. As the weeks passed, the boy's behaviour became more extreme. Whenever he passed near a church, crucifix or religious monument he would suddenly become agitated and fall unconscious to the ground. Only when he was carried away from the object or place was he able to continue his walk. Six months elapsed with no improvement. In desperation, M.'s parents wrote to the Bishop of Augsburg imploring him to proceed with the solemn ritual of exorcism. The outcome of the exorcism has not been recorded.

To understand the nature of possession it will be helpful to consider the esoteric view of the human constitution. We have said that the inner self is the source of mutually interacting fields of energy or 'bodies' that vibrate at different frequencies. The body vibrating at the lowest frequency is the physical and represents the expression of the self in the physical universe. The body closest to the physical, and resembling the physical body in terms of vibration and appearance is the 'etheric body' - hence the name 'etheric double.' (see Chapter 5). Beyond, but close to, the etheric body is the 'vital body' which functions as a conduit for the life force, and beyond the vital body is the 'emotional body' (sometimes called the 'astral body') through which the self expresses *feeling*. Beyond the emotional body is the 'lower mental body' through which the self expresses *concrete* thoughts, and further beyond is the 'higher mental body' through which the self expresses *abstract* thoughts. Collectively, all these bodies may be called the *temporal bodies* and when viewed as a composite whole may be referred to in the singular as the *temporal body* or simply as the *body*. The temporal bodies, other than the physical, are sometimes called the 'subtle bodies' and when viewed as a composite whole may be referred to as the *subtle body*. Linking the temporal body with the self is the 'spiritual body' (or the soul) through which the self (or the individualised spirit) expresses its divine nature. Altogether, this produces *seven* planes of manifestation. The innate qualities of the self are expressed through the spiritual and the temporal bodies and manifest - albeit in a distorted fashion - as the *personality*. Summarising: the physical, etheric, vital, emotional, lower mental and higher mental bodies comprise the 'body,' the spiritual body is the 'soul,' and the self is the 'individualised spirit.' We then have the orthodox trinity of body, soul and spirit. Of all the bodies, only the spiritual body is real. Poetically speaking, the body is a 'dream of the soul.' (See fig. 1)

Fig. 1

BODY	SOUL	SPIRIT
Physical Etheric Vital Emotional Lower mental Higher mental	Spiritual body	the Self
The Temporal	The Eternal	

In some systems the subtle bodies are referred to as the 'auric bodies' because they produce an electro-magnetic field or aura around the physical body like the corona of the Sun. The colours of the aura, which can be seen and 'read' by people with clairvoyant vision, reflect the personality, state of health and the general disposition of the individual. The aura has magnetic properties which can attract and repel spirit entities depending on the condition of the subtle bodies. Low vitality, fear, ill will, hatred, coldness, revenge, aggressive thoughts and feelings 'invest' the aura with a powerful negative charge that can be strongly attractive to negative spirit entities. Conversely, high vitality, courage, goodwill, love, compassion, forgiveness, peaceful thoughts and feelings invest the aura with a powerful positive charge that can be strongly repellent to negative spirit entities. In other words, like attracts like. Low vitality in children, especially following severe illnesses, can render them vulnerable to spirit possession because the aura will be too weak to resist 'psychic' attacks or attempts by spirit entities to possess the child's body.

Fig. 2

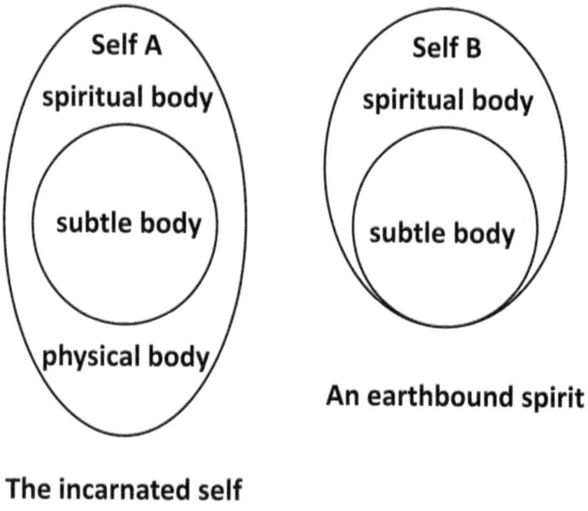

```
    Self A                    Self B
 spiritual body           spiritual body

  subtle body              subtle body

 physical body
```

The incarnated self   **An earthbound spirit**

The left-hand diagram in Fig. 2 shows the incarnated self A (presumed to be sensitive to spirit control), and the right-hand diagram, a potentially controlling spirit B (presumed to be earthbound). In each diagram, the outer loop, enclosing the spiritual and temporal bodies, represents the individuality or spiritual boundary of the self, and the inner loop, enclosing the subtle body - treated as a composite of the subtle bodies - represents the personality.

Fig. 3

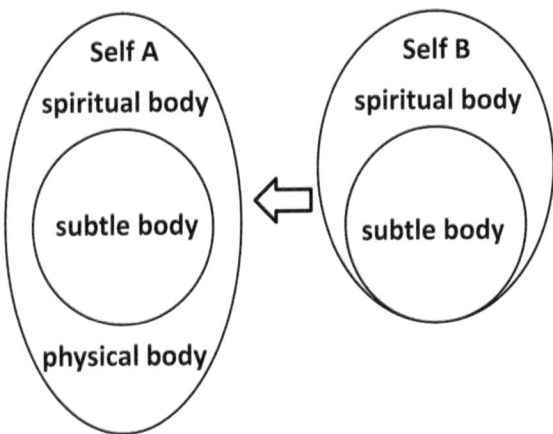

The magnetic pull

Fig. 3 shows the approach of the possessing spirit B, and fig. 4 the possession of A by B. As indicated in fig. 4 the subtle body of A is 'overshadowed' or 'eclipsed' by the subtle body of B. This has a number of consequences: (a) B's personality is impressed upon A's physical body at the expense of A's personality (A loses of consciousness), (b) A's physiognomy, voice and mannerisms change to reflect the personality of B, (c) B controls A's physical body *as if* it were its own. The combined effect of (a), (b) and (c) is to create the impression that B has incarnated in the body of A; but it is no more an incarnation than a marionette is the incarnation of its controller.

Fig. 4

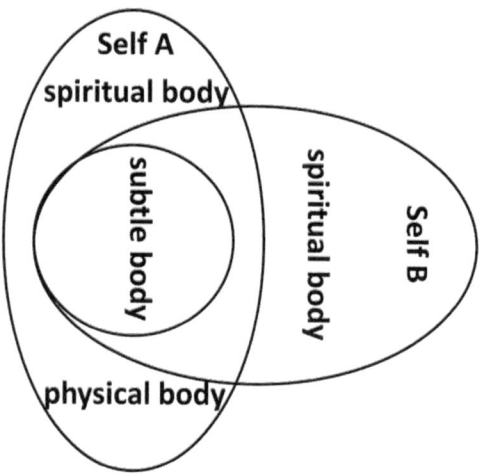

Possession

This is illustrated in fig.4 which shows the physical body of A lying outside the spiritual boundary of B. But, once B has gained control of A's physical body it can utilise its apparatus - such as the vocal cords or hands - to communicate with third parties on Earth.

In the majority of cases, the positive and negative influences in the aura combine in such a way that the subtle body of A is only partially eclipsed by the subtle body of B (see fig. 5).

Fig.5

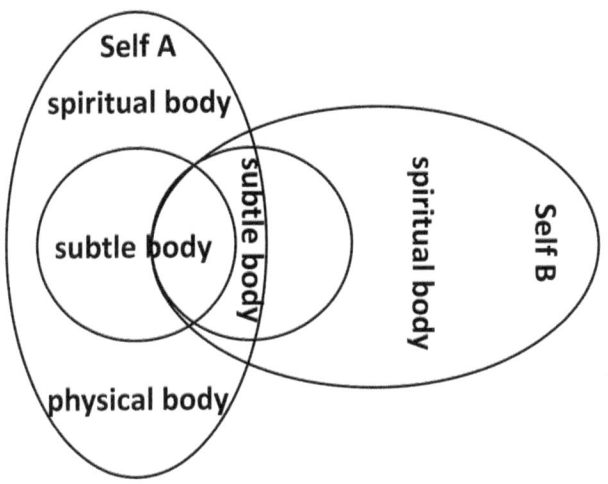

Obsession

The respective subtle bodies then remain in stable equilibrium until: (1) either or both of the opposing forces change, or (2) the equilibrium is disturbed by an external agency. In such a state, A's personality is still present (A remains conscious) albeit in a circumscribed manner. However, the personality of B is also impressed on A's physical body but to an extent determined by the degree of the 'eclipse.' In practice, A's outward behaviour will be modified or influenced by B's personality or there may be an 'alternation' of personalities from one to the other. The 'proximity' of the respective subtle bodies means that A and B will become aware of each other's thoughts, feelings and memories. A will have 'memories' belonging to another person; strange thoughts will intrude on A's mental landscape, and uncharacteristic desires and emotions will surface e.g. A may 'hear' voices. In whatever fashion A chooses to interpret these experiences, A's sense of personal identity or selfhood will be undermined. (In a reincarnationist culture, A may believe that the memories relate to a previous life.) As we shall see in Chapter 8, children who fall prey to spirit intrusions may disown their parents and express a strong desire to go to their 'former home.' If treated, A may be diagnosed as suffering from any of a number of mental illnesses, such as schizophrenia or a multiple personality disorder. This is a classic case of spirit *obsession*.

The obsession of children is illustrated most vividly in the work of Carl Wickland. (We have already discussed the case of Charlie Herrman in Chapter 1.) In his final book, *The Gateway of Understanding (1934) - Part 2* Wickland records how several children with mental illnesses were found to have been obsessed by spirits attempting to reincarnate in their bodies. One such child had been suffering from 'absence seizures' i.e. sudden impairments of consciousness. According to standard descriptions, absence seizures last from a few seconds to about half a minute and are often accompanied by blank stares, an upward roll of the eyes and sudden interruptions in movement and speech. For example, if walking, eating or talking the subject will suddenly stop in mid-motion or mid-sentence and be unresponsive when addressed. Several obsessing spirits had already been removed from this child and during a subsequent session, with the child's mother (Mrs J.) present, the spirit of a reincarnationist was found to be present. The spirit was dislodged from the child's aura and allowed to take control Wickland's wife. Wickland enlightens this

SPIRIT INFLUENCE

spirit by drawing it into conversation. The following is a record of the exchanges:

Wickland: How do you do, and who are you?
Spirit: A man, of course. How could I be anything else. I am born again. I was a Theosophist and was going to reincarnate but when I tried to reincarnate there were about a dozen ahead of me. [Other spirits obsessing patient.] And I don't like it - all of us crowded into one little body. I was a man, a student studying Theosophy, and I died, but I have not yet reached what I am going to become.

Mrs J: How did you find my son?
Spirit: Through you. I found you first. I thought you were quite a nice lady and I saw that if I could get into your family I could have a good home and a quiet, easy life. But circumstances prevented my reincarnating and I only got into a boy. I know better now and I understand that reincarnation is all buncombe. I knew where I was all the time.

Wickland: What is your name?
Spirit: My name is Ralph James and I was a lecturer in London. [The patient's family had lived in England.]

Wickland: Who was the ruler at that time?
Spirit: King Edward. I wish that I could go out and shout to the world how many children are sent to the idiot asylums by spirits of Theosophists who have hovered around mothers trying to reincarnate through a young baby. When one gets into a child and cannot get out it is a great mistake. Sometimes there are two, three or more minds interfering

with one child, the child is declared insane and they all go to the asylum and remain with the child until it dies. Once in a while an obsessing spirit can get away but only by holding continuously the thought of leaving. This is very difficult. Sometimes I was able to slip away but came back again. I have been watching the whole proposition here [removal of obsessing spirits, one by one, from the patient] and watched for my time to get out. I have observed obsession here and the treatments given, the effect of electricity on the vital organs, the magnetic current being cut and the wonderful results accomplished by means of this psychic. [Mrs. Wickland.] Why people cannot master themselves in the earth life I cannot understand. They should study nature instead of growing so negative from following various fads, such as eating only vegetables. They should understand that everything depends upon everything else, from microbes on up. Many Theosophists travel around in the astral world in a blind condition but hold the thought of finding a place to reincarnate. Many want to become leaders and have their own religion.

Wickland: How old are you ?
Spirit: I cannot tell exactly. I think I was about forty-five years old. You can count the interval, as King Edward came to the throne in 1901. I knew all about my own death. After I left my physical body, I wanted to travel with people. so I went to India and elsewhere, following others. If you are conscious of passing out, it is a wonderful study to observe where you are going. Very few travel on, however. Generally they prefer to remain in their own homes. Especially is that so of England. There departed

spirits remain for centuries, abiding in old castles and haunted houses, fighting among themselves. Those in the physical life cannot remain long in such places so in time all of these old castles will be torn down, because people cannot live comfortably in haunted houses, and the owners cannot afford to keep up these places. If only people would understand this influence. Someday I will come to you again and tell you all about my experiences. I am not a bad spirit, merely a foolish one. I visited mediums; some considered themselves controlled by Cleopatra and some by St John, but these were only obsessing spirits pretending to be great personages. It is going to take time to break up false beliefs, but there will be a new religion and it will be a sensible one. I must go now. Thank you for freeing me. (Wickland, pp.214-216)

* * *

The following case from *These Mysterious People (1934)* by Nandor Fodor illustrates how possession or obsession are often incorrectly called 'reincarnation.' The American seer and prophet Andrew Jackson Davis (1826-1910) had received no formal education prior to the age of sixteen. However, three years after his sixteenth birthday - following a mysterious encounter with the spirits of the ancient philosopher Galen of Pergamon and the Christian mystic Emanuel Swedenborg - he became both a healer and a prodigious writer of philosophical and mystical subjects. At the age of nineteen he published the monumental work: *The Principles of Nature, Her Divine Revelations, and a Voice to Mankind (1847)*, a book he had dictated to his amanuensis, William Fishbough, while in a trance state. George Bush, professor of Hebrew at New York University, heard Davis quote correct Hebrew and questioned him while in trance. According to Professor Bush: "Taken as a whole the work is a profound and elaborate discussion of the philosophy of the universe, and for grandeur of conception, soundness of principle, clearness of illustration, order of arrangement and encyclopaedic range of subjects, I know no work of any single mind that will bear away from it the palm." (Quoted in Fodor, Ch. 8)

Following Professor Bush's endorsement, the book was an immediate success but later investigations revealed the *Revelations* to be a reflection of Swedenborg's own thinking. In a number of cases, the style of prose was identical. This accords with Davis's own claim to be possessed by the spirit of Swedenborg when in trance and obsessed by him when not in trance. "If not," inquiries Fodor, "by what sort of recondite mental process could an ignorant country boy get hold of the contents of musty old books of the very existence of which he must have been unaware?" Writing in 1846, Davis made a number of correct astronomical predictions such as the discovery of Pluto but – like Swedenborg – made some highly questionable ones. For example, both Davis and Swedenborg maintained that all the planets, with the exception of the three outer ones, were inhabited. However, Davis went on to publish another monumental work: *The Great Harmonia (1852)* and laid the foundations for much of modern spiritualism. This strongly suggests that the spirits of Swedenborg and Galen had been working through Davis in order to transmit knowledge to humankind.

In spite of Davis' claim to be possessed by the spirit of Swedenborg, some contemporary commentators still thought in terms of reincarnation. In the *Quest for Dean Bridgman Conner*, American journalist Anthony Philpot tells how in 1907 he introduced one Professor Lutoslawsky to Davis while the latter was working in a small office in the rear of a store on Warren Avenue. Lutoslawsky wanted to meet Davis more than "any man in America" and was taken aback when they met. According to Philpot: "They looked at each other for a moment as they clasped hands, and then Professor Lutoslawsky exclaimed: 'Why you are Swedenborg!'"(Fodor, Ch. 8).

Davis replied in and off-hand manner: "Yes, I am." However, Lutoslawsky chatted with Davis as though he were talking to Swedenborg himself. Afterwards, Philpot noted: "The whole thing made a rather curious impression on me . . . and I wondered if Professor Lutoslawsky really believed that Dr. Davis was a reincarnation of Swedenborg and whether Dr. Davis believed it himself. But they were both very serious and I said nothing." It does not seem to have occurred to Philpot that if Davis had been a reincarnation of Swedenborg - because he spoke like Swedenborg - then, by the same reasoning, he must also have been a reincarnation of Galen. It would then follow than Swedenborg himself was a reincarnation of Galen! Yet, we know such a scenario to be impossible because Davis himself claimed to have had mystical encounters with both the spirits of Galen and Swedenborg in his youth. There was never any doubt in the mind of Davis that he had channelled the posthumous thoughts of Swedenborg and Galen, and if such is the case then Swedenborg, Galen and Davis must be three individuals with distinct spiritual identities.

The Possession of Lurancy Vennum

Lurancy Vennum is especially interesting because her case has many features in common with those touted as evidence for reincarnation (see Chapter 8). The impossibility of reincarnation in her case is proven by the fact that Lurancy Vennum and her possessing spirit, Mary Roff, had been contemporaries of one another in the neighbouring states of Iowa and Illinois in the United States of America. When Mary Roff passed away at the comparatively young age of eighteen in July, 1865, Lurancy Vennum was over fourteen months old.

Our narrative follows the account given by spiritualist Dr. E. Winchester Stevens in *The Watseka Wonder (1897)*. The book has the following interesting subtitle: "Probably the most remarkable case of Spirit Return and manifestation ever recorded in history. Fully authenticated by a multitude of witnesses. Over 100,000 copies sold. A girl dead and buried 12 years comes back, identifies herself and lives for 3 months and ten days as the recognized daughter of her parents."

Mary Lurancy Vennum, daughter of Thomas and Lurinda J. Vennum, was born 16th April, 1864 in the town of Midford seven miles south of Watseka. In April, 1871, following several changes of residence, the Vennums moved to Watseka situating themselves just 200 metres from the residence of Mr and Mrs Asa B. Roff. Although neighbours, the Vennums and Roffs remained relative strangers to one another, their only acquaintance being a brief visit by Mrs Roff to the Vennums which was never returned plus a few formal exchanges between the two gentlemen of the family. In the summer of 1871 the Vennums moved yet again settling some distance from the Roffs on opposite sides of Watseka. There was no further contact between the Roffs and the Vennums prior to the events of this story.

Lurancy (commonly known as Rancy) was a healthy child and had never been sick apart from a mild attack of measles in 1873. One day in early July, 1877 she said to her parents: "There were persons in my room last night, and they called 'Rancy! Rancy!!' and I felt their breath on my face." When this is repeated the following day she leaves her room and spends the rest of the night with her mother. A few days later, on 11th July, Lurancy had been busy sewing carpet for most of the afternoon. At about 6pm when her mother called her to supper, Lurancy replied: "Ma, I feel bad; I feel so queer." She then placed her hand on her chest and suddenly fell to the floor apparently dead with every muscle in her body becoming rigid. She lay in this state for five hours. When she regains consciousness she says she feels "very strange and queer." She rests well for the remainder of the night but the next day the rigid state returns. This time, however, she is able to speak and tells her parents she could see spirits, describing them in detail and calling some of them by name. Among those mentioned were her sister and brother, Laura and Bertie who had passed away some years previously. She exclaimed, "Oh, mother! can't you see little Laura and Bertie? They are so beautiful!" Lurancy falls into many of these trance states describing spirits, heaven and the angels.

In September, however, her trances suddenly cease and she returns to her normal self. On 27th November, 1877, however, she begins to experience violent pains in her stomach - as many as six times a day - and, over the next two weeks, they increase in intensity. Then one day, on or around 11th December, 1877 her trances return - as many as twelve a day - and continue until February, 1878. These trances last from one to eight hours during which time she often claims to be in heaven.

Lurancy is placed under the care of two doctors, but friends and relatives of the Vennums believe Lurancy to be mentally ill. The local Methodist minister makes enquiries at a nearby asylum and - in spite of reluctance on the part of Mr and Mrs Vennum - it is the general feeling that Lurancy should go there. Meanwhile, Lurancy's case has come to the attention of the Roffs who had briefly known the Vennums in Watseka some years before. The Roffs, imbued with the Christian spirit, contact the Vennums and advise them not to commit Lurancy to an asylum with all its attendant horrors.

After much persuasion, Mr Roff obtains permission from Mr Vennum to visit Lurancy and bring with him Dr. E. Winchester Stevens of Janesville, Wisconsin to investigate the case. They arrive at the Vennums on the afternoon of 31st January, 1878. According to Stevens: "The girl sat near the stove, in a common chair, her elbows on her knees, her hands under her chin, feet curled up on the chair, eyes staring, looking every way like an "old hag." She sits for a time in silence, until Stevens moves his chair, when she savagely warns him not to come nearer. She appears sullen and crabbed, calling her father "Old Black Dick," and her mother "Old Granny." She refuses to be touched, even to shake hands, and is reticent and sullen with all save the doctor, with whom she enters freely into conversation, giving her reasons for doing so; she says he is a Spiritual doctor and would understand her." (Stevens, pp.17 and 18)

Dr. Stevens asks the name of the person to whom he is speaking. Lurancy replies: "Katrina Hogan." The following is a record of the initial exchanges between Stevens and Lurancy:

Stevens: "How old?"
Lurancy: "Sixty-three years."
Stevens: "Where from?"
Lurancy: "Germany."
Stevens: "How long ago?"
Lurancy: "Three days."
Stevens: "How did you come?"
Lurancy: "Through the air."
Stevens: "How long will you stay?"
Lurancy: "Three weeks."

Lurancy's attitude then changes and she admits she is not really a woman but a young man called Willie Canning. He ran away from home, got into difficulty, changed his name several times and finally lost his life and was now here because he "wanted to be." After a while, Lurancy tires of answering questions and peppers Stevens with questions of her own: "What is your name? Where do you live? Are you married? How many children? How many boys? How many girls? What is your occupation? What kind of a doctor? What did you come to Watseka for? Have you ever been at the South Pole? North Pole? Europe? Australia? Egypt? Ceylon? Benares? Sandwich Islands?" According to Stevens, Lurancy has a fair knowledge of geography. She next inquires after the doctor's habits and morals: "Do you lie? get drunk? steal? swear? use tobacco? tea? coffee? Do you go to church? pray?" She then asks that the same questions be put to

Mr Roff and Mr Vennum but only through Dr. Stevens, making some "very unpleasant retorts."

At about 5.30pm, as Dr. Stevens and Mr Roff prepare to leave, Lurancy suddenly flings her arms up in the air and falls to the floor, laying there straight and rigid. They both sit down again: "The visitors being again seated, he [Dr Stevens] took her hands as they were held straight upward, like iron bars, and by magnetic action soon had the body under perfect control and through the laws of Spiritual science was soon in full and free communication with the sane and happy mind of Lurancy Vennum herself, who conversed with the grace and sweetness of an angel, declaring herself to be in heaven." (Stevens, p.19)

Whilst in this state Lurancy answers Stevens' questions with "great rationality and understanding." She says she knows the evil spirit calling itself Katrina and Willie and others and regretted that they were controlling her. Stevens then encourages Lurancy to look for more enlightened controlling spirits: "Then on being advised, she looked about and inquired of those she saw, and described, and named, to find someone who would prevent the cruel and insane ones from returning to annoy her and the family. She soon said: "There are a great many spirits here who would be glad to come," and she again proceeded to give names and descriptions of persons long since deceased; some that she had never known, but were known by older persons present. But, she said, there is one the angels desire should come, and she wants to come. On being asked if she knew who it was, she said: 'Her name is Mary Roff.'" (Stevens, p.20) Mr Roff says: "That is my daughter; Mary Roff is my girl. Why, she has been in heaven twelve years. Yes, let her come, we'll be glad to have her come."

He assures Lurancy that on Earth, Mary was a good and intelligent soul and would be of great assistance to her.

From that moment, Lurancy's personality changes dramatically. According to Stevens: "From the wild, angry, ungovernable girl, to be kept only by lock and key, or the most distressing watch-care of almost frantic parents; or the rigid, corpse-like cataleptic, as believed, the girl has now become mild, docile, polite and timid, knowing none of the family, but constantly pleading to go home. [A feature recorded by Dr. Ian Stevenson in his cases 'suggestive of reincarnation.'] The best wisdom of the family was used to convince her that she was at home, and must remain. Weeping, she would not be pacified, and only found contentment in going back to heaven, as she said, for short visits." (Stevens, p.26)

The following incidents show how the spirit of Mary Roff had completely overwhelmed the mind of Lurancy Vennum. Mrs Mary Lord had lived opposite the Roffs for a number of years to within a few months of Mary Roff's death. Following the death of her husband, she married a Mr Wagoner and was now living close to the Vennums. On meeting Mrs Wagoner, Lurancy said: "O Mary Lord, you look so very natural, and have changed the least of any one I have seen since I came back." Lurancy - although living close to the Wagoners - was completely oblivious of the fact that Mrs Lord had remarried, greeting her exactly as Mary Roff would have done fifteen years previously.

About a week following Dr. Stevens' visit to the Vennums, Mrs A. B. Roff and her daughter, Mrs Minerva Alter, Mary's sister, visit Lurancy. As they approach the Vennum residence, Lurancy, looking out of the window, calls out: "There comes my ma and sister Nervie!" the pet name by which Mary used to call Mrs Alter. When they enter the house Lurancy throws her arms around them weeping with joy. From that moment onward Lurancy becomes even more homesick becoming, at times, almost frantic to go to the Roffs. According to Stevens: "Mrs Vennum was nearly prostrated, and could not have survived the care and anxiety many months longer, under the same state of affairs."

Eventually, friends of Mr and Mrs Vennum insist that Lurancy be sent away, and on 11th February, 1878 she leaves the Vennums to live with the Roffs. On arrival she greets them as if they were her own parents, embracing them with much love and affection. According to Stevens: "The girl now in her new home, seemed perfectly happy and content, knowing every person and everything that Mary knew when in her original body, twelve years to twenty-five years ago, recognizing and calling by name those who were friends and neighbors of the family from 1852 to 1865, when Mary died, calling attention to scores, yes, hundreds of incidents that transpired during her natural life. During all the period of her sojourn at Mr Roff's she had no knowledge of, and did not recognize any of Mr Vennum's family or neighbors, yet Mr and Mrs Vennum and their children visited her and Mr Roff's people, she being introduced to them as to any strangers." (Stevens, p.28)

Some days after Lurancy had moved to the Roffs, Mrs Parker, who had been a neighbour of the Roffs in Middleport in 1852, and had lived next door to them in Watseka in 1860, arrives at the Roffs with her daughter-in-law, Nellie Parker. Lurancy immediately recognizes both of the ladies, calling Mrs Parker "Auntie Parker" and the other "Nellie," as Mary Roff would have done eighteen years previously. In a conversation with Mrs Parker,

Lurancy asks, "Do you remember how Nervie and I used to come to your house and sing?" According to Mrs Parker, that was the first allusion ever made to that matter. Mary and Minerva used to come to Mrs Parker's house and sing "Mary had a little lamb." This happened twelve years before Lurancy was born.

One evening, when Mr Roff is reading his newspaper and waiting for tea, he asks Mrs Roff if she can find a certain velvet headdress that Mary had worn just before she died. If so, could she lay it on the stand and say nothing about it, to see if Lurancy would recognize it. Mrs Roff readily finds the headdress and lays it on the stand. Lurancy, who had been outside in the yard, comes in and immediately recognises it, saying: "Oh, there is my head-dress I wore when my hair was short!" She then says: "Ma where is my box of letters? Have you got them yet?" Mrs Roff replies, "Yes, Mary, I have some of them." As Lurancy sorted through the letters she says, "Oh, Ma, here is a collar I tatted! Ma, why did you not show to me my letters and things before?" The collar had been fashioned by Mary before Lurancy had been born.

In 1857 the Roffs had moved to Texas and Mr Roff asked Lurancy if she remembered anything about it, to which Lurancy replies: "Yes, pa, and I remember crossing Red River and of seeing a great many Indians, and I remember Mrs. Reeder's girls, who were in our company." According to Mr Roff, Lurancy would, from time to time, mention things that happened thirteen to twenty five years previously. The following is a letter from Mr Roff to Dr. Stevens dated 19th February, 1878: "You know how we took the poor, dear girl Lurancy (Mary). Some appreciate our motives, but the many, without investigation and without knowledge of the facts, cry out against us and against the angel girl. Some say she pretends; others that she is crazy; and we hear that some say it is the devil. Mary is perfectly happy; she recognizes everybody and everything that she knew when in her body twelve or more years ago. She knows nobody nor anything whatever that is known by Lurancy. Mr. Vennum has been to see her, and also her brother Henry, at different times, but she don't know anything about them. Mrs. Vennum is still unable to come and see her daughter. She has been nothing but Mary since she has been here, and knows nothing but what Mary knew. She has entered the trance once every other day for some days. She is perfectly happy. You don't know how much comfort we take with the dear angel." (Stevens, p.31)

Lurancy shows much affection for Dr. Stevens because he had "opened the gate" for Mary Roff to come through and because he has done so much for her family. Expressing her gratitude she sends him the following letter signing it "Mary Roff": "I am yet here. Frank is better. Nervie is here for dinner; Alice Alter is going to stay all night; Mrs. Marsh was here today and read a beautiful letter to us. I wish you could spend the evening with us. I would like to have your picture to look at. Please write to pa when you get time. We all send our love to you. I like it here very much, and am going to stay all the time. I went to heaven and staid about an hour. It seems a long time since I saw you. Forget me not. Good night. MARY ROFF."

When 'Mary' made her brief excursions to 'heaven', other spirits would speak through Lurancy. According to Mr Roff: "A lady came through at our house, who claimed to have lived and died in Tennessee, and says she was afflicted from eight years of age till twenty-five, when she died with a similar disease, and in a similar way that Mary died. She says that Mary has control of Lurancy Vennum, and will retain control until she is restored to her normal condition, when Mary will leave." (Stevens, p.32)

Sometime during the first week of May, 1878 'Mary' hints that Lurancy is about to return. Mr Roff writes: "I want to give you a little scene; time Monday morning, May sixth; place, A. B. Roff's office, Watseka; present, A. B. Roff at table writing; Frank Roff at table at the right of A. B. R.; door behind A. B., and a little to the left; enters unheard the person of Lurancy Vennum; places her arm around the neck of A. B. Roff, kissing him and saying, 'Pa, I am going with Mrs. Vennum to visit today;' A. B. Roff looks around and discovers standing in the door Mrs. Vennum, Lurancy's mother, looking on the scene. The girl then bade an affectionate good-by to Frank; A. B. R. asks: 'How long will you stay?' She replies, 'Till two or three o'clock.' Mrs. Vennum then said to Mr. Roff: 'If she does not get back at that time, don't get alarmed, we will take care of her.' Exit Mrs. V. and the girl. You don't know how my heart aches for that poor mother, yet she is much happier than she was last winter with Lurancy as she was." (Stevens, p.33)

On 7th May, 1878 a tearful 'Mary' prepares Mrs. Roff for Lurancy's return. She sits down, closes her eyes and in a few moments Lurancy is back. Looking wildly around the room she asks: "Where am I? I was never here before." Mrs. Roff replies: "You are at Mr. Roff's, brought here by Mary to cure your body." Lurancy cries and says: "I want to go home." Mrs. Roff asks her if she could stay till her folks are sent for. Lurancy says "No." Mrs Roff then asks Lurancy if she feels any pain in her chest. (Mary had suffered such pains). Lurancy replies: "No, but Mary did." After a few minutes 'Mary' returns and is so happy she sings her favourite song: "We are coming sister Mary."

After her second return, 'Mary' would stroll in the garden with Mrs Alter, saying: "Come, Nervie, put your arm around me and we will take a little walk in the garden or the grove, for I cannot be with you much longer and I want to be with you every minute I can." When asked when or where she was going, 'Mary' would reply: "The angels tell me I am going to heaven, but I don't know just when. Oh, how I wish you could live here at home with us as you used to when I was here before." She tells Mrs Alter that when she got into this body she felt much as she had done twelve years ago; the body seemed so natural she might have been born with it. In conversation with Stevens about her life on earth, 'Mary' spoke of cutting her arm at which point she pulled up her sleeve to show the scar. She then suddenly stopped saying: "Oh, this is not the arm; that one is in the ground," and then informed Stevens where she had been buried, what people were in attendance and how they felt. According to Stevens, 'Mary' had, some years prior to her return, tried to contact her parents from the other side through the hand of a medium, giving name, time and place and, sometime later, rapped and spelled out a message through another medium, giving the same information which her parents confirmed.

Dr. Stevens records the following incident which took place on 21st April, 1878 to illustrate how easily the spirit of Mary Roff took control of suitably sensitive people. "Mary being the last one to join the company in the parlor, took the only vacant seat, next to a gentleman friend. Dr. Steel became influenced by a brother of one of the persons present, and made a very striking address, with a good deal of energy and pathos. On his becoming disentranced and entering into the general conversation, Mary voluntarily disembodied her controlling power, and leaving the girl's form like a corpse, with the head resting against the shoulder of her friend, immediately took control of Dr. Steel, and in every possible way required proved it to be herself; she then through that manly form, turned in a jovial way and laughed at the position of the seemingly untenanted body and its limp condition, with a pleasant jest at the friend who supported it. She soon, however, returned to her own proper control and seemed to enjoy the trick she had played, in the control of the gentleman." (Stevens, pp.38 and 39)

The following incident shows how a possessing spirit can impart skills to its host. After 'Mary' releases Dr. Steel from her control, Lurancy's persona suddenly changes. She calls across to Charlotte (the hired help) and they both exit the room together. A few minutes later Lurancy returns dressed like an elderly lady with gown, cap, cape and spectacles bowed over and leaning on the arm of Charlotte. According to Stevens "not one trace of the girl could be seen save in the youthful skin of the face." She then sits down in an old armchair and announces herself as Charlotte's grand-mother, naming relatives that Lurancy could have known nothing about. The 'old lady' says she died of cancer near the right eye and temple and then asks for tepid water and a soft cloth to bathe and dress the area. When she is finished she calls for food - eating it apparently without teeth - and then smokes afterwards to ease the pain. She then asks for knitting work, which is duly provided, and criticises it because it has not been done properly. She unravels it and instructs Charlotte in the art of knitting. This she does without looking thereby demonstrating a degree of proficiency not possessed by the 'normal' Lurancy.

As Mary Roff's influence begins to fade and the possession weakens, Lurancy Vennum becomes *obsessed* and this condition lasts for approximately one month. As expected, there is an alternation of personalities: "As the time drew near for the restoration of Lurancy to her parents and home, Mary would sometimes seem to recede into the memory and manner of Lurancy for a little time, yet not enough to lose her identity or permit the manifestation of Lurancy's mind, but enough to show she was impressing her presence upon her own body." (Stevens, pp. 41-42).

On another occasion: "Mary left control, and Lurancy took full possession of her own body. Henry [Lurancy's brother] was called in and she caught him around his neck, kissed and wept over him, causing all present to weep. At this juncture Mr. Roff was called and asked Lurancy if she could stay till Henry could go and bring her mother (she had expressed a desire to go and see her father and mother.) She said, 'No,' but if Henry would go and bring her, she would come again and talk with her. She immediately left and Mary came again." (Stevens, pp. 41-42)

On 21st May, 1878, Lurancy returns for good and is asked by Stevens if she had any recollections of the experience. According to Lurancy, she remembered a few things that happened during the last month (i.e. when she was *obsessed*) but that the information was imparted to her by Mary. Stevens concludes the narrative as follows: "In conclusion, let me say to those who doubt or disbelieve the strange, mysterious and wonderful story, call to mind Lurancy's condition at her home last January, surrounded with all the kind care of parents, friends and physicians, everything done to alleviate her suffering and perform a cure that human minds and hands could possibly do, yet growing continually worse (if that were possible), given up by her physicians, her friends without a ray of hope, the insane asylum ready to receive her, a condition terrible to behold! Then view her condition from May twenty-first until today, over three months, a bright, beautiful, happy, healthy girl, and then tell me what produced the change. The narrative furnishes the facts; account for them if you can on any other hypothesis, than power exercised through or by the spirit of Mary Roff having control of Lurancy's body." (Stevens, p.50)

* * *

That discarnate personalities can impress the minds of the incarnate with their memories, thoughts and feelings was a fact well known to the pioneers of modern psychical research. Professor Hyslop maintained that this phenomenon was mistakenly adduced as evidence for reincarnation. In *Contact with the Other World (1919)* he states that: ". . . facts adduced in support of reincarnation can be explained as mediumistic phenomena. That is, discarnate personalities may produce in the minds of psychics the feeling of long past time or of previous existence by the transmission, telepathically perhaps, of their own feelings and states of mind. These would naturally enough be interpreted as evidence of reincarnation." (Hyslop, p.378).

On the doctrine of reincarnation he states that: ". . . it must be said that this belief rests on metaphysics alone. It has no scientific foundation whatever. Some venture to adduce facts to support it, but these will not bear the slightest examination as evidence. For instance, some will tell us that they can remember a previous existence. But they do not reckon with illusions of memory. We sometimes recall something which we locate in a certain time and place, but find later that this location was wrong. When the total experience is recalled we find that we are dealing with two events connected only by similarity. We confused them because of the imperfection of the recall. This imperfect recall will explain most of the alleged instances of recollection of a prenatal past." (Hyslop, p.378)

Dr. Carl Wickland was strongly critical of the doctrine of reincarnation and maintained it was responsible for many cases of obsession in young children. In *Thirty Years Among the Dead (1924)* he states: "That the belief in reincarnation on earth is a fallacious one and prevents progression to higher spiritual realms after transition, has frequently been declared by advanced spirits, while numerous cases of obsession which have come under our care, have been due to spirits who, in endeavouring to 'reincarnate' in children, have found themselves imprisoned in the magnetic aura, causing great suffering to both their victims and themselves." (Wickland, p.333)

Chapter 7
Mind and Body

The mind's power over the physical body is such a self-evident feature of human behaviour that few people would seriously question it. I decide to get up out of my chair and leave the room and, hey presto, my body does exactly that. "Not so fast!" says the materialist. "Your body is merely responding to a complex pattern of physio-chemical reactions in the brain that were set in motion long before you even sat on the chair. Volition doesn't come into it." What has been called the 'naturalisation of the mind' - the notion that mind and consciousness are merely byproducts of the body's nervous system - began to take root in Western consciousness following the philosophical separation of mind and body by René Descartes (1596-1650) and the scientific determinism of Pierre-Simon de Laplace (1749-1827). Descartes believed that the physical body was a machine largely beyond the reach of the human mind. Although human thought controls bodily actions such as walking, talking and dancing, all the vital functions, such as the circulation of the blood and the immune system, are governed by natural laws; the mind - being nonmaterial in essence - cannot influence the body's physiology.

This dualistic view of the human constitution, known as *Cartesian dualism*, created a happy division of labour between those concerned with the human anatomy and those concerned with the human mind. But, it was a division that was doomed to failure for the astonishing success of the 'naturalistic' view of the world ushered in by Sir Isaac Newton brought an end to the cherished belief that mind existed independently of physical matter. Whether or not scientific imperialism rides tandem with political imperialism is a question beyond the scope of this book, but at some point in the expansion of the British Empire the human mind itself came 'up for grabs.' What was once the preserve of theologians and metaphysicians suddenly became the province of physicists and chemists. Thus, when Laplace entered the stage one hundred years after the death of Descartes he could assert, with some confidence, that *all* things are determined by natural laws.

Over the course of the next two centuries, Laplacian determinism steadily created a picture of the human body in which all anatomical events – including thoughts and feelings – could be explained in terms of physiological processes. In this 'naturalistic' view of the world, mind and consciousness are no longer independent variables but states to be determined; in extreme versions, mind and consciousness are dispensed with altogether. These unidirectional and eliminatist models of the human anatomy dominate the fields of physiology and biology today. Yet many physiological reactions are *themselves* the product of mental states. Anxiety and blood pressure, fear and perspiration, nervousness and skin rashes, happiness and health, depression and disease, religious devotion and stigmata (discussed below), trance and transfiguration (see Chapter 6) to name just a few, all testify to the mind's ability to influence the body's physiology in both mundane and startling ways. Statistical surveys tend to support this view. For example, a study of 2,400 patients in Finland revealed a significant correlation between 'hopelessness' and cardiovascular disease and cancer. (See Everson et al in *Psychosomatic Medicine (1996)*, 58, pp.113-121.) Furthermore, a study of one hundred men under the age of 70 who had died suddenly were found to have been under exceptional stress within a half an hour, twenty four hours, or six months preceding the death. (See A. Myers and H. A. Dewar, *British Medical Journal (1975)*, 37, pp. 1133-1143.)

Related to the experiments of Professor Paul Joire and the transfer of sensibility to material objects such as small putty figures (see Chapter 5) is the notion of a 'death curse' in which a powerful suggestion of death (possibly hypnotically induced) is quickly followed by its realisation. Physician Λ. Λ. Watson, who was a medical officer at a mission hospital in Zaire, recorded ten sudden deaths following the application of a death curse. One death concerned a native nurse who had converted to Christianity. Although he had been outspoken about the "foolishness" of believing in such things, he died within three days of learning that he himself had received a death curse. (See *Medicine, Science, and the Law (1973)*, 13, pp.192-194.) Similar cases have been reported in Western countries. J. L. Mathis, for example, records the case of a man who developed asthma following a "curse" from his mother and then promptly died when the curse was repeated during a telephone call. (See *Psychosomatic Medicine (1964)*, 26, pp.104-107.)

A similar case, reported to the editor of the *British Medical Journal (1965)* tells the story of a 43 year old woman who died following a minor operation. Many years before, she had been told by a fortune teller that she would die at the age of 43. Just before surgery the woman had told medical staff that she would not survive the operation. C. K. Meador records the case of an American man who had been "hexed" by a voodoo priest. Although the man was apparently close to death, his physician saved his life by entering into his belief system and introducing a "counter-hex." Meador also records a case in which a man lost all desire to live following the sudden and tragic death of his wife. Six months after her death, he was diagnosed with cancer and told he had only a short time to live. Three months after this prognosis he was admitted to hospital and died the next day. The autopsy revealed that the man's cancer was insufficient to have caused his death. (See *Southern Medical Journal (1992)*, 85, pp.244-247.)

Why conventional medicine has been generally resistant to the notion that critical mental states can influence the body's physiology is probably due to the absence of a plausible explanatory model, though developments in the relatively new field of psychoneuroimmunology are beginning to shed light on the mystery. In a paper entitled: 'Emotions, immunity, and disease' published in *Archives of General Psychiatry (1964)* pp. 657-673; G. F. Solomon and R. H. Moos argue that stress can be immunosuppressive and therefore detrimental to good health. Physiologists, Walter Cannon and Hans Selye have suggested that the body maintains its proper functioning through an internal system of self-regulation called 'homeostasis' and that stress is an important factor in upsetting the balance. Though less dramatic than cardiovascular breakdowns or systemic failures, sudden changes in mental states are known to produce specific physiological responses. A severe fright, for example, can turn a person's hair white, and excessive worry can turn it grey. Summing up recent research, E. M. Sternberg states that: ". . . even the greatest skeptic must now admit that a wealth of evidence exists to prove in the most stringent scientific terms that the functions of the mind do influence the health of the body." (*The Balance Within: The Science Connecting Health and Emotions (2001)* p.xvi)

Stigmata

The physiological impact of extreme religious devotion, manifesting as marks and lesions that imitate the wounds of the Passion - known as stigmata - provide an enduring testament to the power of emotional and mental imagery over the physical body. The term 'stigmata' actually originates in Saint Paul's Letter to the Galatians where he says: "from henceforth let no man trouble me, for I bear branded on my body the stigmata of Jesus." However, it is not generally believed that Saint Paul bore the marks of Christ's Passion on his own body but is alluding to the ill treatment he had received in the service of Christ.

The first person known to have borne the five wounds of the Passion was Saint Francis of Assisi (1181-1226). Two years before his passing, Francis was alone on Mt. Alverna where he had begun a fast of forty days in honour of the archangel Michael. While he was praying on the mountainside, he saw a seraph borne upon six radiant wings descending towards him. When the seraph had drawn near, Francis perceived the form of a crucified man with his hands and feet extended between the wings. Two of the wings rose above his head, two were spread as for the purpose of flying, and the remaining two veiled his body. After the vision had passed Francis noticed that his hands and feet bore exactly the same nail marks as he had seen on the form of the seraph; and on his right side was a wound flowing with blood as if pierced by a lance. The wounds on his hands and feet grew larger and began to flow with blood, and a 'nail' resembling one of iron was set in the midst of each wound. The heads of the nails were turned uppermost and were moveable in every direction but - according to Saint Clare of Assisi who saw Francis' body after his death - could not be withdrawn.

In spite of his wounds, Francis could still move his fingers and was able to use his hands and feet as before; but walking very far became difficult, and for this reason he always rode on horseback in his later travels. According to a fellow Brother, who accidentally touched the wound on Francis' side, it was deep and about three inches in length. Francis' habit was often stained with blood. The wounds never appeared to fester nor did Francis ever make use of any healing remedies. Pope Alexander IV and several cardinals bore witness to Francis' stigmata and, after his death, were seen by more than fifty Brothers of his own order, by Saint Clare and her Sisters, as well as by many pilgrims who were permitted to touch the wounds with their own hands. Those passing by Saint Francis's body witnessed "not the prints of the nails, but the nails themselves formed out of his flesh and retaining the blackness of iron." (*The Life of S. Francis (1904)*, by S. Bonaventure, ch. xiii.-xv.)

Following the death of Saint Francis, stigmatic phenomena began to appear in religious houses. Ida of

Louvain of Belgium (d.1300), a nun of the Cistercian convent of Roosendael, received stigmata resembling coloured circles on her hands and feet; on her side was an oblong-shaped wound. The stigmata were so painful she could not bear them to be touched. After imploring God to remove them, the marks disappeared but the pain persisted. Gertrude van der Oosten (d.1358), born at Voorburch in Holland of peasant parents, received stigmata during deep prayer and meditation. Though not a nun, nor bound by religious vows, her meditations on the Passion were so intense she received bleeding stigmata seven times a day at each of the canonical hours. Distressed at the multitudes that flocked to see her, she prayed that the stigmata might be withdrawn. The blood ceased to flow but the marks remained. Blessed Margareta Ebner (1291-1351) suffered the pains of stigmata, although the wounds were neither visible nor lasting. Saint Catherine Benincasa (1347-1380), better known as Saint Catherine of Siena, received stigmata at the age of 23 but, following a prayer that they might be made invisible, vanished immediately.

In later centuries, stigmatic phenomena were carefully investigated by Vatican authorities. One such case was La Bienheureuse Lucie de Narni (1476-1544). She first received stigmata in 1496 at the age of twenty when in Choir with her sister nuns. According to those present, she would fall into a state of ecstasy and 'observe' the events leading up to the crucifixion of Christ from the trial with Pontius Pilate to the crowning of thorns in the presence of Mary Magdalene and Saint John. At the same time, she would experience their pain and anguish. A committee of investigation was set up by Pope Alexander VI to determine whether the stigmata were naturally occurring wounds or the result of divine grace. The committee was composed of the Grand Inquisitor, the Bishop of Narni, the Prior of Viterbo, several canons, and the physician, Al Gentiari. Following a strict examination, they pronounced the stigmata to be of supernatural origin. However, rumours soon spread that Lucie was a fraud. Duke Hercules of Este - determined to clear up the matter once and for all - implored the Pope to send Lucie to him at Ferrara where he arranged for seven physicians, together with two bishops and the Archbishop of Milan to examine her. Although they confirmed the findings of the first commission this still did not settle the issue. The Pope therefore arranged for his own physician, Bernard de Recanati - one of the most famous physicians of his day - and two bishops to conduct a new investigation in Rome. To test the genuineness of the stigmata Bernard had a special glove made that could only be opened by breaking his personal seal. He fastened it on Lucie's hand where it remained for nine days. If the wound had been natural then, after nine days, it would have begun to suppurate. On removing the glove, Bernard found the wound to be as fresh and red as before. The third commission therefore concluded that the stigmata were genuine.

Saint Gemma Galgani (1878–1903) received all five stigmata before her twenty-third birthday. Her spiritual director and biographer, Father Germanus, leaves a detailed account of her life. When the stigmata began there appeared on the back of Gemma's hands, and in the middle of the palms, a reddish mark. A little later the skin itself broke and the lesion took on the appearance of a fresh wound. The wound in the palm of each hand was about one centimetre in diameter, and on the back of each hand about two millimetres in width and twenty millimetres in length.

Sometimes the laceration was superficial, at other times it was barely perceptible. As a rule, however, each wound was very deep and appeared to pass right through the hand. The wound in the palm of each hand became covered with a hard fleshy protuberance, slightly raised like the head of a nail. In the feet, the wounds were wider, the wound on the top of the left foot being bigger than that of the sole of the right foot. The aperture of the wound in the side was in the form of a crescent lying on its back with the two points turned upwards. Its length in a straight line was six centimetres and its width in the middle, three millimetres. Her clothes were soaked with the blood that flowed from it. After the Friday ecstasy, the blood stopped flowing and the wounds began to heal. By the following Sunday at the latest only a white mark remained which, five days later, would begin to bleed again and then heal.

Monsignor Moreschini, Archbishop of Camerino, gives the following account of Gemma's stigmata: "When it was Vespers time she withdrew quite alone to say her usual prayers before the crucifix. In a few minutes she was in full ecstasy. I entered, and with my own eyes beheld her totally transfigured so that she looked like an angel, although torn by terrible pain. From her face, head and hands there flowed fresh blood, and I suppose it was the same all over her body. That flow of blood lasted for about half an hour, but did not reach the ground, because it dried quickly while flowing." (http://www.stgemmagalgani.com)

Gemma's stigmata, which first appeared in June 1899, stopped in 1901 following a prayer by her for their removal. In spite of her extreme religious devotion, Gemma was initially scorned by the Catholic hierarchy - she claimed that she had spoken with her guardian angel, Jesus, the Virgin

Mary and other saints. However, following a thorough investigation into Gemma's religious life, her spiritual director, the Reverend Ruoppolo, personally became convinced of the authenticity of her mystical experiences. In early 1903, Gemma was diagnosed with tuberculosis and from that moment her health began to deteriorate. According to a nurse who attended Gemma during the last months of her life, there occurred extraordinary mystical phenomena. She states: "We have cared for a good many sick people, but we have never seen anything like this." Following a thorough investigation, Gemma was beatified in 1933 and canonized in 1940. (*The Life of St. Gemma Galgani (2009)* by Germanus.)

Saint Pio of Pietrelcina (1887-1968), born of peasant farmers in the southern Italian region of Campania, is one of the first priests known to have received the stigmata of the Passion. Although he suffered from a number of debilitating illnesses, which required hospitalisation and major surgery, he lived to the ripe old age of 81. Like many saints before him, Padre Pio had decided from a very early age to devote himself entirely to God and become a member of a religious order. As a child it is said he would inflict penances on himself such as using a stone as a pillow and sleeping on the stone floor. Much later, he would teach that the love of God is inseparable from suffering and that through suffering the soul reaches God.

During his novitiate period from 1903 to 1904, Padre Pio had many visions and throughout his priesthood was the subject of frequent 'demonic' attacks. In a series of letters to his spiritual directors he provides a detailed account of his mystical experiences. He states that the Devil attacked him both physically and spiritually and would use all manner of tricks and deceits to torment him, appearing in the guise of people he loved or trusted or as an 'angel of light', as 'Christ Crucified, as a young friend of the friars, as the Spiritual Father or as the Provincial Father; as Pope Pius X, a Guardian Angel, as St. Francis and as Our Lady.' He learnt to distinguish the reality from the imposture by carefully analysing the feelings they produced in him. In a letter to Padre Agostino, dated 18th January, 1912, he states: "The Devil does not want to lose this battle. He takes on many forms. For several days now, he has appeared with his brothers who are armed with batons and pieces of iron. One of the difficulties is that they appear in many disguises. There were several times when they threw me out of my bed and dragged me out of my bedroom. I am patient, however, and I know Jesus, Our Lady, my Guardian Angel, St. Joseph and St. Francis are always with me."

Padre Pio received his first stigmata in 1911. In a letter to his spiritual advisor, Padre Benedetto, he states: " . . last night something happened which I can neither explain nor understand. In the middle of the palms of my hands a red mark appeared, about the size of a penny, accompanied by acute pain in the middle of the red marks. The pain was more pronounced in the middle of the left hand, so much so that I can still feel it. Also under my feet I can feel some pain." In 1915 Padre Pio reports that he found the outwards signs of the stigmata so humiliating that he prayed for their removal but did not wish to be released from the pain. The visible signs then disappeared but the pain remained. He also reports that he experienced the pain of the 'crown of thorns' and the scourging.

In 1918, while the First World War was still being fought, Padre Pio offered himself to God as a victim to end the war and, according to Pio, Christ appeared to him and pierced his side. Following this experience, an actual wound appeared in his side. In another letter to Padre Benedetto he describes what is known as the 'transverberation experience': "While I was hearing the boys' confessions on the evening of the 5th August I was suddenly terrorized by the sight of a celestial person who presented himself to my mind's eye. He had in his hand a sort of weapon like a very long sharp-pointed steel blade which seemed to emit fire. At the very instant that I saw all this, I saw that person hurl the weapon into my soul with all his might. I cried out with difficulty and felt I was dying. I asked the boy to leave because I felt ill and no longer had the strength to continue. This agony lasted uninterruptedly until the morning of the 7th. I cannot tell you how much I suffered during this period of anguish. Even my entrails were torn and ruptured by the weapon, and nothing was spared. From that day on I have been mortally wounded. I feel in the depths of my soul a wound that is always open and which causes me continual agony." However, his pains eventually subsided but the figure who had delivered the agonising blow – believed by Pio to be the wounded Christ - reappeared while he was at prayer in the choir loft in the Church of Our Lady of Grace. This time Pio experienced a religious ecstasy and afterwards received the five wounds of Christ's passion. According to Pio, "the pain was so intense that I began to feel as if I were dying on the cross." However, the stigmata were to remain with him for the next fifty years. In addition to stigmatization, Pio is said to have possessed a number of supernormal abilities such as bilocation, healing powers, and the ability to 'read' souls.

Like Gemma Galgani before him, Pio was initially rejected by the Catholic hierarchy and efforts were made to transfer him to another locality; however all attempts failed in the face of strong local opposition. Investigations by contemporary theologians into Padre Pio's ministry produced a number of critical reports but had no lasting effect. Fourteen years after his passing, a thorough investigation was carried out by Vatican officials and in 1990 Padre Pio was declared a 'Servant of God.' In 1997 he was declared 'venerable' and in 1999 he was 'blessed.' In 2002, he was canonized. (From the *Catholic Web Services*.)

One of the most celebrated stigmatists of the twentieth century was the Catholic mystic Therese Neumann (1898-1962) of Konnersreuth. A member of the Third Order of St. Francis she suffered a series of debilitating ailments that confined her to her bed for long periods of time. Having suffered paralysis and loss of vision following a fall in her uncle's barn – she was attempting to put out a fire – she became bed-ridden and plagued with bedsores. However, on 29th April 1923 - the day of beautification of Therese of Lisieux - her sight was miraculously restored, and on 17th May 1925, when Therese of Lisieux was canonized, her paralysis and bed sores were completely cured.

On 5th March 1926, the first Friday of Lent, Therese Neumann had a vision of Jesus at Mount Olivet with three Disciples, and on the same day, a wound appeared just above her heart. On 12th March, she had another vision of Jesus at Mount Olivet along with a vision of the crowning of thorns. Following these visions, the wound above her heart reappeared, and on 26th March following a vision of Jesus bearing the cross, the wound appeared once again along with a wound on her hand that flowed with blood. On Good Friday she 'saw' the entire Passion and, shortly afterwards, wounds pouring with blood appeared on her hands and feet; at the same time, blood seemed to flow from her eyes. On Easter Sunday she had a vision of Christ's resurrection and, for several consecutive Fridays afterwards, suffered the Passion in her own body; this happened on Good Friday every year. By 5th November 1926, she had nine wounds on her head – the 'crown of thorns' - as well as wounds on her back and on her shoulders corresponding to the scourging. According to a number of sources close to Therese these wounds never healed or became infected and were present on her body at death. (*Life and Death of Therese Neumann, Mystic and Stigmatist (1987),* by Albert Vogl.)

Therese Neumann is also known for her ability to abstain from food or drink for indefinite periods of time (*inedia*) and for her ability to speak in ancient tongues (*xenoglossia*). From 1922 until her death in 1962, she is said to have consumed nothing solid apart from a consecrated rice-flour wafer once every morning at six o'clock, and from 1926 onwards, no fluids. In July 1927 a physician and four Franciscan nurses observed Therese twenty-four hours a day for two weeks. They confirmed that she consumed nothing apart from her daily consecrated Host and had suffered no ill effects, loss of weight, or dehydration. During her Friday visions, Therese would utter phrases which scholars identified as ancient Aramaic, Hebrew and Greek. With permission from her bishop, Therese underwent a number of scientific investigations and no instances of fraud were detected. Fritz Gerlick, editor of a Protestant German newspaper, went to Konnersreuth to "expose the Catholic fraud," but ended up accepting the phenomena as genuine.

The yogi Paramahansa Yogananda tells of a conversation he had with Therese Neumann in 1935 at the home of one

Professor Wurz, in the small village of Eichstatt eighty miles from Konnersreuth. The following extract is from *Autobiography of a Yogi (1946)*:

> "Don't you eat anything?" (I wanted to hear the answer from her own lips.)
>
> "No, except a consecrated rice-flour wafer, once every morning at six o'clock."
>
> "How large is the wafer?"
>
> "It is paper-thin, the size of a small coin." She added, "I take it for sacramental reasons; if it is unconsecrated, I am unable to swallow it."
>
> "Certainly you could not have lived on that, for twelve whole years?"
>
> "I live by God's light." (How simple her reply, how Einsteinian!)
>
> "I see you realize that energy flows to your body from the ether, sun, and air."
>
> A swift smile broke over her face. "I am so happy to know you understand how I live."
>
> "Your sacred life is a daily demonstration of the truth uttered by Christ: 'Man shall not live by bread alone, but by every word that proceedeth out of the mouth of God.'"
>
> (Again she showed joy at my explanation.)
>
> "It is indeed so. One of the reasons I am here on earth today is to prove that man can live by God's invisible light, and not by food only."
>
> "Can you teach others how to live without food?"
> (She appeared a trifle shocked.)
>
> "I cannot do that; God does not wish it."

Yogananda relates: "As my gaze fell on her strong, graceful hands, Therese showed me a little, square, freshly healed wound on each of her palms. On the back of each hand, she pointed out a smaller, crescent-shaped wound, freshly healed. Each wound went straight through the hand. The sight brought to my mind distinct recollection of the large square iron nails with crescent-tipped ends, still used in the Orient, but which I do not recall having seen in the West."

Professor Wurz, who accompanied Therese and Yogananda on their trips round Germany, remarks on Therese's ability to go without food: "Several of us, including Therese, often travel for days on sight-seeing trips throughout Germany. It is a striking contrast - while we have three meals a day, Therese eats nothing. She remains as fresh as a rose, untouched by the fatigue which the trips cause us. As we grow hungry and hunt for wayside inns, she laughs merrily."

The day after his first visit to Therese, Yogananda learns from Therese's brother, Ferdinand, that she "has the power, through prayer, of working out on her own body the ailments of others;" and that her "abstinence from food dates from a time when she prayed that the throat disease of a young man of her parish, then preparing to enter holy orders, be transferred to her own throat."

On departing, Yogananda is graciously invited by Therese to attend her next trance session at Konnersreuth. When Yogananda's arrives at her home the following Friday, he finds a "line of about twenty visitors" waiting to see her. Yogananda enters Therese's chamber and records his astonishment: "Blood flowed thinly and continuously in an inch-wide stream from Therese's lower eyelids. Her gaze was focused upward on the spiritual eye within the central forehead. The cloth wrapped around her head was drenched in blood from the stigmata wounds of the crown of thorns. The white garment was redly splotched over her heart from the wound in her side at the spot where Christ's body, long ages ago, had suffered the final indignity of the soldier's spear-thrust. Therese's hands were extended in a gesture maternal, pleading; her face wore an expression both tortured and divine. She appeared thinner, changed in many subtle as well as outward ways. Murmuring words in a foreign tongue, she spoke with slightly quivering lips to persons visible before her inner sight. As I was in attunement with her, I began to see the scenes of her vision. She was watching Jesus as he carried the cross amidst the jeering multitude. Suddenly she lifted her head in consternation: the Lord had fallen under the cruel weight. The vision disappeared. In the exhaustion of fervid pity, Therese sank heavily against her pillow."

Ethel Chapman, like Therese Neumann, had stigmata *and* visions of the crucifixion. A patient at a British care home in the 1970's, Ethel suffered from multiple sclerosis and was paralyzed from the waist down. A geriatrician attached to the home found no evidence in Ethel of depression, neurosis, psychosis or any indications of skin complaints such as *dermatitis artifacta* caused by excessive scratching. In conversation Ethel was friendly, articulate and mentally sound. A number of witnesses testified to seeing fresh blood on Ethel's hands and feet on Good Friday. In a BBC radio interview in 1973, she described her visions and sensations as follows: "I remember saying quite plainly 'Oh Lord, please show me in some way you're there.' In the early hours of the morning, I thought it was a dream. I felt myself being drawn on to the Cross. I felt the pain of the nails through my hands and through my feet. I could see the crowds, all jeering and shouting and, of course, it was in a foreign language, I don't know what they were saying. I felt myself all the agony and all the pain that the Lord Himself went through. . . ." Like many other stigmatists before her Ethel considered the stigmata a burden and prayed regularly for the healing of the sick. (www. parapsychologyinfo.com)

Stigmatic Type Phenomena

Re-enactments in the physical body of previous injuries - what have been called *somatic* injuries - is proof of the body's ability to mirror the thoughts, images and emotions of the inner self. J. E. Lifschutz records the case of a girl who, when she was 13 years old, was scratched down her back by her father leaving three long scars. When she left home at the age of 17 and was told that her father planned to visit her, the scars - though healed for four years - bled and did so each time her father announced his intention to visit. (See *American Journal of Psychiatry (1957)*, 114, pp. 527-531*)*. In a similar case, R. L. Moody records how a woman, who as a child had suffered repeated physical abuse at the hands of her father, bled and became bruised and swollen when she relived the trauma. According to Moody: "traverse red streaks" appeared on the palms of her hands where her father had whipped them plus a clearly defined pattern of bruising that matched the shape of a stick. (See *Lancet (1948)*, 1, p.964).

Helen Flanders Dunbar, pioneer of psychosomatic medicine, records the cases of two people who were able to produce wheals (i.e. urticaria) on various parts of their bodies through an act of will. According to Dunbar: "the boundary between the self and the outer world, the skin . . . seems to be peculiarly susceptible to suggestion." (*Emotions and Bodily Changes (1953)*, p. 647).

Psychic researcher Hereward Carrington records the case in which a 'stigmatic bruise' is received by one Louise W. Kops. She reports that: "On the afternoon of May 1st, 1916, I was standing in my hall, preparing to go out, when I saw the knob of my front door slowly turn. I stood still, awaiting developments; gradually the door opened, and I saw a man standing there. As he saw me he quickly closed the door and ran down the stairs and out of the front door. (He was, in fact, a burglar, trying to enter my apartment.) The interesting thing about the experience is this: that during the moment he was standing in the door, although he did not actually move, I had the distinct impression that he had run up the hall and grasped me firmly by the arm, and I was for the moment petrified with fear. The next day my arm was black and blue in the exact spot where I thought he had pinched me; and this mark continued for several days until it finally wore off. I told Dr. Carrington about this two days later when he called, and showed him the mark. (Signed) Louise W. Kops." (*Psychic Oddities (1952)* p. 28)

Somatic injuries by proxy i.e. the appearance of injuries relating to *another person*, bear a striking resemblance to the stigmatic wounds of the Passion. D. H. Tuke records how the lips and mouth of a woman became "suddenly enormously swollen" when she thought a child might cut itself on the lips with a sharp knife. (See *Illustrations of the Influence of the Mind upon the Body in Health and Disease (1884)* p.287). A similar case, recorded by Tuke, involved a woman who, on observing a child's ankle being nearly crushed by an iron gate, suddenly felt a sharp pain in her own ankle and limped home with much difficulty. On arrival she "found a circle around the ankle, as if it had been painted with red-current juice." The following day her ankle was inflamed and kept her in bed for several days. (*Op cit* p.285). A similar case was reported by French-Swiss psychoanalyst, Charles Baudouin. A woman who had seen her child narrowly escape being guillotined by a heavy sliding door suddenly developed "a raised erythematous" circle around her neck which matched the exact place where her child would have been struck by the door (See *Suggestion and Autosuggestion (1920)*, p.100).

In the production of stigmatic wounds, suggestion by another person can be at least as powerful as self-suggestion. In *The Riddle of Konnersreuth in the Light of New Cases of Stigmatization (1933)*, German psychiatrist, Alfred Lechler records how he was able to induce bleeding stigmata in a 29-year old peasant woman merely by hypnotising her. Elizabeth K., - who proved to be an ideal subject for Lechler's experiments - had earlier seen a film about the crucifixion of Christ and proceeded to experience pains in her hands and feet. After Lecher had placed Elizabeth in a hypnotic trance, he suggested that she had been pierced by nails in the manner of the crucifixion. After a number of sessions, she displayed the markings of the 'crown of thorns' on her forehead, an inflamed shoulder corresponding to the place where Christ had carried the cross, and bloody tears similar to those shed by Therese Neumann (see above). Elizabeth said she could feel the nails being driven into her hands and feet. According to author I. Wilson: "The significance of all this is profound. Effectively, Lechler can be said to have established more authoritatively than anyone before or since that spontaneous bleedings of the type attributed to stigmatics during the last seven centuries really do happen, and that these can be demonstrated under properly controlled conditions. He can also be said to have established that a fundamental key to the phenomena is hypnosis, and that the stigmatic, even without having been formally hypnotized seems to be, during his or her bleedings, in a mental and physical state effectively indistinguishable from hypnosis." (*The Bleeding Mind (1989)*, p. 97).

This view is echoed by T. X. Barber who states that "the royal road to solving the mind-body problem involves unravelling the mystery of hypnosis." (See *Imagination and Healing (1984)* by A. A. Sheikh (ed.), pp.69-127). Sir William Barrett FRS (see Chapter 1) was able to induce painful burns in a subject by the power of hypnotic suggestion alone, a result that has been repeated on numerous occasions.

In 1917, J. A. Hadfield records how a patient - who was undergoing hypnotherapy for the treatment of shell shock - suddenly withdrew his arm at the touch of a finger when it was suggested to him that he had been touched by a red hot iron rod; it was further suggested that a blister would form. About a half hour after the patient had regained normal consciousness a blister duly appeared. However, since the patient had not been kept under continuous observation, the results were considered inconclusive. The experiment was then repeated but, this time, with a bandage securely applied. Six hours later, after the bandage had been removed, a blister appeared which steadily increased in size and produced a large quantity of fluid. In a third more stringent experiment the patient's arm was bandaged as before and the patient kept under continuous observation for twenty four hours. Once again, a blister appeared and developed in much the same way. (See *Lancet (1917)*, 2, pp.678-679).

Psychiatrist, M. Ullman suggested to a soldier that a piece of shrapnel had struck his hand. Within an hour a blister began to form and soon became a second degree burn. (See *American Journal of Psychiatry (1947)*, 103, pp.828-830). J. M. Bellis suggested to a patient that she was relaxing on a sunny beach; upon wakening, the patient's face, shoulders and upper arms were sunburnt. (See *American Journal of Clinical Hypnosis (1966)*, 8, pp.310-312). To those who insist that all such burns are really self-inflicted, similar results have been obtained under 'immediate observation' proving that the phenomenon is really genuine and not the product of miss-observation or manipulation. Indeed, according to psychiatrist Helen Dunbar, "it is now possible to regulate the occurrence of a blister to the minute. It shoots up before the eyes of the physician at the regulated time, becoming fully developed within five minutes." (See *Emotions and Bodily Changes (1953)* p. 603)

As one might expect, if hypnosis can be used to induce burns and blisters in otherwise healthy people, it can also be used to alleviate them. Dunbar records the case of a physician who had suffered X-ray burns for 14 years with scars so severe that amputation was recommended. Following a four week course of hypnotherapy, the burns were healed within a year. According to psychiatrist Dabney M. Ewin "a burned patient who has accepted the suggestion that his wounded area is "cool and comfortable" is easy to treat, optimistic, and heals rapidly." (See *Hypnosis at its*

Bicentennial (1978), F. H. Frankel & H. S. Zamansky (Eds)). Ewin states that: "Hypnosis is of inestimable value in the care of burns from the onset to discharge. In the first 2 to 4 hours postburn it diminishes the inflammatory response that causes progression of a burn from first to second degree, or from second to third degree. Later, it is helpful for resisting pain, and especially effective for control of pain in those patients with the most excruciating procedural pain. Infection is minimized, suppressed appetite can be restored, and body image and active participation in rehabilitation are enhanced." *(The International Handbook of Clinical Hypnosis (2001),19*)

Hypnosis has also been used in the treatment of haemophilia. Russian mystic and advisor to the Romanovs, Grigori Yefimovich Rasputin allegedly used hypnotic methods to relieve the bleeding of royal haemophiliac, Alexei Nikolayevich Romanov. In addition to haemophilia, hypnosis has also been used in the treatment of warts, burns, eczema, and allergic skin reactions to a variety of substances such as house dust, pollen, and tuberculin. More recently, A. A. Mason reported that lesions caused by skin allergies were reduced in eight out of nine patients following hypnosis. (See *Acta Allergologica (1960),* supplement 7, pp.332-338).

* * *

Related to the above phenomena are 'telepathic impressions.' In *Reincarnation and Biology (1997)* Dr. Ian Stevenson records the case of a woman who, for no apparent reason, had the distinct impression she had received a sharp blow on the mouth. She later discovered that, at about the same time, her husband had been struck on the mouth by the tiller in his sailing boat. Another case, involved twin sisters, one in Pennsylvania and the other, heavily pregnant, in Italy. The sister in Pennsylvania suddenly developed severe pains in her chest and upper abdomen experiencing shortness of breath. It was later discovered that the sister in Italy had gone into premature labour with serious complications involving a blood clot in the lungs. A similar phenomenon occurs in spiritualism when a medium experiences the transition pains of a recently departed personality, especially if the transition had been violent or traumatic. If the person had suffocated, the medium will experience the pains of suffocation; if the person had died of lung cancer, the medium might cough uncontrollably.

Telepathic impressions of the maternal kind - what Stevenson calls 'maternal impressions' - have been recorded in a variety of cultural and historical settings. Such phenomena - generally dismissed by medical orthodoxy as superstition - occur when a pregnant woman, having witnessed a frightful scene or experienced a powerful emotion, gives birth to a baby with corresponding birthmarks or birth defects. Sixteenth century physician, Cornelius Gemma tells how a child was born with his forehead running with blood after his father had made threatening gestures towards his pregnant wife with a sword aimed at her forehead. In *A Treatise of Diseases,* Flemish physiologist, Jan Baptist van Helmont (1580-1644) records how a Mechlin woman went into premature labour after she saw a soldier's hand cut off in an argument. Her child was born with only one hand and a bleeding arm. In Antwerp a pregnant woman gave birth to a baby with one arm struck off and bleeding after she saw a soldier's arm cut off. In a third case a pregnant woman witnessed the beheading of thirteen men and then gave birth to a baby with "the neck bloody as their bodies she beheld that had their heads cut off." A systematic study of maternal impressions was carried out by a paediatrician in the United States from 1853 to 1886. In a review of 90 cases he found that 77% showed "quite a close correspondence" between the mother's impression and her baby's defect. (Stevenson (1997)).

Thus, it is a well-attested fact that a child Y can be born with marks or defects correlating with the wounds of another person X. But, there is no reason to suppose that the pregnancy need be contemporaneous with the wounding. Indeed, the wounding - and possibly the death - of X might occur *prior* to the conception of Y, the critical factor being the impact on the mother's psyche, not the timing of the wounds. The point is that if X had died before the conception of Y, it cannot automatically be inferred that Y is a reincarnation of X.

Such instances notwithstanding, cases do exist in which the mother has had *no* sighting of X but the child Y has, nevertheless, been born with marks or defects resembling X's wounds. Although the great majority of cases can be explained as chance correlations, this explanation becomes implausible when the child Y - usually at the age of about 2 or 3 - also possesses memories of X's life on Earth and can describe exactly how X's wounds were received. If Y's memories of X have not been obtained through normal channels (such as family or neighbourhood gossip) or paranormal ones (such as telepathic rapport between family members) and there has been no collusion, it follows that Y's memories must have been obtained *directly* from X as telepathic impressions, and Y's birthmarks and defects *indirectly* from X (via Y's mother) as maternal impressions.

Thus, when a discarnate personality X attaches itself to the body of a pregnant woman - perhaps attempting to reincarnate - the impact can be twofold.

One such case is that of Sunita Khandelwal reported by Stevenson in *Reincarnation and Biology(1997)*. We shall summarize the main facts here and refer the reader to Stevenson's monograph for a fuller discussion (Page references refer to the synoptic version: *Where Reincarnation and Biology Intersect (1997))*. Sunita Khandelwal, the daughter of a grain merchant, was born in the town of Laxmangarh in India on 19th September, 1969. Sunita was born with a large, heavily pigmented mark on the right side of her head which bled for about three days following her birth. At the age of about 2 she started to talk about a previous life in Kota where she had parents and two brothers; her family had "a silver shop and a safe." She also said she was pushed by her "cousin" and fell down "from a small height" landing directly on to her head. She had been 8 years old at the time. She would then point to the birthmark on her head to indicate where she had been struck.

As she grew older Sunita would occasionally refuse to eat unless she was taken to Kota. By the age of five she had remembered more details of the previous life such as the place in Kota, where the silver shop was located, and the family's caste. At the prompting of friends, Sunita is taken to Kota and, on arrival, the group search for a silversmith who once had a daughter but had died from a fall. As it turns out, shop owner Prabhu Dayal Maheshwari had an 8 year old daughter, Sakuntala who had died after falling from a balcony; she had been playing with her cousin. Sakuntala, had fallen over a railing and landed "head first on the concrete floor below." She was rushed to hospital but died a few hours later. The hospital record showed that death was caused by a "head injury." Stevenson notes that "Sunita had made 25 statements of which 21 were correct for Sakuntala, 2 incorrect an 2 unverified." Whilst in Kota, "she made 4 more statements, 3 correct and 1 unverified." Stevenson stresses that while each statement in isolation from the others could be dismissed as applying to other families, collectively they cannot. Accordingly: "After a careful appraisal of the facts, I became convinced that Sakuntala was the correct child and that she alone had had a life and death with details that matched Sunita's statements." (p.53).

Chapter 8
Suggestive of What?

In Chapter 2 we noted that 'past life' memories retrieved under hypnotic regression are more likely to be the result of suggestions by the hypnotherapist than recollections of a previous life. In the hypnotic state a subject is unusually responsive to commands and instructions and while in this state may be induced to recall images and sensations that ordinarily remain below the threshold of normal consciousness. Long forgotten memories of childhood, for instance, may be recalled in vivid detail. If a subject is instructed to go back to a 'previous life' then, in such a high state of suggestibility, he will do his best to cooperate. In the process he will recover long forgotten memories of books read, films seen, television programs watched, conversations overheard, and so on. These recovered 'memories' – which in practice will be a blend of fact and fiction - may then form the basis of an elaborate confabulation in which the subject reports memories of a previous live.

Although much reincarnation research has been dismissed on these grounds alone, there exist a substantial number of cases that appear to be genuine instances of past life recall. While reincarnation researchers would maintain that these cases either prove or are at least suggestive of reincarnation, we shall prove that they are not. Since reincarnation research is founded on the premise that reincarnation is a fact, bias is inevitably introduced into the handling, interpretation and presentation of the evidence. That this is true is amply demonstrated in the work of psychiatrist and reincarnation researcher Dr. Ian Stevenson who - as we shall see in the case of Jasbir, taken from his book, *Twenty Cases Suggestive of Reincarnation (1974)* - misrepresents the facts in order to support his prior belief in reincarnation. This case is of critical importance in the evaluation of Stevenson's work and of reincarnationism in general because, while it can easily be proven *not* to be a case of reincarnation, Stevenson nevertheless presents it as a case *suggestive* of one. This innate bias towards the reincarnation hypothesis means that reincarnation researchers are not the best people to assess the meaning and significance of their work. As further evidence of bias, we recall Helen Wambach's proclamation: "I don't believe in reincarnation — I know it!"

Many - though not all - of the cases investigated by Stevenson are authenticated instances of past life recall and were so chosen because they were investigated by Stevenson himself. All cases involve children covering diverse parts of the globe and include seven cases from India, three cases from Ceylon, two cases from Brazil, seven cases among the Tlingit Indians of South-eastern Alaska, and one case from the Lebanon. In the introduction to his study, Stevenson explains how errors of reporting, recording and translation inevitably creep into investigations of this kind and what efforts were made to minimise them. Indeed, by far the greatest part of each case study is devoted to establishing the authenticity of each subject's memories and the veracity of witness testimony; this Stevenson does by personally interviewing all people concerned, most notably the subject Y and his family, the family of the person X (now deceased), friends and neighbours of Y and X cross-checking their statements and satisfying himself that Y's memories of a previous life do in fact correspond to the individual X. He then considers the possibility that Y's memories might have been obtained through normal channels - such as village gossip or communication between the families – or through super-normal channels – such as ESP or telepathic rapport between family members and, in the case of birthmarks or birth defects, through genetic transmission. By carefully eliminating all of these possibilities, Stevenson establishes the authenticity of Y's memories, that is to say, he proves beyond reasonable doubt that Y's memories are a genuine instance of past life recall and do in fact correspond to the deceased individual X. Stevenson concludes that these cases are suggestive of reincarnation. The following case proves that they are not.

The Case of Jasbir

This case concerns a three and half year old boy Jasbir who, in the spring of 1954, is suffering from smallpox. His father, Sri Girdhari Lal Jat of Rasulpur, District Muzaffarnarger, Utter Pradesh, mistakenly believes his son to have died from the disease and calls upon his brother and other men of the village to assist him in the burial. However, the hour is late and the burial is postponed till the following morning. A few hours later Sri Girdhari Lal Jat notices a stirring in the body of his son who then revives and makes a complete recovery. However, a number of days pass before Jasbir can speak again and several weeks before he can express himself coherently. At this point he shows "a remarkable transformation of behaviour." Jasbir, who has not yet reached his fourth birthday, states that he is the son of Shankar of Vehedi (a village some twenty miles from Rasulpur) and that he wishes to go there. He also refuses to eat food at the Jat household on the grounds that he belongs to the higher Brahmin caste. To quote Stevenson: "This obstinate refusal to eat would surely have led to a second death if a kindly Brahmin lady, a neighbour of Sri Girdhari Lal Jat, had not undertaken to cook food for Jasbir in the Brahmin manner." (Note that what began as an *apparent* death has now become an *actual* death.) After a while, however, Jasbir's family - unbeknownst to Jasbir – begin to provide him with food not prepared by a Brahmin and when Jasbir discovers this fact - coupled with pressure from his family - he gradually abandons his strict Brahmin dietary habits and eats regularly with his family. Jasbir's resistance lasts for under two years, though he continues to think of himself as a member of the superior Brahmin caste. Jasbir also tells of a life in the village of Vehedi describing how, during a wedding procession from one village to another, he had eaten some poisoned sweets given to him by a man who owed him money. He had become giddy, had fallen off the chariot he was riding and suffered a fatal head injury.

Although Jasbir's father tries to suppress knowledge of Jasbir's troubling behaviour, news gradually reaches the local Brahmin community. Srimati Shyamo, a Brahmin native of Rasulpur who had married Sri Ravi Dutt Sukla of the village of Vehedi, occasionally returned to Rasulpur and on one such trip in 1957 is recognized by Jasbir as his "aunt." She reports this incident to her husband's family and to members of the Tyagi family in Vehedi and it transpires that Jasbir's memories closely correspond to the life and death of a young man of twenty-two known as Sobha Ram, son of Sri Shankar Lal Tyagi of Vehedi. Sobha Ram had died in May 1954 in a chariot accident in the manner described by Jasbir.

At this point the reincarnationist interpretation of events runs into difficulties because Sobha Ram was alive during the first three-and-a-half years of Jasbir's existence. Jasbir, who was born at the end of 1950, was also living and breathing at the same time as Sobha Ram in 1951, 1952, 1953 until the death of Sobha Ram in May 1954. While Jasbir was living in the village of Rasulpur, Sobha Ram was living in the village of Vehedi just twenty miles away. We shall dwell upon this fact because its significance seems to have completely escaped Dr. Stevenson; he merely describes it as "unusual." According to the doctrine of reincarnation when someone dies their physical body perishes and - if they have residual karma - will incarnate in a new body. Now, to each living person there corresponds one and only one inner self and since Jasbir and Sobha Ram were living and breathing at the same time there must have been two unique spiritual entities expressing themselves in physical form. Now, Hindus believe in the immortality of the self - whether incarnate or discarnate - so that the death of Sobha Ram did not deprive him of his spiritual identity; he continued to exist even after he had discarded his physical body. This means that if two immortal spiritual identities were present *before* the death of Sobha Ram, then two immortal spiritual identities were present *after* the death of Sobha Ram - the latter's physical death being an unimportant detail. Since Jasbir was alive at the time of Sobha Ram's death the latter could not have reincarnated in the body of Jasbir unless, of course, Jasbir had really died and the soul of Sobha Ram had somehow reanimated the pox-ridden corpse of Jasbir.

Now, while such beliefs are common in the voodoo religions of the Caribbean they are not found in the doctrine of reincarnation; nevertheless, this is the route Stevenson chooses to follow. Why? - because, in the doctrine of reincarnation, an individual does *not* reincarnate in the body of a living person; therefore, Stevenson needs the body of a dead one. A careful reading of Stevenson's text will show that while he employs the phrase "presumed death" to describe what happened on the night in question he uses it synonymously with the phrase "actual death." In other words, although Jasbir did not really die - he made a complete recovery - the reader is invited to assume that he did. Thus, Stevenson transforms a living body into a dead one. This is confirmed in a follow-up discussion he has with Jasbir in 1971 in which the latter firmly believes he is a reincarnation of the superior caste individual, Sobha Ram. To quote Stevenson: "I asked Jasbir if he had any idea as to what happened to the mind or personality that had occupied the body of Jasbir before it apparently died of smallpox and before that body had seemingly been taken over by the mind of Sobha Ram." Now, if Jasbir had only *apparently* died of smallpox then, of course, nothing would have happened to the mind or personality occupying the body of Jasbir; it would have continued to remain in the body of Jasbir. Yet Stevenson uses the phrase "had occupied the body of Jasbir" to suggest that Jasbir had *actually* died when, in fact, he had not. (We have already seen in Chapter 2 how Stevenson misuses tense to provide a quick philosophical route to the doctrine of reincarnation.) In reply to the question he puts to Jasbir about what happened to the mind or personality that had occupied the body of Jasbir, Stevenson simply says: "He did not know and nor do I" – and leaves the matter there, thus creating a problem where none previously existed.

It should be stressed that in the investigation of Jasbir's family background, Stevenson carefully eliminates all mundane and super-mundane explanations which might have accounted for Jasbir's memories of Sobha Ram. Since Jasbir could not have been a reincarnation of Sobha Ram - they were contemporaries of one another and, in any case, Jasbir did not die - there can only be one possible explanation for Jasbir's memories and behaviour, namely, that Jasbir was obsessed by the spirit of Sobha Ram. The significance of this result cannot be over-emphasised because it proves beyond reasonable doubt that discarnate personalities exist and can impress the living with their thoughts, feelings and memories. But this is evident from Jasbir's dramatic change of personality following the death of Sobha Ram. When Jasbir recovered from smallpox, he talked like an adult. He then refuses to eat with his family and claims to be a member of the Brahmin class. He uses the *present tense* to proclaim himself the son of Shankar of Vehedi and shows a strong attachment to members of the Tyagi family. During a short stay with the Tyagis at the village of Vehedi, he shares the same cot as Baleshwar (the son of Sobha Ram), unusual for strangers, Stevenson notes, but appropriate for a father and son. Furthermore, when someone calls to take him back to Rasulpur he strongly resists. When in Rasulpur, Jasbir remains lonely and something of an outcast. During his visit to the Jats in 1961, Stevenson notes that Jasbir did not play with the other children, but stayed aloof and isolated. Three years later, in 1964, Jasbir is even more isolated and depressed. According to Stevenson: "His face lacked animation. Although on this occasion he talked more than in 1961, he did not seem particularly eager to do so and remained a bystander in our interviews."

Stevenson's pretence that Jasbir had died of smallpox and his insistence on a reincarnationist explanation of Jasbir's behaviour is further evidenced by his efforts to find a local child who is claiming to have been Jasbir in a previous life. To quote Stevenson: "I have from time to time enquired in the area where he lives about the existence of a child who has claimed that in a previous life he was one Jasbir of village Rasulpur who died of smallpox at the age of about three; but I have never found any trace of such a child." (Hardly surprising since Jasbir never died.)

The problem that Stevenson is attempting to solve is this: given that the Jat and Tyagi families were complete strangers to one another and that information could not have passed to the Jats through mundane or super-mundane channels how could Jasbir have acquired such detailed information about Sobha Ram's life? As we have seen, Stevenson's solution is uninspiring: he changes Jasbir's *apparent* death into an *actual* one so that Sobha Ram could - in the minds of readers - be thought to have reincarnated in the vacant body of Jasbir. Thus, Jasbir's memories will be one and the same as Sobha Ram's. But of course

Jasbir's memories are *not* one and the same as Sobha Ram's because Jasbir's memories relate only to Sobha Ram's final days and to his traumatic passing. Nowhere in his conversations with Stevenson does Jasbir report, for example, incidents in Sobha Ram's early life. Furthermore, by focussing entirely on the means by which Jasbir could have obtained his memories in mundane or super-mundane terms, Stevenson misses an essential point, namely, that even if he had identified such a means of communication, it would not have accounted for Jasbir's early emotional attachment to the Tyagi family. According to Stevenson: "Jasbir felt (and still felt in 1964) a strong attachment to the Tyagi family in Vehedi. He threatened to run away from Rasulpur to Vehedi on at least one occasion."

In the course of a conversation with Jasbir in 1961, Stevenson asks Jasbir to describe what happened between the death of Sobha Ram and his own recovery from smallpox with memories of Sobha Ram. According to Jasbir, after Sobha Ram had died he met a sadhu (holy man) in the discarnate state who advised him to "take cover" in the body of Jasbir, son of Girdhari Lal Jat. Assuming that the encounter was a real event and not a post-mortem fantasy, what did the sadhu mean by "taking cover"? From the context of the discussion it is evident that the sadhu was urging Sobha Ram to reincarnate in the body of Jasbir but that the decision was left to Sobha Ram. If so, we are presented with a problem because a member of the Brahmin caste would not willingly reincarnate in the corpse of a lower caste individual. On the other hand, if he were compelled to do so by karma then, in order to merit such a 'demotion', Sobha Ram must have been an evil person during his relatively short stay on Earth. However, no evidence of serious wrongdoing on the part of Sobha Ram can be found in any of the witness statements given to Dr. Stevenson; by all accounts he seemed to have been a fairly normal person. Furthermore, since Sobha Ram had risen to the Brahmin caste in his current incarnation he is unlikely to have been an evil person in his previous incarnation. (Hindus believe that evil people reincarnate as lower animals.) Clearly, there are inconsistencies in Jasbir's story. Following a later meeting with Jasbir, Stevenson admits that "by 1964, Jasbir's images of this period had become confused and he made several statements contradictory with other evidence."

When the reincarnation hypothesis is discarded, it is relatively easy to explain what happened. When Sobha Ram cast his physical body aside, Sobha Ram remained Sobha Ram retaining his beliefs, feelings, desires and memories. However, his strong belief in reincarnation coupled with his expectation of occupying a new body prevented him from passing on to a less material plane of existence. Instead, he hung around waiting for a body to become available, and this he believed he had found in the prostrate body of Jasbir. Whether or not he was urged to "take cover" by the discarnate sadhu – who, incidentally, was probably waiting to reincarnate himself but was repelled by the pox-ridden body of Jasbir – is unimportant because, either way, Sobha Ram became trapped in the magnetic aura of the living body of Jasbir impressing the latter with his thoughts, beliefs, feelings and memories.

In Chapter 1 we discussed the case of Jack T. recorded in Carl Wickland's, *Thirty Years Among the Dead*. Jack, who exhibited a dramatic change of personality at the age of five, was found to have been obsessed by the spirit of

Charlie Herrman - a man who had died some fifteen years before Jack had been born. A direct comparison with the case of Jasbir reveals striking similarities. The following statements have been arranged in pairs (a) and (b):

(a) Wickland: "Jack T. had been normal until the age of five, when he began to manifest precocious tendencies and acted strangely." (page 333).

(b) Stevenson: "Prior to that age [three-and-a-half] Jasbir seemed a normal child." (page 49). "When he recovered the ability to speak he showed a remarkable transformation of behaviour." (page 34).

(a) Wickland: "Formerly he had had the natural disposition of a child but began to fret about things ordinarily foreign to a child's mind and acted in many ways like an adult." (page 333).

(b) Stevenson: "He seems to have thought of himself very much as an adult and at first talked freely in Rasulpur of having a wife and children." (page 39).

(a) Wickland: "He was a boy of good appearance but talked constantly of being old, homely and ugly looking, and was so intractable that efforts at reprimand and correction proved of no avail." (page 333).

(b) Stevenson: "He would eat no food at the home of the Jats on the grounds that he belonged to a higher caste, being a Brahmin. This obstinate refusal to eat would surely have led to a second death . . ." (page 34).

(a) Wickland: "Someone had told him [Charlie Herrman] that after death individuals could reincarnate." (page 333).

(b) Stevenson: "Jasbir said that this sadhu had advised him to 'take cover' in the body of Jasbir who had ostensibly died." (page 51).

It should be noted that whilst Jack T. was released from the negative influence of Charlie Herrman through the timely intervention of the Wicklands, no such help was available to Jasbir. A further comparison of statements shows their relative educational attainments:

(a) Wickland: "In a letter written a few days later by the boy's mother we were informed that a remarkable change had occurred in the child. He remained normal and received excellent grades in school." (page 334)

(b) Stevenson: "During my visit in 1961 I easily noticed that he did not play with the other children, but stayed aloof and isolated . . . always wearing a sad expression on his quiet, pock-marked, but handsome face." (page 39). And again: "Jasbir, who was born at the end of 1950, had continued in school up to the tenth class. But he did not pass the work at that level and in 1969 he stopped school." (page 50).

If Jasbir's condition had been properly diagnosed and treated, his childhood would not have been so blighted. Admittedly, Jasbir's family had tried to weaken his ties with the Tyagis - there is ample evidence of this in Stevenson's study - but there is no evidence that they had tried to break his identification with Sobha Ram. By contrast, the Tyagi family positively encouraged it. According to Stevenson, the Tyagis regarded Jasbir as a full member of their family: they had consulted him about the marriage of Sobha Ram's son and he had attended the wedding ceremony. He had also been consulted about the marriage of one of Sobha Ram's daughters. Although Jasbir eventually shook off much of Sobha Ram's influence, he retained the latter's last memories and feelings of superiority.

In an interview with Stevenson in 1971, Jasbir denied that his memories of Sobha Ram had faded; he clearly remembered falling off the chariot on his return from the wedding he had attended (as Sobha Ram) at the village of Nirmana. He even mentioned the exact place where he fell off the chariot (Dabal Pathak), a detail Stevenson does not recall Jasbir having mentioned earlier. (Stevenson passes over this point but it illustrates how Jasbir used later information – probably acquired from the Tyagis – to fill out gaps in his memories of Sobha Ram.) Jasbir still believed he had been poisoned at the wedding ceremony by a man to whom Sobha Ram had loaned money. (It should be noted here that Jasbir had a strong financial incentive to remain the reincarnation of Sobha Ram because the man in question gave Jasbir 600 rupees!)

That Sobha Ram's influence had faded by 1971 is recorded by Stevenson himself: "I remarked in 1964 that he was noticeably depressed. But in 1971 he had developed into a smiling, self-confident young man." Stevenson, woefully (or wilfully) dismissive of the phenomenon of discarnate spirit influence says: "I think we should allow a large share of credit for this happy change to his parents [i.e. the Jats] who had done their best to adjust to a situation which must at times have been very difficult for them." Jasbir also says that his older brother, who had formerly been particularly hostile to his pretensions of superiority, fully accepted him in the family. Sobha Ram's weakening influence is also evidenced by Jasbir's willingness to marry a girl of the Jat caste.

In Chapter 2 we recorded claims that the possession of recondite, historical information by people under hypnotic regression provides convincing evidence of reincarnation.

In view of Jasbir's case, it is worth repeating the remarks of Victor Zammit concerning the work of Helen Wambach: "The recall by subjects of clothing, footwear, type of food and utensils used was better than that in popular history books. She found over and over again that her subjects knew better than most historians — when she went to obscure experts her subjects were invariably correct." He then repeats Wambach's conclusion: "I don't believe in reincarnation — I know it!" That this conclusion is unwarranted is proven by the case of Jasbir. He was not only impressed with thoughts, feelings and memories he was impressed with detailed information relating to Sobha Ram's life on Earth. Following his illness, when he regained his powers of speech, Jasbir gave the exact name of Sobha Ram's father, and said that he lived in the village of Vehedi; he employed language and terms of speech characteristic of the Brahmin caste, saying "haveli" not "hilli" for a house, and "kapra" not "latta" for clothes. According to Stevenson: "The higher levels of society, e.g. Brahmins, use the former words and the lower levels the latter ones." Jasbir also knew that Brahmins cooked their meals in metal vessels as opposed to earthen ones, and he also wore around his neck the sacred thread which is a distinctive habit of upper caste Hindus. When Sobha Ram's father and other members of his family had visited Rasulpur in 1954, Jasbir recognized them and "correctly placed them as to their relationships with Sobha Ram." A few weeks later, when Jasbir is taken to Vehedi, he is put down near the railway station and asked to lead the way to the Tyagi quadrangle; according to Stevenson: "This Jasbir did without difficulty." Jasbir remained in the village for some days and demonstrated to the Tyagi family and other villagers "a detailed knowledge of the Tyagi family and its affairs."

Stevenson provides a long list of items that Jasbir knew about Sobha Ram, his family, where he lived and his immediate environment. We itemise them as follows:

(1) Sobha Ram was the son of Shankar of Vehedi.
(2) Sobha Ram was a Brahmin.
(3) There was a culvert in the village where Sobha Ram had lived.
(4) There was a peepal tree in front of his house.
(5) The wife of Sobha Ram lived in the village of Molna.
(6) Sobha Ram had a chariot he used for weddings.
(7) Sobha Ram had died while returning from Nirmana in a marriage party.
(8) Sobha Ram was poisoned by sweets given to him at the party.
(9) Sobha Ram died after falling off a chariot.
(10) The chariot was pulled by two oxen, one white and one black.
(11) Jasbir recognised the road to Vehedi.
(12) Jasbir recognized Srimati Shyamo.
(13) Jasbir recognised Sri Ravi Dutt Sukla.
(14) Jasbir said there was a tamarind tree in front of a certain courtyard.
(15) Jasbir said the Tyagis had a well that was half in and half outside the house.
(16) Jasbir recognized Sri Shankar Lal Tyagi, giving his name correctly.
(17) Sobha Ram had a son, Baleshwar.
(18) Sobha Ram had an aunt, Ram Kali.
(19) Sobha Ram's mother was Sona.
(20) Sobha Ram had a sister, Kela.
(21) Sobha Ram had a mother-in-law, Kirpi.

(22) Jasbir recognized Sri Santoshi Tyagi.
(23) Sobha Ram's wife was called Sumantra.
(24) When Sobha Ram died he had ten rupees in a black coat in a box.
(25) Jasbir recognized Surajmal, younger brother of Sobha Ram.
(26) Jasbir recognized a certain neighbour of the Tyagis.
(27) Sobha Ram had been bitten by a certain dog.
(28) Jasbir recognized Prithvi, maternal uncle of Sobha Ram.
(29) Jasbir recognized the way from the railway station to the Tyagi quadrangle.
(30) Jasbir recognized Baleshwar, son of Sobha Ram.
(31) Jasbir recognized Sobha Ram's aunt.
(32) Jasbir remembered villagers of Vehedi with whom the Tyagis were not on good terms.
(33) Jasbir recognized Sri Ram Swaroop, brother-in-law of Sobha Ram.
(34) Jasbir recognized Sri Birbal Singh, younger cousin of Sobha Ram.
(35) Jasbir recognized Sri Mahendra Singh Tyagi, younger brother of Sobha Ram.
(36) Jasbir recognized fields belonging to the Tyagi family in Vehedi.
(37) Jasbir recognized Sri Raja Ram, grandfather of Sobha Ram.
(38) Sobha Ram's white ox had longs horns, his black ox short horns.

Helen Wambach and Victor Zammit maintain that the possession of such information - often impossible to obtain through normal channels - is convincing evidence for reincarnation.

Yet Jasbir - who was not a reincarnation of Sobha Ram - possessed more detailed information about a previous life than Helen Wambach's subjects.

The case of Jasbir alone is sufficient to refute all claims that recondite or hard-to-obtain information retrieved under hypnotic regression is evidence of reincarnation. That Jasbir's case has been woefully ignored by reincarnationists is a testament to their lack of objectivity. This means that all other cases of past life recall studied by Dr. Stevenson must be reinterpreted as instances of discarnate spirit influence.

The Case of Ravi Shankar

This case illustrates how, following a traumatic and violent death, the discarnate personality can impress an unborn child with marks similar to the wounds it may have received at the time of its passing. Although the mechanism is not fully understood, such marks are likely to have been impressed via the mother as maternal impressions. (see Chapter 7).

Ravi Shankar, the son of Sri Babu Ram Gupta, was born in July, 1951 in Kanauj, a city of Uttar Pradesh near Kanpur. At the age of about two or three, Ravi Shankar asks his parents for various toys he used to play with in another house (understood by them to relate to a previous life) and by the age of four, he is describing himself as the son of Jageshwar, a barber of Chhipatti District. He also claims to have been murdered by two people who had cut his throat; he names the murderers, the place of the crime, and other relevant details.

In January, 1951 the six-year old son of Sri Jageshwar Prasad, familiarly known as Munna, had been lured from his home by two neighbours, brutally murdered with a knife or razor cut to the throat and then decapitated. The motive for the murder appears to have been the desire to eliminate Jageshwar Prasad's principal heir to his estate so that one of the murderers (a relative) might inherit the property. Although the alleged murderers, Jawahar and Chaturi are detained by the police, they are eventually released through lack of evidence.

Some years later, Munna's father hears of a boy in another district of Kanauj who is describing himself as the son of Jageshwar, a barber of Chhipatti district, and that he had been murdered in a manner similar to his son. The boy had also named the murderers, the place of the crime, and had given other details of the life and death of Munna. Since Sri Jageshwar Prasad is still seeking justice for his murdered son, he visits the home of Ravi Shankar to obtain further information but is treated very brusquely by Sri Babu Ram Gupta who fears that his son might be taken away from him. However, some time later, Sri Jageshwar Prasad arranges to meet Ravi Shankar's mother who lets him to talk to the boy. According to Sri Jageshwar Prasad, Ravi Shankar recognised him as his father of a "previous life," gave details of a murder which corresponded closely to what he had been able to piece together about the murder of his own son Munna and other details. However, Sri Babu Ram Gupta opposes further discussion of the issue and beats his son severely to stop him talking about it. He then sends him away to live in another district for a year or more. Apparently, Ravi Shankar is not only afraid of his father, but is also afraid of the murderers of Munna. On one occasion when he happens to see one of them, he trembles with fear, or possibly anger, expressing a desire for revenge.

One of the most interesting features of this case is the presence of a "linear mark resembling closely the scar of a long knife wound" across Ravi Shankar's neck. His mother, who first noticed the mark when he was three to four months old, says he was born with it. Ravi Shankar believes the mark to be related to the murder of Munna at the hands of Jawahar and Chaturi. As Ravi Shankar grows, the mark slowly changes its position so that by 1964 it is "high on his neck just below his chin"; the mark has also faded. Also faded are his memories of Munna. By 1962, at the age of eleven, he has largely forgotten the events of the previous life. Indeed, he cannot remember either the statements he had made earlier about the life of Munna or even that he had made them at all. However, a vestige of fear remains within him because whenever he sees Jawahar or Chaturi, he feels apprehensive. By 1969, he has completely forgotten the memories of Munna, and by 1971 (Stevenson's last visit) the birthmark had shifted closer to his chin but is still visible.

The Case of Wijeratne

This case - one of three from Ceylon - illustrates how obsession by a discarnate personality can lead to mental illness. Wijeratne, the son of H. A. Tileratne Hami, was born in January, 1947 in the village of Uggalkaltota, Ceylon. Although he was born with a physical deformity of his right arm - a deformity his parents attributed to karma - we shall concentrate on his mental development. At the age of about two and a half, Wijeratne begins wandering around the house in a solitary fashion saying to himself that his arm is deformed because he had murdered his wife in a previous life. He also mentions other details - unknown to his mother at the time - about the commission of this crime, his arrest and execution. She informs her husband and it transpires that H. A. Tileratne Hami had a younger brother, Ratran Hami, who had been hanged in 1928 for the murder of his wife, Podi Menike. H. A. Tileratne tries to discourage Wijeratne from talking about these things but the boy persists and, to quote Stevenson, "often in a brooding solitary way to himself and at other times to persons who asked him about his arm." (Behaviour reminiscent of Jack T.'s in Chapter 1 in which "He constantly fretted over his looks, talking about his ugly and homely appearance and lay awake at night muttering strange things.") However, when Wijeratne reaches the age of five he stops talking spontaneously about the murder but will do so when questioned. By the age of fourteen, his memories of the previous life are much fainter, though he recalls the main events of the last year of Ratran Hami's life more vividly than the early events of his own life.

As part of the authentication process, Stevenson compares the witness testimony at the trial of Ratran Hami with the statements given by Wijeratne. Although Ratran Hami gives a spirited defence - it was an accident that occurred during a scuffle started by Podi Menike's family - the jury is not convinced and they pronounce a guilty verdict. According to Stevenson, Wijeratne's statements strongly support the jury's verdict, namely, that Ratran Hami had killed his wife intentionally. After the sentence is passed, H. A. Tileratne Hami visits his younger brother in prison and asks him how he feels. He says: "I am not afraid. I know that I will have to die. I am only worried about you." Later, Ratran Hami tells his brother that he "would return."

During an interview with Stevenson in the summer of 1961, Wijeratne expresses no remorse about the murder of Podi Menike. If he were confronted with a similar situation today, that is to say, if a legally wedded wife of his behaved in a similar fashion, he would probably murder her. Furthermore, he says: "I had an unbearable temper at that time. I did not think of the punishment I would get." However, he states that his temper in the present life is milder. As someone nurtured on the doctrine of reincarnation, Wijeratne regards his deformity as a fitting punishment for the murder of Podi Menike but, nevertheless, insists that Ratran Hami behaved correctly as an injured husband. As further evidence of his confusion, Wijeratne still regards his father as his older brother. During a later meeting with Stevenson in 1968, Wijeratne modifies his view about the murder of Podi Menike, not through any sense of guilt but because he feels that the transient satisfaction of revenge is not worth the penalty.

In 1969 Wijeratne becomes mentally ill and is admitted to a psychiatric hospital at Ratnapura where he stays for nearly a month. He is diagnosed as having 'hebephrenic schizophrenia' which, according to standard definitions, means that his emotional and behavioural responses had become strange and his facial responses inappropriate. (One of the three characteristics of possession noted in Chapter 6.) When he is discharged, he is placed on tranquilisers but remains moderately to severely ill for about five months. By 1970 he has stopped taking medication. When Stevenson interviews him in November of the same year, he finds him much improved though there are traces of abstractness in his manner and his contact with the environment is still slightly impaired. Stevenson notes that

Wijeratne had difficulty sleeping, that his thoughts had become confused and that he suffered from delusions, one of which was that he was a bird. At this point in the narrative, Stevenson suggests that Wijeratne may have been a bird in a previous life. Quoting from the text: "Both the presumptive precipitating factor of Wijeratne's psychosis and the delusion of being a bird during it *may* have some connection with his memories of a previous life." However, Stevenson modifies this view by redefining Wijeratne's delusion as a memory attributable to Ratran Hami who may himself have believed he was destined to reincarnate as a bird.

Needless to say, Wijeratne's education suffers as a result of his mental illness. In 1969, at the age of twenty-three, he was still at school - about four or five years behind his contemporaries - though still aiming for college. The problem was that he would prepare for the entrance examination, then not take it. On one occasion he was physically ill, but on at least two other occasions he failed to turn up without apparent reason. On a fourth occasion, his mental illness prevented him from taking the examination. When Wijeratne finally leaves school in 1970, he continues his studies, initially alone, then with the help of a private tutor. In December, 1970 and May 1971, he manages to pass the college entrance examinations to study scientific subjects at a university in Ceylon with a view to entering medical school. When Stevenson next meets Wijeratne in 1973, Wijeratne has learned to speak English well and they can communicate without an interpreter. Wijeratne is in good spirits and seems to have fully recovered; he has also had surgery to correct the deformity in his right hand. But, it seems that Stevenson is overly optimistic because, in the summer of 1973, Wijeratne suffers a relapse and is admitted to a psychiatric hospital in Ratnapura from which he is transferred to Angoda. However, after a short stay, he recovers sufficiently to return home - and there the story ends.

The Case of Marta Lorenz

The following case (from Brazil) shows how a young woman who died in tragic circumstances - actually a *de facto* suicide - can overwhelm a child to the point where the child's identification with the obsessing spirit is complete. The story begins with Maria Januaria de Oliveiro (known as Sinhá) (b. circa 1890, d. 1917), the daughter of a prosperous rancher in the southernmost state of Brazil. Sinhá lived with her father and often felt lonely in the relative isolation of his estate. In search of friends and companions, she would visit the village of Dom Feliciano twelve miles from her father's ranch. One such friend was Ida Lorenz - wife of the local school teacher F.V. Lorenz - about whom we shall hear more.

Sinhá did not marry, twice falling in love with men who were unacceptable to her father. One of the men, Florzinho, committed suicide and Sinhá fell into a state of depression. From then on she began to seriously neglect her health. She would deliberately expose herself to cold, damp weather, exhaust herself, and drink cold water in order to make herself unwell. She developed a severe infection of the larynx which soon spread to her lungs causing her voice to become permanently hoarse. Sinhá died of a severe pulmonary infection, probably tuberculosis, at the comparatively young age of twenty eight. On her death bed she confided to her friend, Ida Lorenz, that she wanted to die, that she had deliberately made herself ill, and vowed to return as her daughter. Sinhá also said: "when reborn and at an age when I can speak on the mystery of rebirth in the body of the little girl who will be your daughter, I shall relate many thing of my present life, and thus you will recognize the truth." Ten months after Sinhá's death, Ida Lorenz gave birth to a daughter, Marta. On Earth, a believer in reincarnation, Sinhá had died with the clear intention of returning to Earth as Ida Lorenz's daughter. With such an intention fixed in her mind, the discarnate Sinhá would have stayed close to Ida Lorenz waiting for the opportunity to be reborn. At the moment of Marta's birth, or sometime later, she would have 'attached' herself to the baby in the mistaken belief she had been reborn as the daughter of Ida Lorenz impressing Marta with her thoughts, feelings and memories leading Marta to believe she had been Sinhá in a previous incarnation.

When Marta is two and a half years old, she begins to talk about Sinhá, describing the farm where she lived and various events in her life. On one occasion, when Marta and her older sister, Lola, are returning home from doing the household washing at a nearby stream, Marta asks Lola to carry her on her back. Lola replies: "You can walk well enough, I don't need to carry you." Marta then says: "When I was big and you were small, I used to carry you often." Lola laughs at this but Marta continues: "At that time I did not live here; I lived far from here where there were many cows, oxen, and oranges and where also there were animals like goats, but they were not goats." (Apparently a reference to sheep).

At that time, her siblings knew nothing of Sinhá's vow to return because her parents had deliberately withheld the information "with a view to observing what would develop in Marta spontaneously." After her initial remarks, Marta goes on to make many more statements (estimated to be 120) about the life of Sinhá. She also recognises people who were known to Sinhá. Many of Marta's remarks are recorded by her father, Herr Lorenz, in German shorthand but, because they are incomprehensible to everyone except Herr Lorenz, they get thrown away. In 1946, however, he publishes an account of Marta's case from memory, unfortunately omitting many relevant facts known to other members of the family. According to Stevenson: "If it had been possible to publish the 120 items contemporaneously recorded by F.V. Lorenz, the case of Marta would perhaps have become the best witnessed and most thoroughly documented case suggestive of reincarnation ever observed in a child." Marta, like other cases of obsession, often asked to visit her old home but is not taken there until she is twelve years old.

Marta becomes so obsessed by the spirit of Sinhá, her personality begins to mirror Sinhá's. For example, both Sinhá and Marta were afraid of rain, and both had a fear of blood amounting to a phobia, and, like Sinhá, Marta often wished to die. Marta also worries about the fate of Florzinho, and as she grows older and has children of her own, becomes increasingly preoccupied with the notion that Florzinho might return as her own child and, unsurprisingly, convinces herself that one of her sons is, in fact, Florzinho reborn. Marta also exhibits mediumistic-type phenomena – what Stevenson calls "internal birthmarks." We recall that Sinhá had deliberately neglected herself by exposing herself to cold, damp weather contracting a severe infection of the larynx and a permanently hoarse voice resulting in her death from an acute pulmonary infection. Up to the age of ten, Marta suffered frequent attacks of laryngitis and remembers having a permanently hoarse voice until the age of nine. According to Marta, she had painful throat infections about once a month and, during these attacks, felt "large in her body and thought she was going to die."

In 1962, when Stevenson first meets Marta, she is married with children of her own. He notes that she has forgotten much of Sinhá's life but still recalls quite vividly Sinhá's last days and her tragic death from tuberculosis. When Stevenson meets her again in 1972 she has established a degree of an autonomy that was absent in her early years. She is able to make clear distinctions between her own life and Sinhá's and - even though Sinhá had died at the relatively young age of twenty eight - judges them to have been roughly equal in terms of happiness. The principal difference is that, while Sinhá's marriage plans were frustrated by her father resulting in the tragic death of Florzinho, Marta was able to marry and raise a family of her own. However, Marta experienced more than her fair share of grief with the sad and untimely deaths of her brothers, Paulo and Carlos. The case of Paulo – the subject of the next section - is of special importance because it demonstrates how belief in reincarnation can have disastrous consequences. As we shall see, Paulo believed he was the reincarnation of his own sister, Emilia.

The Case of Paulo Lorenz

We begin with Emilia, the second child of F. V. and Ida Lorenz, born in February 1902 some years after the death in infancy of their first child, Emilio. Throughout her short and unhappy life, Emilia seems to have been very uncomfortable with her gender, telling her brothers and sisters that if reincarnation were possible, she would return as a man. She also says she would never marry. As Emilia approaches the age of nineteen, she has several offers of marriage but rejects every one of them. She tries to commit suicide on a number of occasions and finally succeeds in October, 1921 after taking cyanide.

Sometime after Emilia's death, Frau Ida Lorenz attends a spiritualist meeting and receives a communication directly from a spirit claiming to be Emilia. The substance of the communication is that "Emilia" regretted committing suicide and that she wished to return to the family as a boy. According to Stevenson, Frau Lorenz is doubtful about "Emilia's" desire to change sex and Herr Lorenz is incredulous. At any rate, the spirit "Emilia" is persistent, saying on three separate occasions: "Mamma, take me as your son. I will become your son." About a year later, in 1922, Ida Lorenz gives birth to a son, who is named Paulo.

Up to the age of about five, Paulo's sexual orientation appears to be feminine. He insists on wearing girls' clothes, prefers to engage in activities normally associated with the fair sex, such as needlework and playing with dolls, and prefers to be with girls rather than boys. In light of Emilia's declared intention to return as a boy, Paulo's behaviour would seem, at this stage of his development, to be the result of overprotective mothering coupled with a *belief* that he might be Emilia reborn. If Ida Lorenz had believed that Paulo was a reincarnation of Emilia (as she believed Marta was a reincarnation of Sinhá) it would be hard for her to think of Paulo as exclusively Paulo and, indeed, might even relate to him as she had related to Emilia. In such circumstances mixed cues would be transmitted to Paulo suggesting, not only that he was a boy *and* a girl, but that he was both Paulo *and* Emilia. Such gender and identity confusion would certainly be reinforced by Ida Lorenz's determination - having lost Emilia once - not to lose her a second time. In other words, Paulo's behaviour could be a self-fulfilling prophecy brought on by Ida Lorenz's *belief* that Emilia had reincarnated as Paulo.

In his investigations of Emilia and Paulo, Stevenson learns of remarkable similarities in their skills and preferences. For example, both Emilia and Paulo had an unusual aptitude for sewing (not shared by other members of the family); they were both interested in travelling; both tried, but failed, to play the violin; they preferred their sister Lola to their other siblings; they had little interest in cooking, both had a habit of breaking off the corners of new loaves of bread, and so on.

Although much of this can be explained as a result of Paulo's strong identification with Emilia encouraged, no doubt, by a family who believed he was Emilia reborn, there is sufficient evidence to suggest he was, in fact, obsessed by the spirit of Emilia. Paulo (considered to be a late talker) uttered his first words at the age of three and a half. When seeing another child put something into its mouth, he says: "Take care. Children should not put things in their mouths. It may be dangerous." Bearing in mind that Emilia had taken her own life by swallowing cyanide, the remarks are highly suggestive and - like the other cases we have discussed in which children make adult-sounding remarks – strongly suggests the influence of a discarnate spirit. Not only does Paulo make comments beyond his years, he has memories of another domicile and can give accurate descriptions of its interior. He also remembers one Dona Elena who gave Emilia sewing lessons and recognises Emilia's sewing machine. He also recognises a dress that had once belonged to Emilia.

Paulo also demonstrates how a discarnate spirit can impart skills to its 'host'. Before he reaches the age of five he shows an aptitude for needlework that cannot be explained by Ida Lorenz's unconscious attempts to rekindle Emilia's old sewing skills. Interestingly, as he grows older his sewing skills decline (he falls behind his sisters) suggesting that the skills imparted by an obsessing spirit diminish in quality as the spirit's influence fades.

When Stevenson meets Paulo in 1962 he administers what is called "the modified drawing test" to identify homosexual and effeminate men, taken from L. Whitaker's paper in the *Journal of Consulting Psychology*. In this test, the subject is asked to draw three human figures. The choice of sex for the first and third figures is left open to the subject, but the second figure must be a person of the opposite sex. For both optional choices, Paulo draws female figures (they both had long hair) from which Stevenson concludes that Paulo showed a greater orientation towards the feminine gender than most men of his age (now thirty-nine years old). Unfortunately, that is the last time Stevenson sees Paulo because, during a follow-up visit to Brazil in 1967, he learns that Paulo committed suicide the year before. Paulo's relatives - especially his brother, Waldomiro - are so distraught they cannot enlighten Stevenson as to why Paulo should have taken his own life; he has to wait until 1972 to learn the full story.

Paulo had joined the Brazilian army but retired due to ill health - he had been suffering from pulmonary tuberculosis - but managed to find employment in the Department of Highways. Some years later he became politically active on the side of the Trabhalista (the Labour Party) and forged a close relationship with one of the party leaders. Following a coup in 1963, Brazil fell under the rule of a military dictatorship and his friend was forced to flee to Uruguay leaving Paulo unhappy and depressed. These feelings were exacerbated when Paulo himself was watched by agents of the regime. At some point he was arrested and beaten up during an "interrogation". From then on, he suffered a steady mental and emotional decline becoming obsessed with the idea that he was under permanent surveillance. In spite of his arrest and rough treatment at the hands of the military regime, Paulo's family believed his fears to be largely delusional. Several months before his death, he made a number of suicide threats and attempted to kill himself on at least one occasion. His brother, Waldomiro had planned to arrange medical treatment for Paulo but before these plans could materialise, Paulo killed himself by covering himself with inflammable liquid and setting himself on fire. He died ten hours later expressing no regret for his actions.

Clearly, Paulo had taken his own life while the balance of his mind was disturbed but one can only surmise as to the possible causes. It is abundantly clear, however, that he showed many of the classic signs associated with suicide: he gave prior indications about his intentions (he told his brother, Waldomiro that he was going to shoot himself); and he made one serious attempt to kill himself (he tried to inject air into is vein but was rescued in time.) Although, Paulo was under extreme mental and emotional stress he was never diagnosed as mentally ill and may have seen suicide as the only possible way of escaping his perceived difficulties. A possible clue, however, may be found in the life of Emilia who seems to have obsessed Paulo for much of his childhood and may have continued to do so - though not to the same extent - for much of his adulthood. Emilia, herself, had tried to commit suicide on several occasions: once by taking poison and once by trying to strangle herself. Significantly, one method she used was by injecting air into her vein - as did Paulo. This leads us to ask: did Emilia impart her suicidal tendencies to Paulo, or did he subsequently learn of them through his family relationships and try to emulate them? On the other hand, Paulo's strong identification with Emilia coupled with a knowledge of her suicide may have contributed to a frame of mind which regarded suicide as the most natural way to end his life. Whatever the reason, the moral of the tale is clear. If Paulo's condition had been properly recognised and treated in childhood he may have developed exclusively as Paulo and not as a hybrid version of two distinct entities created largely by the beliefs of his parents.

As we shall see in the following case study, the desire to return to the family group and the subsequent obsession of family members is a recurring theme among the Tlingit Indians of south-east Alaska - an ethnic group in which belief in reincarnation forms an important part of their religious and social behaviour. Although Stevenson chronicles seven cases in all, the majority of cases cannot be regarded as genuine instances of past life recall since the testimony of independent witnesses (such as non-family members) is almost entirely absent. Much of the testimony depends on the subject's own word and the corroboration of family members who themselves believe in reincarnation.

However, there is enough evidence to suggest that at least some of the cases are genuine instances of past life recall.

A Prophecy

The case we shall briefly outline is trumpeted by Stevenson as a convincing case of reincarnation because it involves a "prophecy" coupled with the "fulfilment" of tests. However, the story begins with William George, Sr., a Tlingit Indian of south-east Alaska and fisherman by occupation. William Senior, like many Tlingit Indians, believed in reincarnation, and towards the end of his life, expressed a strong desire to return. On a number of occasions he told his son (Reginald George) and daughter-in-law (Susan George) that: "If there is anything to this rebirth business, I will come back as your son." He also said: ". . . you will recognise me because I will have birthmarks like the ones I now have." William Senior had two prominent moles, each about a half inch in diameter, one on his left shoulder and one on his left forearm about two inches from the crease of his elbow. When William Senior reached the age of sixty he gave his son, Reginald a gold watch (a family heirloom) saying: "I'll come back. Keep this watch for me. I am going to be your son. If there is anything like that [i.e. rebirth], I'll do it." The watch was placed in a jewel box where it remained for five years.

A few weeks later, William Senior went missing from his boat. None of his crew knew what had happened and his body was never recovered. It was assumed he fell over board and was swept out to sea by heavy currents. Nine months later, Susan gives birth to a boy. On the baby's left shoulder and left forearm are pigmented moles similar to those possessed by William Senior but only half the size. This identification with his grandfather leads the parents to name the baby William. As William Junior develops, he seems to grow in the likeness of his grandfather. Not only does William Junior have a facial appearance similar to his grandfather, his likes and dislikes are much the same, his posture is similar, and he also walks with a gait characteristic of his grandfather. William Senior's gait was the result of an injury sustained to his right ankle in his youth; he limped with his right foot turned outward. According to his parents, William Junior also walked with his right foot turned outward, though Stevenson notes that the abnormality is only slight and would probably not be noticed unless one's attention is drawn to it.

To what extent William Junior's physical and behavioural similarities to his grandfather were due to heredity, positive encouragement from his parents, William Junior's own desire to emulate his grandfather, or the encouragement of close relatives will never be known. However, there is evidence to suggest that William Junior was obsessed by the spirit of his grandfather. For example, when William Junior was about four and a half years old, he saw his mother remove William Senior's gold watch from the jewellery box and, without prior prompting, said: "That's my watch!" This was the first time the watch had been taken out of the box in five years. Furthermore, like his grandfather, William Junior had a tendency to worry and fret and give cautionary advice to those around him. He showed a precocious knowledge of fishing and boats, the best places for fishing, and he had a natural aptitude for handling nets. He also referred to his great-aunt as "sister," which was William Senior's relationship to her, and to his uncles and aunts as his "sons" and "daughters." Interestingly, he expressed fatherly concern over the excessive drinking habits of two of his uncles. (Compare this with Jasbir's fatherly relationship with Baleshwar, the son of Sobha Ram.) In Chapter 6 we saw how a person's physical mannerisms change to reflect the disposition of a possessing spirit. William Junior's gait appears to be an instance of this phenomenon.

* * *

In all the cases reviewed, it is evident that Dr. Ian Stevenson has provided abundant evidence for human survival beyond bodily death. By carefully eliminating mundane and super mundane explanations, he has shown that, in a significant number of cases, the only reasonable explanation for a child's past life memories, with or without correlated birthmarks, is the influence of a discarnate personality. The importance of this cannot be overestimated because it supports the work of the early psychical researchers Frederick W. Myers, James Hyslop, William Crookes and others (see Chapters 5 and 6) who demonstrated in a number of scientific investigations that human personality survives the death of the physical body. That Stevenson's reincarnationist interpretation of the evidence is wrong is demonstrated by the case of Jasbir.

In the introduction to *Where Reincarnation and Biology Intersect (1997)* Stevenson briefly considers alternatives to the reincarnation hypothesis and casually dismisses the phenomenon of spirit intrusion by asking why possessing spirits should all withdraw their influence when children reach the ages of 5 to 8 - the age group in which children, on the basis of Stevenson's research, lose their memories of past lives. A more pertinent question - a question Stevenson fails to address - is how exactly does reincarnation account for the loss of memories between the ages of 5 and 8? To an educational psychologist there is no mystery. Between those ages (what is commonly termed middle childhood) a child attains a degree of personal autonomy and ego development which enables it to resist the intrusion of obsessing spirits and assert its own identity in much the same way that adolescents, between the ages of 13 and 16, assert their independence and resist the intrusion of their parents - two stages of development well understood in educational psychology. Indeed, under the hypothesis of obsession, the fading of past life memories between the ages of 5 and 8 is to be expected - not to be puzzled about. Stevenson might just as well ask why parents relax their control when adolescent children reach the ages of 13 to 16. The point is that the continued presence of an obsessing spirit is a stimulus to the child's memories. When the child resists, the spirit's influence weakens. When the spirit departs, the stimulus disappears and the impressed memories fade accordingly. Since the degree of resistance varies from one individual to another, the complete fading of memories is not universal. Indeed, some memories survive as memories of memories.

Stevenson also asserts that possessing spirits do not explain the existence of correlated birthmarks "unless we suppose that possession occurs before the child's birth." (p.11) In that case, Stevenson asks: "how does possession differ from reincarnation?" (It should be noted that Stevenson accepts that a possessing spirit can impress an unborn child with birthmarks - a fact he establishes over and over again in his monograph.) However, Stevenson's claim that the spirit's possession of the unborn child is the same as reincarnation is wrong on *three* counts. Firstly, the timing of the self's association with its physical expression - which in any case is meaningless from the self's point of view - is not subject to earthly definitions. If the self is associated with its physical expression at all stages *after* the child's birth then it is associated with its physical expression at all stages *before* the child's birth. An external spirit entity would, therefore, have no legitimate claim on a body already earmarked for incarnation; the spirit entity would, so to speak, be superfluous to requirements. Secondly, if having discarded its physical expression, the self - for whom time has no reality - reincarnated in the body of an unborn child, it would be incarnating in two bodies simultaneously - a clear violation of individuality. Thirdly, there is nothing in principle to distinguish the unborn child from the grownup child (i.e. the adult). From the self's point of view, a child's existence in or out of the womb is a minor detail, each marking a different stage in the physical expression of the self. Why should spirit intrusion be called 'reincarnation' at the prenatal stage and 'possession' at the postnatal stage? Indeed, the distinction is wholly arbitrary for if spirit intrusion could be called 'reincarnation' at an early stage it could just as easily be called 'reincarnation' at a later stage which would be absurd because the child and the possessing spirit would obviously be contemporaneous entities. Since time has no reality for the self, the possessing spirit and the child are, from the self's point of view, contemporaneous entities at *all* stages of the child's development. Stevenson's self-serving assumption that no spirit entity is associated with the unborn child other than the reincarnating one is an assumption without any foundation whatsoever.

The logical error in Stevenson's arguments is to confuse *ex ante* with *ex post* i.e. intentions with actualities. He supposes that a discarnate personality's *intention* to reincarnate in the body of a child - born or unborn - is synonymous with an *actual* reincarnation. This is evidenced by his conversion of Jasbir's apparent death into an actual death, and his conversion of Sobha Ram's intention to reincarnate into an actual reincarnation.

In conclusion, Stevenson may be criticised on a number of grounds. The examples cited below are illustrative rather than exhaustive.

(1) His research has no theoretical basis.

In Chapter 2 we analysed his philosophical justification for reincarnation and found it to be based on an erroneous view of *tense*. Instead of employing a coherent model of consciousness he draws on local beliefs and superstitions to buttress his explanations. The more people who subscribe to an idea, the more convinced Stevenson becomes of its reality.

(2) His research methodology is flawed.

When interviewing subjects, his questions are couched in the language of reincarnationism. This means that, by and large, he gets the results he wants. Although it might be argued that this is inevitable because his subjects already believe in reincarnation, it is fatal from an investigative point of view because the exercise becomes a self-fulfilling prophecy.

(3) He misleads with his sources.

In *Reincarnation: Field Studies and Theoretical Issues (1977)*, for example, he cites John McTaggart's *Human Immortality and Pre-Existence (1916)* as supporting the doctrine of reincarnation, but fails to mention McTaggart's better known paper *The Unreality of Time (1908)* (see Chapter 11) which is clearly incompatible with any doctrine based on the concept of real time. In fact, McTaggart's *Human Immortality and Pre-Existence* is consistent with pre-existence beyond the body.

(4) He misrepresents the facts to support his belief in reincarnation.

We saw in the case of Jasbir how Stevenson treats an *apparent* death synonymously with an *actual* one. Although Jasbir could *not* have been a reincarnation of Sobha Ram, Stevenson, nevertheless, presents it as a case suggestive of one. Moreover, in his discussion of the unborn child, spirit intrusion is arbitrarily called 'reincarnation.'

(5) He uses language in a misleading manner

We have already noted that he uses the term 'apparent' synonymously with 'actual,' but he also uses the term 'suggestive' synonymously with 'indicative,' and the term 'possession' synonymously with 'obsession.' Furthermore, he makes no distinction between *ex ante* and *ex post*, confusing intentions with actualities. In Chapter 2 we noted how he equates eternity with infinite time and discusses issues of immortality in the *past* tense - an obvious logical error since an eternal being is necessarily timeless.

(6) His dismissal of spirit intrusion is unwarranted

In particular, he fails to draw a distinction between possession and obsession, using the word 'possession' as a generic term for both. However, because Stevenson fails to distinguish between the two, he misses golden opportunities to probe the nature of the phenomena he is investigating. For example, a question he never puts to any subject is: "Looking back to when you were only 2 or 3 years old do you ever remember talking like an adult?" To the parents he might have asked: "Has your child ever suffered from *petit mal*?" (sudden impairments of consciousness). Indeed, any question that might suggest the presence of an obsessing or possessing spirit has been studiously avoided. Finally, he fails to mention the work of Dr. Carl Wickland and James Hyslop and the many researchers who have spent much of their lives demonstrating the reality of spirit influence. The fruitfulness of their approach has been demonstrated on numerous occasions.

PART 3
TIME & ETERNITY

Chapter 9
Newton's Universe

The law of cause and effect - often trumpeted as a fundamental truth applicable to everyone and everything - is a "truth" of fairly recent origin. It began with the writings of Galileo, Kepler and Descartes, reached its apotheosis in Newton and Laplace, then spread to every area beyond the physics of matter before collapsing as a fundamental principle of science with the arrival of quantum mechanics. To illustrate how modern physics has abandoned this fundamental "truth" we need only quote from Stephen Hawking's and Leonard Mlodinow's book, *The Grand Design (2010),* which postulates a universe that spontaneously created itself out of nothing: "Spontaneous creation is the reason there is something rather than nothing, why the universe exists, why we exist. It is not necessary to invoke God to light the blue touch paper and set the universe going." (p.180) In other words, there is no first cause; and if there is no first cause then, ultimately, everything else is without cause. This also follows from Proposition D, Chapter 3 which states that to an eternal being - such as the human self - all events are simultaneous. If all events are simultaneous then no event can be said to be the cause of any other event. This is not to say that from a *temporal* perspective different events cannot be linked to one another in causal relationships though, it should be said, such relationships are largely the product of social and cultural conventions. For example, if A pushes B over a cliff, we say that B was killed by A - not by gravity or by the rocks at the foot of the cliff.

Although causal law began with the aforementioned scientists, the foundations were laid when the Ptolemaic system of astronomy collapsed in favour of the heliocentric (sun-centred) models of Copernicus and Kepler. Claudius Ptolemaeus (90-168), known in English as Ptolemy, is best known for his astronomical treatise the *Almagest* (Mathematical Compilation), the only comprehensive treatise on astronomy to have survived from the ancient world. In the *Almagest*, Ptolemy provided a set of geometric models which could be used to construct tables of planetary motions - seven in all - and predict their future positions in the night sky. In his later work, *Planetary Hypotheses,* Ptolemy uses the epicycles of his model to compute the dimensions of the universe, estimating the Sun to be at an average distance of 1210 Earth radii and the radius of the sphere of the fixed stars at 20,000 Earth radii.

Although Ptolemy's model is called "geocentric," Ptolemy's Earth is not actually located at the centre of planetary motion (see fig. 1).

A model from the Almagest   Fig. 1

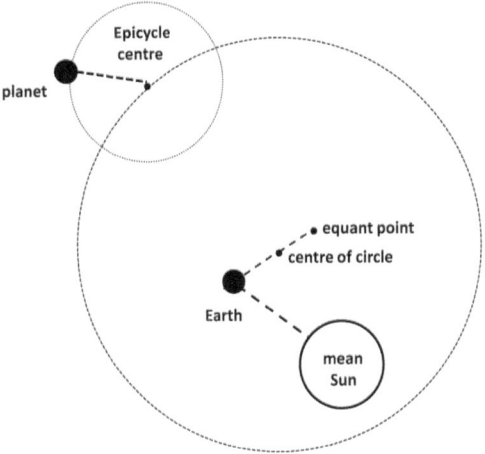

By placing the Earth some distance from the planet's orbital centre (believed to be the centre of a circle), with the equant point symmetrically placed on the opposite side, Ptolemy was able to account for the apparent uniform motion of planets as seen from the Earth. The purpose of the epicycle (a superimposed circle) is to account for the planet's occasional retrograde motion. The "mean Sun" locates an empty point in space marking the mean distance of the Sun from the Earth. Although Ptolemy's models provided reasonable approximations to the observed motion of the planets, planetary motion is in fact *elliptical*, as later described by Kepler in his Laws of Planetary Motion (see below).

Medieval Christian cosmology was firmly rooted in Ptolemaic astronomy. The Earth was at the hub of creation and bounded by the "ninth sphere" of stars beyond which lay the heavenly Empyrean. Christians identified the sphere of stars with the Biblical firmament and sometimes posited an invisible layer of water above the firmament to accord with Genesis. In this cosmology all was divided between Heaven, Earth and Hell, and everything and everyone had its proper place in the order of creation - God, man, angels and demons. Needless to say, the Temporal Power was ecclesiastical authority; to question the Ptolemaic scheme was not merely to challenge the prevailing orthodoxy, it was to challenge the power of the Holy Church. The major contemporary criticism of Ptolemy's system was that it violated the fundamental precept that all celestial motions should be circular or combinations of circular motions. Other critics complained that his system was *ad hoc* in the sense that he organised his model around the data and adjusted the model's parameters to get the best possible "fit." Nevertheless, in terms of astronomical predictions Ptolemy's models outperformed all other ancient systems of astronomy and were not improved upon even by Copernicus.

Nicolaus Copernicus (1473 - 1543), a man of German and Polish descent, was accomplished in a variety of disciplines and could, equally, be described as a mathematician, astronomer, physician, Catholic cleric, classical scholar and economist. He is generally considered to be the first astronomer to create a comprehensive "heliocentric" model of the universe, although his Greek predecessors also thought that the Sun was at the centre of planetary motion. His book, *De revolutionibus orbium coelestium* (On the Revolutions of the Celestial Spheres) published in 1543 just before his death, is often regarded as the starting point of modern astronomy. The change from the "geocentric" to the heliocentric cosmology is generally known as the Copernican Revolution, the first hint being published in manuscript form as a short treatise, called the *Commentariolus* (Brief Outline) setting out seven axioms of planetary motion. They are remarkably modern in outlook and laid the foundations of a broad view of the solar system that has largely survived unchanged to this day. We list them as follows:

(1) The heavenly bodies do not all move round the same centre
(2) The earth is not the centre of the universe, only of the moon's orbit and of terrestrial gravity.
(3) The sun is the centre of the planetary system and therefore of the universe.
(4) Compared to the distance of the fixed stars, the earth's distance from the sun is negligibly small.
(5) The apparent daily revolution of the firmament is due to the earth's rotation about its own axis.
(6) The apparent annual motion of the sun is due to the fact that the earth, like the other planets, revolves round the sun.
(7) The apparent 'stations and retrogressions' of the planets are due to the same causes

Contrary to popular belief, Copernicus did not create a heliocentric model of planetary motion in order to simplify the Ptolemaic system. He had two purposes: firstly, he was seeking conformity with the motions produced by Ptolemy's models, and secondly, he wanted planetary motions to be circular and uniform. This could be achieved by shifting the centre of planetary motion away from the Earth to an empty point in space which located the "mean

Sun" - rather than to the Sun itself. Therefore, the models of Copernicus are not strictly heliocentric but "heliostatic." Instead of a moving Sun, his models utilise the concept of a moving Earth. The first truly heliocentric model was not introduced until the publication of Kepler's *Treatise on Mars* in 1609.

As an exercise in astronomical system building, the work of Copernicus is not generally regarded as superior to the work of Ptolemy. Later research has shown that Copernicus's system did not produce more accurate results than Ptolemy's. The continued use of epicycles and the dependence on Ptolemy's data tend to weaken the claim that Copernicus's contribution to astronomy was revolutionary. In the *Commentariolus*, Copernicus concedes that Ptolemy's planetary models produce better numerical results but insisted, nevertheless, that the principle of uniform and circular celestial motion be obeyed. The move from the Ptolemaic to the Copernican system has been described as a move from instrumentalism to realism. Copernicus wanted to construct a model which, he believed, conformed to the "real" world in its essential details; he did not want any artifice that happened to agree with the data. In the Preface to the *De revolutionibus*, Copernicus wrote that "the astronomical tradition has inherited a monster" - a clear reference to the astronomy of Ptolemy. For more than half a century *De revolutionibus* attracted little attention from either professional astronomers or clerics. In fact the Copernican Revolution did not really begin until the appearance of Kepler and Galileo at the beginning of the seventeenth century.

Johannes Kepler (1571-1630), German mathematician and astronomer, is best known for his three Laws of

Planetary Motion derived from the remarkably accurate data of the Danish astronomer Tycho Brahe (1546 -1601). Kepler's laws are as follows:

Law of Ellipses (1609): *The orbit of each planet is an ellipse, with the sun located at one of its foci.*

Law of Equal Areas (1609): *A line drawn between the sun and the planet sweeps out equal areas in equal times as the planet orbits the sun.*

Harmonic Law (1618): *The square of the sidereal period of a planet is directly proportional to the cube of the major semi-axis of the planet's orbit.*

In fig. 2, the Laws shows that a planet moves fastest when closest to the Sun and slowest when furthest from the Sun.

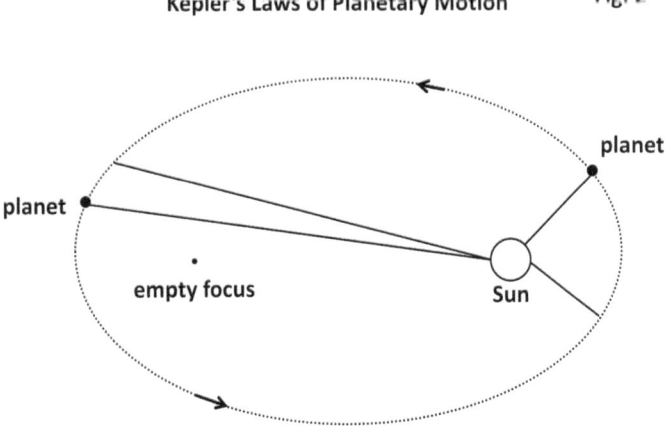

Kepler's Laws of Planetary Motion — Fig. 2

This enables us to understand what Ptolemy must have observed when viewing the night sky. Suppose an observer is located at the empty focus. When the planet is furthest from the Sun (i.e. closest to the observer) the planet is moving through space more slowly, but this fact is disguised by its proximity to the observer. When the planet is closest to the Sun (i.e. furthest from the observer) the planet is moving more quickly, but this fact is disguised because of its remoteness from the observer. Consequently, the planet appears to be moving round the sky with almost uniform angular velocity. The empty focus in Kepler's model corresponds to Ptolemy's equant. Kepler's agreement with Copernicus was first announced in his book *Mysterium Cosmographicum (1597)* (The Cosmographic Mystery), a work that is considered to be the first public expression of support for the Copernican system of astronomy. In the book's introduction Kepler is unequivocal, describing the system as "an inexhaustible treasure of truly divine insight into the wonderful order of the world and all bodies therein." However, Kepler had influential friends and managed to avoid the wrath of the Church; not so for Galileo.

Galileo steps in

Galileo Galilei (1564-1642), Italian physicist, astronomer, and philosopher, has been described as the midwife of modern science. To comprehend his work and achievements it is necessary to look at the world through the eyes of Aristotle, the creator of a paradigm that had dominated the world of thought for nearly two thousand years. Employing powerful arguments, Aristotle created an *a priori* physics based largely on appearances and commonsense observations. For example, a force was needed to keep an object in motion, even at constant speed; all earthbound objects eventually came to rest unless acted upon by a force; and heavy objects fell faster than lighter ones. In the heavens, perfection reigned and circular motion was maintained without need of any forces whatsoever. At a superficial level, these things are actually observed. Planets *do* appear to move in circular orbits, and – due to friction - physical objects *do* require forces to keep them moving at constant speed. For example, a force is needed to move a crate along the ground at a constant speed to overcome the force of friction between the ground and the crate; and a lump of lead reaches the ground faster than a sheet of paper due to the differential effects of air resistance. For Aristotle appearances were deceiving; if he had been aware of all the subtle effects of friction and air resistance and carried out precise and controlled experiments, he may well have formulated laws akin to Newton's, and the history of the world may have been very different.

One of the most important laws of physics, the so-called law of inertia, commonly attributed to Galileo, was actually formulated by René Descartes (1596–1650). According to the law of inertia, material bodies have a natural tendency to persist in their state of motion in a straight line. This is the basis of Newton's first law of motion. Strangely enough Descartes came to this conclusion, not by experiment, but by pure reason. Galileo, on the other hand carried out precise and controlled experiments with pendulums, freely falling objects, and masses sliding down inclined planes. Making brilliant generalisations, he came close to formulating the first two laws of motion now associated with Newton. Galileo's experiments with moving bodies led him to the famous conclusion that, if the effects of air resistance could be removed, all objects would fall with equal speed.

In the celestial sphere, Galileo was a provocative and controversial advocate of the Copernican system of astronomy, and it was this advocacy that brought him into conflict with the Catholic Church. The events leading up to Galileo's trial in 1633 are outlined in Arthur Koestler's book *The Sleepwalkers (1959)* and are only summarized here. Galileo's letters and replies can be found in the aforementioned work.

In 1613, Galileo's relationship with the Catholic Church began to deteriorate following the publication of a letter to the Dowager Duchess Christina of Lorraine. In this letter Galileo attempts to silence all theological objections to Copernicus: "Some years ago, as Your Serene Highness well knows, I discovered in the heavens many things that had not been seen before our own age. The novelty of these things, as well as some consequences which followed from them in contradiction to the physical notions commonly held among academic philosophers, stirred up against me no small number of professors - as if I had placed these things in the sky with my own hands in order to upset nature and overturn the sciences.... Showing a greater fondness for their own opinions than for truth, they sought to deny and disprove the new things which, if they had cared to look for themselves, their own senses would have demonstrated to them. To this end they hurled various charges and published numerous writings filled with vain arguments, and they made the grave mistake of sprinkling these with passages taken from places in the Bible which they had failed to understand properly."

Galileo continues the argument that the Bible should not be taken literally because it is expressed in a language suitable for ordinary people who are "rude and unlearned."

The letter continues: "Hence, in expounding the Bible, if one were always to confine oneself to the unadorned grammatical meaning, one might fall into error. Not only contradictions and propositions far from true might thus be made to appear in the Bible, but even grave heresies and follies. Thus it would be necessary to assign to God feet, hands, and eyes, as well as corporeal and human affections, such as anger, repentance, hatred, and sometimes even the forgetting of things past and ignorance to come. ... For that reason it appears that nothing physical which sense-experience sets before our eyes, or which necessary demonstrations prove to us, ought to be called in question (much less condemned) upon the testimony of biblical passages which may have some different meaning beneath their words."

In the following passage Galileo attempts to shift the burden of proof on to the Church. In other words it is the responsibility of the Church to prove that the Copernican system is *false*: "Now if truly demonstrated physical conclusions need not be subordinated to biblical passages, but the latter must rather be shown not to interfere with the former, then before a physical proposition is condemned it must be shown to be not rigorously demonstrated - and this is to be done not by those who hold the proposition to be true, but by those who judge it to be false. This seems very reasonable and natural, for those who believe an argument to be false may much more easily find the fallacies in it than men who consider it to be true and conclusive..."

Almost two years passed before the Church reacted. On a visit to Pisa in December 1615, a Father Lorini attended a sermon delivered by the rabble-rousing Dominican monk, Father Thommaso Caccini. In his sermon, Caccini attacks all mathematicians (i.e. astronomers) in general and Copernicus in particular. Afterwards, Father Lorini is shown a copy of Galileo's letter to the Dowager Duchess Christina. Lorini is deeply shocked and sends the following letter to Cardinal Sfondrati: "All our Fathers of this devout convent of St Mark are of opinion that the letter contains many propositions which appear to be suspicious or presumptuous as when it asserts that the language of Holy Scripture does not mean what it seems to mean; that in discussions about natural phenomena the last and lowest place ought to be given to the authority of the sacred text; that its commentators have very often erred in their interpretation; that the Holy Scriptures should not be mixed up with anything except matters of religion. . ... Ever mindful of our vow to be the 'black and white hounds' of the Holy Office...when I saw that they [the 'Galileists'] expounded the Holy Scriptures according to their private lights and in a manner different from that of the common interpretation of the Fathers of the Church; that they strove to defend an opinion which appeared to be quite contrary to the sacred text; that they spoke in slighting terms of the ancient Fathers and of St Thomas Aquinas; that they were treading underfoot the entire philosophy of Aristotle which has been of such service to Scholastic theology; and, in fine, that to show their cleverness they were airing and scattering broadcast in our steadfast Catholic city a thousand saucy and irreverent surmises; when, I say, I became aware of all this, I made up my mind to acquaint your Lordship with the state of affairs, that you in your holy zeal for the Faith may, in conjunction with your most illustrious colleagues, provide such remedies as will appear advisable. ... I, who hold that those who call themselves Galileists are orderly men and good Christians all, but a little overwise and conceited in their opinions, declare that I am actuated by nothing in this business but zeal for the sacred cause."

Galileo's letter is forwarded to the Consultor of the Holy Office for examination. However, it is felt that the views expressed are not objectionable and, in any case, do not depart from Catholic doctrine. The case is dismissed. One month later, Caccini appears before the Holy Office to give his own testimony. A number of witnesses are called, and the contradictions in their evidence convince the Inquisitors that Caccini's charges of heresy and subversion are a fabrication. The case is dismissed again, and the matter dropped; but the controversy continues. Three months later, Galileo is cleared of all charges, and Copernicus's book *De revolutionibus orbium coelestium* is placed on the Index, 'pending corrections.'

About this time, Cardinal Robert Bellarmine, the most respected theologian in Christendom, a general of the Jesuit Order and Consultor of the Holy Office becomes involved. Cardinal Bellarmine assures Galileo that he has nothing to fear from the Church so long as he confines himself to physics and mathematics and refrains from theological interpretations of the scriptures. In a long and authoritative letter to a Father Foscarini (who wrote a book in favour of the Copernican system), but also addressed to Galileo, Cardinal Bellarmine shifts the burden of proof back onto Galileo and the advocates of Copernicus. In other words: it is Galileo's responsibility to prove that the system is *correct*. Galileo is given only two alternatives:

(1) Supply the required proof that the Copernican system is correct.
(2) Agree that the Copernican system should be treated only as a hypothesis.

Since Galileo is not prepared to supply proofs, and the alternative would expose him to ridicule, he rejects the compromise formula. Galileo's answer to Cardinal Bellarmine is contained in a letter to a Cardinal Dini: "To me, the surest and swiftest way to prove that the position of Copernicus is not contrary to Scripture would be to give a host of proofs that it is true and that the contrary cannot be maintained at all; thus, since no truths can contradict one another, this and the Bible must be perfectly harmonious. But how can I do this, and not be merely wasting my time, when those Peripatetics who must be convinced show themselves incapable of following even the simplest and easiest of arguments?"

Against the advice of friends, Galileo travels to Rome, and continues to be controversial; in fact, he does everything possible to provoke a showdown with the Church. Up until now, he had desisted from supplying proofs - as requested by Cardinal Bellarmine; but now, in Rome, he is armed with his final "proof" – the 'theory of tides'. Some years earlier, Kepler had provided the correct explanation in the *Astronomia nova;* the tides were due to the moon's influence. But this theory had been rejected by Galileo as astrological nonsense. Galileo had declared, incorrectly, that the tides were due to the combined orbital and diurnal motions of the Earth. However, Galileo's "final proof" was presented to Pope Paul V on Galileo's behalf by a young Cardinal Orsini; but the Pope was not impressed.

On 23rd February, 1616, the Qualifiers ruled against Galileo.

Two propositions had been submitted to them:

(1) The Sun is the centre of the world and wholly immovable of local motion.

(2) The Earth is not the centre of the world, also with a diurnal motion.

The unanimous ruling was that the first proposition was: "....foolish and absurd, philosophically and formally heretical inasmuch as it expressly contradicts the doctrine of Holy Scripture in many passages, both in their literal meaning and according to the general interpretation of the Fathers and Doctors." The second proposition was also rejected and declared: "....to deserve the like censure in philosophy, and as regards theological truth, to be at least erroneous in faith."

However, the Qualifiers were overruled under pressure from the more progressive Cardinals, and on 5th March the General Congregation of the Index issued a more moderate decree in which the word 'heresy' is absent, but which suspended the work by Copernicus, *De revolutionibus orbium coelestium* but condemned and prohibited the book by Father Foscarini (referred to above).

However, the following Injunction was issued (prior to the decree) but not served: "Thursday, 25th February 1616. The Lord Cardinal Mellini notified the Reverend Fathers, the Assessor, and the Commissary of the Holy Office that the censure passed by the theologians upon the propositions of Galileo - to the effect that the Sun is the centre of the world and immovable from its place, and that the Earth moves, and also with a diurnal motion - had been reported; and His Holiness has directed the Lord Cardinal Bellarmine to summon before him the said Galileo and admonish him to abandon the said opinion; and *in case of his refusal to obey,* that the Commissary is to enjoin on him, before a notary and witnesses, a command to abstain altogether from teaching or defending this opinion and doctrine and even from discussing it; and, if he do not acquiesce therein, that he is to be imprisoned." This injunction remained on the Inquisition files until Galileo's trial in 1633.

Galileo published nothing for seven years following the decree, but gained a powerful ally in Maffeo Barberini, who became Pope Urban VIII in 1623. Urban and Galileo agreed that the system of Copernicus was only a hypothesis and not reality. However, Galileo continued to make enemies - especially among the leading members of the Jesuit Order, such as Father Firenzuola and Father Grassi, by his attacks on their works. As a result, the Jesuit Order as a body became hostile to Galileo. Unfortunately for Galileo, Father Firenzuola was the Inquisition's Commissary General at Galileo's trial.

Galileo's next work, *Dialogue on the Great World*, completed in 1623 and to be published in Rome, is thinly disguised propaganda for Copernicus and Galileo's own theory of tides. However, he gained an *imprimatur* for the book on condition he censors out the parts supporting Copernicus. This Galileo does not do and, consequently, loses the support of his chief ally, Pope Urban. According to the Jesuits, by publishing the *Dialogues* uncensored, Galileo:

(1) Broke the agreement with pope Urban to treat Copernicus's system as only a hypothesis.
(2) Obtained the *imprimatur* on false pretenses.
(3) Based one of the simple-minded characters of the *Dialogue* on Pope Urban.

The latter charge was untrue, but it persisted in the mind of Urban. However, it was enough to initiate proceedings against Galileo. A special commission was appointed to investigate the affair and found that:

(1) Galileo had transgressed orders in deviating from the hypothetical treatment of Copernicus, and maintaining absolutely the Earth's motion.
(2) He had erroneously ascribed the phenomena of the tides to it.
(3) He had been deceitfully silent about the command laid upon him by the Holy Office in 1616 "to relinquish altogether the said opinion...nor henceforth to hold, teach, or defend it in anyway whatsoever verbally or in writing."

The report was handed over to the Inquisition which issued its summons in October, 1632. However, Galileo's interrogations did not take place until the following year. According to inquisitorial custom, the charges are not communicated to the accused. At the trial, Galileo was, merely, asked if he knew why he had been summoned. The Injunction of 1616 was, then, read out to him, and all the various complaints against Galileo were repeated.

Galileo, who had reached the age of seventy and was in poor health, recanted. He, falsely, claimed to have written the *Dialogue* in refutation of Copernicus, and made a number of contrite statements in his defence. But the Inquisition was not impressed. It found against Galileo on two counts:

(1) Of having contravened Cardinal Bellarmine's admonition and the injunction of 1616, and having "artfully and cunningly extorted the licence to print by not notifying the censor of the command imposed upon him."

(2) Having rendered himself "vehemently suspect of heresy, namely, of having believed and held the doctrine which is contrary to sacred Scripture that the sun is the centre of the world".

The following sentence is issued: "... Sanctissimus decreed that said Galileo is to be interrogated as to his intention [in writing the Dialogue] under the threat of torture; and if he kept firm he is to be called upon to abjure before a plenary assembly of the Congregation of the Holy Office, and is to be condemned to imprisonment at the pleasure of the Holy Congregation, and ordered not to treat further, in whatever manner, either in words or in writing, of the mobility of the Earth and the stability of the Sun; otherwise he will incur the penalties of relapse. The book entitled *Dialogo di Galileo Galilei Linceo* is to be prohibited. Furthermore, that these things may be known by all, he ordered that copies of the sentence shall be sent to all Apostolic Nuncios, to all Inquisitors against heretical pravity, and especially the Inquisitor in Florence, who shall read the sentence in full assembly and in the presence of most of those who profess the mathematical art."

From a legal standpoint the sentence was a miscarriage of justice because the Injunction of 1616 was never served on Galileo. It remained in the Inquisition files, and was not produced until the start of Galileo's trial seventeen years later. Moreover the heliocentric system of Copernicus had never been officially declared a heresy. Hence, there was no legal basis for Galileo's trial. However, Galileo's imprisonment was not punitive; part was spent at a Grand Duke's villa, and part in the palace of the Archbishop Piccolomini in Sienna. Afterwards, Galileo returned to his farm at Arcetri, and then to his house in Florence, where he spent the remaining years of his life. In the years following the trial, Galileo completed his book on the science of dynamics: *Dialogues Concerning Two New Sciences,* the work on which his fame rests. He died at the age of 78 in 1642 - the year of Sir Isaac Newton's birth.

* * *

At the time of Galileo's death, theoretical physics was fragmented and intellectually confused. There were the celestial motions of Kepler, the principle of inertia of Descartes, and the terrestrial dynamics of Galileo, but no unifying principle or agreement about fundamental causes. The disparate nature of physics is evidenced by the diversity of opinion among leading scientists of the day. In *Revolution in Science (1985)* Professor I. Bernard Cohen lists a number of propositions associated with Galileo, Kepler and Descartes that are at variance with the work of Isaac Newton.

Galileo:
(1) The acceleration of bodies falling toward the earth is constant at all distances, even as far out as the moon.
(2) The moon cannot possibly have any influence on (or be the cause of) the tides in the sea.

Kepler:
(1) A solar force exerted on the planetary bodies diminishes directly as the distance and acts only in or near the plane of the ecliptic.
(2) The sun must be a huge magnet.
(3) Because of its "natural inertia", a moving body will come to rest whenever the motive force ceases to act.

Descartes:
The planets are carried around by a sea of aether moving in huge vortices.

Sir Isaac Newton (1642-1727), physicist, mathematician, astronomer, alchemist and theologian is generally regarded as the greatest scientist of the last millennium. Newton's *Mathematical Principles of Natural Philosophy (1687)* (known by its Latin abbreviation as the *Principia*), laid the foundations of classical physics and created a paradigm of the universe which dominated science for the next three hundred years. In the *Principia*, Newton describes the three laws of motion and the law of universal gravitation, showing that the motions of terrestrial and celestial bodies are governed by the same set of laws. At the same time, he demonstrates the consistency between Kepler's laws of planetary motion and his theory of gravitation, thus removing the last doubts about the heliocentric nature of the heavens. Newton's Laws are commonly expressed as follows:

1. Law of Inertia: *Every body continues in its state of rest, or of uniform motion in a straight line, unless it is compelled to change that state by forces impressed upon it.*

Generally attributed to Descartes, the inertial property of mass is the innate tendency of a physical body to persist in its current state of motion. Inertia is described in the *Principia* as a law governing the behaviour of physical bodies in the absence of resultant forces, and is now known as Newton's First Law.

2. Law of Acceleration: *A change in motion [i.e. momentum] is proportional to the motive force impressed; and is in the direction of the line in which that force is impressed.*

Newton's Law of Acceleration is the fundamental principle of classical mechanics and formalizes a commonplace phenomenon. For example, if a football is kicked twice as hard as previously it will accelerate twice as much in the direction in which it is kicked.

3. Law of Reciprocal Action and Reaction: *To every action there is always imposed an equal reaction; in other words, the actions of two bodies upon each other are always equal in magnitudes but opposite in direction.*

In the *Principia*, Newton's Third Law is accompanied by a number of examples: "if anyone presses a stone with a finger, the finger is also pressed by the stone"; "if a horse draws a stone tied to a rope, the horse will (so to speak) also be drawn back equally toward the stone, for the rope, stretched out at both ends, will urge the horse toward the stone and the stone toward the horse by one and the same endeavour..." The Third Law means that all forces are interactions between physical bodies, and that, consequently, there is no such thing as a force that acts on only one body.

The first three Laws - known as Newton's Laws of Motion - have survived unchanged and account for all known terrestrial motions. So entrenched have these Laws become that any physicist or engineer attempting to "suspend" any one of them, in order to account for strange or anomalous phenomena, is automatically branded a "heretic". A famous example is that of Eric Laithwaite, professor of electrical engineering at the Imperial College (University of London) and inventor of the linear motor. He had been invited to deliver a lecture at the Royal Institution in London in recognition of his original contributions to the science of engineering. However,

Laithwaite had been experimenting with gyroscopes and noted their unusual behaviour: a heavy gyroscope, when spinning, becomes very easy to lift up; this was the subject of his lecture. Laithwaite had constructed a large gyroscope and attached it to the end of a three foot pole. The rotor could be spun up to high speeds on a low-friction bearing driven by a small but powerful electrical motor. He first demonstrated that the apparatus was heavy - it weighed more than 50 pounds. It took all his strength and both hands to raise the pole and gyroscope much above waist level. When he started to spin the rotor at high speed, the apparatus became so light that he could, effortlessly, raise it above his head with just one hand. (See fig. 3)

Fig. 3

The demonstration was intended to surprise and delight the audience of distinguished scientists, and Professor Laithwaite went on to suggest that Newton's Third Law of Action and Reaction did not apply to gyroscopic motion. The response took Laithwaite completely by surprise; there was a stunned and embarrassed silence. According to Laithwaite: "I was very excited about it because I knew I had something to show them that was startling. And I did it rather in the spirit of 'come and see what I've discovered - come and share this with me.' It was only afterwards that I realised no one wanted to share it with me. The reaction was 'the man's obviously a lunatic. There must be some trick' was what people said. I was simply trying to tell them, 'look, here's something very unusual that's worth investigating. I hope I've got sufficient reputation in electrical engineering not to be written off as a crank. So when I tell you this, I hope you'll listen.' But they didn't want to."

Following the Royal Institution lecture, there was a furore, followed up by articles in the morning press with headlines such as "Laithwaite defies Newton" with speculations about anti-gravity machines and space travel. The disapproval of his audience continued long afterwards. For the first time in two hundred years, there were no published proceedings to record an Institution lecture. The Royal Institution erased all record of Professor Laithwaite and his gyroscopic demonstration. Laithwaite became a non-person and his professional reputation ruined – he became a "heretic." However, Laithwaite continued his work on gyroscopes and, eventually, came to the conclusion that the apparent weight loss, associated with spinning gyroscopes, could, in fact, be explained by Newton's Laws, and that the third Law of Action and Reaction still applied. Since the time of the *Principia*, Newton's Third Law has remained unchanged; not so the Law of Gravity.

Law of Gravity: *Every particle in the universe attracts every other particle with a force whose magnitude is proportional to the product of the masses of the two particles and inversely proportional to the square of the distance between them. The direction of force lies along the straight line connecting the two particles.*

Although the Law of Gravity accounted for the planetary motions described by Kepler, Newton was deeply troubled because it involved the occult idea of 'action-at-a-distance.' In a letter to Richard Bentley in 1692, Newton wrote: "That one body may act upon another at a distance through a vacuum without the mediation of anything else, by and through which their action and force may be conveyed from one another, is to me so great an absurdity that, I believe, no man who has in philosophic matters a competent faculty of thinking could ever fall into it." However, Newton's concerns were largely forgotten, and by the turn of the nineteenth century, the Law was generally regarded as the most successful theory of physics. To be sure, there were minor discrepancies between theory and observation such as the secular advance of Mercury's perihelion; but, the majority of physicists felt that these problems could be solved by simply incorporating factors previously ignored such as the influence of hidden planets. The principal difficulty with the Law of Gravity is that a change in the relative position of two bodies causes an instantaneous change in the gravitational pull experienced by both. In the case of planets, the bodies could be light years apart, but the effect is immediate. For this to happen, gravitational causes must propagate with infinite speed, an idea at variance with the electromagnetic theory of physicist, James Clerk Maxwell and, indeed, with ordinary experience. In the absence of a propagating mechanism all actions-at-a-distance must necessarily be instantaneous.

Action-at-a-distance remained an unsolved problem in physics until Einstein formulated his general theory of relativity in 1915. Two years earlier, at the 1913 Congress of Vienna he had told the meeting: "After the untenability of the theory of action-at-a-distance had thus been proved in the domain of electrodynamics, confidence in the correctness of Newton's action-at-a-distance was shaken. One had to believe that Newton's Law of Gravity could not embrace the phenomena of gravitation in their entirety." According to Einstein, gravity is not the result of a force propagated between physical bodies but an attribute of curved space-time. In the general theory of relativity, large bodies like stars and planets distort space-time in their vicinity and cause smaller passing bodies – like satellites or particles of light - to move in trajectories determined by the geometry of space-time; this enabled a description of the behaviour of light that was consistent with current astronomical observations. In the general theory the gravitational acceleration of a mass in free fall is due to its 'world line' being a geodesic of space-time. Given two points on a curved surface the geodesic is defined as the shortest distance connecting them; if the surface is flat the geodesic is a straight line; hence, for terrestrial motions, general relativity reduces to Newtonian mechanics.

* * *

In the formulation of his Laws, Newton found it necessary to impose certain restrictions on the motion of a particle. Expressed graphically, the key postulate was that a particle's displacement-time curve should be smooth and continuous or, equivalently, that the curve should contain no "corners" or "sharp" points. This ensured that key variables of interest, such as displacement, velocity and acceleration, could be analysed by the methods of Euclidian geometry and later by the methods of calculus. In fig. 4, the curve on the left is smooth and continuous while the curve on the right has "corners" at points a, b, and c and is discontinuous at points d and e.

Fig. 4

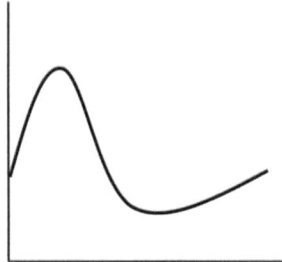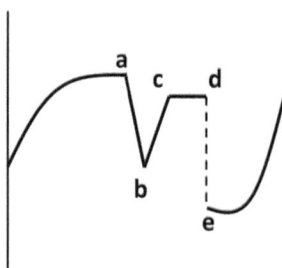

But to understand how smoothness and continuity gave rise to the concept of mechanical causality it is necessary to go back to Newton's earlier work, *Method of Fluxions and Infinite Series* compiled in 1671 in which he develops techniques that enabled him to articulate the Laws of Motion and Gravity. In the *Fluxions,* Newton approaches the problem of particle motion by analysing the motion of a *point* in one dimension (i.e. along a line). Since, at any moment of time, a particle can move in only one direction, the results can be generalised to three dimensions. Using Cartesian coordinates, a point's displacement (from some starting position) can be plotted in two dimensions, displacement measured along a vertical axis and the time elapsed along a horizontal axis (see fig. 5).

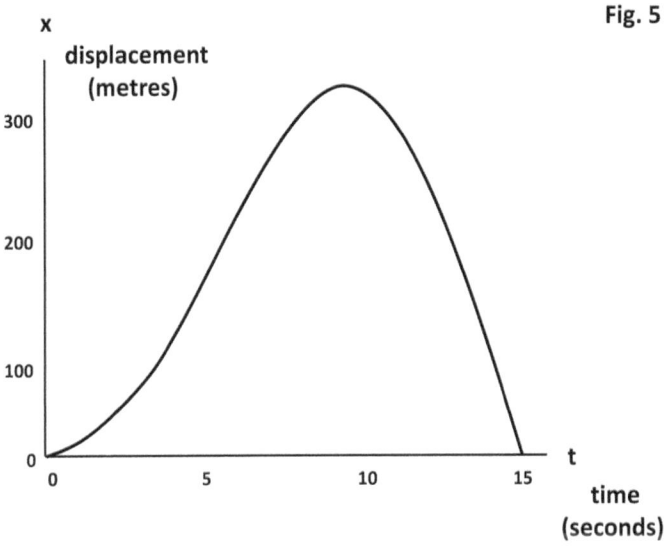

Fig. 5

The origin (bottom left-hand corner) represents the starting point of the motion. After 5 seconds the point is 167 metres from the origin. After 10 seconds it is at its maximum displacement of 333 metres. From then on, the point moves back towards the origin arriving there 15 seconds from the start of the motion. The graph, then, shows either the future of the point's path looking *forwards* from the origin or the history of the point's path looking *backwards* towards the origin.

The technique Newton employs for the analyses of smooth curves he calls the "method of fluxions." A curve is described as a "flowing point," and the infinitesimally short path traced by the point in an infinitesimally small amount of time he calls the "moment" of the flowing quantity. The ratio of the moment to the corresponding time is called the "fluxion" of the variable. The infinitesimally small quantities Newton employs in the *Fluxions* are not equal to zero but are arbitrarily close to zero – a technique involving the limit of an infinite series. The nomenclature and notation of the *Fluxions* are no longer used, but the underlying concepts and techniques have survived. In modern notation we have:

(a) ... moment of the flowing quantity = dx
(b) ... the corresponding time = dt

where dx refers to an infinitesimally small displacement and dt an infinitesimally small period of time. The ratio of these two quantities is then dx/dt. In other words, the "fluxion" of the variable x is the rate of change of the displacement x with respect to time t - what physicists call the velocity of x. We may then write v = dx/dt where v stands for the velocity.

It is a geometric property of a smooth curve that to each and every point on the curve, one and only one tangent may be drawn. In fig. 6a the curve on the left is everywhere smooth (disregarding the end points) whereas the curve on the right has a corner at point B. Only *one* tangent may be drawn at point A but *two* may be drawn at point B - one for each section of the curve (see fig. 6b.)

NEWTON'S UNIVERSE

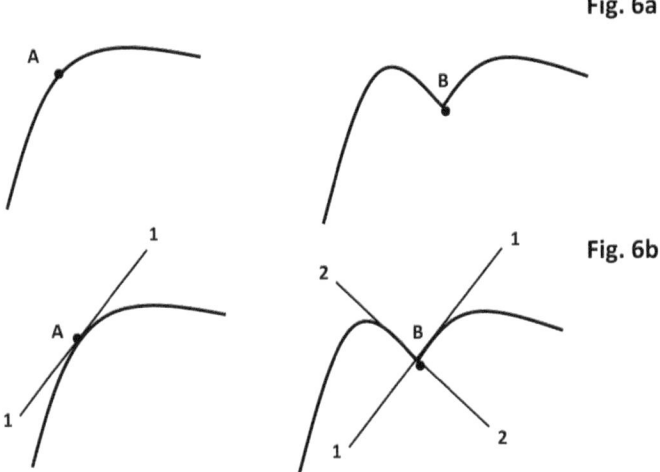

Fig. 6a

Fig. 6b

It is a well known proposition in the mechanics of particle motion that the gradient of the tangent to a displacement-time curve measures the velocity of the particle at the specified point of time (see fig. 7)

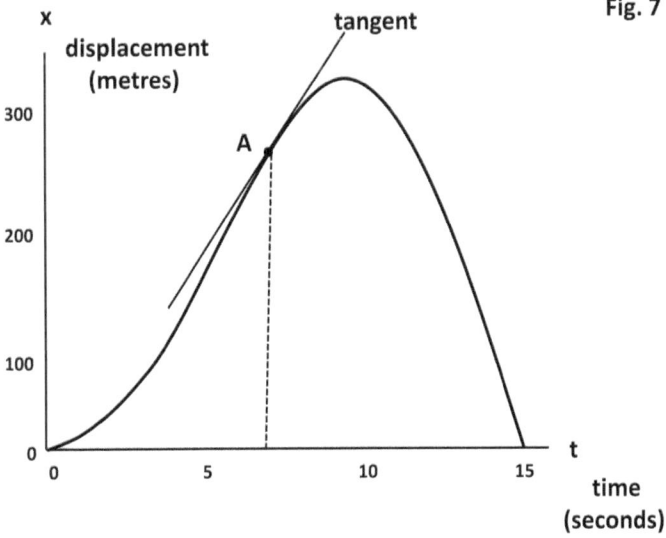

Fig. 7

It then follows that to each and every point on a smooth and continuous displacement-time graph there corresponds one and only one velocity. In other words, the velocity of the particle at point A is uniquely determined. Since the displacement-time curve is smooth and continuous, the velocity-time curve will also be smooth and continuous (see fig. 8), and this, in turn, ensures that the particle's velocity at each point of time is uniquely determined.

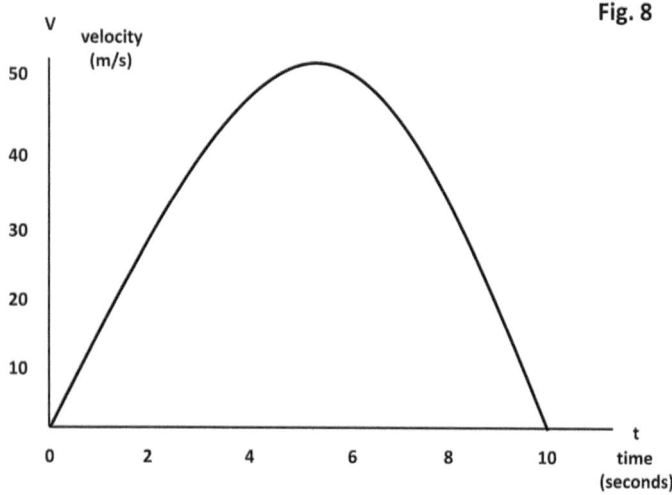

Fig. 8

The acceleration of a particle is defined as the rate of change of velocity with respect to time or, alternatively, the ratio of an infinitesimally small change in velocity to an infinitesimally small change in time i.e. $a = dv/dt$, where a stands for the particle's acceleration. Given this definition, it follows that the gradient of the tangent to a velocity-time curve measures the acceleration of the particle, and since the velocity-time curve is smooth and continuous, the acceleration-time curve will also be smooth and continuous.

Hence, the acceleration of the particle will be uniquely determined at each point of time. Newton's Law of Acceleration is often expressed as F = ma (force = mass x acceleration), and since the acceleration is uniquely determined it follows that the force acting on the particle is uniquely determined (see fig. 9).

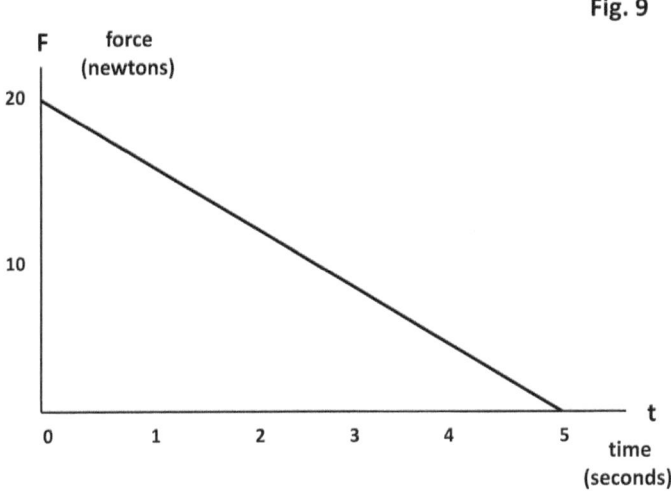

Fig. 9

It is the uniqueness of the relationship that gives it the character of a causal law. As we shall see in Chapter 10, if particle motion is not smooth and continuous the Law of Acceleration is no longer applicable.

It is a curious feature of Newton's Laws that a force cannot be observed directly and must be calculated indirectly via the equation F=ma. Since mass and acceleration can both be measured independently of force, this does not normally pose a problem. However, some Continental mathematicians, notably Joseph-Louis Lagrange (1736-1813), thought the approach unsatisfactory and transformed

Newtonian mechanics into a branch of analysis that dispenses with the notion of force. Lagrange showed that Newton's mechanics can be derived from variational principles - a branch of mathematics called the calculus of variations. However, in practice, Newton's Laws are much easier to apply than Lagrangian methods and have generally retained their popularity as scientific and engineering tools.

* * *

In *The Structure of Science (1961)* Ernest Nagel states that: "Classical mechanics is the generally acknowledged paradigm of a deterministic theory, and current discussions of determinism are heavily indebted to mechanics for many of the distinctions and much of their language." (p.278) Newton's Laws provided justification for what has been called the 'mechanical philosophy' of nature – a view of the world that evolved into the more sophisticated ideology of determinism. Determinism in science is the belief that all physical events are causally determined by other physical events, that is to say,

(1) Every cause uniquely determines its effect.
(2) Actions and consequences are connected in necessary causal relationships.

This rules out all effects other than the one that actually occurs. In classical mechanics, causality is expressed through Newton's Laws of Motion and the Law of Gravity. A free body will necessarily move with uniform speed in a straight line unless compelled to do otherwise by an externally impressed force (The Law of Inertia). Every action will necessarily produce an equal reciprocal reaction (The Law of Action and Reaction). The motion of a satellite in a planet's gravitational field will necessarily be a conic i.e. a circle, ellipse, parabola, or hyperbola (The Law of Gravity). The trajectory of a particle near the surface of a planet will necessarily be parabolic; and objects released from rest at the same time and in the same locality will necessarily fall with equal speed (The Law of Acceleration.)

Although Newton's Laws provided the foundations for the deterministic view of the universe, the principal architect of seventeenth century determinism was not Newton but Descartes. In his *Principles of Philosophy* published in 1644, Descartes expounded the philosophical view - known as Cartesian dualism - that mind or spirit existed independently of the physical universe. According to Descartes, matter is divided into discrete particles which interact with one another, altering their motions, coming to rest, speeding up or changing direction, but the total quantity of motion in the universe remains constant. The physical universe is then a gigantic machine operating - as all machines must - in accordance with the laws of mechanics. This ensured that non-mechanical agents, such as the mind or spirit, never entered the picture. Although a person is capable of moving his own body around and manipulating physical objects, the vast majority of natural phenomena, including the biological functions of the human body, are never affected by the human will at all. Non-human animals, where mind and spirit were presumed to be absent, were thought to be biological machines. In *De homines (1662)*, for example, Descartes argues that animals can be reductively explained as automata.

One hundred years later, the mechanical philosophy of nature finds its full expression in the works of French mathematician Pierre-Simon de Laplace (1749-1827). Laplace maintained that if a superior intelligence were acquainted with the positions of all the material particles in the universe, and with the forces acting between them, "the future as well as the past would be present to its eyes." In his *Probability Theory (1812)*, he states: "We ought to regard the present state of the universe as the effect of its antecedent state and as the cause of the state that is to follow. An intelligence knowing all the forces acting in nature at a given instant, as well as the momentary positions of all things in the universe, would be able to comprehend in one single formula the motions of the largest bodies as well as of the lightest atoms in the world, provided that its intellect were sufficiently powerful to subject all data to analysis; to it nothing would be uncertain, the future as well as the past would be present to its eyes. The perfection that the human mind has been able to give to astronomy affords a feeble outline of such intelligence. Discoveries in mechanics and geometry, coupled with those in universal gravitation, have brought the mind within reach of comprehending in the same analytical formula the past and the future state of the system of the world. All the mind's efforts in the search for truth tend to approximate to the intelligence we have just imagined, although it will forever remain infinitely remote from such intelligence." All activity then is a chain of events - or more generally a complex network of events - governed by the law of cause and effect. Provided enough information is given, all physical phenomena can, in principle, be predicted, retrodicted and explained. In this view, human volition is an illusion because all mental processes are ultimately the product of physical interactions which, in turn, are governed by physical laws.

Thus were the foundations of modern scientific determinism laid. When physicists began to penetrate the mysteries of the atom, determinism become increasingly *reductionist* in character i.e. tending to reduce the behaviour of complex systems to the behaviour of increasingly smaller parts. Classical mechanics is reductionist in the sense that the motion of a mechanical system is the sum of the motions of its component parts. The momentum of a rigid body, for example, is calculated as the sum of the momenta of the parts comprising the body. Reductionist approaches in psychology attempt to explain human behaviour through a descending hierarchy of disciplines, beginning at the level of biology and descending to chemistry and particle physics. In *A Theoretical Basis of Human Behaviour (1925)* psychologist, A. P. Weiss (1879 – 1931) argues that psychological data ought to be reducible to descriptions of physiochemical processes; and in *The Behaviour of Organisms (1938)* and *Science and Human Behaviour (1953)* behaviourist B. F. Skinner argues that psychology should seek to establish empirical laws that describe stable and precise relationships between stimuli (causes) and responses (effects).

* * *

Following the triumph of Newtonian physics, classical thinkers adjusted their vision of the world to accommodate the Newtonian paradigm of continuity, mechanism and causal law. Beneath the surface of visible phenomena it was believed that causal processes were at work which guaranteed the continuous and orderly progress of natural, social and economic events. Deviations from causal law were regarded as aberrations to be ignored, minimized or eliminated from descriptions of the world. In the Newtonian spirit, it was believed that all phenomena were amenable to scientific analysis, prediction and control; scientists who departed from this paradigm were often marginalised, ignored and sometimes persecuted.

The influence of Newtonian thinking in areas beyond the physical sciences can be seen most clearly in the field of economics. The expressions: "laws of supply and demand", "price determination", "the price mechanism", "the market mechanism", "market equilibrium", "general equilibrium", and the "accelerator," have their origins in mechanical concepts. Adam Smith (1723–1790), moral philosopher, pioneer economist and author of the book, *An Inquiry into the Nature and Causes of the Wealth of Nations (1776),* postulated a hidden adjustment mechanism - called the 'invisible hand' - which governed the allocation of scarce resources between the various agents of the economy. It was argued that, free of government intervention, markets will operate smoothly, quickly and efficiently to produce an overall distribution of wealth that was, in some sense, the 'best of all worlds' for society as a whole. This powerful notion is the foundation of free market ideology and has survived, virtually intact, to this day.

One hundred years after Adam Smith, Newtonian thinking finds its full expression in the marginal utility theories of Jevons, Menger and Walras. According to their theories a consumer will purchase a product to the point where the price equals the additional utility (i.e. marginal utility) derived from the product. The consumer's utility function is smooth and continuous and can be analysed using the very same methods developed by Isaac Newton for the study of particle motion. William Stanley Jevons, British economist and logician, developed the mathematical theory of marginal utility in his seminal work, *The Theory of Political Economy (1871);* but remarkably similar ideas were expounded by the Austrian economist, Carl Menger in his *Principles of Economics (1871),* and by the French economist, Leon Walras in *Elements of Pure Economics*

(1874–1877). This convergence of thinking has been noted by economist Mark Blaug. In his standard work, *Economic Theory in Retrospect (1968),* he states: "The striking similarity in the basic approach of these three books, coupled with the fact that each writer developed his ideas in total ignorance of the others' works, suggests the existence of some underlying force to which they were all responding." (p.298)

Marginal utility theories in economics are based on the assumption that consumers (or households) derive incremental amounts of utility or satisfaction from incremental amounts of commodities. Marginal productivity theories, on the other hand, assume that suppliers (or firms) produce incremental amounts of products from incremental amounts of a factor of production, such as labour or machinery. In order to apply the differential calculus all quantities are treated as continuous variables. Functional or causal relationships are then established between them to obtain:

(1) a household's utility function which relates a household's utility to the consumption of commodities and,
(2) a firm's production function which relates the output of commodities to inputs of capital and labour.

Marginal utility is defined as the increment of utility per increment of consumption, and marginal product is defined as the increment of output per increment of a factor of production. Hence, all marginal quantities are the ratio of two incremental variables. These formulations may be sharpened if:

(a) utility and production functions are mathematically continuous and,
(b) all increments are infinitesimally small quantities.

The ratio of two infinitesimally small increments is the first derivative of a function that relates the two variables - an idea directly attributable to Isaac Newton.

The neoclassical school of economics, founded by the Cambridge economist, Alfred Marshall (1842 – 1924) and developed by his intellectual successor, Arthur Pigou (1877-1959), popularized, among other things, the use of supply and demand curves as analytical tools for the study of price determination. Known as partial equilibrium analysis, the technique investigates the equilibrium of a single market operating in isolation from the rest of the economy. A demand function for a commodity shows, *ceteris paribus*, how much buyers (i.e. households) would wish to purchase at various prices. A supply function for the commodity shows, *ceteris paribus*, how much suppliers (i.e. firms) would wish to sell at various prices (see fig. 10).

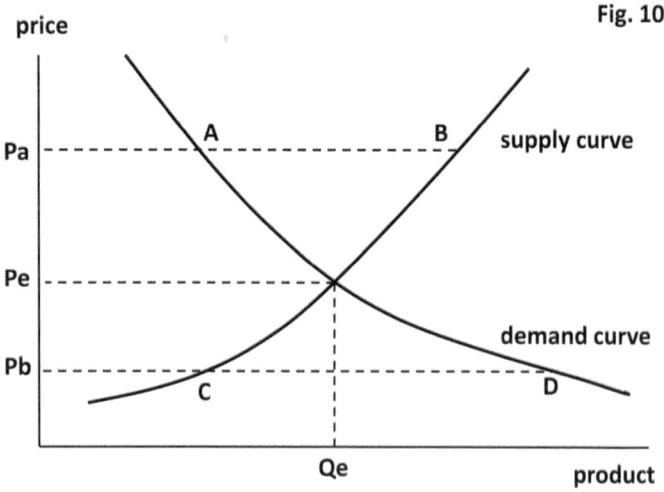

Fig. 10

Demand varies inversely with price (higher price, lower demand) while supply varies directly with price (higher price, greater supply). Hence, the demand curve for a commodity is downward-sloping and the supply curve upward sloping. If the market price is too high (say, Pa) total supply exceeds total demand by AB units and competition between sellers will cause the price to fall. If the price is too low (say, Pb) demand will exceed supply by CD units and competition between buyers will cause the price to rise. Only when the price is equal to Pe will total demand equal total supply, Qe. All commodities can then be exchanged at the ruling price and there will be no pressure on buyers or sellers to adjust their positions. If buyers' preferences or production techniques remain unchanged, all commodities will continue to be exchanged at the price Pe. The market for the commodity is then said to be in equilibrium. In fig. 10, buyers as a whole are happy to purchase the quantity Qe at the price Pe and sellers as a whole are happy to sell the quantity Qe at the price Pe. Hence, there will be no tendency for the price to change.

The principal assumption behind the construction of supply and demand curves is that firms maximise profit and households maximise utility - an idea borrowed from the differential calculus involving 'stationary points.' The smoothness and continuity exhibited by these curves reflects the smoothness and continuity of the decision-making functions of households and firms. The assumption of continuity, then, enabled price determination to be studied by the methods of calculus (see, for example *Microeconomic Theory: A Mathematical Approach (1958)* by M. Henderson and Richard E. Quandt.) However, since the time of Jevons, Menger and Walras mathematical economists have tended to depart from the traditional assumptions of continuity and base their theories on more general set-theoretic foundations.

To see how Newtonian thinking influenced the development of economic theory we need only compare the forces acting on a particle with the 'forces' acting on the price of a commodity. Suppose a number of forces are suddenly applied to a particle that is moving with constant velocity. Now, some forces may assist the particle's motion and some forces may oppose it. If the forces assisting the motion are exactly counterbalanced by the forces opposing it, the resultant force is zero and the particle's velocity will remain unchanged. The system is then said to be in equilibrium. If the forces assisting the particle's motion are greater than the forces opposing it, the resultant force is positive and the particle will accelerate in the direction of the resultant force. If the forces assisting the particle's motion are less than the forces opposing it, the resultant force is negative and the particle will accelerate in the *opposite* direction. In a commodity market, if the forces of demand are exactly counterbalanced by the forces of supply, the resultant excess demand is zero and the price of the commodity will remain unchanged. The market is then said to be in equilibrium. Motion is expressed through price changes. If the forces of demand exceed the forces of supply, the resultant excess demand is positive and the price will accelerate in the direction of the excess demand i.e. upwards. If the forces of supply exceed the forces of demand, the resultant excess demand is negative and the price will accelerate in the opposite direction i.e. downwards.

Unlike partial equilibrium theory, which investigates the behaviour of a single market, general equilibrium theory analyses the behaviour of all markets in the economy and how they interact with one another. In particular, it attempts to establish the conditions under which equilibrium for all markets may be attained simultaneously. As an all-encompassing model of explanation, general equilibrium theory reached its peak in the writings of modern mathematical economists such as Gerard Debreu. In *The Theory of Value (1959)* Debreu establishes, the precise conditions for the existence and uniqueness of general equilibrium in a free market economy.

General equilibrium theory is an impressive intellectual structure, but its depiction of actual economies can be highly misleading. In such models all markets are cleared simultaneously and no resources are left unemployed. When underlying parameters change - such as consumer tastes or production techniques - the system moves smoothly and swiftly to a new state of equilibrium. The principal result is that all significant market movements are changes in equilibrium positions. Since decision makers are assumed to behave rationally and possess full information, such models describe a world of complete certainty. Once the initial conditions have been set, all economic activity unfolds mechanically and predictably – like a machine in a Newtonian universe.

Chapter 10
Law and Disorder

In *Natural Philosophy of Cause and Chance (1949)*, physicist Max Born sets out three postulates that define the classical concept of causality:

(1) Causality postulates that there are laws by which the occurrence of an entity B of a certain class depends on the occurrence of an entity A of another class, where the word entity means any physical object, phenomenon, situation, or event. A is called the cause, B the effect.
(2) Antecedence postulates that the cause must be prior to, or at least simultaneous with, the effect.
(3) Contiguity postulates that cause and effect must be in spatial contact or connected by a chain of intermediate things in contact.

Firstly, it is incorrect to say that antecedence postulates that cause must be "at least simultaneous with effect." According to the Oxford Dictionary of English, antecedence means: preceding in time or order. If two events are simultaneous, one cannot be said to be the cause of the other. Postulate 1 implies that all events are governed by a law of cause and effect.

Needless to say, there are serious problems with the classical concept of causality (see Chapter 3). According to David Hume (1711-1776), a principal figure in the history of Western philosophy and the Scottish Enlightenment, it is not even necessary that an event have a cause - an assertion later confirmed by the spontaneous emission of radiation. In his seminal work, *A Treatise of Human Nature (1739)*, he states: "It is a general maxim in philosophy that whatever begins to exist must be caused to do so. This is commonly taken for granted in all reasonings, without any proof being given or asked for. It is supposed to be based on intuition, and to be one of those - immediately self-evident - maxims that men can't really doubt in their hearts, even if they deny them with their lips. But if we examine this maxim in terms of the idea of knowledge that I have explained, we shan't discover in it any mark of any such intuitive certainty. Quite the contrary: we'll find that it is of a nature quite foreign to what can be known intuitively." (Book 1, Part iii, Section 3). Hume maintains that no particular events can *a priori* be connected in causal relationships: "According to my doctrine, there are no objects which we can, by merely surveying them and without consulting experience, discover to be the causes of anything else." (Book 1, Part iii, Section 15)

In *An Enquiry concerning Human Understanding (1748)*, Hume argues that: "If we reason a priori, anything may appear able to produce anything. The falling of a pebble may, for all we know, extinguish the sun; or the wish of a man may control the planets in their orbits. Only experience teaches us the nature and limits of cause and effect, and enables us to infer the existence of one object from that of another." (Section 12, Part iii). In other words, no events can be connected with one another in necessary causal relationships *before* they happen. If such is the case then no events can be connected with one another in necessary causal relationships *after* they happen.

In classical mechanics notions of causality are based on *law* not experience. In practice, objects do not fall with equal speed (because of air resistance) and bodies *do* need a force to keep them in motion (because of friction). In order to establish the mechanics of terrestrial motion Galileo was forced to abstract from, rather than synthesise, the complex details of everyday experience. Only by conducting a series of idealized experiments in artificially controlled situations - none of which bore much relation to the events or happenings of ordinary experience - was Galileo able to demonstrate the existence of underlying regularities which we refer to as 'natural laws.' For example, he showed that objects fall with equal speed by rolling spheres of different sizes down inclined planes. But spheres, and the motion of spheres, are not connected in necessary causal relationships because the spheres may never be set in motion. A more mundane example is the following: a motorist gets into a car, starts the engine and the car moves. Commonsense dictates that the actions of the motorist caused the car to move. But anything could have prevented it from happening e.g. the petrol tank may have been empty, the car's ignition may have been faulty, the wheels may have been clamped, the tyres may have been flat, the car may have been facing a brick wall etc. etc. In other words, although the motorist caused the car to move, the motorist's actions and the car's motion are not connected in a necessary causal relationship. The fact that A caused B does not mean that A *necessarily* caused B because B may never have happened. Hence, there is no law of cause and effect operating between A and B.

In 1898, American logician and philosopher Charles Sanders Peirce (1839-1914) – described by Bertrand Russell as "one of the most original minds of the later nineteenth century, and certainly the greatest American thinker ever," - wrote: "Those who make causality one of the fundamental categories of thought - of whom you will find that I am not one - have one very awkward fact to explain away. It is that men's conceptions of a cause are in different stages of scientific culture entirely different and inconsistent. The great principle of causation which, we are told, it is absolutely impossible not to believe, has been one proposition at one period in history and an entirely disparate one at another is still a third one for the modern physicist. The only thing about it which has stood... is the name of it." (*Reasoning and the Logic of Things*). In other words, the so-called the law of cause and effect is nothing more than a form of words strung together to service a particular ideology.

Nearly one hundred years later, Jaegwon Kim, Professor of Philosophy at Brown University and the author of a number of influential papers on causation, has stated that attempts to analyze the concept of causation have reached an impasse. Writing in 1995, Kim expresses his concern as follows: "The attempt to "analyze" causation seems to have reached an impasse; the proposals on hand seem so widely divergent that one wonders whether they are all analyses of one and the same concept." (wikipedia.org/wiki/Causality). Five year later, computer scientist John F. Sowa writes: "In modern physics, the fundamental laws of nature are expressed in continuous systems of partial differential equations. Yet the words and concepts that people use in talking and reasoning about cause and effect are expressed in discrete terms that have no direct relationship to the theories of physics. As a result, there is a sharp break between the way that physicists characterize the world and the way that people usually talk about it." (wikipedia.org/wiki/Causality)

At a superficial level cause and effect would seem to be a statement of the obvious. A cause, by definition, must be the cause of something, and this something must be the effect. The effect, by definition, must be the effect of something; and this something must be the *cause*. But, if the law of cause and effect merely asserts that every cause has an effect and that every effect has a cause, then the 'law' is nothing more than an empty truism. Hume dismisses such notions in the following way: "Even more frivolously, some say that every effect must have a cause because having-a-cause is implied in the very idea of effect. It is true that every effect must have a cause, because 'effect' is a relative term of which 'cause' is the correlative. But this doesn't prove that everything real must be preceded by a cause, any more than it follows from 'Every husband must have a wife' that every man must be married." (*A Treatise of Human Nature (1739)* Book 1, Part iii, Sect. 3)

Discontinuity and Indeterminism

In Chapter 9, we saw how Newton's assumptions of smoothness and continuity gave rise to the Law of Acceleration. Let us revisit the motion of a particle and see what happens when these assumptions no longer apply. Suppose a particle's velocity steadily increases from 0 m/s to 50 m/s and then suddenly falls to 0 m/s, and that the motion is repeated every 5 seconds. This produces the displacement-time graph in fig. 1.

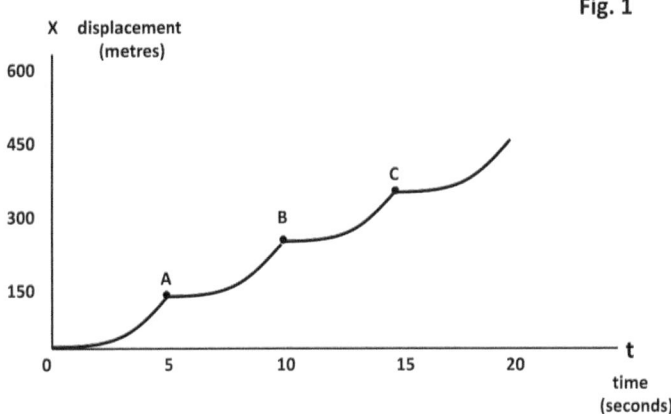

Fig. 1

The 'corners' at A, B, C correspond to the sudden changes of motion. Notice that each corner possesses *two* tangents: one for each part of the curve (see fig. 2).

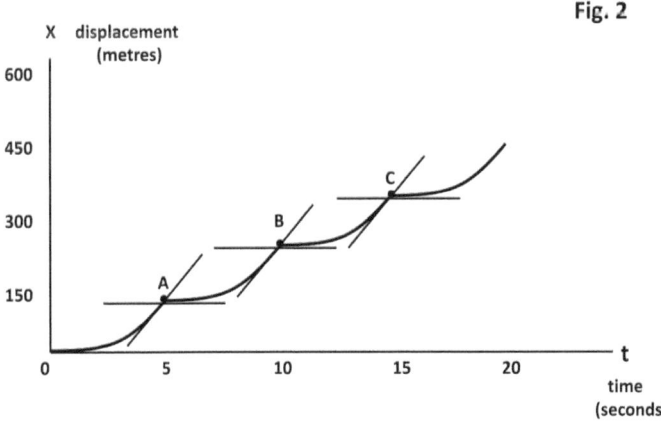

Fig. 2

We know from Chapter 9 that the gradient of the tangent to a particle's displacement-time curve measures the velocity of the particle, therefore each corner corresponds to *two* velocities: 0 m/s and 50 m/s. The derived velocity-time graph shows more clearly how the particle's velocity suddenly changes from 50 m/s to 0 m/s every 5 seconds (see fig. 3).

Fig. 3

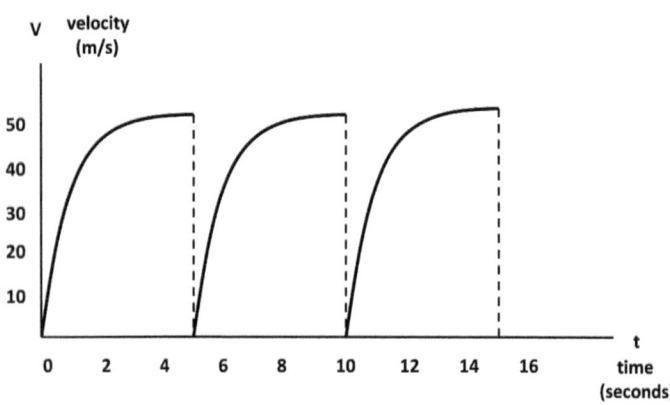

At the moment of the 'jump,' the particle's velocity is indeterminate within the range 0 to 50 m/s. From Chapter 9 we also know that the gradient of the tangent to a velocity-time curve measures the particle's acceleration. If we set $m = 1$ (chosen for simplicity) we obtain the force-time graph shown in fig. 4.

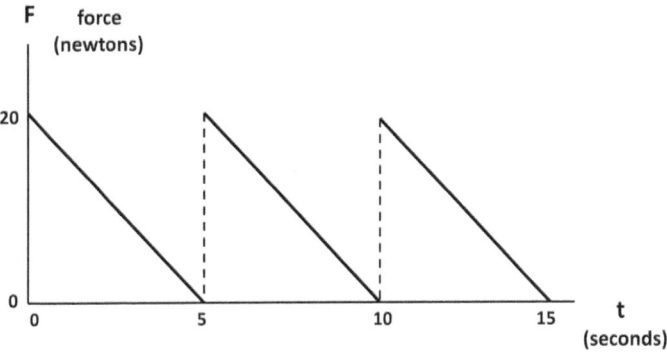

Every 5 seconds, the force suddenly jumps from 0N to 20N. At the moment of the jump the force is indeterminate within the range 0 to 20N, therefore, the equation F = ma is indeterminate every 5 seconds. If discontinuities had arisen at *one* second intervals, the equation F = ma would have been indeterminate every second. If discontinuities had been present everywhere, the equation would have been completely indeterminate. We recall from Chapter 9 that the smoothness postulate enabled Newton to employ the methods of Euclidian geometry to analyse the motion of a particle and to develop the differential calculus. A necessary condition is that for two related variables, infinitesimal increases in one may *only* be associated with infinitesimal increases in the other. In figs. 3 and 4, it is clear that at 5 second intervals infinitesimally small changes in time are definitely not associated with infinitesimally small changes in either velocity or force. For the differential calculus - and by implication the equation F = ma - to be applicable throughout the entire range of motion, these points of discontinuity must not exist.

* * *

Although Newtonian thinking dominated areas beyond the physical sciences evidence of cataclysms, geological upheavals, extinction of species and, more recently, wars, revolutions and mass unemployment belied the notion that the Earth was – in any sense of the word - a smooth and continuously evolving planet. In the field of economics, general equilibrium theory - the theory that all markets clear swiftly and continuously - conspicuously failed to explain the phenomena of mass unemployment, galloping inflation and the collapse of banking systems, arguably sharp discontinuities in the normal state of affairs.

As a response to these crises, economists tended to depart from orthodox theories and construct *ad hoc* models at variance with the theoretical foundations of their subject, the most famous being *The General Theory of Employment, Interest and Money (1936)* by John Maynard Keynes, a work that marked a significant departure from the classical theory of employment. Prior to the *General Theory*, the predominant view among economists was that unemployment did not exist or, if it did, it was caused by trade unions holding the real wage rate above the marginal product of labour. Following the 1929 Wall Street crash and the appearance of mass unemployment throughout the Western world in the face of falling wage rates, this position was swiftly abandoned. By the middle of the 1930's it was clear that if the capitalist system was to survive, new theories were needed. The sudden change of approach signalled by the *General Theory* reflected deep discontinuities in the structure of Western economies beyond the powers of orthodox theory to explain.

Although Keynes' *General Theory* provided a satisfactory explanation of mass unemployment – a phenomenon due to investment deficiency - it singularly failed to predict the 'stagflation' (runaway inflation with unemployment) of the 1970's. Indeed, some economists, notably Milton Friedman of the Chicago school, argued that Keynesian demand management policies were the principal cause of the inflation. According to Friedman, "inflation is always and everywhere a monetary phenomenon" and, if that is the case, it follows that the great inflation of the 1970's must have been caused by an over-expansion of the money supply brought about by the application of Keynesian demand management policies. Subsequent reflections and analyses of this historic failure culminated in a series of lectures given by the distinguished economist Sir John Hicks, and published under the heading: *The Crisis in Keynesian Economics (1975)*. Thus, while classical economics collapsed in the presence of discontinuities in the interwar period, Keynesian economics collapsed in the presence of discontinuities in the post-war period.

Two of the most fundamental laws of economics - the Laws of Supply and Demand - can also be shown to fail in the presence of discontinuities. In Chapter 9 we saw how supply and demand curves determine the equilibrium price of a commodity. When a discontinuity exists, they singularly fail to do so.

Example

Consider the supply and demand for private education. The supply of private education is defined as the number of pupil places offered by the private sector. The demand for private education is defined as the demand for pupil places. The "price" of private education is the fee charged by private schools. We shall suppose, for the sake of simplicity, that competition between schools ensures that: a) all fees are equal, and b) standards among schools are uniform. The supply of private education varies directly with the price. The higher the price, the greater the number of places offered (because more profitable) and the lower the price, the smaller the number of place offered (because less profitable). The demand for private education varies inversely with price. Fig. 5 shows the supply and demand curves for private education.

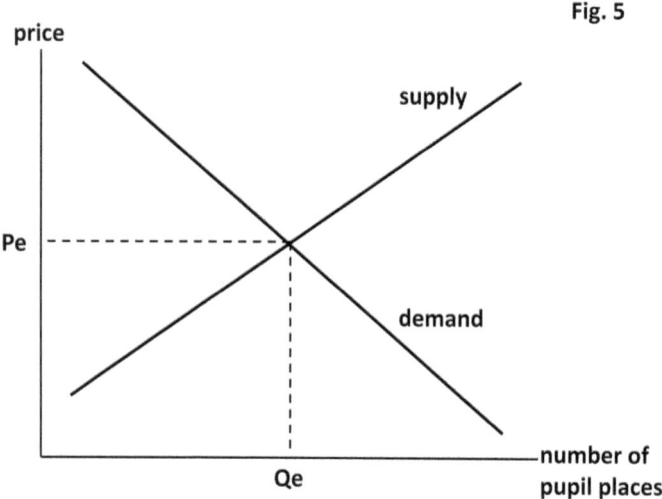

Fig. 5

When the price is equal to Pe the demand for pupil places is equal to the supply of pupil places. We shall assume that initially the market for private education is in equilibrium. Let us suppose that the government decides to expand the number of places offered by the private education sector to Qm (see fig. 6).

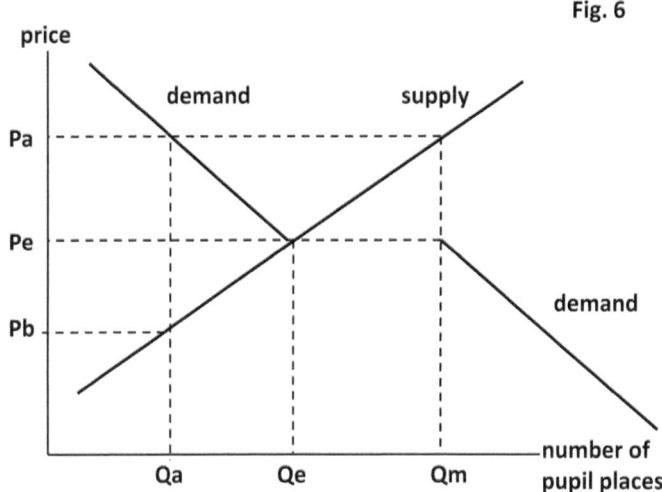

Fig. 6

It does this by issuing "education vouchers". The maximum number of subsided places will then be (Qm - Qe) (i.e. the total number of places now on offer minus the original number of places). Let us suppose, further, that the government is only prepared to operate the voucher scheme while the price is Pc or lower. This means that the cost to the taxpayer will not exceed the amount Pe x (Qm - Qe) (i.e. the price of private education multiplied by the number of subsidised places). If the price rises above Pe the government will honour its commitments to existing parents but will turn away new applicants.

At the price Pe the demand for private education will now be any number from Qe to Qm depending on the demand for subsidized education. The number of vouchers taken up by parents is undetermined within the framework of the analysis and must, therefore, be treated as a parameter. Let us assume that all vouchers are taken up. In fig. 6 the section of the demand curve below the price Pe shifts to the right by the amount (Qm - Qe). The cost to the taxpayer reaches its maximum amount Pe x (Qm - Qe). In order to meet the extra demand, schools must expand their teaching staff and capital stock (i.e. classrooms, buildings etc) and this involves additional expenditures. As schools try to recover the extra costs - it may take several years - the price of private education steadily rises to Pa. But, by this time, all the subsidized pupils have left, and the voucher scheme has been scrapped (due to a change of government) and the detached section of the demand curve shifts back to its original location. The higher price Pa causes the demand to fall to Qa creating an excess supply of places equal to (Qm - Qa). The end result is that schools find themselves with excess capacity. Some schools go bankrupt but others adapt to the changed circumstances. At any rate, the price of private education slowly falls to Pb to match the lower demand.

A new government decides to restore the private education sector to its former glory and reintroduces the voucher scheme – and so the cycle is repeated. However, this time, the number of vouchers taken up is different and this results in a different pattern of price changes. The point is that while the discontinuity exists, the equilibrium price of private education remains indeterminate.

Enter the quantum

On 14th December, 1900, the German physicist, Max Planck delivered a paper at a meeting of the German Physical Society entitled: *"On the Theory of the Energy Distribution Law of the Normal Spectrum"*. Planck had derived a formula for the energy distribution of a certain kind of thermal radiation - called "blackbody" radiation. In physics, a black body is an idealized object that *absorbs* all incident electromagnetic radiation and *emits* thermal radiation in a continuous spectrum that depends on the object's temperature. Black body radiation does not occur naturally but may be approximated by the radiation from a tiny aperture in a large enclosed container. Since absorption is perfect at all wavelengths, it is also the best possible emitter of thermal radiation. Planck also introduced a number which, when inserted into his formula, gave the best possible fit between his theory and the experimental data of his fellow physicist, Wilhelm Wien. This number – which Planck had determined through a process of trial and error - turned out to be a number of fundamental significance. It is now called "Planck's constant" and is designated by the letter h.

Before 1900, energy was assumed to be a continuously variable quantity, like mass or height. Under the assumption of continuous variation, classical physics made an absurd prediction: at ever higher frequency levels of the spectrum, thermal radiation will approach infinity. This prediction has been called "the ultraviolet catastrophe" and highlighted a major weakness in the classical theory of radiation. To address the problem Planck proposed that atoms emit or absorb energy E only in discrete bundles – called quanta – that are integer multiples of his constant h multiplied by the frequency f of the emitted radiation i.e.

(1) . . . $E = nhf$

where $n = 1, 2, 3, \ldots$ If energy is so measured, Planck found that it is possible to construct a theory of energy distribution that closely agrees with experimental data. It is this constant h that characterises quantum physics. Although h depends on the system of units used to measure it, its magnitude, in everyday terms, is so small it is normally written in the scientific notation. The number is:

(2) ... $6.62606957 \times 10^{-34}$ J.s.

To gain some idea how small it is, imagine a tiny piece of string whose length is equal to Planck's constant. If the units are in centimetres, then approximately twenty billion, trillion, trillion of these lengths of string, end to end, would be needed to span the width of a postage stamp. The date of Planck's paper on energy distribution has been called the birthday of quantum physics.

There the matter rested until 1905 when Albert Einstein published a paper on the 'photo-electric' effect - a phenomenon first discovered by Heinrich Hertz in 1887 - in which light energy displaces electrons from the surface of a metal. Classical physics was unable to account for this phenomenon and made a number of predictions which conflicted with experimental evidence. Following the work of James Clerk Maxwell on the propagation of electromagnetic waves, it was generally believed that wave energy was continuously distributed over the wave front. However, Einstein - harking back to Isaac Newton's corpuscular theory of light - postulated that light travelled in discrete, localized "packets" of energy which he called photons. The energy of each photon was found to be equal to the frequency of the light multiplied by Planck's constant:

(3) ... $E = hf$

a remarkable confirmation of Planck's theory. However, Einstein's description of light was completely at variance with the orthodox view in which light propagated as an electromagnetic wave. At any rate, the wave nature of light had been firmly established in 1801 by the experimental physicist, Thomas Young in a "double-slit" experiment which involved passing a beam of light through two closely-spaced slits. Upon exit, the component beams are found to interfere with each other as evidenced by the pattern of alternating bright and dark regions on a detection screen opposite the slit apparatus. This alternating pattern would be produced if light was a wave of energy. Nevertheless, Einstein had shown that a beam of light behaved like a stream of particles. How could light be both a wave of energy and a stream of particles?

The need to account for this extraordinary phenomenon – which is now called the 'wave-particle duality' - led to some extraordinary explanations. The Danish physicist, Niels Bohr suggested that an "observer-effect" might be in operation. To paraphrase Bohr, if the measuring apparatus is designed to observe particle behaviour, then particles are detected; if it is designed to observe interference effects (associated with waves) then waves are detected. In other words: the act of observing determines the outcome. Observing a "wave-particle" is like a blind man observing an elephant. If he approaches the elephant from one direction he detects a pair of tusks, from the opposite direction, a tail. But, this insoluble conundrum raised a more fundamental question: had physics misunderstood the nature of matter at its most fundamental level – the atom?

When Planck delivered his paper in 1900, it was known that atoms contained tiny indivisible particles with negative charges – called electrons – and regions of positive charge. By 1911, a decade after Planck's historic paper, Ernest

Rutherford, Hans Geiger and his student, Ernest Marsden had localized the positive charge in the tiny - but relatively massive - nucleus of the atom. However, these epoch-making discoveries created a new problem. According to classical theory, the negatively charged electrons in an atom should orbit the positively charged nucleus under the influence of the electric force and - as they accelerated in their orbits - radiate electromagnetic energy. But, calculations showed that orbiting electrons will quickly lose all their energy and spiral into the nucleus of the atom. In other words: the atom should collapse, and matter – as we know it – should not exist!

Another problem - involving radiation from atoms - had existed for over a hundred years. In 1802, the English chemist and physicist, William Hyde Wollaston passed sunlight through a prism and observed dark demarcation lines in the spectrum of colours. Twelve years later, the German optician, Joseph von Fraunhofer, with more refined techniques at his disposal, performed a similar experiment and discovered as many as 574 dark lines. What Wollaston and von Fraunhofer had seen in the solar spectrum were absorption lines arising from diffuse gases overlaying the bright visible surface of the Sun. These absorption lines – now called Fraunhofer lines - occur when the atoms in a diffuse gas absorb certain discrete frequencies of light from a continuous source. The resulting spectrum is called an absorption spectrum. A different kind of spectrum is produced when the atoms of a diffuse gas are excited by electric discharges and emit light of discrete frequencies. In the case of hydrogen gas, the spectrum is a series of bright coloured lines against a dark background. These bright lines are called spectral lines and the resulting spectrum an emission spectrum.

Why atoms should absorb and emit light of discrete frequencies remained unknown. But, in 1884 – three decades before a satisfactory explanation was given - a Swiss mathematician and physicist, Johann Balmer had shown that the wavelengths of the first four lines in the visible spectrum of hydrogen were related by a simple formula - a formula that was later generalised to include many more lines. Although the rationale of the formula was not understood, it demonstrated that the absorption and emission of electromagnetic radiation by atoms and molecules followed definite rules.

In 1913 - amid the growing chaos and confusion in physics - Danish physicist Niels Bohr proposed a new model of the atom. This model – which was based on the atomic theories of Ernest Rutherford – was constructed in order to explain the spectral lines of hydrogen. Bohr proposed that the single electron of the hydrogen atom can exist only in special states of motion, called stationary states. In a stationary state, the electron orbits the nucleus of the atom (the positively charged proton) without radiating electromagnetic energy. In Bohr's model, the angular momentum (i.e. mass x angular velocity) L of an electron in a stationary state assumes a value that is an integer multiple of Planck's constant divided by 2π i.e.

(4) ... $L = (nh)/2\pi$

where n = 1, 2, 3, . . . The integers, 1, 2, 3 . . . are called quantum numbers. From these conditions, Bohr was able to calculate the radii of each stationary orbit and the corresponding energy level. As might be expected, the greater the orbital radius, the greater the energy level. Since each angular momentum is an integer multiple of a constant quantity $h/2\pi$ the calculations produce a series of discontinuous energy levels.

According to Bohr, an electron will reside only in a stationary orbit, but it can "jump" from one stationary orbit to another. When this happens the electron emits or absorbs a photon whose energy is equal to the energy difference between the two orbital levels. For example, when an electron jumps to a lower energy level, a photon is emitted. Conversely, when a photon is absorbed, the electron jumps to a higher energy level. The lowest energy level at which an electron can reside is called the ground state (when $n = 1$ the corresponding orbital level defines the Bohr radius.) This ensures that the atom does not collapse. The jump from one orbital level to another may also be described as a discontinuous transition or quantum jump and the combined effect of trillions of quantum jumps to lower energy levels produces the phenomenon of electromagnetic radiation. It can be shown that the discontinuous energy levels of the hydrogen atom are responsible for the spectral lines observed in the hydrogen spectrum.

But, why electrons should behave in the manner proposed by Bohr was not explained until 1923 when the French physicist Louis de Broglie established a connection between the wave-particle behaviour of light and the discontinuous motion of electrons. De Broglie postulated that all particles of matter – not just photons - had wave-like properties and, if this was the case, then it should be possible to calculate their wavelengths. Starting with Einstein's formula for the energy of a photon and applying results from relativity theory, de Broglie showed that the wavelength λ of a particle is equal to Planck's constant divided by the particle's linear momentum i.e.

(5) ... $\lambda = h/(mv)$

This calculated wavelength – now called the de Broglie wavelength - characterises a particle (or wave) travelling in a straight line. Nevertheless, de Broglie used this result to explain why an electron orbit should be quantized. He proposed that Bohr's stationary orbits were only those in which standing waves were possible – like the vibrations of a wire loop. When a wave is localised in space – as happens when an electron orbits the nucleus - only a discrete set of wavelengths, and corresponding energy levels, are possible. In fig. 7, the standing wave oscillates between two extremes: the heavy wave and the broken wave.

Fig. 7

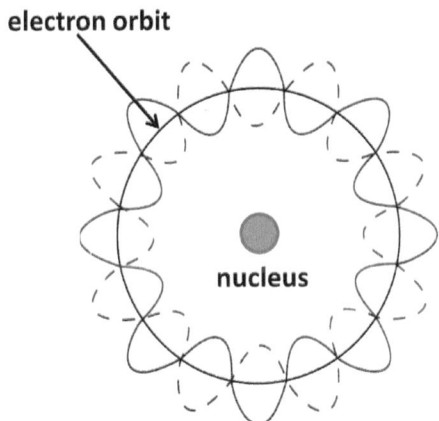

An electron can circle the nucleus only if its orbit contains an integral number of de Broglie wavelengths. We shall refer to this as the de Broglie condition. The diagram shows a standing wave with eight wavelengths. A fractional number of wavelengths - such as 4.7 - cannot persist; as the wave travels round the loop, destructive interference will occur and the vibrations will quickly die out.

Using his formula for the wavelength of a particle – in this case the electron - De Broglie derived Bohr's quantized conditions and so explained the existence of discontinuous energy levels within the atom. In 1927 the American physicists Clinton J. Davisson and Lester H. Germer confirmed De Broglie's matter-wave postulate in a convincing experiment involving the diffraction of electrons by crystals. As further confirmation, it was found that "double-slit" experiments with electron beams also produce the characteristic interference patterns associated with waves.

From the very moment Bohr introduced his model, it was apparent that matter, at its most fundamental level, could not be described in the language of classical physics. Furthermore, some extraordinary things seemed to be happening. When an electron jumps to a higher energy level, it must do so instantaneously otherwise it would emit electromagnetic radiation continuously during the transition. This would conflict with observations – as well as the Bohr model - that radiation is absorbed in the transition to a higher energy level. Now, an instantaneous jump has some very strange implications. In the Bohr model, an electron orbits the nucleus at a certain distance from the nucleus - this distance being the radius of the orbit - and is determined by the de Broglie condition. Therefore, when an electron jumps to a higher energy level its distance from the nucleus increases instantaneously. In other words, it makes an instantaneous jump through space. Atomic distances are very small but electrons are even smaller; hence, a jump between energy levels is – for an electron - a very large distance. Now, if an entity traverses space instantaneously, it traverses space in zero time. But, if it can traverse space in zero time, then it must necessarily exist everywhere at once – though focusing in only one place at a time. For such an entity, time and space is no barrier. This raises the fundamental issue of location. Can an electron be located anywhere at all? The alternative – which lies very much within the realm of speculation - is to reject the notion of instantaneous jumps and argue that when an electron begins to jump between energy levels, it is instantly destroyed and a new electron is created at the new energy level - destruction and creation occurring simultaneously. This, of course, raises the question of identity. If the disappearance of the old electron occurs simultaneously with the appearance of the new one, does it make sense to speak of an electron jumping between energy levels when it ceases to exist at the jump? Furthermore, if creation and destruction are simultaneous events, how is the process coordinated?

Bohr's model of the atom was highly influential and marked a watershed in the understanding of the atomic structure of matter. But, it was a model constructed to serve a particular purpose. While the model accounted for the spectra of hydrogen and hydrogen-like atoms it did not account for the spectra of more complicated atoms and molecules. Hence, it did not provide a complete description of matter at its most fundamental level. Nevertheless, the notion of 'discontinuous jumps' – now referred to as 'quantum jumps' or 'quantum leaps' - has entered into the lexicon of modern physics.

Between 1925 and 1926 Bohr's description of the hydrogen atom was replaced by a more general theory. Erwin Schrödinger, Werner Heisenberg, Max Born, Pascual Jordan, Paul Dirac and others developed methods and techniques which transformed the study and description of atomic phenomena into a mathematically rigorous discipline. These methods - collectively known as quantum mechanics - began as two separate approaches. Werner Heisenberg, Max Born and Pascual Jordan formulated quantum mechanics in the abstract mathematical language of matrices (rectangular arrays) – called matrix mechanics. At about the same time, the Austrian physicist, Erwin Schrödinger developed an alternative version called wave mechanics - soon showing that matrix and wave mechanics were equivalent representations. Since wave mechanics can be interpreted in terms of the well-known properties of waves, Schrödinger's approach is generally preferred by physicists.

Heisenberg and Schrödinger had published their seminal papers during a period of unprecedented disquiet in the state of physics. Ten years before, Einstein had published work on the spontaneous and stimulated emission of radiation in which energy exchanges could occur spontaneously without a direct cause. This work had followed hot on the heels of Bohr's theory of discontinuous jumps which flatly contradicted the classical concept of continuous motion. By 1920, Einstein was very dissatisfied with the state of physics and, in a letter to Max Born, said he would be "very unhappy to renounce complete causality." According to one modern physicist, chronicling the development of quantum mechanics in the 1920's: "theoretical evidence was building for a discontinuous physics in which energy exchanges happened 'spontaneously', unpredictably and with a complete lack of respect for the notion that there should be a direct connection between cause and effect." (*Beyond Measure (2004)*, Jim Baggott, p.22).

Einstein's work on spontaneous radiation, combined with Bohr's theory of discontinuous jumps, served to undermine the classical concept of causality which, among other things, requires that: (a) motion be continuous (b) all effects have causes. It was clear that physics was moving in a radically new direction. We saw in the previous section how causal theories collapse in the presence of discontinuities and that the fundamental principle of classical mechanics F=ma is vulnerable to the existence of discontinuities. By the middle of the 1920's, it was evident that the whole of classical physics – which included Newton's Laws of Motion - was collapsing in the presence of discontinuities within the atom. When Erwin Schrödinger, a classical physicist by temperament, published his paper in 1926 he was attempting to reverse this trend and restore continuity to the heart of physics.

Schrödinger's problem was to find a continuous wave function Ψ (psi) that described the matter-waves of de Broglie and was consistent with the discontinuous energy levels within the hydrogen atom. With what has been described as stroke of inspiration, he took the classical wave equation and simply inserted the de Broglie wavelength. There was no precedent for such an approach and it could not be justified by an appeal to existing theory. Contemporary and later physicists felt that Schrödinger's derivation was somewhat obscure. Nevertheless, his equation was remarkably successful, casting considerable light on the whole of physics and chemistry. Moreover, at the macroscopic level i.e. the level perceivable by the human senses, it was consistent with classical mechanics. Although, Schrödinger's equation appeared like a rabbit out of a hat, physicists emphasise that its validity lies not with its derivation but with the accuracy of its predictions; it has proven to be in remarkable agreement with physical data. Schrödinger's work was hailed as a triumph by the scientific community, and in 1933 he was awarded the Nobel Prize for Physics. The Schrödinger wave equation is now regarded as a fundamental principle of quantum mechanics – like Newton's $F = ma$ in classical mechanics.

Although Schrödinger's equation was a great success, there were a number of problems. In water waves, the quantity that changes periodically is the height of the water; in sound waves, it is the pressure. But what, one wonders, changes periodically in a matter-wave? Moreover, how did Schrödinger's theory account for the particle-like behaviour of electromagnetic waves? Schrödinger himself believed he had answered the last question by introducing the notion of "wave packets" i.e. bundles of electromagnetic waves which combine to produce a wave with an unusually large amplitude (see fig.8).

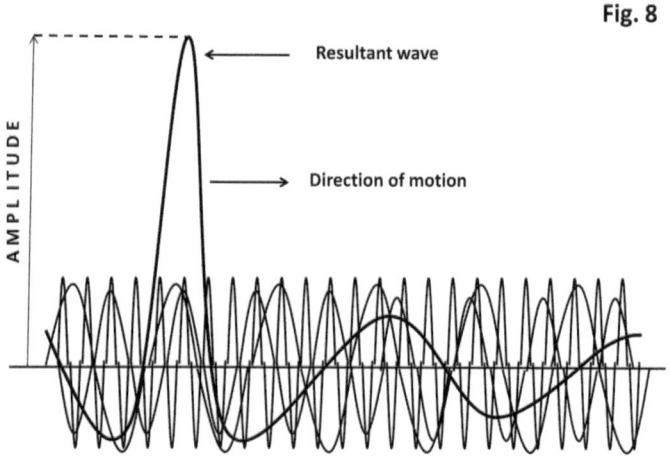

Fig. 8

Vibrations in the electromagnetic field

According to Schrödinger, these high amplitudes would be detected as particles. Such an interpretation, he believed, would solve the wave-particle duality by eliminating particles altogether. In other words, only waves would exist.

Unfortunately (for Schrödinger), a wave packet can persist only if its dimensions are large in relation to the wavelength. When confined to a small region of space, superpositions of tightly packed waves spread out very quickly, dispersing into a resultant wave with a more uniform distribution of amplitudes. This means that particle-like characteristics cannot be the result of wave superpositions, a fact pointed out to Schrödinger by the distinguished physicist, Hendrik Lorentz in a letter dated May, 1926. As further confirmation, any physicist looking at the track left by an electron in a cloud chamber would be convinced that an electron was a particle – not a wave.

Perhaps the more pressing question, namely, what was oscillating in a matter-wave, was provided by Max Born in 1926. He proposed that the de Broglie matter-wave – now represented by the Schrödinger wave function Ψ – corresponded to a wave of probability. While Ψ itself was given no physical interpretation, Born proposed that the quantity Ψ^2 (psi-squared), evaluated over a region of space, gave the probability that an electron will be detected there. Under Born's interpretation, it is possible to calculate the probability that an electron will be detected in a certain region of space but this will not be enough to determine its precise location: there will always be an element of uncertainty. By providing the Schrödinger wave equation with a probabilistic interpretation, Born discarded a cornerstone of classical physics, namely, that causes and effects are linked together in deterministic relationships that precludes uncertainty. Given the laws of mechanics and various initial conditions, all effects can be calculated uniquely from their causes; therefore, it should be possible, at least in principle, to calculate an electron's precise location. But, under Born's interpretation this is impossible. In fact, the electron's position is the product of chance – like the throw of a die.

At first, it was thought that imprecision or uncertainty flowed from imperfection – imperfections in quantum theory. This, indeed, was Einstein's view. In a letter to Max Born dated December, 1926, Einstein states that: "Quantum mechanics is certainly imposing. But an inner voice tells me that it is not yet the real thing. The theory says a lot, but does not bring us any closer to the secret of the 'Old One.' I, at any rate, am convinced that He is not playing dice." Heisenberg disagreed. He felt that uncertainty lay at the heart of physics. In a sense, Heisenberg went back to the drawing board. He asked: how do physicists measure the position and momentum of an electron? To answer this question, he devised a 'thought experiment' in which a hypothetical gamma-ray microscope detects an electron through its collisions with other particles. In a gamma-ray microscope, gamma-ray photons are 'bounced' off an electron and collected on a detection device which produces a magnified image. Unfortunately, this creates a problem. In 1923, the American physicist, Arthur Holly Compton had shown that when a gamma-ray photon collides with an electron, the electron is given a severe jolt. (This is now known as the Compton Effect). Immediately after impact, the position and momentum of the electron change in a way that is unpredictable. According to Born's interpretation of the wave function, only probabilities may be calculated. Now, one could improve the accuracy of measurement by using a more powerful microscope i.e. one with a higher resolution. In this case, the electron's position will be less uncertain but, since the disturbance will be greater, the electron's momentum will be more uncertain. Using a less powerful microscope i.e. one with lower resolution, the electron's momentum will be less uncertain, because there will be less disturbance, but the electron's position will be more uncertain.

Heisenberg formalized the argument in his famous 'uncertainty principle' which places a limit on the accuracy with which two complementary variables – such as position and momentum - may be known. The more one knows about one variable, the less one can know about the other. This means that if - contrary to Born's interpretation of the wave function - a particle's position could be measured precisely, then *nothing whatsoever* could be known about its momentum, and vice versa. If an electron's precise position and momentum can never known simultaneously, then its future path can never be determined. In other words, causal law at the level of the atom does not exist.

The measurement of an electron's position and momentum is a special case of a more general problem in quantum mechanics known as the 'problem of measurement.' In any quantum mechanical system: "The measurement of an observable causes the state of the system to change in a way that is inherently uncontrollable and unpredictable, via a mechanism the nature of which we do not know." (*Understanding Quantum Physics (1990),* Michael A. Morrison, p.590). The underlying process is random and the governing laws are probabilistic. Moreover, there is an interaction between the observer and the observed which cannot be eliminated. These fundamental facts are built into the mathematical structure of quantum mechanics and provide a coherent and consistent description of the quantum world – a description that has been confirmed by countless experiments.

But, that is not all. According to quantum mechanics, *prior* to the act of measurement, a particle's position is not a meaningful quantity but exists only as a potential property that is realized or made meaningful only through the act of observation. This phenomenon applies to *all* the particle's properties. But, if this is the case, then a particle cannot be said to exist as an entity independent of the observer. Since particles are the building blocks of the physical cosmos, and since these building blocks exist only as potential entities until they are actualized through measurement or observation, it follows that the cosmos as a whole is realizable only through measurement or observation. Such a result supports the notion that consciousness is the primary reality and that the human self exists outside the fabric of time and space.

Deterministic chaos

For nearly three hundred years, the scientific establishment believed that causal laws made the world an inherently predictable place, a paradigm of certainty expressed in Newton's Laws of Motion. The Laplacian worldview, which grew out of Newtonian physics, maintained that the future course of the universe could, in principle, be completely predicted once the initial conditions were known. This view of the world began to crumble, even before the arrival of quantum mechanics. In 1887, the King of Sweden, Oscar II, offered a prize to anyone who could find the general solution to a problem that had perplexed mathematicians since the time of Newton. It was the problem of how three or more bodies, obeying Newton's Law of Gravitation, interact in free space. The most notable example of a three-body problem is the Sun-Earth-Moon system (see fig. 9).

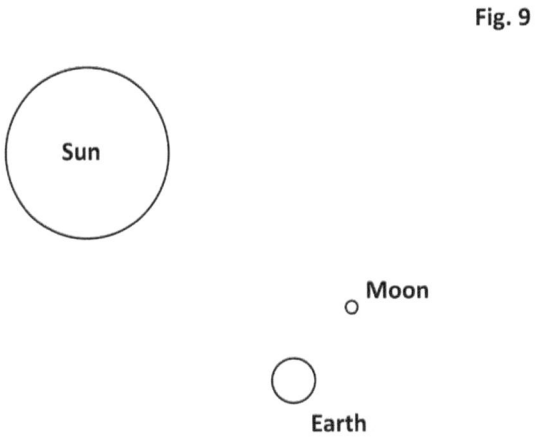

Fig. 9

The precise wording of the problem, which was clearly addressed to mathematicians, was as follows: "Given a system of arbitrarily many mass points that attract each other according to Newton's law, under the assumption that no two points ever collide, try to find a representation of the coordinates of each point as a series in a variable that is some known function of time and for all of whose values the series converges uniformly."

Two hundred years before this challenge, Isaac Newton had solved the *two*-body problem. He showed that if the common centre of mass of the two bodies is considered to be at rest, then each body travels along a conic section (i.e. a circle, ellipse, parabola or hyperbola) which has a focus at the centre of mass of the system; the two conics will be in the same plane. However, if another mass is added to the system, the problem becomes much more difficult. Newton himself had made some progress towards its solution in the *Principia* but his arguments were verbal and geometrically based. Precisely how three bodies interact under the influence of gravity remained a famous, unsolved problem in mechanics.

In response to the King of Sweden's challenge, French mathematician, Henri Poincaré made a highly original, though unsuccessful, attempt at a solution. He showed that three interacting bodies under the influence of gravity behave in a way that is inherently unpredictable. Mathematicians would later call the motion *chaotic*. According to Poincaré: " . . it may happen that small differences in the initial conditions produce very great ones [differences] in the final phenomena. A small error in the former will produce an enormous error in the latter. Prediction becomes impossible." (Quoted in *Chaos and Fractals (1992)*, Peitgen, Jürgens, Saupe pp.41 to 42).

Poincaré won first prize, making contributions that would lead to the modern theory of chaos.

Some of the simplest dynamical systems exhibit chaotic behaviour e.g. a bouncing ball on a vibrating table, and the double pendulum. Chaotic behaviour is also exhibited in electrical circuits, lasers, in oscillating chemical reactions, in fluid dynamics, and mechanical and magneto-mechanical devices, as well as computer models of chaotic processes. Although the future behaviour of the system is fully determined, long-term prediction is impossible because the system behaves chaotically. Chaotic behaviour is easy to demonstrate in the case of a double pendulum.

In the fig. 10 the path of the lower weight is traced out as it swings through space.

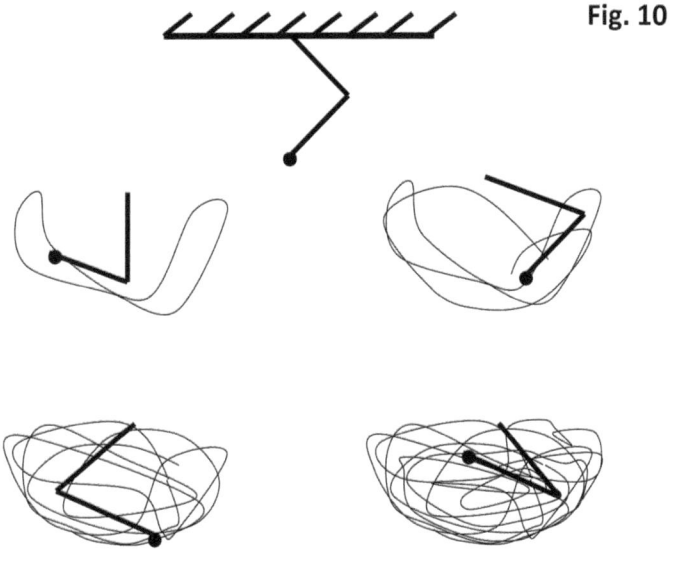

Fig. 10

The motion soon becomes chaotic and unpredictable. The most famous case of how chaos can emerge from a simple non-linear dynamical system is the 'logistic map':

(L) ... $x_{n+1} = \alpha x_n(1 - x_n)$

first used by the mathematician Pierre François Verhulst in 1845 to study the dynamics of population change. Equation (L) demonstrates how chaos and unpredictability can arise from a simple deterministic model. The sequence of graphs in fig. 11 show how the behaviour of x responds to changes in the parameter α when the initial value of x is 0.1 (The horizontal axis denotes the number of iterations.)

Fig. 11

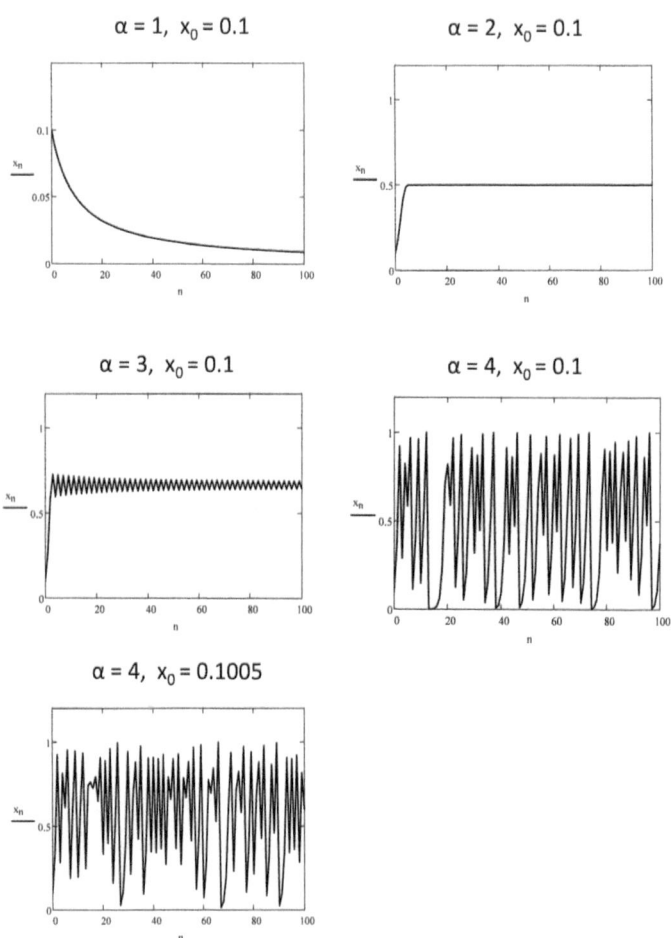

When α = 4 the path of x becomes chaotic. If the initial value of x is increased very slightly to 0.1005, the path of x changes in a completely unpredictable way'

In 1963, American meteorologist, Edward Lorenz published a paper in the Journal of Atmospheric Sciences entitled: *Deterministic Turbulent Flow*. He had carried out a number of computer simulations and found that weather patterns were sensitive to initial conditions. For example, very slight changes in atmospheric pressure could lead to dramatic changes in weather patterns throughout the globe within a few days. One meteorologist remarked that if his results were correct "one flap of a seagull's wings could change the course of weather forever."

The word "butterfly" first appeared in 1972 in the title of a talk Lorenz gave to the American Association for the Advancement of Science: *Does the flap of a butterfly's wings in Brazil set off a tornado in Texas?* This sensitivity to initial conditions, popularly known as the "butterfly effect," has rendered long-term weather forecasting extremely difficult – if not impossible - even though the weather is governed by deterministic laws. More significantly, it shows how deterministic chaos undermines the relationship between causality and predictability.

Chapter 11
The Unreality of Time

The nature of time has been a puzzle to philosophers since antiquity and a source of bewilderment to physicists ever since the publication of Isaac Newton's *Mathematical Principles of Natural Philosophy* in 1687. According to Professor J. Alexander Gunn: " . . the problem [of time] has been recognized as exceedingly difficult. Dean Inge has referred to the problem as 'the hardest in metaphysics,' and 'we know that from the first dawn of speculation till now, from the time of Parmenides and Zeno to that of Mr. Bradley and M. Bergson, there has been no other problem that has seemed so baffling as that of Time.'" (*The Problem of Time (1929)*, sect. 241)

In Newton's *Principia* time is described as follows: "Absolute, True, and Mathematical Time, of itself, and from its own nature flows equably without regard to anything external, and by another name is called Duration. Relative, Apparent, and Common Time is some sensible and external (whether accurate or unequable) measure of Duration by the means of motion, which is commonly used instead of True time; such as an Hour, a Day, a Month, a Year.... For the natural days are truly unequal, though they are commonly considered as equal, and used for a measure of time. Astronomers correct this inequality for their more accurate deducing of the celestial motions. It may be, that there is no such thing as an equable motion, whereby time may be accurately measured. All motions may be accelerated and retarded, but the True, or equable progress, of Absolute time is liable to no change. The duration or perseverance of the existence of things remains the same, whether the motions are swift or slow, or none at all. "[Translated from the original Latin text by Andrew Motte, 1729.]

Newton distinguishes between absolute time, which "flows equably without regard to anything external," and relative time which is measured by the Earth's axial motion. Furthermore: "It may be, that there is no such thing as an equable motion, whereby time may be accurately measured. All motions may be accelerated and retarded." The apparent solar day, which is defined as the interval between two successive returns of the Sun to the local meridian, varies in length due to the Earth's axial tilt and elliptical orbit around the sun. Consequently, astronomers use a mathematical construction called the mean solar day which is an average of all the apparent solar days throughout the year. It is significant that Newton does not regard relative time as fundamental but as a symbolic measure of absolute time. However, his definition of absolute time "without reference to anything external" violates one of his own principles, namely, that one should investigate only what may be observed (*hypotheses non fingo* - I feign no hypotheses.)

Gottfried Wilhelm Leibniz (1646 – 1716) attacked Newton's concept of absolute time because it contradicted two fundamental philosophical principles:

(1) the 'principle of sufficient reason' which states that there must be a reason for something to exist rather than not to exist, or an event to occur rather than not to occur, or something to be true rather than not to be true.
(2) the 'identity of indiscernibles' which states that two or more objects or entities are identical (i.e. are one and the same entity) if they have all their properties in common.

Leibniz argued that if the universe had been created at a particular time, there is no conceivable reason why it should have been created at *that* time as opposed to any other time. Consequently, absolute time must contradict the principle of sufficient reason. But suppose the universe had been created in time. In that case, time would have been empty for an infinite duration before the universe had been created and would therefore have consisted of an infinite number of indiscernible – and hence identical - moments. This contradicts Newtonian theory, which requires that all moments of time be distinct.

In *Einstein's Theory of Relativity (1923),* Max Born, modern physicist and pioneer of quantum mechanics, criticises Newton's concept of absolute time on the grounds that "what exists without reference to any external object whatsoever is not ascertainable and is not a fact." (p. 57). In other words: absolute time is not a fact of nature and as far as modern physics is concerned does not exist. Relative time, derived from the motion of bodies, cannot be used as a measure of absolute time because all motions from which relative time is measured may vary in ways which, ultimately, cannot be known. The mean solar day may appear to be constant against the stellar background but the background stars are themselves moving in relation to the galactic centre, and the galactic centre is moving in relation to the nearest group of galaxies. Since the universe is expanding, everything is, in fact, moving relative to everything else; nothing is at absolute rest and therefore nothing can be used as an ultimate yardstick against which absolute time may be measured. This continual flux is unnoticed in everyday affairs because the motion of the Earth seems regular and the background stars seem fixed.

Newton does not discuss the experience of time in human consciousness - sometimes called subjective or psychological time - but it does appear in the writings of physicist James Clerk Maxwell (1831-1879). In *Matter and Motion (1877)*, Maxwell states that: "The idea of Time in its most primitive form is probably the recognition of an order of sequence in our states of consciousness. If my memory were perfect, I might be able to refer every event within my own experience to its proper place in a chronological series. But it would be difficult, if not impossible, for me to compare the interval between one pair of events and that between another pair—to ascertain, for instance, whether the time during which I can work without feeling tired is greater or less now than when I first began to study. By our intercourse with other persons, and by our experience of natural processes which go on in a uniform or a rhythmical manner, we come to recognize the possibility of arranging a system of chronology in which all events whatever, whether relating to ourselves or to others, must find their places." (p. 11). As we shall see, Maxwell's concatenation of time and memory is echoed in the writings of Augustine of Hippo.

On the question of absolute time, Maxwell is close to Newton: "Absolute, true, and mathematical Time is conceived by Newton as flowing at a constant rate, unaffected by the speed or slowness of the motions of material things. It is also called Duration. Relative, apparent, and common time is duration as estimated by the motion of bodies, as by days, months, and years. These measures of time may be regarded as provisional, for the progress of astronomy has taught us to measure the inequality in the lengths of days, months, and years, and thereby to reduce the apparent time to a more uniform scale, called Mean Solar Time." (p. 12) Although Maxwell recognizes the role of time in human consciousness, it is apparent that the concept of time in physics changed very little between the publication of Newton's *Principia* and Maxwell's *Matter and Motion*. Maxwell recognises the difference between absolute and relative time but there is no hint that absolute time might have no objective reality.

Similar remarks apply to Newton's concept of absolute space. Quoting from the *Principia:* "Absolute Space, in its own nature, without regard to anything external, remains always similar and immoveable. Relative Space is some moveable dimension or measure of the absolute spaces; which our senses determine, by its position to bodies; and which is vulgarly taken for immoveable space . . And so instead of absolute places and motions, we use relative ones; and that without any inconvenience in common affairs: but in Philosophical disquisitions, we ought to abstract from our senses, and consider things themselves, distinct from what are only sensible measures of them. For it may be that there is no body really at rest, to which the places and motions of others may be referred." Newton distinguishes between absolute space and relative space but, does not regard relative space as a fundamental feature of the universe: "it may be that there is no body really at rest, to which the places and motion of others may be referred."

Newton's concept of absolute space was controversial from the very beginning. According to Leibniz, space made no sense except as the relative location of bodies, and time made no sense except as the relative movement of bodies. Indeed, he maintained: "There is no space where there is no matter." Bishop Berkeley suggested that, "lacking any point of reference, a sphere in an otherwise empty universe could not be conceived to rotate, and a pair of spheres could be conceived to rotate relative to one another, but not to rotate about their centre of gravity." In modern physics the concept of absolute space is considered to be unnecessary even in the context of Newtonian mechanics. Instead, physicists employ the notion of 'inertial frames of reference' i.e. a set of preferred frames of reference that move with uniform velocity relative to one another. Since the laws of physics are the same in all inertial frames, the concept of absolute space is effectively redundant. In *Gravitation and Gauge Symmetries (2002)* Milutin Blagojević states that:

(1) Absolute space contradicts the internal logic of classical mechanics since, according to the Galilean principle of relativity, none of the inertial frames can be singled out.
(2) Absolute space does not explain inertial forces since they are related to acceleration with respect to any one of the inertial frames.
(3) Absolute space acts on physical objects by inducing their resistance to acceleration but it cannot be acted upon.

Although absolute space has been rejected in favour of inertial frames of reference, modern physics is still grappling with the notion of time. Physicist Richard Feynman, co-creator of quantum electrodynamics, and winner of the Nobel Prize for Physics in 1965, claims that time cannot be defined at all. In his famous lectures, Feynman asks: "What is time? It would be nice if we could find a good definition of time. Webster defines 'a time' as 'a period,' and the latter as 'a time,' which doesn't seem very useful. Perhaps we should say: 'Time is what happens when nothing else happens.' Which also doesn't get us very far. Maybe it is just as well if we face the fact that time is one of the things we probably cannot define (in the dictionary sense), and just say that it is what we already know it to be: it is how long we wait! What really matters anyway is not how we *define* time, but how we measure it." (*The Feynman Lectures* – Volume 1, 8-2.) According to Feynman, then, time is not defined but *measured*; the quantity being measured merely called time. Of course, measuring something and calling it "time" does not mean that time exists any more than measuring something and calling it "green elephants" means that green elephants exist. The Greek philosopher, Plotinus (205 –270) said: "The measurement of a quantity of time does not help us know its nature. Not only is measurement not necessary to its existence, but the problem of measuring leaves its nature entirely undiscussed." (Quoted in: *The Problem of Time(1929),* sect. 31 - J. Alexander Gunn)

* * *

To show that time as measured by the motion of the Earth is purely conventional, consider the following example. Suppose a 'master' clock exists and is perfectly synchronized to the axial motion of the Earth, and that all other clocks in existence are synchronized to the master clock. When the Earth has made one complete rotation on its axis, the clock shows that one "day" has elapsed; 1/24 of a rotation corresponds to one "hour," and 1/1440 of a rotation to one "minute," and so on. A commuter, Alice, travels 60 miles to work by train, and the train driver ensures that the average "speed" of the train is always maintained at 60 miles per "hour;" hence, her journey takes exactly one "hour." Through long experience Alice knows when the journey is coming to an end because her subjective experience of waiting closely corresponds to one "hour" on the clock. Suddenly, the Earth's rate of rotation begins to decrease but it happens so slowly that no one is aware of the fact and life continues as normal. Let us pick up the story when its rate of rotation has fallen by half. To an 'outside' observer standing on a 'fixed' star, all clocks – which are synchronized to the master clock – are now running at half their original speed. As mentioned, the driver of the commuter's train must ensure that the "speed" is exactly 60 miles per "hour." In other words, the train must cover the usual distance of sixty miles as the Earth completes one twenty fourth part of its "daily" axial motion. He does this by slowing the train down to half its original "speed." Alice now finds that the journey is taking twice as long. Although the train is still travelling at 60 miles per "hour" in terms of the new measurement of "hours," Alice experiences a "speed" of only 30 miles per "hour" in terms of the old measurement of "hours." In other words the journey seems twice as long, though the measurement of "speed" is unchanged.

As the rotation of the Earth continues to decrease, all clocks including the train slow down to match its slower rotation. The "speed" of the train is always maintained at an average of 60 miles per "hour" but Alice feels that the journey is taking longer and longer. Eventually the Earth stops rotating (relative to the stars), all clocks stop, and the train stops relative to the Earth. Time has stopped but the subjective experience of waiting continues. However, the train is still 'travelling' at 60 miles per "hour." Eventually, Alice gets off the train and hitches a lift! The motion of the Earth has failed to provide a measure of time which corresponds to the human experience of waiting. The point is, of course, that absolute time cannot be measured by the motion of bodies, let alone the Earth, unless the motion is known to be regular. But, of course, there is no way of knowing that the motion of a body is regular unless some method of measuring time already exists. In *The Problem of Time (1929)* Gunn asks the question: "how can we consistently affirm that time is a measure of movement and that it is itself measured by movement? We can only know equal times by some constant velocity of rotation, but we can only know that any rotation is constant if we already know and can measure equal times." (sect. 54). In physics, time is used to measure the motion of bodies – not the other way round. Although our example has shown that motion cannot measure absolute time, it might be thought that atomic clocks can. Unfortunately, the same problem arises because it cannot be known if atomic clocks provide accurate measures of absolute time unless a method for measuring absolute time already exists. If it is asserted that atomic clocks measure the passage of time by definition then, of course, the assertion is no more valid than the assertion that polygraphs detect lies by definition.

Given that absolute time has been rejected by modern physics and that relative time as measured by the rotation of the Earth, or by the motion of some other physical body, is purely conventional, we are still left with the notion of *time* itself – however measured or defined. Time, of course, refers to the *passage* of time but if time is an objective phenomenon it ought to be the same for everyone irrespective of the person's motion. Not so for Albert Einstein. In fact time depends on the speed at which an observer is moving – a result derived from the two fundamental postulates of Einstein's theory of relativity:

Postulate I. The principle of relativity.
All inertial observers are equivalent.

Postulate II. Constancy of the velocity of light.
The velocity of light is the same in all inertial frames

According to the principle of relativity there are an infinite number of frames of reference (inertial frames) moving with uniform velocity with respect to one another, in which the laws of physics are the same. To illustrate, consider any inertial system j were $j = 1, 2, \ldots \infty$. Let F_j, m_j and a_j be the force, mass and acceleration respectively of a body in inertial frame j. Newton's Law of Acceleration in frame j is then expressed as:

(L) $\ldots F_j = m_j a_j$

where $j = 1, 2, \ldots \infty$. If the laws of physics changed from one inertial frame to another, then the formulae expressing those laws would be functions of velocity. The principal of relativity is completely consistent with Newtonian theory since all Newton's equations remain unchanged when expressed in different inertial frames. Hence, the subscripts are unnecessary. The radical departure from Newtonian theory is Postulate II – which asserts that the velocity of light is the same in every inertial frame.

Historically, Einstein's second postulate arose from the inability of Michelson and Morley in 1887 to detect the 'luminiferous ether' then believed to be a unique medium or frame of reference for the transmission of light. If the velocity of light is constant in all inertial frames (as proposed by Einstein) it is easy to show that time becomes a function of motion, giving rise to the strange phenomenon of 'time dilation.' This means, for example, that a clock moving away from an observer will tick more slowly in relation to a clock held by the observer. To illustrate, suppose a space craft is travelling away from the Earth at one tenth of the speed of light, and suppose further that an astronaut inside the craft walks from one part of the craft to another in 5 seconds. To someone on Earth the astronaut (according to the time dilation equation of relativity theory) would take 5.025 seconds; the greater the velocity of the craft, the slower the apparent motion of the astronaut. If time slows down in relation to the Earth, then everything slows down – even the aging process.

It may be objected, of course, that whatever applies to the astronaut also applies to an observer on Earth; therefore, if the astronaut's time dilates relative to an observer on Earth, the observer's time should dilate relative to the astronaut on the spacecraft leaving their relative times unchanged. This argument is correct as far as it stands. So long as the astronaut is travelling with constant velocity, the symmetrical relationship between the astronaut and the Earth is maintained. However, when the astronaut momentarily stops in space to return home the symmetry is broken and he finds he has aged less than his contemporaries on Earth. This is an example of the so-called "twin paradox" i.e. a twin travels into space in a high-speed rocket and returns home to find he has aged less than his identical "stay-at-home" twin. Although a paradox of sorts, it is not a paradox within the theory of relativity. On the outward journey the relative positions of the two twins are unchanged until the travelling twin turns round to make the journey home. At the turnaround the travelling twin switches inertial frames leading to a recalculation of time. Suppose the travelling twin measures the time elapsed on the outward journey immediately before the turnaround to be T_1 and then recalculates the time elapsed immediately after the turnaround to be T_2. The difference between the two measures of time ($T_2 - T_1$) represents a "jump discontinuity" and is the amount by which time has dilated during the whole journey. It is also the difference between the ages of the two twins which becomes apparent when the travelling twin returns home and finds his twin ($T_2 - T_1$) years older. This result has been confirmed experimentally with real clocks – one stationary (relative to the Earth) and one moving. Needless to say, the elasticity of time in relativity theory has profound implications for the notion of time. Given that planets, stars and galaxies are moving away from the Earth with different relative velocities, the measurement of time will be different for each astronomical object; it follows that time for the cosmos as a whole has no meaning. In *A Brief History of Time (1988),* Stephen Hawking - discussing the technical difficulties of solving Feynman's quantum equations - makes the novel suggestion that time is "imaginary." According to Hawking: "To avoid the technical difficulties with Feynman's sum over histories, one must use *imaginary* time. That is to say, for the purposes of the calculation one must measure time using imaginary numbers, rather than real ones. This has an interesting effect on space-time: the distinction between time and space disappears completely." (p.134). It would seem that modern physics is moving ever closer to the view that time and space are unreal. But, the unreality of time is an ancient idea.

Greek Thoughts

Parmenides of Elea (c. 520 – 430 BCE), Greek philosopher, poet and the founder of the discipline of logic, has been described as a towering figure in the history of western thought. Credited with the discovery of the true shape of the Earth (his contemporaries insisted it was flat or saucer-shaped) he was also the first to argue that time is unreal. Parmenides eliminated time from his philosophical view of the world by appealing to the logical characteristics of language and thought. His principal thesis was that whatever can be spoken of, thought of, or inquired into "is without creation or destruction; whole unique, unmoved and perfect. Nor was it ever, nor will it be, since it now is, all together, one continuous." (Quoted in *The Presocratic Philosophers: A Critical History with Selected Texts (1983)* by G. S. Kirk, J. E. Raven, and M. Schofield). In other words: anything real exists as a complete unchanging whole; therefore, anything that is not a complete unchanging whole is unreal. Anything that appears in parts, or is in any way incomplete or imperfect is unreal. Time, of its nature, is not a complete whole because the past, present and future do not co-exist.

Time appears only as fleeting instants of the present; therefore time is unreal. Parmenides made a clear distinction between appearances and reality, time being a characteristic feature of the phenomenal world of appearances, not of reality – a view endorsed by Plato himself. For Plato: "Time is a corruption of Eternity as Becoming is a corruption of Being. Time is regarded as the form, sign, and measure of the impermanence of the imperfect. Presumably, if the Perfect were fully manifested to us Time would vanish." (Quoted in *The Problem of Time (1929)* - J. Alexander Gunn, Sect. 23).

Aristotle (384 –322 BCE), who was a student of Plato, presents a number of arguments in his book *Physics* intended to cast doubt on the existence of time. These arguments were taken up and developed into a general critique of time by a number of later philosophers, notably Sextus Empiricus (c. 200 CE) of the Skeptic school. Sextus presents three arguments adapted from Aristotle to show that time cannot possess either, or must possess both, of a pair of contradictory qualities. In each case, Sextus shows that time does not exist. The three qualities that time possesses are: (a) finiteness (b) divisibility and (c) mutability. Finiteness means that time has a beginning and an end. Divisibility means that time can be divided into past, present and future. Mutability is time's changing nature, changing its state from non-being (when it is future) to being (when it is present) to non-being (when it is past). When future becomes present, time is generated; when present becomes past, time is destroyed. Hence, mutability also represents time's capability of being generated and destroyed. The following arguments, used by Sextus to show that time does not exist, are based on Philip Turetzky's

Time (1998). For a more detailed discussion the reader is referred to Turetzky's book.

Sextus' argument concerning finiteness:
If time is finite, it must begin at some time and end at some time. But if time begins at some time and ends at some time, then there must have been times before and after time exists, which is nonsense. Therefore time is not finite. Suppose time is infinite. Part of time is past, part of time is present, and part of time is future. If the past and future do not exist, then only the present exists. If only the present exists, then time is not infinite. But under the hypothesis that time is infinite, the past and future must exist. If the past and future exist, then the past and future must be present, which is nonsense. Therefore, time is not infinite. Since time is neither finite nor infinite, and everything existent must be one or the other, time does not exist.

Sextus' argument concerning divisibility:
Since time can be divided into past, present and future, time is divisible. But anything divisible into parts can be expressed against a (standard) part of itself. If the present can be expressed in terms of the past, then the past is the same as the present. If the future can be expressed in terms of the present and the past, then the present and past are the same as the future. But these results are nonsense, therefore time is not divisible. Since time cannot be both divisible and indivisible, time does not exist.

Sextus then argues that each part of time does not exist. The past and future do not exist, because if they did they would be present. But the past and future cannot be present because otherwise all events would be simultaneous.

Furthermore, the present does not exist. If something changes, it changes in the present. If the present is indivisible, then something can change in an indivisible amount of time – which is impossible. Therefore the present is not indivisible. If the present is divisible, then its parts must be past, present, or future. If an existent thing has parts, then the parts must also exist. But neither the future nor the past exist; therefore the present cannot be divided into parts that are past and future. Hence the present is not divisible. Since the present is neither divisible nor indivisible and since it must be one or the other, it does not exist.

Sextus' argument concerning mutability:

Part of time is future and does not yet exist; but time comes into being when it becomes present. Therefore, time is capable of being generated. But since the future does not exist, and if time is generated out of the future, time is generated out of something that does not exist. Since something can be generated only out of something that exists, time is not capable of being generated. Part of time exists as present; but time no longer exists when it becomes past. Therefore time is capable of being destroyed. But since the past does not exist, and if time is destroyed into the past, time is destroyed into something that does not exist. Since something can be destroyed only into something that exists, time is not capable of being destroyed. We conclude that time is both capable and incapable of being generated and destroyed. Since this result is contradictory, time does not exist.

Sextus uses other arguments to show that time does not exist by assuming that time comes into being. If time becomes, then it becomes in time. But if time becomes in time, then time exists before it becomes. Since this result is absurd, time does not become in itself. If time does not become in itself, then it becomes in another time. In particular, if the present becomes in another time, then it becomes in either the past or future. But if the present becomes in the past or future then the present is the same as the past or future. Since this result is nonsense the present cannot become in the past or future. The same argument applies to the past and the future. Therefore time cannot become in another time. Since time cannot become in itself or in another time, time cannot be generated. However, time *is* capable of being generated because parts of it (i.e. the future) do not exist. Therefore time is neither capable nor incapable of being generated and, since everything existent must be capable or incapable of either, it follows that time does not exist.

Augustine

One hundred and fifty years after Sextus, the Christian theologian Augustine of Hippo (354 – 430) also cast doubt on the reality of time. In the *Confessions,* Book XI (xiv to xxxi), Augustine asks the question: what is time? He takes the two tenses, past and future and wonders how the past can exist when it is no longer present, and how the future can exist when it is not yet present? If the present were always present, it would not flow into the past but be eternity. But can any time be present? In particular, can the current year be present? Since a year can be divided into months, some months are in the past and no longer exist, and some months are in the future and do not yet exist. Hence, only the current month can be present. But since a month can be divided into days, some days are in the past and no longer exist, and some days are in the future and do not yet exist. Hence, only the current day can be present. But since a day can be divided into hours, some hours are in the past and no longer exist, and some hours are in the future and do not yet exist. Hence, only the current hour can be present. But this argument can be repeated for any division of the day, however small. Given any division, some instants are in the past and no longer exist, and some instants are in the future and do not yet exist. No interval of time, however, small, can claim to be present since some part of the interval belongs to the past and no longer exists, and some part of the interval belongs to the future and does not yet exist. In the limit the duration of the present is exactly *zero*. In the words of Augustine: "the present occupies no space" or "has no extension." It follows that no time can be present. But if the past no longer exists, the future does not yet exist and no time can be present, then time cannot exist.

Nevertheless, Augustine feels that time must exist. He asks: "When time is measured, where does it come from, by what route does it pass, and where does it go?" If time comes from the future, it comes from something which does not yet exist. If time passes through the present, it passes through something which has no extension. If time passes into the past, it passes into something which no longer exists. But time is measured over some extension i.e. some lengths of time are longer than others. In what extension, then, is it measured? It cannot be the future because the future does not yet exist. It cannot be in the present because the present has no extension. It cannot be the past because the past no longer exists. Augustine then considers the recitation of a poem. The poem is long because "it consists of so many lines. The lines are long, for they consist of so many feet. The feet are long, for they extend over so many syllables. The syllable is long, for it is double the length of a short one." But it may happen that a short line, recited slowly, may take longer than a long line recited quickly. Therefore, "time is simply distension." But what is this distension? When someone speaks, their voice sounds and time passes. But how is this time measured? It cannot be measured before the voice has sounded because it lay in the future and the future does not yet exist. Nor can it be measured in the present because the present has no extension. Nor can it be measured after the voice has sounded because it lay in the past and the past no longer exists. Yet, according to Augustine: "We do measure periods of time." If time cannot be measured in the future, the present or the past, then time, if it exists, must be measured in some other way.

Gradually, Augustine realizes that time is experienced in the mind. He does this by analysing the phrase *Deus Creator omnium* (God Creator of all things). The phrase (in Latin) consists of eight syllables in which short and long syllables alternate. The first, third, fifth and seventh syllables are short in relation to the second, fourth, sixth and eight syllables which are long. Each of the long syllables (Augustine perceives) takes twice as long to pronounce as the short syllables. But since the syllables are pronounced sequentially - each syllable ceasing to exist before the next is pronounced - how can the short syllable be retained in order to verify that the next syllable is long? Augustine concludes: "it is not the syllables which I am measuring, but something within my memory which stays fixed there" and that, consequently, "it is in you, my mind, that I measure periods of time." In other words, time is the inner experience of *waiting* (See also Feynman's remarks above.) Moreover, to quote Turetzky on Augustine: "Time does not belong to the physical order. There is no time in itself, only a field of relations among changeable beings, which become temporal when measured" and "that there is no creation in time because time itself is created as an aspect of consciousness." (pp. 63 and 64). Since the experience of waiting is different for each individual it might be supposed that time is an illusion. Not so for Augustine; he concludes that time is a universal characteristic of the human soul. Augustine's use of the term "soul" probably corresponds with the modern use of the word "mind" but, either way, time is an inner subjective experience – it can fly or drag depending on the circumstances and the state of mind – but it is definitely not an objective phenomenon.

The experience of time in human consciousness has been called the "specious present." First coined by E. Robert Kelly under the pseudonym "E. R. Clay" in 1882 and developed by Harvard professor of philosophy William James (1842 – 1910), the specious present revisits the problems raised by Augustine: "The relation of experience to time has not been profoundly studied. Its objects are given as being of the present, but the part of time referred to by the datum is a very different thing from the conterminous of the past and future which philosophy denotes by the name Present. The present to which the datum refers is really a part of the past — a recent past — delusively given as being a time that intervenes between the past and the future. Let it be named the specious present, and let the past, that is given as being the past, be known as the obvious past.

All the notes of a bar of a song seem to the listener to be contained in the present. All the changes of place of a meteor seem to the beholder to be contained in the present. At the instant of the termination of such series, no part of the time measured by them seems to be a past. Time, then, considered relatively to human apprehension, consists of four parts, viz., the obvious past, the specious present, the real present, and the future. Omitting the specious present, it consists of three . . . nonentities — the past, which does not exist, the future, which does not exist, and their conterminous, the present; the faculty from which it proceeds lies to us in the fiction of the specious present." (*The Principles of Psychology(1893)*

The past, future and present are thus "non-entities" and the specious present is a "fiction" – a fiction based on an observer's experience of change. The specious present, as an element of human consciousness, can be established as follows:

(1) What an observer sees, the observer sees as present.
(2) The observer sees motion.
(3) Motion occurs over an interval.

Therefore, what the observer sees as present occurs over an interval. But, of course, the interval is contained within the memory of the observer, and what is contained within the memory does not necessarily correspond to a feature of the "external" world.

McTaggart

One of the most implacable opponents of the reality of time was John McTaggart (1866 – 1925). A fellow and lecturer in philosophy at Trinity College, Cambridge from 1897 to 1923, and teacher to Bertrand Russell and G. E. Moore, McTaggart is best known for his philosophical paper *The Unreality of Time,* first published in the journal *Mind* in 1908. According to McTaggart "nothing that exists can be temporal, and that therefore time is unreal." McTaggart argues that time is unreal because our descriptions of time are either contradictory, circular, or insufficient.

McTaggart derives his result using the method of *reductio ad absurdum.* He assumes that time exists and then proves that it is circular or leads to an infinite regress in which case it cannot exist. He begins by introducing the notion of a position or location in time. Temporal occurrences, more commonly called events, occupy positions in time. The class of positions can be ordered by the relation 'earlier than' or 'later than'. Each position is earlier than some positions and later than others. The relation 'earlier than' satisfies two mathematical relations:

(a) **transitivity**: If P is earlier than Q, and Q is earlier than R, then P is earlier than R.
(b) **asymmetry**: If P is earlier than Q, then Q is not earlier than P.

For any two distinct positions P and Q it must be true that either P is earlier than Q or that Q is earlier than P (The same applies to the relation 'later than'). Furthermore, each position may be classified as past, present or future. While the distinctions of the first class are permanent, the distinctions of the second are not. If event E is earlier than event F, then E is always earlier than F. But an event which is now present, was future, and will be past. It is here that McTaggart draws his battle lines: "the distinction of past, present, and future is as essential to time as the distinction of earlier and later, while in a certain sense it may be regarded as more fundamental than the distinction of earlier and later. And it is because the distinctions of past, present, and future seem to me to be essential for time that I regard time as unreal."

The series of positions which runs from the distant past, the near past to the present, and then from the present to the near future and to the distant future, McTaggart calls the A-series. Every moment or event changes with respect to its A-series characteristics: it is first future, becomes present and then past. For example, a visit to a museum is a future event when it is anticipated; it is a present event when it is experienced, and is a past event when it is remembered. In terms of moments: future moments become present moments, and present moments become past moments. Fig. 1 shows how a visit to a museum (event E) changes with respect to its A-series characteristics. Change with respect to these characteristics constitutes the passage of time.

Fig. 1

The A-series

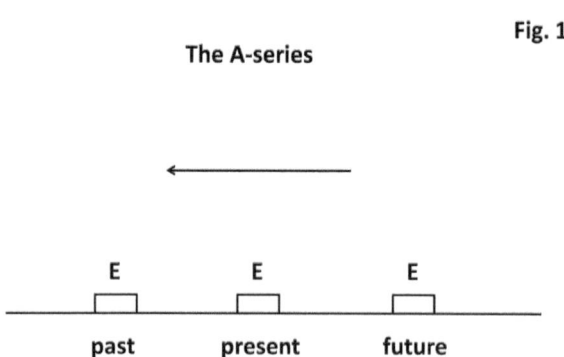

The series of positions which runs from earlier to later, or from later to earlier, McTaggart calls the B-series. In the

B-series moments and events are in fixed relationships with one another. Any set of events E, F, G, H will always occupy the same relative positions: if event E is earlier than event F, and event F is earlier than event G, and event G is earlier than event H, then these events will always stand in that relationship. For example, the American Declaration of Independence will always be earlier than the bombing of Pearl Harbour, and the bombing of Pearl Harbour will always be earlier than the Korean War. The same applies to moments. Fig. 2 shows that events and moments maintain their relative positions.

Fig. 2

The B-series

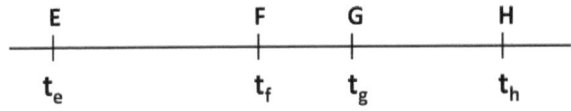

The essential difference between the two series is that the A-series is dynamic and the B-series is static. The A-series represents change or the passage of time, and the B-series represents fixed relationships between moments or events. McTaggart argues that the A-series is necessary for time because time involves change and that an event can only change with respect to its A-series characteristics. For example, John Fitzgerald Kennedy, thirty-fifth President of the United States, was assassinated at 12:30 p.m. Central Standard Time on Friday, November 22, 1963, in Dealey Plaza, Dallas, Texas. That event is fixed and unchangeable but at all dates prior to Friday, November 22, 1963 it was a future event, and at all dates after Friday, November 22, 1963 it was a past event. The fact of President Kennedy's assassination can therefore change only with respect to its A-series characteristics. This is true in general: no fact about anything can change, unless it is a fact about its place in the A-series. If nothing changed, however, there would be no time because everything would be permanently 'frozen'. McTaggart, therefore, rejects the notion of absolute time since absolute time, if it existed at all, would exist independently of change.

In 'Time without Change,' *Journal of Philosophy*, 66 (1969): 363-81, Sidney Shoemaker says: "The claim that time involves change must of course be distinguished from the truism that change involves time." In fact, it is not a truism that change involves time. McTaggart argues that time involves change but does not argue that change involves time. The distinction may be clarified using a Venn diagram (see fig. 3).

Fig. 3

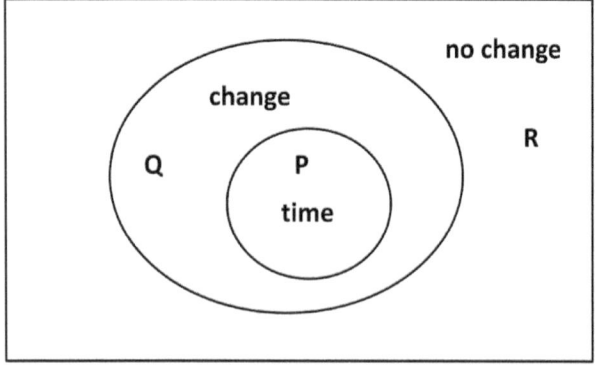

In position P, time involves change but in position Q change does not involve time. In position R, if nothing changed there would be no time. The best known example of change without time can be found in mathematics. To illustrate, consider the set of positive integers $\{1, 2, 3, \ldots \infty\}$. Using x to denote a positive integer, we may also write this as $\{x\}$. Initially, $x = 1$, then $x = 2$, then $x = 3$, then $x = 4$ and so on, until all the positive integers are listed. Since the set of positive integers exists as a time-independent entity the listing is a purely conceptual process. Beginning with the integer 1 and moving to the right, x changes its value from 1 to ∞ in a completely timeless fashion. In other words: x changes without time. But this is true of all mathematical formulae which express time-independent relationships. For example, a change in the radius of a sphere results in a change in its volume; a change in the side of a square results in a change in its area. In general, if two variables are functionally related, a change in one variable results in a change in the other. But these changes are completely time-independent i.e. they are changes without time.

However, there is a more fundamental objection to the notion that change involves time, namely, that if change is used to measure time, then time cannot be used to measure change without contradiction. To see this, let us suppose that time passes when something changes. Consider a car moving along a straight road. As the car moves from A to B, the total distance travelled changes from a smaller to a larger amount. Let the change in distance be Δx and the time elapsed be Δt where the symbol Δ denotes a change. Since we are assuming that time passes with the motion of the car, we can use the motion of the car to measure the passage of time. Let us suppose that the time elapsed is proportional to the distance travelled. We then have the simple relationship:

(1) ... $\Delta t = k \Delta x$

where $k > 0$. If the distance travelled doubles, trebles, quadruples etc. the time elapsed also doubles, trebles, quadruples. This seems reasonable and encapsulates the common (but, as we shall see, erroneous) belief that when things change time necessarily passes. Let us define the units of time in such a way that $k = 1$. We then have,

(2) ... $\Delta t = \Delta x$

We shall show that given equation (2) time cannot pass without contradiction. From elementary mechanics if x is displacement and t is time then $\Delta x/\Delta t$ measures average velocity (change in displacement divided by the time elapsed.) Since the car is travelling with uniform velocity, displacement and distance travelled are one and the same thing. Suppose the car is travelling with a velocity of, say, 5 m/s then,

(3) ... $\Delta x/\Delta t = 5$

From (2), substituting for Δt in equation (3) we have $\Delta x/\Delta x = 5$

i.e. $1 = 5$, which is, of course, a contradiction. It should be noted that the contradiction is not a consequence of our choice of k; left undetermined a contradiction still arises. To see this, suppose another car is travelling along the same stretch of road with a uniform velocity of 8 m/s i.e.

(4) ... $\Delta x/\Delta t = 8$

For the first car: using equation (1) and substituting for Δt in (3) we have $\Delta x/(k\Delta x) = 5$ implying that $k = 1/5$. For the second car: using equation (1) and substituting for Δt in (4) we have $\Delta x/(k\Delta x) = 8$ implying that $k = 1/8$. Therefore, $5 = 8$ which is, of course, another contradiction.

Against this result, it might be argued that the motion of the Earth measures time without contradiction. As we have already seen, the motion of the Earth measures *conventional* time – not absolute time. Conventional time in astronomy measures fractional rotations of the Earth - nothing more. To say that one hour has elapsed is merely to say that the Earth has made one twenty-fourth of a complete turn on its axis. But, to then argue that one hour has elapsed during this one twenty-fourth of a turn is obviously circular. If the Earth stopped rotating, conventional time would stop altogether although the subjective experience of waiting would continue.

The fallacy that when things change time necessarily passes derives directly from the experience of waiting. The reasoning is as follows: (A) change necessarily entails waiting, (B) waiting marks the passage of time. Therefore change necessarily entails the passage of time. Both statements A and B are false. Firstly, change per se does not entail waiting. As we have seen, change in mathematics is a timeless concept; and if there is no time, there is no waiting. Therefore, change does not necessarily entail waiting. Statement B is also false because the subjective experience of waiting varies from one individual to another and from one situation to another; indeed, waiting is an infinitely elastic experience that cannot be measured by physical instruments. In precisely the same circumstances waiting can fly for one person and drag for someone else.

For an anxious patient the experience of waiting for an operation may seem like an "eternity," but during the general anaesthetic, the experience of waiting is zero. A boring film will drag but an enjoyable one will pass quickly. A dreaming person may experience a lifetime between dusk and dawn; an innocent person may experience a prison sentence as endless duration. It is often said that a drowning person sees a whole lifetime pass before his eyes. If, on the contrary, waiting marked the passage of time – assuming that time existed as an objective phenomenon - the experience of waiting would be a constant and inelastic feature of the personal and social landscapes. Since we know this not to be the case, it is incorrect to assert that waiting marks the passage of time - or even that waiting is loosely correlated with the passage of time. Therefore, statement B is a fallacy and it follows that the conclusion - that change necessarily entails the passage of time - is also a fallacy.

Returning to McTaggart, while he argues that an A-series and a B-series are both essential to the nature of time, a B-series alone cannot account for change: in a B-series, all events and moments are in permanent relationships. Even if absolute time existed, change could not be found in the different moments of time since each moment would have its own place in the B-series: each would be earlier or later than each of the others. If there is any change at all it can only be found in the A-series. Moreover, since the relations 'earlier than' and 'later than' are temporal relationships, a B-series cannot exist without an A-series: events are ordered with respect to a B-series only if they are located within an A-series. In other words, while a B-series is necessary for time it is not sufficient.

McTaggart firmly rejects Bertrand Russell's view of time outlined in the latter's *Principles of Mathematics (1903)*, section 442. According to Russell: "Change is the difference, in respect of truth or falsehood, between a proposition concerning an entity and the time T_0 and a proposition concerning the same entity and the time T_1, provided that these propositions differ only by the fact that T_0 occurs in the one where T_1 occurs in the other." For example, there is change if the proposition: 'At the time T_0 my poker is hot' is true, and the proposition: 'At the time T_1 my poker is hot' is false. McTaggart notes that Russell looks for change not in the events in the time series, but in the object to which those events happen: "If my poker is hot on a particular Monday, and never before or since, the event of the poker being hot does not change. But the poker changes, because there is a time when this event is happening to it, and a time when it is not happening to it." However, McTaggart argues that "this makes no change in the qualities of the poker." It is always a quality of the poker that it is hot on that particular Monday, and it is always a quality of the poker that it is not hot at any other time. Both these qualities are true – the time when it is hot and the time when it is cold. The fact that the poker is hot at one point in a series and cold at other points cannot give change, if neither of these facts change – and neither of them does. Furthermore, "nor does any other fact about the poker change unless its presentness, pastness, or futurity change."

As a further example, McTaggart considers the Greenwich meridian which passes through a series of degrees of latitude. Two points in this series S_0 and S_1 can be found such that the proposition: 'At S_0 the meridian of

Greenwich is within the United Kingdom' is true, and 'At S_1 the meridian of Greenwich is within the United Kingdom' is false. If proponents of the view that time is real argue that this does not account for change, why should they argue that the propositions concerning the poker *do* account for change? The answer is that the propositions concerning the poker involve a time series whereas the propositions concerning the Greenwich meridian do not. If the A-series characteristics are removed from a series of positions, the remaining series is non-temporal and cannot account for change any more than the series of latitudes. The point is that there can be no change unless facts change and a fact can only change with respect to its futurity, its presentness, and its pastness i.e. with respect to its A-series characteristics.

Having argued that the distinctions of past, present and future are essential to time i.e. there can be no time without an A-series, McTaggart goes on to prove that an A-series is either circular or leads to an infinite regress in which case an A-series cannot exist. If an A-series cannot exist, then time cannot be real. McTaggart begins his refutation by noting that: "if anything is to be rightly called past, present, or future, it must be because it is in relation to something else. And this something else to which it is in relation must be something outside the time series. For the relations of the A-series are changing relations, and no relations which are exclusively between members of the time series can ever change." For example, the bombing of Pearl Harbour (event E), and the assassination of President Kennedy (event F) are in exactly the same places in the time series, relatively to one another a million years before they take place, while each of them is taking place, and when they are a million years in the past. The same is true of the relationship of moments to one another, and of the relationship of events to moments. The point is that while the relationship between the events E and F does not change, the A-series characteristics of each event do change. The assassination of President Kennedy was a future event (before it happened) was a present event (when it happened) and became a past event (after it happened).

If future moments and events become present moments and events, and present moments and events become past moments and events, then all moments and events must be moving relative to something outside themselves. This can be visualised in fig. 4.

Fig. 4

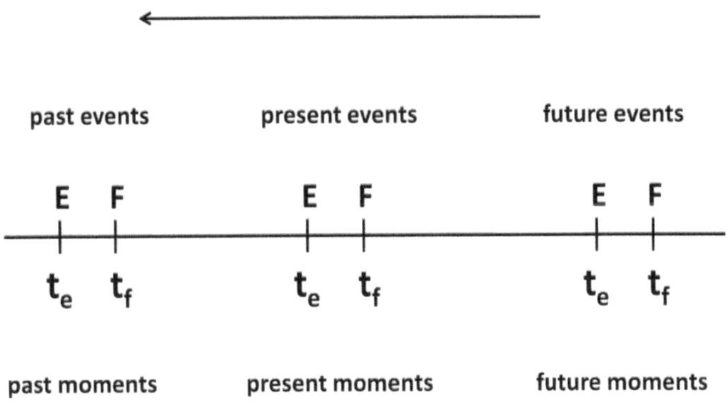

past events	present events	future events
E F	E F	E F
t_e t_f	t_e t_f	t_e t_f
past moments	present moments	future moments

The horizontal line through the moments t_e and t_f - more commonly called the timeline - represents the collection of all moments. Events E and F and the corresponding moments t_e and t_f do not change relative to each other but move relative to the page in the direction indicated by the arrow. Relative to the page the whole timeline shifts from right to left as future moments become present moments, and present moments become past moments - all events and moments maintaining their relative positions on the timeline. We have already noted that the concept of absolute motion is meaningless which, in the present context, means that the timeline cannot move relative to itself. The flow of time - if any meaning can be attached to the expression - must flow relative to something external to itself in the same way that a river flows relative to the river bed. But because, in reality, there is no external something against which time can flow - nothing in reality corresponds to the page of the book - it follows that past, present and future must move with the timeline; all events possess all A-series characteristics simultaneously from the future, through the present, to the past. But pastness, presentness and futurity are incompatible properties and since nothing can have incompatible properties, the A-series cannot exist. According to D. H. Mellor: "An event which is yesterday cannot also be tomorrow. Past, present, and future tenses are mutually incompatible properties of things and events. But because they are forever changing, everything has to have them all. Everything occupies every A-series location, from the remotest future, through the present, to the remotest past. But nothing can really have incompatible properties, so nothing in reality has tenses. The A-series is a myth." (*The Unreality of Tense (1993)*). Since the A-series does not exist, McTaggart concludes that time is unreal. The only way of making sense of the flow of time is to postulate another timeline against which the original timeline can be compared. But this merely shifts the problem back one stage because the second timeline would only make sense in relation to a third timeline and so on *ad infinitum*, thus producing an infinite regress.

The Reduction Principle

A direct route to the unreality of time is by way of the Reduction Principle. This principle derives from a simple application of polar opposites in which a thing or quality has meaning only in relation to its opposite or inverse. For example, right has meaning only in relation to left; right and left then form a 'polar pair.' Other pairs are: finite and infinite, light and darkness, spirit and matter, north and south, positive and negative, real and unreal, time and eternity. Alternatively, one might say that the finite is a 'shadow' of the infinite; darkness is a 'shadow' of the light; matter is a 'shadow' of the spirit, time is a 'shadow' of eternity, and so on. Instead of the word 'shadow' the word 'illusion' may be used instead. There are other aspects of the relationship which may be expressed just as easily. For example, the finite cannot comprehend the infinite; darkness cannot comprehend the light; time cannot comprehend eternity. Alternatively, one might say that to the infinite, the finite is unreal; to the light, darkness is unreal; to spirit, matter is unreal; to eternity, time is unreal. The last polarity leads directly to the notion that to an eternal being time has no reality.

We shall let $(-\alpha, \alpha)$ represent any polar pair, where $-\alpha$ is the negative or inverse component of the real component α. The assertion that the negative (unreal) component of the polarity to the positive (real) component has no reality can then be expressed as follows:

(1) . . . $-\alpha : \alpha = \Phi$

where the null symbol "Φ" represents nothingness or unreality. We shall refer to this as the 'null relationship.' The inverse relation to equation (1) is as follows:

(2) ... $\alpha : -\alpha = R$

where the symbol R represents reality. We shall refer to this as the 'real relationship.' Equations (1) and (2) belong to a system of axioms governing the relationship between polar pairs which we list as follows:

Axiom 1: $-\alpha : \alpha = \Phi$
Axiom 2: $\alpha : -\alpha = R$
Axiom 3: $-(-\alpha) = \alpha$
Axiom 4: $-(-\alpha : \alpha) = \alpha : -\alpha$.

Axiom 3 says that the inverse of the negative (unreal) component is equal to the positive (real) component. Axiom 4 says that the inverse of the null relationship is the real relationship. From axioms 1, 2 and 4 we have $-\Phi = R$ i.e. the inverse of nothingness is reality. Using Axiom 3, Axiom 4 may be rewritten as follows:

(3) ... $-(-\alpha : \alpha) = -(-\alpha) : -(\alpha)$

where $-(-\alpha)$ refers to α. In mathematical parlance, the inverse operator "-" is distributive over ":" Using the distributive property, we have:

(4) ... $-R = -(\alpha : -\alpha) = -(\alpha) : -(-\alpha) = -\alpha : \alpha = \Phi$

i.e. the inverse of reality is nothingness. A special case of the null relationship is the (finite, infinite) polarity. Replacing the null symbol by zero, we have

(5) ... (finite : infinite) = 0.

In mathematics, the ratio of a number to infinity is equal to zero e.g. $(5 : \infty) = 0$. Normally, the division sign is used to express the ratio between numbers i.e. $5/\infty = 0$ but the more general symbol ":" is preferable since it can relate any pair of objects in a polarity.

The temporal cosmos to the eternal cosmos is a special case of the null relationship. If **T** stands for the temporal cosmos and **E** the eternal cosmos, we have:

(6) ... $\mathbf{T} : \mathbf{E} = \Phi$.

This says that the temporal cosmos to the eternal cosmos has no reality. The inverse relation is:

(7) ... $\mathbf{E} : \mathbf{T} = \mathbf{R}$.

This says that the eternal cosmos to the temporal cosmos is reality. If T is a quantity of time and **E** is eternity, we may also write $T : \mathbf{E} = 0$. This says that time to eternity is relatively zero, or has no reality. The inverse relation is:

(8) ... $\mathbf{E} : T = \infty$

which says that eternity to time is relatively infinite. To a time-bound being, eternity seems like an infinitely long period of time. But this is merely to say that to a time-bound being, eternity is beyond comprehension.

The expression 'reduction principle' was devised by the author to mirror the increasing tendency in science to reduce all human activity to the interaction of subatomic particles i.e. to increasingly smaller amounts of matter (in effect, to nothing). The Reduction Principle works in the opposite direction, reducing the temporal universe to unreality. As Professor Keith Ward emphasises in his book: *Why There Almost Certainly Is a God (2008):*

"All the great classical philosophers . . . Plato, Aristotle, Aquinas, Descartes, Leibniz, Spinoza, Locke, Berkeley, Kant, Hegel . . . all argued that the ultimate reality, often hidden under the appearances of the material world of time and space, is mind or Spirit." In II Corinthians, 4:18 it is said that: "The things which are seen are temporal but the things which are not seen are eternal." In the Koran: "All that is with you passeth away, but that which is of God abideth." In the Talmud: "Unhappy is the man who mistakes the branch for the tree, the shadow for the substance." In Hinduism, the material universe is an illusion or dream of the eternal – the great Maya. In Buddhism, only *nirvana* is real - everything else is impermanent. The current scientific position, correctly interpreted, is not dissimilar. According to Hawking and Mlodinow: "Spontaneous creation is the reason there is something rather than nothing. . ." (quoted from *The Grand Design*). Since it is self-contradictory to assert that something can create itself out of nothing, Hawking's statement permits of only one interpretation, namely, that the temporal cosmos is *unreal*. In effect, Hawking and Mlodinow have provided a scientific proof of the Reduction Principle, $\mathbf{T} : \mathbf{E} = \Phi$.

Chapter 12
From Here to Eternity

In Chapter 4 reincarnation was refuted without reference to the self or the soul or, indeed, to anything that might exist independently of the process of rebirth, the crucial concept being a series of noncontemporaneous personalities whose primary function was the elimination of karma. Whatever serves to link these personalities together - whether a 'stream of consciousness' or an immortal self - is ultimately irrelevant to the refutation of reincarnation in this scenario. If karma is a perfect law - as it ought to be - we found that the probability of any series of personalities eliminating karma and therefore attaining liberation is precisely *zero*. On the other hand, if karma operates within a small margin of error, the probability of every series of personalities eliminating karma and attaining liberation is so small it can be equated to zero. This enabled us to formulate the Impossibility Theorem proving that reincarnation cannot be a fact of nature.

In a scenario in which time is *unreal*, however, the refutation of reincarnation must proceed in a different manner. In Chapter 3 this was accomplished by employing the Temporal Postulates and demonstrating that any system of thought embodying the concepts of immortality, individuality and reincarnation is logically incoherent. Towards the end of this chapter we shall augment the Temporal Postulates with the postulates of immortality and individuality and present the Refutation as a series of formal propositions. But first, some discussion of the term 'soul' is in order.

In much of the spiritualist literature, the term 'soul' is treated as a member of a triune self of body, soul and spirit, a mediator between the body and the spirit that is similar in some respects to both but maintaining its own identity (see also Chapter 6). Unfortunately, this usage has tended to confuse discussion because immortality of the soul is often equated with immortality of the spirit with the result that the terms 'soul' and 'spirit' are used interchangeably. This has led to a dual usage of the word soul referring, on the one hand, to something one *has* and, on the other, to something one *is*.

Traditionally the soul is the 'harvester' of all the experiences acquired in the worlds of matter, the record keeper of all the deeds and misdeeds carried out by the personality during its earthly incarnation. When used in this sense, the soul must necessarily survive bodily death otherwise the record of the incarnated life could not be carried forward; and it is here that survival is often confused with immortality because it is automatically assumed (through its identification with the spirit) that the soul is necessarily indestructible. This confusion is by no means confined to the literature of spiritualism. For example, in a well known text: *An Introduction to Philosophical Analysis (1973)* by John Hospers it is stated that: "If someone survived his bodily death, it would constitute no proof of theism; it could be just another fact about the universe, perhaps a surprising one. *It would constitute proof of immortality,* but what would constitute proof of God?" (p.488) [emphasis added].

As mediator between the body and the spirit, the soul is divided into a higher part (the part in contact with the spirit) and a lower part (the part in contact with the body.) The higher part necessarily belongs to the eternal because any contact with an eternal entity, such as the spirit, must take place in the eternal. This follows because anything not belonging to the eternal is unreal in relation to the eternal (Post. I, Prop. A, Ch.3). The lower part necessarily belongs to the temporal otherwise the body would have no reality in relation to the lower part. This follows because anything belonging to the temporal is unreal in relation to the eternal (Post I, Ch.3). Hence, part of the soul belongs to the temporal and part to the eternal. Crucially, this permits the soul to exist in both time and eternity, travelling through time in the material worlds and residing in eternity in the spirit worlds.

Such a description of the soul is easily incorporated into the reincarnationist view of the world because, once it is granted that part of the soul can travel through time, it is a short step from granting that it can 'hop' from one body to another along a notional timeline. While the lower part transmigrates from one body to another in the temporal, the higher part resides in the eternal, presumably unmoved by the activities of the lower. The problem with this scenario is that an entity cannot belong to both the temporal and the eternal because the temporal and the eternal are mutually exclusive (Prop. A, Ch.3). If an entity belongs to the eternal it cannot then transmigrate through time because time has no reality for any being existent in the eternal (Post. I,

Ch.3); and if an entity belongs to the temporal it is unreal in relation to the eternal (Post. I, Ch.3). Only an undivided immortal soul can exist, and the proper domain for an immortal soul is the eternal (Prop. C, Ch.3). Clearly, when the concept of the divided soul is enlisted in the reincarnationist cause, it fails spectacularly. But, it also fails when it is enlisted as an undivided entity. If the soul transmigrates from one body to another in time then it must belong to the temporal, and what belongs to the temporal is of finite duration (Prop. B, Ch.3). Hence, a transmigrating soul cannot be immortal.

However, there is a further difficulty. To a being existent in the eternal, time and space are unreal; therefore what is impossible across space is equally impossible across time. If the soul cannot be associated with more than one physical body across space, it cannot, for the same reason, be associated with more than one physical body across time. From the eternal perspective there is no difference between contemporaneous physical bodies and noncontemporaneous ones – all are simultaneous. In other words, multi-incarnation and reincarnation are one and the same thing. Since nobody would seriously claim that a group of people living and working at the same time are in joint possession of a single soul – each member of the group being an individual – nobody can sensibly claim that a group of people living and working in different historical time periods are in joint possession of a single soul. If spiritual identity is preserved across space then it is preserved across time. This is illustrated in fig. 1.

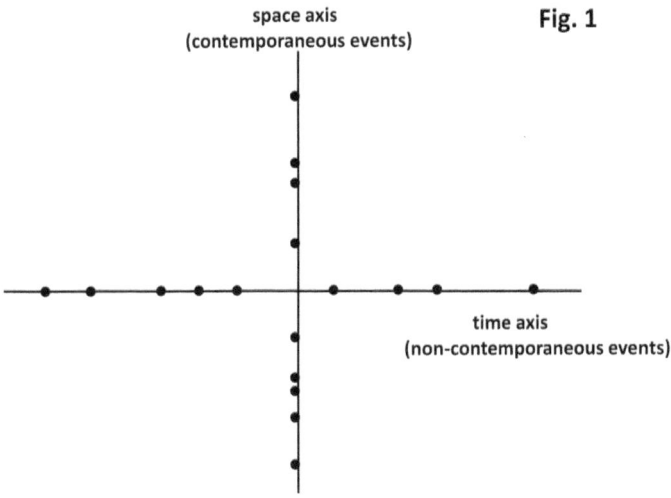

Fig. 1

The space axis represents events occurring at the same time (contemporaneous events) and the time axis represents events occurring at different historical time periods (noncontemporaneous events). Points on the space axis correspond to human beings living and working at the same time, whereas points on the time axis correspond to human beings living and working in different historical time periods. An eternal being would be located off the page along a line perpendicular to the page through the origin. From an eternal being's perspective – and indeed from a time-bound perspective – all people located along the space axis are contemporaneous individuals with unique spiritual identities. From the eternal perspective, the space and time axes are indistinguishable (see also Chapter 11 in which the introduction of 'imaginary' time by Stephen Hawking leads to the same conclusion) so that all people located along the time axis are also contemporaneous individuals with unique spiritual identities. If different people - wherever they are located in time and space – have different spiritual identities then reincarnation is meaningless because all incarnations would then be unique expressions of coexistent souls.

Now, some believers, encouraged by spirit communications from beyond, imagine that reincarnation can be explained in terms of the 'group soul' concept. But what does this really mean? It means *one* soul per group of personalities. What, then, is the relationship between these personalities? They cannot be contemporaneous personalities because contemporaneous personalities are different individuals with different souls; therefore, they must be noncontemporaneous ones. But, if the group soul is an immortal entity it must belong to the eternal (Prop. C, Ch. 3); and since time to the eternal is unreal (Post. I, Ch. 3) all the personalities must be simultaneous (Prop. D, Ch. 3) in which case the group soul cannot be uniquely expressive. In short, the group soul concept reduces human beings to little more than flocks of pigeons or colonies of termites.

As an alternative route to reincarnation the concept of the greater Self is sometimes employed (see also Chapter 2). This posits a greater Self which somehow becomes fragmented into lesser selves, each self corresponding to a different incarnation. The fallacy of this approach is that while the greater Self exists in the eternal the fragmented lesser selves exist in the temporal. Since the temporal is unreal in relation to the eternal (Post. I, Ch.3) the parts have no reality in relation to the whole. But, since the parts collectively comprise the whole, the whole has no reality in relation to itself, which is absurd.

Another source of confusion noted above is the dual usage of the word soul. A person is said to *have* a soul and also to *be* a soul. Some philosophers regard the word soul as untenable. According to John McTaggart: "It is better to speak of the immortality of the self, or of men, than the immortality of the soul. The latter phrase suggests untenable views. For, in speaking of the identity of a man during different periods of his bodily life, we do not usually say that he is the same soul, but the same self, or the same man. And to use a different word when we are discussing the prolongation of that identity after death, calls up the idea of an identity less perfect than that which lasts through a bodily life . . . Moreover, it is customary, unfortunately, to say that a man has a soul, not that he is one. Now if our question is put in the form 'Has man an immortal soul?' an affirmative answer would be absurd. So far as it would mean anything it would mean that the man himself was the body, or something which dies with the body – at any rate was not immortal – and that something, not himself, which he owned during life, was set free at his death to continue existing on its own account. For these reasons it seems better not to speak of the soul, and put our question in the form 'Are men immortal?" (*Human Immortality and Pre-Existence (1916)* pp. 10,11).

To avoid misunderstandings we shall, henceforth, dispense with the word soul and express the propositions of the Refutation in terms of the *self*.

Postulate I and the spheres of consciousness

According to Postulate I of the Temporal Postulates, the temporal to the eternal is unreal. This can be illustrated geometrically as a relationship between the sequential and the simultaneous. In fig.2, points E, F, G, H represent a sequence of events beginning with E and ending with H.

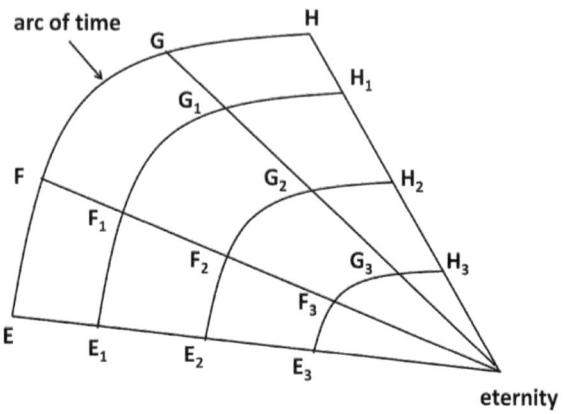

Fig. 2

The outer arc, on which events E, F, G and H are located, represents the broad experience of time in the physical universe (though experiences will vary from one individual to another and from one circumstance to another.) The distance along the arc between any two events, such as E and G, represents the experience of time between those events; we shall call this distance, EG. The inner arcs, between the physical universe and eternity, represent the experience of time in spheres of consciousness less material than the physical. Arcs beyond the physical universe (not shown) represent the experience of time in spheres more material than the physical. The experience of time varies inversely with the sphere of consciousness. The higher the sphere of conscious, the less is the experience of time. The lower, more gross, the sphere of conscious, the greater is the experience of time. In 'heaven' there is no experience of time; in 'hell' any length of earthly time - even a split second - is experienced as endless duration.

Event E in the physical universe is seen as event E_1 in sphere 1, event E_2 in sphere 2, event E_3 in sphere 3, and event En in sphere n; likewise for events F, G and H. The experience of time EG in the physical universe corresponds to the experience of time $E_1 G_1$ in sphere 1, $E_2 G_2$ in sphere 2, $E_3 G_3$ in sphere 3, and EnGn in sphere n. Events may occur in spheres other than the physical. For example, $P_8 Q_8$ in sphere 8 corresponds to $P_6 Q_6$ in sphere 6, $P_{20} Q_{20}$ in sphere 20, and PQ in the physical universe. In general, PnQn in sphere n corresponds to PmQm in sphere m. It can be seen that the time between any two events in the physical universe, say FG, corresponds to ever smaller amounts of time in spheres closer and closer to the eternal, approaching zero in the limit i.e.

(1) ... FG, $F_1 G_1$, $F_2 G_2$, $F_3 G_3$, ... 0

More concisely:

(1a) ... limit FnGn = 0 as n→∞.

From the eternal perspective events F and G coincide. But, this is true for any sequence of events not belonging to the eternal. If all events coincide in eternity then, from the eternal perspective, all events are simultaneous. What may take centuries on Earth, will pass by in the "twinkling of an eye" in spheres of consciousness close to eternity and simultaneously in eternity.

In spheres more material than the physical, the broad experience of time increases at greater distances from eternity approaching infinity in the limit i.e.

(2) ... FG, $F_{-1} G_{-1}$, $F_{-2} G_{-2}$, $F_{-3} G_{-3}$ ... ∞

More concisely,

(2a) ... limit $F_{-n}G_{-n} = \infty$ as $n \to \infty$.

Hence, in spheres of consciousness grosser than the physical, a day on Earth may be experienced as centuries. At death, when the physical body is cast aside, the individual will be drawn to the sphere of consciousness appropriate to his or her spiritual condition. If the individual is enshrouded in a body grosser or more restrictive than the physical one, time will drag; if finer or less restrictive, time will fly. Prop. D, Ch. 3 is applicable to all spheres of consciousness, that is to say, any sequence of events in any sphere of consciousness will appear to be simultaneous when viewed from the eternal. Furthermore, since individuality is indestructible, reincarnation is meaningless in every sphere of consciousness from here to eternity and, in the opposite direction, in every sphere of consciousness from here to hell.

Why the human self is immortal

In this book, immortality and individuality are 'givens' since it is sufficient to show that either one is incompatible with reincarnation. Though no rational person would seriously dispute that individuals are fundamentally distinct from one another, many feel that immortality needs some justification. In the reincarnationist literature, immortality is often equated with survival of bodily death so that evidence of the latter is regarded as evidence of the former. In fact (as we shall prove below) reincarnation implies that the human self is mortal; thus, survival of bodily death does not imply immortality. If human immortally means anything at all, it means much more than bodily survival.

The question: "What evidence is there that we survive bodily death?" places the burden of proof on believers. Of course, one could just as easily ask: "What evidence is there that we do *not* survive bodily death?" and place the burden of proof on sceptics. It is interesting to note that believers have the advantage over sceptics. If sceptics are right they will never know, but will definitely know if they are wrong. On the other hand, if believers are wrong they will never know, but will definitely know if they are right. The argument is similar to Pascal's Wager about the existence of God. French philosopher, Blaise Pascal (1623-1662) argued that if the existence of God could not be determined through reason, a rational person should wager as though God exists, because he has everything to gain, and nothing to lose. Pascal's wager is set out in *Pensées (1669)*, part III, note 233 as follows:

(1) God is, or He is not
(2) A Game is being played where heads or tails will turn up.
(3) According to reason, you can defend neither of the propositions.
(4) You must wager. It is not optional.
(5) Let us weigh the gain and the loss in wagering that God is. Let us estimate these two chances. If you gain, you gain all; if you lose, you lose nothing.
(6) Wager, then, without hesitation that He is. There is here an infinity of an infinitely happy life to gain, a chance of gain against a finite number of chances of loss, and what you stake is finite. And so our proposition is of infinite force, when there is the finite to stake in a game where there are equal risks of gain and of loss, and the infinite to gain.

Expressing this in the language of statistics:

(i) Probability of an infinite gain (if God exists) = 1/2
(ii) Probability of a zero gain (if God does not exist) = 1/2
Therefore,
(iii) The expected value = $(\infty \times 1/2) + (0 \times 1/2) = \infty$.

Hence, any finite wager in favour of God will produce an infinite gain.

Opting for immortality against oblivion can be presented in a similar fashion by substituting the statement: "the human self is immortal" for the statement: "God is." A wager in favour of immortality then has an expected value of infinity. Alternatively, one could argue that since God exists in the eternal, and since His creations are eternal (see Chapter 3), the human self - a creation of God - must be immortal. To prove that the human self is immortal, it is sufficient therefore to prove that God exists.

Some arguments *against* the existence of God are based on the notion that He is not all powerful and therefore cannot be an absolute deity. This is sometimes argued from the following kinds of premises:

(i) God is the supreme power in the cosmos.
(ii) God is all powerful.
(iii) God cannot create a being more powerful than Himself.
(iv) Therefore, God is not all powerful

Another popular argument is that given the definition 2+2=4 God cannot make it otherwise. In other words, if God accepts the above definition as true, he cannot make it untrue. This is saying, in effect, that God cannot contradict Himself; therefore, God is not all powerful. But, of course, if God chooses not to contradict Himself, the issue of contradiction becomes irrelevant.

In a good-humoured and measured response to Richard Dawkins' book, *The God Delusion (2006),* Professor Keith Ward, formerly Regius Professor of Divinity at the University of Oxford systematically dismantles the atheistic view of the world. Ward's book: *Why There Almost Certainly Is a God (2008)* has been described as "A deft, enjoyable, courteous – yet completely devastating – critique of Richard Dawkins' latest foray beyond his sphere of scientific expertise." Ward describes his book as "yet another reply to Dawkins by one of those believers in God whom Dawkins describes as arguably the most unpleasant character in all fiction." Furthermore, Ward advises the reader: "In this short book I want to challenge his arguments, to show that they are not at all strong, and to show that there are much stronger arguments in favour of believing in a God – in fact, that it is almost certain that there is a God." (p.10)

Unsurprisingly, Ward agrees with Dawkins' God hypothesis: "there exists a superhuman, supernatural intelligence who deliberately designed and created the universe and everything in it, including us." Dawkins' alternative view that "any creative intelligence, of sufficient complexity to design anything, comes into existence only as the end product of an extended process of gradual evolution" is, according to Professor Ward, "a very recent, highly contentious, minority philosophical world view" (p.14), a worldview that, incidentally, is comprehensively rebutted by the Oxford University mathematician John C. Lennox (see Chapter 2).

The case against God is rooted in the materialist creed i.e. the philosophical theory that physical matter is the only reality and that psychological states such as emotions, reason, thought, and desire will eventually be explained as physical interactions. Unfortunately (for materialists) since the arrival of quantum physics, it is unclear what physical matter is. It is certainly not – as the Greek philosopher Democritus thought – a conglomeration of tiny lumps of hard "atoms" bumping into each other in real time to form trees, mountains and people. Quantum physicists now speak in terms of 'imaginary time,' ten or eleven-dimensional curved space-time, and electrons being probability waves in Hilbert space. In *The Matter Myth (1992),* Paul Davies and John Gribbin argue that matter is essentially an illusion produced by a mysterious interaction between the mind and some unknown reality; and quantum physicists, such as Bernard d'Espagnat speak in terms of a "veiled reality." Ward asks the question: "What is the point of being a materialist when we are not sure exactly what matter is?" (p.15)

Although Professor Ward comprehensively rebuts Dawkins' case against God, his arguments for the existence of God, which incidentally are based on the work of Thomas Aquinas, are not entirely consistent with the belief that God is an eternal being. Crucial to Ward's 'proofs' is the notion of a first cause: "Everything, says Aquinas, that comes into being is brought into being by something else." Ward, then, incorrectly states that: "Modern science is founded on this postulate – that every event has a cause." (p.106). (See Chapters 3 and 10 for a contrary view). Clearly, Ward believes that God exists in time for, without time, there can be no cause and effect relationships. But to God, who exists in eternity, such things do not exist because all events are simultaneous. At any rate, the notion of God in time is problematical since (i) time would need to be infinite otherwise God would be perishable and (ii) His existence would require the occurrence of time before the universe was created - in fact before time was created.

In *Eternal God: A Study of God without Time (1988)*, Professor Paul Helm considers a recent argument against the timeless existence of God. It is presented as a series of propositions beginning with the statement that God exists timelessly leading to the final conclusion that the first statement is incoherent:

(1) God's existence is timeless.
(2) God exists simultaneously at all moments of human time (from 1.)
(3) God is simultaneously present at what I did yesterday, am doing today, and will do tomorrow.
(4) If time t_1 is simultaneous with time t_2, and t_2 is simultaneous with time t_3, then time t_1 is simultaneous with time t_3,
(5) If God is simultaneously present at what I did yesterday and what I am doing today then yesterday and today are simultaneous (from 3. and 4.)
(6) But the idea that yesterday and today are simultaneous is absurd.
(7) Therefore, (1) is incoherent.

If statement (1) is incoherent it follows that God exists in time. But, we have already seen in Chapter 11 that the concept of time is problematical. Absolute time is meaningless, clock time is conventional, space-time is relative, imaginary time is technical, and psychological time is flexible. In what time, then, does God exist? It is evident that time, however measured or defined, cannot provide a meaningful foundation for God's existence. Since time is an undefined concept, the above argument against the timelessness of God is unsound. However, Helm demonstrates unsoundness in another way. By constructing a parallel argument he is able to show that similar reasoning leads to the conclusion that the spacelessness existence of God is also incoherent. In like fashion, the argument begins with the statement that God's existence is spaceless and leads to the conclusion that the first statement is incoherent.

(1) God's existence is spaceless.
(2) God is wholly spatially present at different places.
(3) God is wholly spatially present at what I am doing here and you are doing there.
(4) If an individual A is wholly spatially present with another individual B, and A is wholly spatially present with a third individual C then B is wholly spatially present with C.
(5) Thus if God is wholly spatially present at what I am doing here and you are doing there then where you are and where I am are the same place.
(6) But the idea that this place and that place are the same place is absurd.
(7) Therefore, (1) is incoherent.

If statement (1) is incoherent, then God exists in space. But such a notion is absurd because God is Spirit, and Spirit does not occupy space (see also Chapter 6); hence, the reasoning is unsound. If the general method is unsound, it cannot be reasoned that God exists in time. Much of this argument, however, can be simplified by appealing to the Temporal Postulates. If God is eternal, He does not exist in the Temporal (Prop. A, Ch.3), and if He does not exist in the Temporal, He does not exist in time.

On the question of human immortality, we maintain that God's existence is necessary because (a) something exists and (b) something cannot create itself out of nothing. Since God is the creator of the human self - it cannot be self-created - and since God's creations belong to the eternal (see Chapter 3) it follows that the human self is immortal.

Now many of the arguments directed against the timelessness of God are arguments against the timelessness of any eternal being, including the human self. For example, it is claimed by some philosophers that nothing that exists timelessly could be a person. In other words, a timeless being could not act, have intensions or remember – all capabilities necessary for being a person. If this is the case then the human self – indubitably a person – cannot be timeless. According to Robert C. Colburn: "Surely it is a necessary condition of anything's being a person that it should be capable (logically) of, among other things, doing at least some of the following: remembering, anticipating, reflecting, deliberating, deciding, intending, and acting intentionally. . . But now an eternal being would necessarily lack all of these capacities inasmuch as their exercise by a being clearly requires that the being exist in time." (Quoted in *Eternal God: A Study of God without Time (1988),* p.57)

But if personhood exists in time, what is the nature of the time in which it is supposed to exist? Does it exist in absolute time, relative time, conventional time, space-time, imaginary time, or psychological time? Without a clear understanding of the nature of time, Colburn's claim that no timeless being could be a person is meaningless. Professor Helm notes that the concept of personhood is itself a "philosophical minefield" (p.57). For example, some philosophers claim that embodiment is necessary for personhood while others claim that it is not. It is also claimed by some - and denied by others - that only language-users are persons. It is both claimed and denied that only individuals living in communities are persons, and it is both claimed and denied that only individuals who are capable of being conscious are persons etc. etc. Helm dismisses such claims as self-cancelling and considers four of the most cited arguments against timelessness. These are the arguments from: (a) memory (b) purpose (c) knowledge (d) power.

The argument from memory asserts that to be a person it is necessary to remember things or to have memories. Remembering must take place in time because what is remembered or experienced is past, and what is past implies the passage of time. Furthermore, remembering implies temporal duration because to recall something is to think about it and thinking can only take place in time. Since a timeless being can have no memories, it cannot be a person. Helm rebuts this argument in the following way. Firstly, remembering is not something which necessarily requires time. Remembering that P is true is equivalent to knowing that P is true and not forgetting that P is true. In the case of a timeless being this becomes: "a timeless being remembers P when he knows P and it is impossible for him to forget P." In other words, what a timeless being knows and what he remembers are one and the same thing. Furthermore, what a timeless being knows is not the result of a time-taking process but is innate. For an eternal being, therefore, memory and knowledge are equivalent – neither requiring the passage of time.

The argument from purpose asserts that a timeless being cannot act purposefully, since purposeful behaviour or intentionality is linked to the future result of an action and futurity implies the passage of time. Helm notes that this argument is based on a premise which is accepted without argument - namely, that an eternal being acts and that actions have beginnings and endings. Although Helm agrees that an eternal being does not initiate actions, since in eternity there are no beginnings and endings, he disputes the notion that this is in any way inhibiting because an eternal being may have timeless purposes. These purposes may or may not have effects in the physical world; if they do, then the effects and purposes are simultaneous. The point is that, for an eternal being, purposes and effects are produced timelessly i.e. they do not require the passage of time. Furthermore, since purposes and effects are simultaneous, the claim that they are in a cause and effect relationship is erroneous. But, purposes do not necessarily have effects. For example, the purpose of an eternal being could be to glorify God or to awaken from the illusion of the physical world. At any rate, according to Helm, the distinction between eternal purposes and their effects is not a temporal distinction but a logical one. The effect may be physical but the purpose is timeless. For example, a timeless being's eternal purpose could be that its physical incarnation be pleasant and uneventful.

The argument from knowledge claims that omniscience - or unlimited knowledge - is sufficient for personhood. According to philosopher Nelson Pike: "If a timeless individual could have knowledge – at least if it could have unlimited knowledge – then we could at least conceive of the case in which a timeless individual would have to be counted as a person. This is true if it is also true that a timeless individual could not deliberate, anticipate or remember." (*God and Timelessness (1970)* - page 125).

However, Pike goes on to argue that a timeless being could not be omniscient. His reasons are that a timeless individual could not act in any of the ways suggestive of knowing, believing or being aware of something. Furthermore, a timeless being could not communicate anything whatsoever to us or provide any reasons or evidence for believing that it is omniscient or that it knows anything at all.

Although, Pike's arguments are directed principally against the timelessness of God, they apply equally to the human self because it could be reasonably argued that the latter is omniscient within its own sphere of consciousness. Helm believes there is a basic confusion in Pike's argument. The confusion is between:

(1) those conditions which are necessary for P being true.
(2) the conditions necessary for someone being warranted in believing that P is true.

Helm summarizes Pike's position in the following way: "If we could not ourselves be convinced, upon evidence, that a timeless being is omniscient, then the very idea of a timeless, omniscient being is not possible." (p.65). This is dangerously close to the logical positivist position: i.e. if we have no warrant for statement P then statement P is meaningless – an extreme position not actually held by Pike himself since, according to Helm, Pike "explicitly draws back from the idea that it is meaningless to speak of a timeless being as having knowledge or as being aware of something" (p.65).

Helm offers a provisional definition of omniscience by saying that an individual is omniscient "if that individual knows all true propositions and has no false beliefs." He then poses the question: Could an individual who is timeless know all true propositions and holds no false beliefs? "Why not?" Helm asks. Pike himself provides no arguments against such a possibility and unless any arguments are produced the proposition stands. Helm, then, considers the claim that a timeless being could not be given knowledge or acquire it directly because it would lack the necessary sensory equipment. To this Helm replies that a timeless being could know and understand whatever was being communicated to it provided it had an appropriate conceptual scheme – and there are no reasons to suppose it has not. Secondly, a timeless being would not need to acquire knowledge directly since its knowledge would be 'innate' and, furthermore, it could well be the sole source of knowledge within its sphere of consciousness.

The argument from power claims that a timeless individual could not produce, create, or bring about an object, circumstance, or state of affairs. In other words, a timeless being could not be potent or powerful – let alone omnipotent. According to Pike: "The point seems that if God were to create or produce an object having a position in time, God's creative activity would then have to have occurred at some specific time. The claim that God timelessly produced a temporal object (such as a mountain) is absurd." (*God and Timelessness (1970),* p.105). Pike concludes that a timeless God cannot create anything at all. Helm notes that Pike's arguments betoken confusion. This confusion derives from a false premise – namely, that the universe exists in time. Although it may be meaningful to ask what happened before an individual was born, it is meaningless to ask what happened before the universe was created because the universe does not exist in time. The point is that God creates everything simultaneously because, to God, time has no reality; therefore His entire creation – including the creation of particular things like trees and mountains – is a timeless, simultaneous creation.

According to Augustine (see also Chapter 11): "It is not in time that you precede times. Otherwise you would not precede all times. In the sublimity of an eternity which is always in the present, you are before all things past and transcend all things future, because they are still to come, and when they have come they have past. But you are the same and your years do not fail. Your 'years' neither go nor come. Ours come and go in succession. All your 'years' subsist in simultaneity, because they do not change. Your today is eternity." (*Confessions* - page 230)

Clearly, God does not exist in time but since He is the creator of the cosmos, the cosmos must be a timeless creation (see also Chapter 3). Therefore the argument from power fails.

* * *

The philosophical and theological arguments in favour of God's existence underpin the assertion that the human self is immortal because God's creations are eternal and the human self cannot be a self-creation. Once it is recognised that the human self belongs to the eternal and is uniquely expressive it is easy to prove that the human self does not reincarnate. The following Postulates are sufficient to refute the doctrine of reincarnation:

Postulate I: The Reduction Principle
The temporal to the eternal is unreal.

Postulate II: The Principle of Inclusion
All things belong to the temporal or the eternal

Postulate III: Immortality
The human self is immortal

Postulate IV: Individuality
The human self is uniquely expressive

Before we proceed to the propositions of the Refutation some clarification of Postulate IV is in order. The assertion that the human self is uniquely expressive means that the human self does not incarnate in more than one physical body simultaneously. If this were not the case, then different people living and working at the same time would be manifestations of a single individuality. Reincarnation is refuted by showing that all people who have ever lived or will live are unique expressions of coexistent individualities, that is to say, there is a one to one correspondence between individuals and physical bodies, both contemporaneous and noncontemporaneous. If the individual expressing itself as Janet Smith is coexistent with the individual expressing itself as the Tudor monarch Elizabeth I, then Janet Smith cannot be a reincarnation of Elizabeth I.

In any analysis of human individuality, one would want the relationship between individuals and *contemporaneous* physical bodies to be one to one i.e. to each physical body there should be associated only one individual, and to each individual there should be associated only one physical body. Hence, pointing to a physical body would be the same as pointing to an individual. If one individual could incarnate in more than one physical body, multi-incarnation would be a fact - a scenario specifically ruled out by Postulate IV (see also Chapter 5).

We need then consider only the possibility that more than one individual might be incarnated in the *same* physical body such as conjoined twins. In this scenario, pointing to one physical body would be the same as pointing to two individuals. Cases of 'multiple possession' bear some resemblance to conjoined twins, though our analysis in Chapter 6 has shown that possession is an *intrusion* of the body - not an incarnation. The self is associated with the physical body from conception to death, so that any other entity - whether it be a discarnate personality attempting to reincarnate or some other obsessing entity - would be superfluous to requirements and at best a transitory influence.

However, there remains the strange possibility of 'multiple individualities' being incarnated in one and the same physical body from conception to death. Such a phenomenon might, in practice, be indistinguishable from 'multiple personalities' or 'multiple possession' casting doubt on the utility of such concepts. If such is the case, then the relationship between individuals and physical bodies is 'many to one.' In fig. 3, the individual incarnated in body G is different to the individual incarnated in body K, and the individuals incarnated in body F are different to the individuals incarnated in body L.

Fig. 3

Contemporaneous Individuals

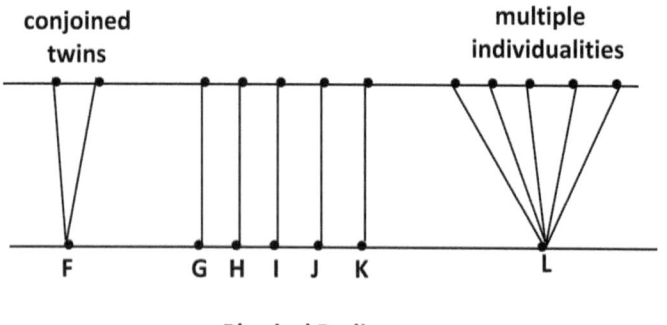

Physical Bodies

Crucially, however many individuals may be incarnated in one physical body they must be different to the individuals incarnated in another physical body. Thus, no individual can simultaneously be incarnated in more than one physical body. This is explicitly ruled out by Postulate IV. (See fig. 4).

Fig. 4

NOT PERMITTED BY POSTULATE IV

Contemporaneous Individuals

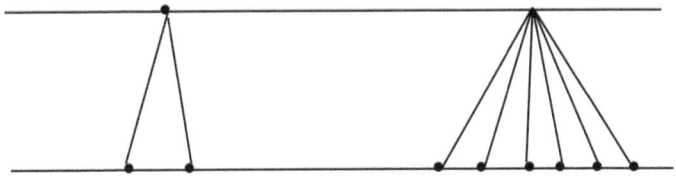

Physical Bodies

The question we need to ask is this: do the special cases of conjoined twins or 'multiple individualities' compromise the concept of individuality? In the case of conjoined twins, it could reasonably be argued that two individuals are really expressing themselves through *two* physical bodies that happen to be joined together. 'Multiple individualities' certainly compromise the one to one relationship between physical bodies and individuals but it does not compromise the concept of individuality itself because individuality does not depend on the physical body. When the physical body is discarded, each individuality will continue to exist.

However one chooses to interpret the phenomenon of 'multiple individualities' it has no bearing on the refutation of reincarnation because Postulate IV requires only that a given individual not be incarnated in more than one physical body simultaneously. No matter how many individuals may be incarnated in the *same* physical body, no member of the group may be incarnated in another physical body. This means we can proceed as though these complications do not exist. We shall assume, therefore, that the relationship between physical bodies and individuals is one to one. Thus, pointing to a physical body is the same as pointing to an individual, as shown in fig. 5.

Fig. 5

Contemporaneous Individuals

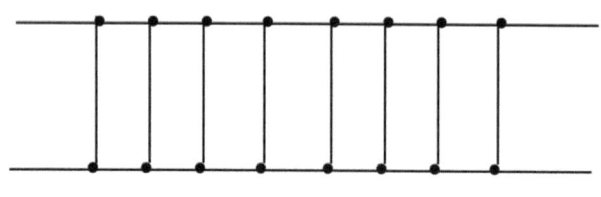

Physical Bodies

The propositions of the Refutation

In Chapter 3, Propositions A, B, C and D were deduced from the two temporal postulates and are listed here for convenience.

Proposition A
The temporal and the eternal are mutually exclusive.

Proposition B
Anything belonging to the temporal is of finite duration, and anything of finite duration belongs to the temporal.

Proposition C
A *mortal* human self belongs to the temporal, and an *immortal* human self belongs to the eternal.

Proposition D
To an eternal being all events are simultaneous.

Proposition E
The human self does not incarnate more than once.

Proof

Our method of proof is by *reductio ad absurdum*. Let us assume that the human self *does* incarnate more than once. If the human self incarnates more than once then it expresses itself through its incarnations sequentially; and if the incarnations are expressed sequentially, the human self is uniquely expressive. Since the human self is immortal (Post. III) it belongs to the eternal (Prop. C); and to an eternal being all events are simultaneous (Prop. D). If all events are simultaneous, the human self expresses itself through its incarnations simultaneously. But, if the expressions are simultaneous, the human self is not uniquely expressive. Since this result is a contradiction, the original assumption that the human self incarnates more than once is *false*. Therefore, the human self does *not* incarnate more than once. [QED]

Proposition F
Reincarnation implies that the human self is mortal.

Proof

If the human self reincarnates, its incarnations are expressed sequentially in time. If the incarnations are expressed sequentially in time, the self cannot exist in the eternal otherwise the incarnations would be simultaneous (Prop. D). If the human self does not exist in the eternal, then it must exist in the temporal (Post. II), and if it exists in the temporal it must be of finite duration (Prop. B). Since anything of finite duration cannot be immortal, the human self must be mortal. [QED]

Proposition G:
All theories of reincarnation violate Postulates III or IV.

Proof

If no permanent self exists (as in Buddhism) then Postulate III is violated. Hence we need consider only cases in which a permanent self *does* exist i.e. in which Postulate III is satisfied (as in modern Hinduism and Western reincarnationism). We shall show that Postulate IV is violated. Since the human self is immortal (Post. III) it belongs to the eternal (Prop. C); and if it belongs to the eternal, all incarnations are simultaneous (Prop. D). Hence, the human self expresses itself through its incarnations simultaneously. If the expressions are simultaneous, the human self cannot be uniquely expressive. Hence, Postulate IV is violated. [QED]

MATHEMATICAL APPENDIX

A Smooth Approximation

We wish to obtain a smooth approximation for the equation:

$$A(x+1) - A(x) = \rho A(x-1).$$

Since the LHS represents a change per unit interval, the equation can be written more generally as:

$$[A(x+1) - A(x)]/1 = \rho A(x-1).$$

Dividing the interval between each integer into N equal parts, the width of each interval becomes $1/N$. Let $\Delta x = 1/N$ then,

$$[A(x+\Delta x) - A(x)]/\Delta x = \rho A(x-\Delta x).$$

As the number of intervals N approaches infinity, the length of each interval approaches zero i.e. as N $\to$ infinity, $\Delta x \to 0$. The limiting equation then becomes:

$$A'(x) = \rho A(x)$$

where $A'(x)$ is the first derivative of the function $A(x)$.

Proposition 2, Chapter 4

If the random variables $0 \leq A^G(1) \leq 1$ and $0 \leq -A^B(1) \leq 1$ each have uniform probability distributions, and $\alpha \equiv \lambda - \mu$, then the random variable,

$x = (1/\alpha)\log_e[-A^B(1)/A^G(1)] + 1$ has the pdf:
  $P(x) = (\alpha/2)\exp[\alpha(x-1)]$ for $-\infty < x \leq 1$
  $P(x) = (\alpha/2)\exp[\alpha(1-x)]$ for $1 \leq x < \infty$

Proof
Let $A_1 \equiv -A^B(1)$ and $A_2 \equiv A^G(1)$ then,

$x = (1/\alpha)\log_e[A_1/A_2] + 1.$

Define system S as follows:

(S1) ... $x_1 = (1/\alpha)\log_e[A_1/A_2]+1$
(S2) ... $x_2 = A_2$

We shall find the joint pdf $g(x_1, x_2)$ of the random variables x_1 and x_2. Firstly, let $f(A_1, A_2)$ be the joint pdf of A_1 and A_2. Since A_1 and A_2 are statistically independent we have:

$f(A_1, A_2) = f_1(A_1)f_2(A_2) = P(A_1) \times P(A_2) = 1 \times 1 = 1.$

The inverse of system S is:

(T1) ... $A_1 = x_2 \exp[\alpha(x_1 - 1)]$
(T2) ... $A_2 = x_2$.

From a well-known theorem in calculus:

$g(x_1, x_2) = f(A_1, A_2)|J|$

where J is the Jacobian of the system T.
Since $f(A_1, A_2) = 1$ we have:

$g(x_1, x_2) = |J|.$

By finding the partial derivatives in J, it is easy to show that:

$J = \alpha x_2 \exp[\alpha(x_1 - 1)] > 0.$

It then follows that the joint pdf of x_1 and x_2 is:

$g(x_1, x_2) = \alpha x_2 \exp[\alpha(x_1 - 1)].$

To find the marginal distribution $g_1(x_1)$ we integrate out the variable x_2. The domain of A_1 and A_2 is shown in fig.1.

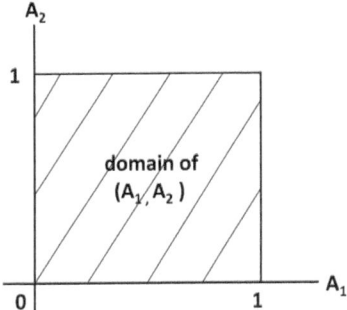

Fig. 1

Its image - the domain of x_1 and x_2 - is shown in fig.2 and consists of *two* regions.

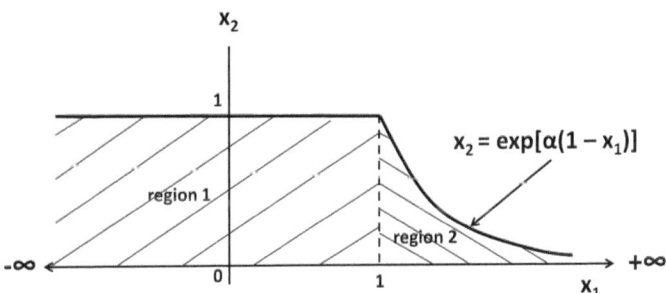

Fig. 2

1st region:
$-\infty < x_1 \leq 1$ and $0 \leq x_2 \leq 1$
$g_1(x_1) = \int \alpha x_2 \exp[\alpha(x_1 - 1)]dx_2 = (\alpha/2)\exp[\alpha(x_1 - 1)]$

integrated from 0 to 1.

2nd region:
$1 \leq x_1 < \infty$ and $0 \leq x_2 \leq \exp[\alpha(1 - x_1)]$
$g_1(x_1) = \int \alpha x_2 \exp[\alpha(x_1 - 1)]dx_2 = (\alpha/2)\exp[\alpha(1 - x_1)]$

integrated from 0 to $\exp[\alpha(1 - x_1)]$.
Since $x \equiv x_1$ and $P(x) \equiv g_1(x_1)$ we have:

$P(x) = (\alpha/2)\exp[\alpha(x - 1)]$ for $-\infty < x \leq 1$
$P(x) = (\alpha/2)\exp[\alpha(1 - x)]$ for $1 \leq x < \infty$ [QED]

Proposition 3, Chapter 4

Let ε be the error in the operation of karma and p be the probability that x is close to an integer greater than 1 then $p = \varepsilon$.

Proof

$\Pr(n - \varepsilon < x < n + \varepsilon) = \int (\alpha/2)\exp[\alpha(1 - x)]dx$

integrated from $n + \varepsilon$ to $n - \varepsilon$. Evaluating and simplifying it can be shown that:

$\Pr(n - \varepsilon < x < n + \varepsilon) = \sinh[\alpha\varepsilon]\exp[\alpha(1 - n)]$.

Since n is any number from 2 to infinity we sum from 2 to infinity. Thus:

$p = \sum\sinh[\alpha\varepsilon]\exp[\alpha(1 - n)] = \sinh[\alpha\varepsilon]\sum\exp[\alpha(1 - n)]$.

Now $\exp[\alpha(1 - n)] = (\exp[-\alpha])^{n-1}$ and $\Sigma(\exp[-\alpha])^{n-1}$ is the sum of a geometric series with common ratio $\exp[-\alpha]$. Since $\alpha > 0$, $\exp[-\alpha] < 1$, the series converges. Evaluating the sum of the series we find that:

$\sum\exp[\alpha(1 - n)] = \exp[-\alpha]/(1 - \exp[-\alpha])$.

Summarising and simplifying:

$p = \sinh[\alpha\varepsilon]/(\exp[\alpha] - 1)$.

Since ε and α are both small, $\sinh[\alpha\varepsilon] \approx \alpha\varepsilon$ and $\exp[\alpha] \approx 1 + \alpha$. It then follows that $p \approx \alpha\varepsilon/\alpha = \varepsilon$. [QED]

The pdf of karma

From Chapter 4:

$K(x) = pA^G(1) + qA^B(1)$
where $p \equiv \exp[\lambda(x-2)]$ and $q \equiv \exp[\mu(x-2)]$.

Let $A_1 \equiv -A^B(1)$, $A_2 \equiv A^G(1)$ then:

$K(x) = pA_2 - qA_1$

Define system U as follows:

(U1) ... $K_1 = pA_2 - qA_1$
(U2) ... $K_2 = A_2$

We shall find the joint pdf $h(K_1, K_2)$ of the random variables K_1 and K_2. The inverse of system U is:

(V1) ... $A_1 = (p/q)K_2 - K_1/q$
(V2) ... $A_2 = K_2$

As before:

$h(K_1, K_2) = f(A_1, A_2)|J|$
where J is the Jacobian of the system V.

Since $f(A_1, A_2) = 1$ we have:

$h(x_1, x_2) = |J|$.

By finding the partial derivatives it can be shown that:

$h(x_1, x_2) = 1/q$

We shall find the marginal distribution $h_1(K_1)$ by integrating out the variable K_2. The domain of A_1 and A_2 is shown in fig.1. Its image - the domain of K_1 and K_2 - is shown in fig.3 and consists of *three* regions:

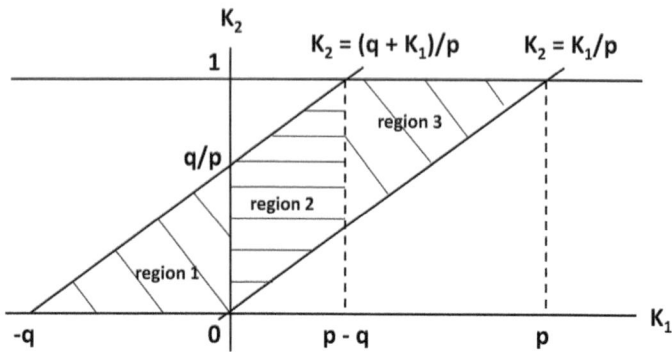

Fig. 3

1st region:

$-q \leq K_1 \leq 0$ and $0 \leq K_2 \leq (q + K_1)/p$
$h_1(K_1) = \int 1/q \, dK_2 = (q + K_1)/(pq)$
integrated from 0 to $(q + K_1)/p$

2nd region:

$0 \leq K_1 \leq (p - q)$ and $K_1/p \leq K_2 \leq (q + K_1)/p$
$h_1(K_1) = \int 1/q \, dK_2 = 1/p$
integrated from K_1/p to $(q + K_1)/p$.

3rd region:

$(p-q) \leq K_1 \leq p$ and $K_1/p \leq K_2 \leq 1$
$h_1(K_1) = \int 1/q \, dK_2 = (p - K_1)/(pq)$
integrated from K_1/p to 1.

Since $K \equiv K_1$ and $P(x) \equiv h_1(K_1)$ we have:

$P(K) = (q + K_1)/(pq)$ for $-q \leq K_1 \leq 0$
$P(K) = 1/p$ for $0 \leq K_1 \leq (p - q)$
$P(K) = (p - K_1)/(pq)$ for $(p-q) \leq K_1 \leq p$

The equations correspond to the 1st, 2nd and 3rd sections respectively of the graph in fig. 12, Chapter 4.

Bibliography

1) Austin, The Rev, H. (trans.), *Stigmata: A History of Various Cases (1883),* Internet Archive.
2) Baggott, Jim *Beyond, Measure: modern physics, philosophy and the meaning of quantum theory*, Oxford UP, 2004.
3) Barrett, William F. and Hyslop, James H., *On The Threshold of the Unseen (1918)* - Kessinger.
4) Blaug, Mark, *Economic Theory in Retrospect*, Heinemann Educational Books Ltd., 1968.
5) Boddington, Harry, *The University of Spiritualism*, Psychic Press Ltd., 1985
6) Bonaventure, *The Life of St. Francis (1904)*, Internet Archive.
7) Borden, Robert S., *A Course in Advanced Calculus,* Dover, 1998.
8) Born, Max, *Einstein's Theory of Relativity,* Dover, 1962.
9) Boyer, Carl B., *The History of the Calculus and its Conceptual Development*, Dover, 1959.
10) Brent, Peter, *Charles Darwin: A Man of Enlarged Curiosity,* William Heinemann Ltd., 1981.
11) Browning, Rev. William (trans.) *The Autobiography of Saint Gemma Galgani*, www.stgemmagalgani.com.
12) Campbell Holms, A., *The Facts of Psychic Science and Philosophy,* Kegan Paul, Trench, Trubner & Co., Ltd., 1925.
13) Cantor, Georg, *Contributions to the Founding of the Theory of Transfinite Numbers*, Dover, 1955.
14) Carrington, Hereward,
    1. Psychic Oddities, Rider and Company, 1952.
    2. Eusapia Palladino and Her Phenomena (1909), Internet Archive
15) Chadwick, Henry (trans.). *Saint Augustine: Confessions,* Oxford UP, 1991.
16) Cohen, I, Bernard. *Revolution In Science,* Harvard UP, 1985.
17) Conner, Steven, *The Book of Skin*, Cornell UP, 2004.
18) Davies, Paul and Gribbin, John. *The Matter Myth,* Penguin books, 1992.

19) Dawkins, Richard,
    1. *The Blind Watchmaker (1986),* Penguin Books, 2006.
    2. *Climbing Mount Improbable (1996),* Penguin Books, 2006.
20) Denton, Michael. *Evolution: A Theory in Crisis,* Adler & Adler, 1985.
21) d'Esperance, Elisabeth, *Shadow Land (1897)* http://survivalebooks.org
22) Dunbar, Helen Flanders, *Emotions and Bodily Changes: A Survey of Literature on Psychosomatic Interrelationships, 1910-1953,* Ayer, 1976.
23) Eiseley, Loren, *Darwin's Century*, Doubleday Anchor Books, 1958.
24) Ferris, Timothy (ed.). *The World Treasury of Physics, Astronomy and Mathematics,* Little, Brown and Co., 1991.
25) Feynman, Richard P., Leighton Robert B., Sands, Matthew, *The Feynman Lecture on Physics, Vols. 1, 2, 3*, Addison-Wesley, 1963, 64, 65.
26) Fodor, Nandor, *An Encyclopaedia of Psychic Science (1933)*, University Books Inc., 1966.
27) Fowles, Grant R. and Cassiday, George L., *Analytical Mechanics,* Harcourt Brace & Co., 1993.
28) Goldberg, Samuel, *Difference Equations,* John Wiley & Sons 1958.
29) Gunn, Alexander, *The Problem of Time,* Unwin, 1929.
30) Gurney, Edmund, Myers, Frederic and Podmore, Frank, *Phantasms of the Living (1886)*, Kessinger.
31) Hawking, Stephen
    1. *A Brief History of Time,* Bantam Books, 1988.
    2. *The Grand Design*, (with Leonard Mlodinow) Bantam Books, 2010.
32) Helm, Paul, *Eternal God: A Study of God without Time,* Oxford UP, 1988.

33) Henderson, James M. and Quandt, Richard E., *Microeconomic Theory*, McGraw-Hill, 1958
34) Hicks, John, *The Crisis in Keynesian Economics,* Wiley-Blackwell, 1975.
35) Hinnells, John R. (ed.), *A Handbook of Living Religions,* Penguin Books, 1984.
36) Hodges, Wilfred, *Logic,* Penguin Books, 1991.
37) Hogg, Robert V. and Craig, Allen T, *Introduction to Mathematical Statistics*, Macmillan, 1958.
38) Hoskin, Michael, *The Cambridge Illustrated History of Astronomy*, Cambridge UP, 1997.
39) Hume, David, *An Enquiry concerning Human Understanding (1748)*, Oxford UP, 2007.
40) Hyslop, James H.
    1. *Life After Death: Problems of the Future Life and its Nature (1918),* Internet Archive.
    2. *Contact With the Other World: The Latest Evidence As to Communication With the Dead (1919),* Kessinger.
41) Joire, Dr. Paul, *Psychical and Supernormal Phenomena: Their Observation and Experimentation (1916),* Internet Archive.
42) Kiely, David M. and McKenna, Christina, *The Dark Sacrament,* HarperCollins e-books, 2007.
43) Koestler, Arthur, *The Sleepwalkers,* Penguin Books, 1964.
44) Krane, Kenneth, *Modern Physics,* John Wiley & Sons, 1996.
45) Kuhn, Thomas S., *The Structure of Scientific Revolutions,* University of Chicago, 1970.
46) Lennox, John C.,
    1. *God's Undertaker: Has Science Buried God?* Lion, 2007.
    2. *God and Stephen Hawking,* Lion, 2007.
47) Lombroso, Cesare, *After Death - What? (1908),* The Aquarian Press, 1988.

48) Mackie, John L., Causes and Conditions in *Causation*, Ernest Sosa and Michael Tooley (eds.) Oxford UP, 1993.
49) Maxwell, James Clerk, *Matter and Motion (1877)*, Dover, 1991.
50) McConnell, Brian, *The Possessed*, Brockhampton Press, 1995.
51) McGrath, Alister, *Dawkin's God,* Blackwell Publishing, 2005.
52) McTaggart, J. M. E., The Unreality of Time (1908) in *The Philosophy of Time,* Robin Le Poidevin and Murray MacBeath (eds.) Oxford UP, 1993.
53) Mellor, D. H., The Unreality of Tense (1981) in *The Philosophy of Time,* Robin Le Poidevin and Murray MacBeath (eds.) Oxford UP, 1993.
54) Milton, Richard, *The Facts of Life: Shattering the Myth of Darwinism,* Fourth Estate Ltd., 1992.
55) Morrison, Michael A., *Understanding Quantum Physics,* Prentice Hall, 1990.
56) Nagel, Ernest, *The Structure of Science,* Routledge & Kegan Paul, 1961.
57) Oesterreich, T. K., *Possession - Demoniacal and Other*, Kegan Paul, Trench, Trubner & Co., Ltd., 1930.
58) Ostaszewski, Adam, *Advanced Mathematical Methods*, Cambridge UP, 1990.
59) Owen, Robert Dale, *Footfalls on the Boundary of Another World (1868),* Kessinger.
60) Peikoff, Leonard, *Objectivism: The Philosophy of Ayn Rand,* Penguin Books, 1991.
61) Peitgen, Heinz-Otto (et al), *Chaos and Fractals,* Springer-Verlag, 1992.
62) Richet, Charles, *Thirty Years of Psychical Research (1923)*, Kessinger.
63) Stevens, Dr. E. Winchester, *The Watseka Wonder (1928),* Internet Archive.

64) Stevenson, Dr. Ian
   1. *Twenty Cases Suggestive of Reincarnation*, University of Virginia Press, 1966.
   2. Reincarnation: Field Studies and Theoretical Issues (1977) in *Handbook of Parapsychology*, 631-663, Wolman, Benjamin B. (ed.) McFarland & Company, 1986.
   3. *Where Reincarnation and Biology Intersect*, Praeger, 1997.
65) Stove, David, *Darwinian Fairytales,* Encounter Books, 1995.
66) Strawson, P. F. *Introduction to Logical Theory,* Methuen & Co. Ltd., 1952.
67) Turetzky, Philip. *Time,* Routledge. 1998
68) Tyrrell, G. N. M., *Apparitions*, Society for Psychical Research, 1953.
69) Walsh, Michael (ed.), *Butler's Lives of the Saints,* Burnes & Oates, 1985.
70) Ward, Keith, *Why There Almost Certainly Is a God,* Lion, 2008.
71) Webster, James
   1. *The Case Against Reincarnation: A Rational Approach,* Grosvenor House Publishing Limited, 2009.
   2. *Life Is ForEver,* Woodside Publications, 2000.
72) Westfall, Richard S., *Never at Rest: A Biography of Isaac Newton,* Cambridge UP, 1980.
73) Wickland, Dr. Carl
   1. *Thirty Years Among The Dead (1924)*, Spiritualist Press, 1978.
   2. *The Gateway of Understanding,* Psychic Book Club 1934.
74) Wilson, Ian, *The Bleeding Mind: An Investigation into the Mysterious Phenomenon of Stigmata,* HarperCollins, 1988
75) Yogananda, Paramahansa, *Autobiography of a Yogi (1946)*, Internet Archive

General Index

GENERAL INDEX

A

A-series 398, 399, 404, 406-408
Advaita Vedanta 66, 67
absence seizures 212
absorption spectrum 358
acceleration time curve 330
action-at-a-distance 40, 324, 325
actions function 134-153
agnosticism 88, 89, 106
apparitions 182, 200
archetypal form 42
astral body 206
attacks, demonic 242
autosuggestion 252
average velocity 402
axial motion 377, 382, 383
axioms of karma 127

B

B-series 398, 399, 404
bilocation 169, 170, 174, 176, 184, 187, 188, 200, 244
Brahman 35, 66, 67
Buddhism 5, 24, 32, 33, 67, 412
black body radiation 355
Bohr's model 359, 363
butterfly effect, 375

C

Cantor's Theorem 146
Cartesian dualism 234
catastrophe, ultraviolet 355
causal necessity 114
chance mutations 74, 75, 81, 84, 85
chaotic processes 372
Chicago school 351
Christ's Passion 237, 244
circumscriptive replication 170-172
Compton Effect 368
confabulations 12, 59, 260
contiguity postulates 342
contradictory statements 97, 99
Copernican Revolution 305, 306
correlated birthmarks 18, 20, 21, 293, 294
curved space-time 426
cryptids 106

D

Darwinism 47-50, 72, 76, 81, 85
Dawkins' God hypothesis 425
de Broglie wavelengths 362, 365
death curse 235
demand curves 338, 339, 351, 352, 354
demons 198
determinism 233, 234, 332-334

difference equations 137, 143, 145
discontinuous energy levels 359, 360, 362, 365
displacement-time curves 326, 330, 348
domino metaphor 90
Dvaita Vedanta 67

E

ectoplasmic forms 176
electron jumps 360, 362
electrostatic field 202
elementals 198
emission spectrum 358, 364, 365
emissions, spontaneous 343
energy, living fields of 201, 202
epicycles 302, 306
equilibrium economics 336, 340, 341, 350
etheric body 184-190, 202, 206
evolution 47, 49, 69-77, 80, 84, 85, 118, 119
exorcism 196, 205
exteriorisation 169, 170, 176, 178, 181, 184, 187, 188,

F

feedback 121-124, 133
finite duration 416, 439, 440
fluxions 326, 328
force-time curve 331, 349
fragmented selves 418
frame, preferred 381, 385-387
Fraunhofer lines 358

G

geodesic 325
generalising inferences 90, 91, 93, 94
geometric series 446
gravity 32, 113, 114, 302, 305, 323-326, 332, 333, 372, 381
gyroscopes 322

H

heliocentric cosmology 305
homeostasis 236
hydrogen spectrum 360
hypnosis 12, 60, 188, 253-255
hypnotic regression 4, 11, 59, 260, 272, 276

I

immortality 32, 34-38, 46, 51-56, 67, 101-106, 168, 169, 191, 264, 265, 296, 297, 413-422, 424, 429, 434, 439, 440
Impossibility Theorem xi, xvi, 150, 413

GENERAL INDEX 461

individuality xi, xii, 18, 19, 37, 40, 41, 43-45, 51-56, 67, 104, 115, 168, 169, 176, 190, 191, 204, 208, 295, 414, 422, 435, 437
induction, proof by 90, 92
inductive reasoning 88-92
inertia, law of 309, 319, 320, 332
infinite regress 397, 406, 409
infinite series 326, 328
injury, somatic 250, 251
irrefutability, principle of 49, 87

K

Karma xi, xiii, xvi, 5, 6, 25-32, 36, 39, 41, 57, 58, 64-66, 115-153, 168, 264, 268, 278, 413, 446, 447
karmic function 134-153
karmic paths 117
Kepler's Harmonic Law 307
Kepler's Law of Ellipses 307
Kepler's Law of Equal Areas 307
Keynesian Economics 351

L

Lagrangian mechanics 331, 332
Laplacian determinism 234

Law of Conservation of Energy 86
linear differential equation 144, 145
Lorenz's computer simulations 375
Lyell's concept of uniformitarianism 69, 70

M

marginal productivity theories 337
market equilibrium 336
materialisation 170, 176, 184, 188, 189, 201
materialism 193, 194
maternal impressions xii, 13, 19, 256, 257, 276
measurement of change 400-403
measurement of karma 125
measurement of time 387
mental body 206
metempsychosis 53, 54, 63
micro-to macroevolution 85
multi-incarnation 169, 170, 172, 190, 416, 435
multilocation xii, 170, 190
mutations 74-76, 81-85

N

natural selection 70, 72, 74, 75, 79

neoclassical school 338
Newtonian mechanics 133, 325, 332, 381
Newtonian paradigm of causality 335
Newtonian paradigm of continuity 335
Newton's action-at-a-distance 325
Newton's concept of absolute space 380
Newton's concept of absolute time 377, 378
Newton's Law of Acceleration 321, 331, 385
Newton's Law of Gravity 325
Newton's Law of Inertia 320
Newton's Third Law 321

O
obsessing spirits 3, 212, 214, 215, 294
obsession 10, 15, 17, 18, 20, 21, 23, 41, 169, 170, 195, 197, 199, 212, 214, 215, 232, 278, 284, 290, 294, 297
obsession hypothesis 294

P
paradigm 74, 96, 192, 193, 308, 320, 332, 335, 370
Pascal's Wager 423
past life memories xii, xiv, 4-6, 13, 20, 21, 55, 60, 260, 293, 294
pendulum, double 372
phantasmal replication 170, 172
philosophy, mechanical 332, 333
photo-electric effect 356
Planck's constant 150, 355, 356, 359, 360
possession, demonic 10, 197, 204
Postulates I and II 100, 103, 168, 413, 414, 419, 428, 434, 438
Postulates I to IV 434, 435, 440
Poulain's definitions 199
principle of equity 129, 130
principle of sufficient reason 378
probability density function 147-152, 443, 444, 447
Ptolemaic system of astronomy 302
Ptolemy's models 303-305
punctuated equilibria 72, 73

Q
quantifying karma 125
quantum non-locality 39, 40

quantum physics 36, 39, 40, 96, 97, 356, 369, 426

R

Reduction Principle xiv, 100, 409, 411, 412, 434
reductionism in science 333-335, 411
reincarnation hypothesis 60, 61, 261, 269, 293
reincarnation research xv, 15, 20, 21, 260, 261
relativity theory 360, 386, 387
resolution, single incarnation 120
response coefficients 140
revolution, marginal 336, 337, 350

S

schizophrenia, hebephrenic 280
Schrödinger's wave equation 364-367
self-contradictory statements 32, 33, 52, 69, 97-100, 102-106, 191, 412
self-refuting statements 35, 97
sensation, community of xii, 169, 170
sensibility, exteriorisation xii, 169, 170, 178, 181, 184, 188

space-time 325, 388, 426, 427, 429
specious present 395, 396
spirit control 3, 178, 188, 198, 202, 208-210, 212, 215, 222, 227-231
spirit entities 10, 201, 207, 208
spirit influence 10, 11, 14, 192-232
spirit intrusions 212, 293, 295, 297
spirit obsession 10, 15, 17, 18, 20, 21, 23, 41, 169, 170, 195, 197, 199, 212, 214, 215, 232, 278, 284, 290, 294, 297
spirit possession xii, 10, 195, 196, 202, 208
stasis 73
stigmata 169, 170, 235, 237-250
stigmatic type phenomena 250-255
subtle bodies 206-211
survival, bodily 192-194, 293, 414, 422

T

telepathy 14, 231, 255-257, 262
temporal cosmos 411, 412

temporal duration 38, 56, 101, 102, 376, 380, 393, 416, 420, 430, 439, 440
temporal order 55
Temporal Postulates xi, xvi, 100, 103, 168, 413, 414, 419, 428, 438
temporal sequence 54
Theosophical Society 24, 57
thermal radiation 355
time
  clock 427
  conventional 403, 429
  imaginary 387, 388, 417, 426, 427, 429
  psychological 379, 427, 429
  relative 377, 378, 380, 384, 386, 429
  unreality of xiv, xvi, 55, 297, 376-412
time dilation 386
time series 405, 406
timeless creation 434
timeless purposes 432
timeline 407, 408, 409, 415
trance mannerisms 42
trance mediumship 203
transfiguration 235
transmigration 53, 57, 58, 63, 67, 119
transverberation 244
travelling clairvoyance 201
travelling twin 387
trillion outcome problem 83

U

uncertainty principle 97, 369
uniformitarianism 69, 70
units of karma 125, 131, 133
utility 336, 337, 339

V

velocity of light 385, 386
velocity-time graph 330, 348
Venn diagram 400
vision, clairvoyant 207

W

wave energy 356
wave-particle duality 357, 367
wave superpositions 366, 367

X

xenoglossia 246

Index of Names

INDEX OF NAMES

A

Aquinas, Thomas 312, 412, 426
Aristotle xiv, 308, 309, 312, 389, 412

B

Baggott, Jim 364
Balmer, Johann 359
Barberini, Maffeo 316
Barrett, Sir William 14, 253
Baudouin, Charles 252
Bellis, J. M. 254
Bentley, Richard 324
Berkeley, George 381, 412
Bishop of Augsburg 205
Bishop of Narni 240
Blagojevi, Milutin 381
Blaug, Mark 337
Blavatsky, H. P. 4, 24, 35, 57-59
Bloxham, Arnall 13
Bohr, Niels 357, 359-365
Bonaventure, S. 238
Born, Max 342, 363, 364, 367, 368, 378
Brahe, Tycho 307
Bush, Dr. George 215

C

Cannon, Walter 236
Cantor, George 146
Capra, Fritjof 36
Cardinal Dini 314
Cardinal Mellini 315
Cardinal Orsini 314
Cardinal Sfondrati 312
Carrington, Hereward 184, 251
Cayce, Edgar 4, 21-23, 25
Chapman, Ethel 249
Christina, Dowager Duchess 310, 312
Cohen, Bernard 319
Colburn, Robert C. 429
Compton, Arthur Holly 368
Copernicus, Nicolaus xiii, 302, 304-306, 308, 310, 312-318
Correns, Carl Erich 73, 74
Courtier, M. 183
Crookes, William 193, 293
Curie, Marie 183
Curie, Pierre 182
Cuvier, George 71

D

Darwin, Charles 50, 69-85
Davies, Paul 426
Davis, Andrew Jackson 58, 215-217
Dawkins, Richard 50, 76-78, 81, 82, 425, 426
de Broglie, Louis 360-362, 365, 367

de Narni, La Bienheureuse Lucie 239
de Recanati, Bernard 240
de Vries, Hugo 73, 74
Debreu, Gerard 341
Democritus 426
Denton, Michael 72
Descartes, René 233, 234, 301, 309, 319, 320, 333, 412
d'Esperance, Elisabeth 176-178, 188, 189
Dewar, A. 235
Dirac, Paul 363
Dunbar, Helen Flanders 250, 251, 254

E

Ebner, Blessed Margareta 239
Einstein, Albert 325, 356, 357, 360, 364, 365, 368, 378, 385, 386
Eiseley, Loren 72
Eldredge, Niles 72
Euclid 98, 326, 349, 368
Euphorbus 57
Ewin, Dabney M. 254

F

Father Agostino 243
Father Alberto 175
Father Benedetto 243, 244
Father Firenzuola 316
Father Foscarini 313, 315
Father Germanus 240, 242
Father Grassi 316
Father Lorini 311, 312
Father Thommaso Caccini 311, 313
Feynman, Richard 382, 387, 388, 395
Fishbough, William 215
Flournoy, Théodore 203, 204
Fodor, Nandor 215-217
Frankel, F. H. 255
Fraunhofer, Joseph von 358
Friedman, Milton 351

G

Galen of Pergamon 215-217
Galileo Galilei xiii, 301, 306, 308-319, 344
Geiger, Hans 358
Gemma, Cornelius 256
Gerlick, Fritz 246
Germer, Lester H. 362
Gertrude van der Oosten 239
Gould, Stephen Jay 72, 73
Gribbin, John 426
Gunn, Alexander 376, 382, 384, 389
Gurney, Edmund 185

INDEX OF NAMES

H
Hadfield, J. A. 253
Hawking, Stephen xiv, 301, 387, 412, 417
Heisenberg, Werner 363, 364, 368, 369
Helm, Paul 427-433
Henderson, M. 339
Hercules, Duke of Este 240
Herrman, Charlie 15-18, 22, 23, 41, 212, 270, 271
Hertz, Heinrich 356
Hicks, John 351
Hinnells, J. R. 67
Home, Daniel Dunglas 58
Hospers, John 414
Howitt, William 58
Hoyle, Fred 76
Hume, David 343, 346
Hutton, James 69
Huxley, T. H. 74
Hyslop, James H. 193-195, 231, 232, 293, 293

I
Ida of Louvain 239, 240

J
James, William 395
Janet, Pierre 204
Japhet, Celina 57
Jevons, William Stanley 336, 339

Joire, Paul 178-180, 188, 189, 235
Jordan, Pascual 363
Jürgens, Hartmut 372

K
Kant, Immanuel 412
Kardec, Allan 4, 57-59
Kelly, E. Robert 395
Kepler, Johannes xiii, 301-303, 306, 307, 308, 314, 319, 320, 324
Keynes, J. M. 350
Kiely, David M. 199
Kim, Jaegwon xiii. 345
Kingsford, Anna 58
Kirk, G. S. 388
Koestler, Arthur 310
Kops, Louise W. 251
Kuhn, Thomas S. 192

L
Lagrange, J. 331, 332
Laithwaite, Eric 321-323
Laplace, P. 233, 234, 301, 333
Lechler, Alfred 252
Leibniz, G. W. 377, 378, 381, 412
Lendrum, Canon W. H. 199
Lennox, John C. 75, 81, 82, 425
Leroux, Pierre 57
Lifschutz, J. E. 250
Locke, John 412

Lombroso, Cesare 189
Lorenz, Edward 375
Lutoslawsky, Professor 217
Lyell, Charles 69, 70

M

Mackie, John L. xiii, 107, 108
Maitland, Edward 58
Marsden, Ernest 358
Marshall, Alfred 338
Mathis, J. L. 235
Maxwell, James Clerk 325, 356, 379, 380
McConnell, Brian 199
McKenna, Christina 199
McTaggart, John xiv, 296, 297, 396-409, 419
Meador, C. K. 236
Mellor, D. H. 56, 408
Mendel, Gregor 73, 74
Menger, Carl 336, 339
Mlodinow, Leonard 301, 412
Moore, G. E. 397
Moos, R. H. 236
Morrison, Michael A. 369
Motte, Andrew 377
Müller, M. 204
Myers, A. 235
Myers, Frederic W. 185, 293

N

Nagel, Ernest 332
Neumann, Therese 245, 246, 249, 252

Newton, Isaac xiii, 52, 53, 56, 133, 234, 301-341, 346, 349, 350, 356, 365, 366, 370-372, 376-381, 385, 386

O

Ochorowitz, Julien 184
Oesterreich, T. K. 198, 203-205
Olcott, Henry 24, 57

P

Palladino, Eusapia 181, 182, 187, 189
Parmenides of Elea xiv, 376, 388, 389
Pascal, Blaise 423
Peirce, C. S. xiii, 345
Philpot, Anthony 217
Pigou, Arthur 338
Pike, Nelson 431-433
Planck, Max 15, 354-357, 359, 360
Plato 57, 389, 412
Playfair, John 69
Plotinus 382
Podmore, Frank 185
Poincaré, Henri 372
Pope Alexander IV 238
Pope Alexander VI 239
Pope Paul V 314
Pope Pius X 243
Pope Urban VIII 316

INDEX OF NAMES

Poulain, Augustin 197-199, 202
Prior of Viterbo 240
Ptolemy, Claudius xiii, 302-306, 308
Pythagoras 57

Q
Quandt, Richard E. 339
Quinn, Susan 183

R
Ramanuja 67
Rand, Ayn 56
Ranga Hilyod 24, 25, 42
Rasputin, Grigori Yefimovich 255
Raven, J. E. 388
Reverend Ruoppolo 242
Reynaud, Jean 57
Richet, Dr. Charles 175, 183
Roberts, Jane 42
Rochas, Albert 181
Romanov, Alexei Nikolayevich 255
Russell, Bertrand 345, 397, 405
Rutherford, Ernest 358, 359

S
Sabatier, M. 181
Saint Alphonse de Liguori 175, 189
Saint Anthony of Padua 174, 186, 189
Saint Augustine of Hippo xiv, 379, 392-396, 434
Saint Catherine Benincasa 239
Saint Clare 238
Saint Francis of Assisi 237, 238
Saint Gemma Galgani 240-242
Saint Gerard Majella 175, 186
Saint John 239
Saint Joseph 243
Saint Mark 312
Saint Paul 237
Saint Pierre du Queyroix 174
Saint Pio of Pietrelcina 175, 189, 242
Saint Therese of Lisieux 245
Saint Thomas Aquinas 312, 412, 426
Saupe, Dietmar 372
Schofield, M. 388
Schopenhauer, Arthur 55
Schrödinger, Erwin 363-367
Selye, Hans 236
Sextus Empiricus xiv, 389-392
Shankara 67

Sheikh, A. A. 253
Siddhartha Sakyamuni 24, 25
Skinner, B. F. 335
Smith, Adam 336
Smith, Hélène 203
Sowa, John F. 345
Spinoza 412
Stanley, Steven 72
Sternberg, E. M. 237
Stevens, Dr. E. Winchester xii, 218, 220-231
Stevenson, Dr. Ian 4, 13, 14, 18, 19, 50, 55, 56, 59, 223, 255-259, 260-298
Swedenborg, Emanuel 215-217

T
Tuke, D. H. 251
Turetzky, Philip 389, 390, 395
Tyrrell, G, N. M. 200, 201

U
Ullman, M. 254

V
van Helmont, Jan Baptist 256
Vogl, Albert 246

W
Walras, Leon 336, 339
Wambach, Dr. Helen 12, 13, 20, 60-62, 261, 273, 275, 276
Ward, Keith 411, 425
Watson, A. A. 235
Webster, James iii, v, xvi
Weiss, P. 335
Whitaker, L. 288
Wickland, Dr. Carl 3, 15-17, 24, 212-215, 232, 269-271, 298
Wickramasinghe, Chandra 76
Wien, Wilhelm 355
Wilberforce, Samuel 74
Wilson, I. 252
Wollaston, William Hyde 358
Wurz, Professor (friend of Therese Neumann) 247, 248

Y
Young, Thomas 357
Yogananda, Paramahansa 172-174, 186, 189, 246, 248

Z
Zamansky, H. S. 255
Zammit, Victor 61, 273, 275

www.ingramcontent.com/pod-product-compliance
Ingram Content Group UK Ltd.
Pitfield, Milton Keynes, MK11 3LW, UK
UKHW041409180426
11947UKWH00007B/25